NONVERBAL COMMUNICATION

Nonverbal Communication

READINGS WITH COMMENTARY

Edited by
SHIRLEY WEITZ
Graduate Faculty New School for Social Research

New York
OXFORD UNIVERSITY PRESS
London   Toronto   1974

Copyright © 1974 by Oxford University Press, Inc.
Library of Congress Catalogue Card Number: 73-90367
Second printing, 1975
Printed in the United States of America

ACKNOWLEDGMENTS

I would like to thank Harmon Hosch, Vivian Shayne, and David Fineman for their help, particularly in compiling the name index.

Nobility and dignity, self-abasement and servility, prudence and understanding, insolence and vulgarity, are reflected in the face and in the attitudes of the body whether still or in motion.

—Socrates (Xenophon, *Memorabilia III*)

CONTENTS

NONVERBAL COMMUNICATION

INTRODUCTION

Best sellers like Julius Fast's *Body Language* have safely established the study of nonverbal communication in the popular mind as a short cut to an understanding of human motivation and interaction. But, what is the more enduring place of nonverbal research in the behavioral sciences? When the fad passes and sensitivity groups are no longer the vogue, will interest in this area similarly fade? The opinion of this writer and many others in the field is an emphatic "no," because simultaneously with the emergence of "body language" as a popular pastime has come an avalanche of serious scientific work, on both the theoretical and the empirical levels. Indications are that nonverbal research will become an integral part of social psychological theories of interpersonal communication, person perception, and emotional expression, as well as contribute heavily to such applied fields as psychotherapy and intergroup relations. Workers in fields allied to psychology, such as linguistics, anthropology, and communications, have also invested heavily in this research, and their different methodological and theoretical approaches have given a breadth and variety to this field that is unusual in the behavioral sciences. The development of videotape equipment (Berger, 1970) and computer-assisted video analysis techniques (Ekman, Friesen, and Taussig, 1969) have provided the methodological basis for further advances in the field.

The last year alone has produced five major books in the area, devoted to theory and research of important investigators (Dittmann; Ekman, Friesen and Ellsworth; Hinde; Mehrabian; Scheflen, all 1972). The latest volume of the prestigious Nebraska Symposium on Motivation (Cole, 1972) has a major section on nonverbal communication, including articles by Ekman, Exline, and Mehrabian. Two textbooks entirely devoted to this area have been published (Eisenberg and Smith, 1971; Knapp, 1972), along with a reader emphasizing the communications aspect of nonverbal research (Bosmajian, 1971). *Semiotica,* a new journal largely devoted to research in nonverbal communication, has been created within the past five years. The *Journal of Communication* (Harrison and Knapp, 1972) has produced an entire issue on the subject. Hardly an issue of the *Journal of Personality and Social Psychology* goes by without two or three articles utilizing nonverbal or paralinguistic variables. Laurence Wylie, the well-known anthropologist and author of *Village in the Vaucluse,* a study of a French village, is now turning his attention to body movement research, investigating national differences in nonverbal signs. A report on Wylie's preliminary findings (Robertson, 1973) indicates that "even the way Frenchmen and women move and think about their bodies expresses the 'tension and rigidity' he perceived in the society long ago."

Certainly, attention to nonverbal variables is not a new development in the arts and communication, but its treatment as a serious scientific domain for psychology has been a relatively recent development. The art of the theater, especially mime and dance, is heavily dependent upon the universal language of nonverbal signs, as is painting and sculpture (Lawson, 1957; Shawn, 1954; Gombrich, 1972; Arnheim, 1966). Music and song reflect the influence of paralinguistic effects. Politicians and other persuaders have long known the value of gesture in oratory, and communications research has not neglected nonverbal variables (Mortensen, 1972). The emphasis in this book will be on the place of nonverbal research in the psychological literature, to indicate how work in the study of emotion, cognition, social interaction, and the ethology of human behavior has been enhanced by attention to nonverbal communication.

The interest in nonverbal measures has come from varied sources in psychology. In social psychology, the interest in the analysis of dyadic and small group interactions has grown out of the work of symbolic interactionism (see Stone and Farberman, 1970) and the dramaturgical perspective of Erving Goffman (1959, 1963, 1967, 1971). Goffman provided a goad to the field by proposing a provocative model of human interaction, in which actors achieve goals by manipulating various aspects of their performance on verbal and nonverbal levels to control the outcome to their own advantage. Although Goffman's work depends heavily upon anecdote, it suggests a definite perspective to take in interaction, one in which nonverbal messages play an integral part.

Concomitant with an interest in the analysis of interactions has come a turning away from the traditional experiment in social psychology. A disenchantment with the validity of attitude measures and conventional verbal scales has predisposed many workers to turn to more subtle measures of behavior, often nonverbal. The resurgence of interest in ethology has given new respectability to observational studies, carried out with appropriate controls in real-life settings rather than in artificial laboratory contexts (e.g., Hinde, 1972; Blurton-Jones, 1972; McGrew, 1972). Rosenthal (1966) found that psychological experiments could not follow the natural science model without incurring the danger of biasing the results due to unintended communication between experimenter and subject. In other words, experimenters would often transmit their expectancies of performance to the subject and thus predispose their hypothesis to confirmation. Although Rosenthal suggests ways to avoid this bias effect (by experimenters "blind" to the condition of the *S*, tape-recorded instructions, and so on), his focus on it led to looking at the experiment as an interaction worthy of study in itself (Rosenthal, 1967). Later research has emphasized paralinguistic cues in experimenter-subject communication (Scherer, Rosenthal, and Koivumaki, 1972).

A ready-made interaction exists in psychology as a focus of practical concern and professional scrutiny, that is, the psychotherapeutic relationship between therapist and patient. Freud, in his concept of transference, put primary emphasis on the importance of this relationship, and subsequent researchers have also investigated it (usually from the one-sided view of therapist appraising patient, however, rather than in a true dyadic communications model). Ekman and Friesen (1968; and related papers in Shlien, 1968) emphasized the importance of nonverbal variables in the psychotherapeutic relationship, and others (e.g., Mahl, 1956; Matarazzo, Wiens, Matarazzo, and Saslow, 1968) turned to the study of speech behavior in interviews, using paralinguistic techniques.

Closely allied to the study of the psychotherapeutic relationship is that of the expression and recognition of emotional states (e.g., see Knapp, 1963; Ekman, Friesen, and Ellsworth, 1972). Various theories of emotional expression have been proposed (see Arnold, 1970), and the relevance to nonverbal research is evident, although it is not clear that *all* nonverbal signs are necessarily manifestations of emotional state; some may be related to cognitive processes (see Dittmann paper, p. **169;** also Wiener, Devoe, Rubinow, and Geller, 1972). Traditional studies in the nonverbal conveyance of emotion have relied on subjects' recognition of actors' posed re-creations of emotional states. Ekman, Friesen, and Ellsworth (1972) have recently attacked this tradition and have suggested a component approach based on separate areas of the face as conveying different affective information (see Ekman, Friesen, and Tomkins article, p. **34**). Using a computer-based retrieval system to match facial expressions, Ekman is attempting to systematize research in this area.

Aside from the psychotherapeutic dyad, other important interactions have received increasing attention from psychologists, many using nonverbal indices. Stern (1971, 1973) has done extensive work in the verbal and nonverbal analysis of mother-infant interactions, on the assumption that such interactions can indicate crucial facts about the affective tone of the relationship and can be predictive of future personality development of the child. Work by

Milmoe et al. (p. **122**) in this volume indicates that paralinguistic information from mothers' voices can be postdictive of their children's behavior. Other related work has looked at linguistic communications patterns in the mother-child dyad (Baldwin and Baldwin, 1973) and at a time-series analysis of the interaction (Rosenfeld, 1973).

Abnormal communication patterns have long been considered indicative of mental illness, particularly schizophrenia. The double-bind hypothesis of disordered and conflicting communication has been looked at in a nonverbal context (Bugental, Love, Kaswan, and April, 1971). Conflicting cues in nonverbal communication are considered at length in this volume (see Part 5, p. **263**). Differences between channels in the direction of nonverbal and verbal cues may be a normal part of potentially conflicted interaction, for example, interracial interaction (Weitz, 1972).

In addition to the more venerable psychological concern with emotion, the newer interest in cognition, so much a part of present-day psychology, has also shaped nonverbal research. Dittmann's paper reprinted here (p. **169**) concerns itself with nonverbal evidence of verbal encoding processes and Freedman, O'Hanlon, Oltman, and Witkin's (1972) work relates the cognitive style of field-dependence-independence to nonverbal communication. The explosion of interest in psycholinguistics (Slobin, 1971; Brown, 1973), spurred by Chomsky's (1957, 1965, 1968) work in transformational grammar has spilled over into nonverbal research by generating interest in paralinguistic variables (see Part 2, p. **93**). A broad interest in language in all its manifestations (see Haugen and Bloomfield, 1973) has included the study of the use of language in interpersonal relationships (Hays, 1973). Work in sociolinguistics (Fishman, 1971; Gumperz and Hymes, 1972) and the social context of language (Giglioni, 1972; Robinson, 1972) has also turned attention to the nonverbal sphere, in order to create a complete model of human communication. Harold Garfinkel's ethnomethodology (see Garfinkel, 1967; Sudnow, 1972) has led to the close sociolinguistic study of everyday interactions.

Nonverbal communication, then, has a natural place in both the classical and modern concerns of psychology and allied social sciences. Moreover, technological advances, in the form of film and videotape (Berger, 1970), should not be underestimated as forces in the growth of the field. Without videotape, for example, or slow motion film techniques, the recording of nonverbal signs would be a hopeless endeavor. Emphasis on other visual media, such as television, has probably also stimulated interest in the field. Lastly, the popularity of psychology in general and work in interpersonal sensitivity in particular (for example, encounter groups) among the general public has had an effect in focusing scientific concern on the area. It seems, then, that many forces, both within psychology and in the culture as a whole, have culminated in the growth and development of nonverbal research. This book attempts to highlight some of the recent trends in nonverbal communication and to indicate the direction in which the field is moving. There can be little doubt that both popular interest and serious research in this area will continue to grow in the years ahead.

A note on the arrangement of this book

Since the various areas of nonverbal research have mainly developed independently of one another, background material is included at the head of each chapter instead of in one grand introduction. The reader might like to read all the chapter introductions at once as a general introduction or just select the ones of special interest as a prelude to reading the selections themselves. The chapter introductions do not comprehensively cover the literature in each field (see Knapp, 1972; Davis, 1972; Duncan, 1969; Argyle, 1969) but suggest the past and future directions of development by citing relevant research.

REFERENCES

Argyle, M., *Social Interaction*, Aldine, Chicago, 1969.

Arnheim, R., *Toward a Psychology of Art*, University of California Press, Berkeley, 1966.

Arnold, M., ed., *Feelings and Emotions: The Loyola Symposium*, Academic Press, New York, 1970.

Baldwin, A. L., and Baldwin, C. P., "The study of mother-child interaction," *American Scientist*, 1973, **61**, 714–21. (Also presented at the biennial meeting of the Society for Research in Child Development, Philadelphia, March 1973).

Berger, M. M., ed., *Videotape Techniques in Psychiatric Training and Treatment*, Brunner/Mazel, New York, 1970.

Blurton-Jones, N., ed., *Ethological Studies of Child Behavior*, Cambridge University Press, Cambridge, 1972.

Bosmajian, H. A., ed., *The Rhetoric of Nonverbal Communication*, Scott Foresman and Company, Glenview, Ill., 1971.

Brown, R., *A First Language: The Early Stages*, Harvard University Press, Cambridge, 1973.

Bugental, D. E., Love, L. R., Kaswan, J. W., and April, C., "Verbal-nonverbal conflict in parental messages to normal and disturbed children," *Journal of Abnormal Psychology*, 1971, 77, 6–10.

Chomsky, N., *Syntactic Structures*, Mouton, The Hague, 1957.

Chomsky, N., *Aspects of the Theory of Syntax*, MIT Press, Cambridge, 1965.

Chomsky, N., *Language and Mind*, Harcourt, Brace and World, New York, 1968.

Cole, J. K., ed., *Nebraska Symposium on Motivation, 1971*, University of Nebraska Press, Lincoln, 1972.

Davis, M., *Understanding Body Movement: An Annotated Bibliography*, Arno Press, New York, 1972.

Dittmann, A. T., *Interpersonal Messages of Emotion*, Springer, New York, 1972.

Duncan, S., "Nonverbal communication," *Psychological Bulletin*, 1969, 72, 118–37.

Eisenberg, A. M., and Smith, R. R., *Nonverbal Communication*, Bobbs-Merrill, Indianapolis, 1971.

Ekman, P., and Friesen, W. V., "Nonverbal behavior in psychotherapy research," in *Research in Psychotherapy*,

Vol. III, J. M. Shlien, ed., American Psychological Association, Washington, D.C., 1968, pp. 179–216.

Ekman, P., Friesen, W. V., and Ellsworth, P., *Emotion in the Human Face: Guidelines for Research and an Integration of Findings,* Pergamon Press, New York, 1972.

Ekman, P., Friesen, W. V., and Taussig, T., "VID-R and SCAN: Tools and methods in the analysis of facial expression and body movement," in *Content Analysis,* G. Gerbner, O. Holsti, K. Krippendorff, W. Paisley, and P. Stone, eds., Wiley, New York, 1969.

Fast, J., *Body Language,* M. Evans, New York, 1970.

Fishman, J. A., *Sociolinguistics,* Newbury House, Rowley, Mass., 1971.

Freedman, N., O'Hanlon, J., Oltman, P., and Witkin, H. A., "The imprint of psychological differentiation on kinetic behavior in varying communicative contexts," *Journal of Abnormal Psychology,* 1972, 79, 239–58.

Garfinkel, H., *Studies in Ethnomethodology,* Prentice-Hall, Englewood Cliffs, N.J., 1967.

Giglioni, P. P., ed., *Language and Social Context,* Penguin, Baltimore, 1972.

Goffman, E., *The Presentation of Self in Everyday Life,* Doubleday Anchor, New York, 1959.

Goffman, E., *Behavior in Public Places,* Free Press, New York, 1963.

Goffman, E., *Interaction Ritual: Essays on Face-to-Face Behavior,* Doubleday Anchor, New York, 1967.

Goffman, E., *Relations in Public: Microstudies of the Public Order,* Basic Books, New York, 1971.

Gombrich, E. H., "Action and expression in Western art," in *Nonverbal Communication,* R. A. Hinde, ed., Cambridge University Press, Cambridge, 1972, pp. 373–93.

Gumperz, H., and Hymes, D., eds., *Directions in Sociolinguistics: The Ethnography of Communication,* Holt, Rinehart and Winston, New York, 1972.

Harrison, R. P., and Knapp, N. L., eds., A special issue on nonverbal communication, *Journal of Communication,* 1972, 22(4).

Haugen, E., and Bloomfield, M., eds., *Language as a Human Problem, Daedalus,* 1973, 102(3).

Hays, D. G., "Language and interpersonal relationships," *Daedalus,* 1973, 102, 203–16.

Hinde, R. A., ed., *Nonverbal Communication,* Cambridge University Press, Cambridge, 1972.

Knapp, M. L., *Nonverbal Communication in Human Interaction,* Holt, Rinehart and Winston, New York, 1972.

Knapp, P. H., ed., *Expression of the Emotions in Man,* International Universities Press, New York, 1963.

Lawson, J., *Mime. The Theory and Practice of Expressive Gesture,* Pitman and Sons, Ltd., London, 1957 (reprinted by Dance Horizons, 1972).

McGrew, W. C., *An Ethological Study of Children's Behavior,* Academic Press, New York, 1972.

Mahl, G. F., "Disturbances and silences in the patient's speech in psychotherapy," *Journal of Abnormal and Social Psychology,* 1956, 53, 1–15.

Matarazzo, J. D., Wiens, A. N., Matarazzo, R. G., and Saslow, G., "Speech and silence behavior in clinical psychotherapy and its laboratory correlates," in *Research in Psychotherapy,* Vol. III, J. M. Shlien, ed., American Psychological Association, Washington, D.C., 1968, pp. 347–94.

Mehrabian, A., *Nonverbal Communication,* Aldine, Chicago, 1972.

Mortensen, C. D., *Communication: The Study of Human Interaction,* McGraw-Hill, New York, 1972.

Robertson, N., "Body language helps U.S. professor read French psyche and his own," *New York Times,* June 26, 1973, p. 47.

Robinson, W. P., *Language and Social Behavior,* Penguin, Baltimore, 1972.

Rosenfeld, H. M. "Time series analysis of mother-child interaction," paper presented at the biennial meeting of the Society for Research in Child Development, Philadelphia, March 1973.

Rosenthal, R., *Experimenter Effects in Behavioral Research,* Appleton-Century-Crofts, New York, 1966.

Rosenthal, R., "Covert communication in the psychological experiment," *Psychological Bulletin,* 1967, 67, 356–67.

Scheflen, A. E., *Body Language and the Social Order,* Prentice-Hall, Englewood Cliffs, N.J. 1972.

Scherer, K. R., Rosenthal, R., and Koivumaki, J., "Mediating interpersonal expectancies via vocal cues: differential speech intensity as a means of social influence," *European Journal of Social Psychology,* 1972, 2, 1963–76.

Shawn, T., *Every Little Movement— A Book about François Delsarte,* Witmark and Sons, 1954 (reprinted by Dance Horizons, 1968).

Shlien, J. M., ed., *Research in Psychotherapy,* Vol. III, American Psychological Association, Washington, D.C., 1968.

Slobin, D. I., *Psycholinguistics,* Scott Foresman and Company, Glenview, Ill., 1971.

Stern, D. N., "A micro analysis of mother-infant interaction," *Journal of the American Academy of Child Psychiatry,* 1971, 10, 501–17.

Stern, D. N., "Mother and infant at play: the dyadic interaction involving facial, vocal and gaze behaviors," in *The Origins of Behavior,* M. Lewis and L. Rosenblum, eds., Wiley, New York, 1974.

Stone, G. P., and Farberman, H. A., eds., *Social Psychology Through Symbolic Interaction,* Xerox College Publishing, Waltham, Mass., 1970.

Sudnow, D., ed., *Studies in Social Interaction,* Free Press, New York, 1972.

Weitz, S., "Attitude, voice and behavior: a repressed affect model of interracial interaction," *Journal of Personality and Social Psychology,* 1972, 24, 14–21.

Wiener, M., Devoe, S., Rubinow, S., and Geller, J., "Nonverbal behavior and nonverbal communication," *Psychological Review,* 1972, 79, 185–214.

one

FACIAL EXPRESSION AND
VISUAL INTERACTION

Facial expression is perhaps the area in nonverbal communications research that comes closest to the more traditional concerns of psychology. The question of nature versus nurture as the origin of behavior is very much present here, as is the issue of the components of human emotionality. We will consider these two aspects of facial expression and the first three articles in this section highlight their importance. We will then consider the related area of visual interaction, which is covered by Exline's review.

Facial expression

The nature-nurture controversy in psychology has been a volatile one in areas such as intelligence and sex role behavior. Most researchers seem to favor a middle ground, advocating the existence of some biological substratum but also recognizing the heavy influence of the environment (or what anthropologists usually call "culture") on human behavior. In studies of nonverbal communication, it is the ethological approach which has been most clearly identified with the nature side of the nature-nurture controversy. We will first consider the ethological perspective and then look at the nurture side of the controversy.

Ethology can be thought of as a way of studying behavior in the same way that any other biological process, for example, digestion, is studied. Naturalistic observation is the chief technique used, without experimental intervention, the hallmark of behavioral psychology. Guiding theoretical concerns are absent, at least at this stage of ethological work. The whole animal is taken as the unit of analysis, within its natural setting, although certain behavioral patterns may be isolated for special attention. If this animal happens to be human, no special adaptation of technique is considered necessary. The ethologist, who almost always comes out of a natural science rather than a psychological background, is a committed evolutionist and thus does not need to be convinced of the continuity of form and function between humans and other animals.

According to Tinbergen (1951), the ethological perspective on behavior is characterized by four major concerns: the immediate cause of the behavior; the development of the response through the life cycle of the animal; the survival value of the behavior to the animal; and the relationship of the response to similar behaviors in other animals. The classic example of the use of this technique is Konrad Lorenz's (1966) work on aggression. Critics of the ethological approach to human behavior (for example, Montagu, 1968, on Lorenz's work) point out that the differences, chiefly cultural and linguistic, between man and animals call for the application of techniques that recognize the cognitive, linguistic, and social complexity of man and ones that do not treat him as simply some more advanced animal. Ethologists are also somewhat prone to blur over their joint use of animal and human evidence in proving a point about human behavior. They usually draw their evidence from animal research and then generalize to human behavior. Thus, Lorenz's work emphasizes animal studies, many on species not even remotely related to humans (for example, stickleback fish), and generalizes to verbal, cultured man, living in a highly structured social setting.

Despite the oversimplification of some ethologists in their analyses of such complex behavioral patterns as aggression, there is an important place for ethological research in the study of nonverbal communication. Nonverbal behavior can be seen in some sense as predating verbal behavior, and perhaps as being a more primitive response system (for example, under conditions of extreme stress, humans resort to nonverbal signs, such as screaming or crying, with accompanying facial expressions, rather than undertaking a complex verbal analysis of the situation). Therefore, techniques of comparative analysis, with the evolutionary perspective of ethology, might be particularly appropriate. Evidence already indicates clearcut similarities between primates and man in their nonverbal response systems (Hinde, 1972; Goodall, 1971; Chevalier-Skolnikoff, 1973). Even with considerable cultural filtering mechanisms at work on regulating emotional expression, universal human cross-cultural trends seem to be maintained (Ekman, 1972). For example, the "eyebrow flash" of recognition on greeting seems to be characteristic of all studied cultures and many primate groups (see Eibl-Eibesfeldt, p. 22).

The use of the ethological perspective in studying nonverbal communication has a long and venerable history. In 1872, Charles Darwin published *The Expression of the Emotions in Man and Animals,* stressing the continuity in form and function of emotional expression, suggesting an evolutionary approach to expressive behavior. No one can claim that this work shook up the psychological world in any measure like the earlier works of Darwin did the biological one, but his voice remained a persistent one to be quoted with respect and admiration by workers in the field throughout the years. Darwin's essential point was that expressive behaviors have survival value to the species and are maintained or dropped in the same way as physical structures. Expressive behavior was viewed as being the vestige of biologically useful movements, which later became innately linked to emotional experience. Darwin felt that emotions were expressed in similar ways across species and that the expressive system was an important innate component of human and animal behavior. He suggested study of infants and blind children as test cases for innateness, and this suggestion has been followed by subsequent investigators (see Eibl-Eibesfeldt, p. **27**). Recently, Ekman (1973) has prepared an excellent commentary on Darwin's work, compiling some new material relevant to his original ideas.

After Darwin, the ethological approach fell out of favor among behaviorally oriented psychologists, who emphasized manipulation and controlled experimentation. Important work by Lorenz (1966), Tinbergen (1969), and Goodall (1971), among others, has earned a place of respect for ethological research, and the turning away from strict behaviorism in psychology has made controlled observation acceptable again. This technique seems particularly well suited to studying spontaneous nonverbal behavior in humans. British investigators have been especially active in this area (see Hinde, 1972). Blurton-Jones (1972) has compiled a series of ethological studies of child behavior (done in Britain), using nonverbal indices of play behavior, mother-child interaction, and so forth. Alloway, Krames, and Pliner (1972) have collected a series of studies on comparative communication of affect. A large body of existing research on animal communication (Evans, 1968) remains to be combed for applicability to human concerns.

Paul Ekman is another supporter of the nature side of the nature-nurture controversy, although he tempers this support by allowing an important role for the effects of culture on emotional expression (Ekman, 1972). His position on innate determinants is primarily a matter of empirical experience rather than of theoretical conviction based on the tenets of ethology. Ekman and Friesen (1971) found that even members of preliterate cultures (who had had little exposure to the media and literate cultures) responded in much the same way as Western subjects when asked to match a particular facial expression to a story. Previously, many studies have shown that among literate cultures, emotional labeling is quite similar (see Ekman, 1972, for a review). Even though he basically supports an innate position, Ekman (1972) thinks that cultural constraints play a very important role in shaping emotional expression. He has developed what he calls a "neuro-cultural theory of facial expressions of emotion," advocating both an innate basis for the connection between certain emotional states and given facial muscles (the "facial affect program"),

and a cultural overlay of display rules which can intensify, deintensil-
ize, or mask the facial display to comply with the normative demands of specific situations in a culture.

Other recent theories of emotional expression give some role to innate factors. Tomkins (1962, 1963) believes that the primary affects are innate but
sees a possibility for cultural influence on their expression (a position similar
to Ekman's). Izard (1971) has posited a role for the innate components of
muscular patterns and postures in emotional expression, but also thinks that attitudes toward emotions, which help determine their expression, are of cultural
origin.

The article reprinted here, by Eibl-Eibesfeldt (p. **20**), presents evidence for
the innate side of the nature-nurture controversy. Eibl-Eibesfeldt cites cross-
cultural similarities in basic emotional expression, similarities which are unlikely to be caused by instances of cultural diffusion or contact. The book by
Hinde (1972), from which the Eibl-Eibesfeldt selection is taken, contains many
excellent papers on the ethological perspective. In the Hinde book, Edmund
Leach provides a direct response to Eibl-Eibesfeldt's position, taking a cultural
position. Very recently, Kreutzer and Charlesworth (1973) have demonstrated
characteristic reactions to different emotions among very young infants, also
providing evidence for an innate basis for emotional expression and reaction.

The nurture side of the nature-nurture controversy has been far from silent.
One proponent of the culturally based view has been Weston La Barre (1947)
who directly challenged the innate position by citing evidence of cultural differences in emotion and gesture. For example, weeping is reported to arise in
many culturally defined contexts, not all of which have to do with sadness.
Earlier, Klineberg (1938) took the same relativistic position, discussing the
differences between Chinese and Western emotional expression. Ekman's
model of a cultural filter of display rules over an innate base might well explain some of these seemingly disparate examples of cultural influence on expressive behavior. Recently, Birdwhistell (1970) has become the most persistent voice for cultural relativism. We discuss his structural approach to
nonverbal behavior in the chapter on body movement and gestures.

The second issue in studies of facial expression is that of the recognition of
emotion and its relationship to dimensional theories of emotion. Ekman, Friesen, and Ellsworth (1972) criticize the traditional studies of "accuracy" of
emotional judgments, in which posed pictures are given to *S*s for identification
of the emotional state portrayed therein. Instead, they advocate a broad sampling of persons, eliciting circumstances, behavior, emotions, and labels, and a
component approach rather than one of judgment. In the component study,
"facial behavior is treated as a response, and the question addressed is whether
a certain position or movement of the subject's face is related to some measure
of the subject's emotional state or circumstances" (Ekman, Friesen and Ellsworth, 1972, p. 31). The FAST system, reported in Ekman, Friesen, and

Tomkins' paper (p. **34**), develops this perspective with the help of a computer retrieval system so that sections of the stimulus face can be matched to items known to be correlated with prior expression of an emotional state. In judgment studies, according to Ekman, Ss are to report the emotion demonstrated in the stimulus material given to them (usually a posed photograph). The advantage of the component system is that the mechanism of emotional expression can be broken down into its component facial parts and the investigator can isolate just which parts or combinations are responding or responded to in a given situation.

Some recent judgment studies, however, have contributed to an insight into the emotional communication process. Work by Lanzetta and Kleck (1970) has shown that persons who are good at judging others' emotions are poor at sending emotional signals to others, and vice versa. Subjects whose emotions were poorly identified by others had higher physiological reactivity than those well identified, and good judges of others' emotions had high physiological arousal when confronted with emotional stimuli. The investigators hypothesize that overt displays of emotion may be suppressed in some individuals, but that inner arousal continues and is compounded by the additional pressure of having to inhibit the display. Such individuals will be overly sensitive to the display of emotion in others, and hence be better judges of such stimuli. Buck, Savin, Miller and Caul (reprinted here, p. **51**) distinguished between "internalizers" and "externalizers" in the expression of emotion. Internalizers tended to react physiologically rather than in overt facial displays to emotional stimuli, whereas externalizers wear their emotion for all the world to see, but do not show as high a degree of internal turmoil. Buck and his associates further found that internalizers were poorer stimuli for others than externalizers. In addition, males were found to predominate among internalizers and females among externalizers, which might have implications for the greater incidence of stress-related diseases in men. Recent work by Buck (1973) indicates that preschool children show individual differences in accuracy of emotional communication when their reactions to slides of emotional stimuli were judged by their mothers and unrelated undergraduates. These differences seem to be tied to personality traits, with outgoing, active, more aggressive, and popular children being better senders than their more introverted, controlled, and shy peers. Sex differences in sending ability did not appear, as they did in adult samples, leading Buck to speculate that socialization pressures for male inhibition of emotional expression do not become effective until later in the life of the child. The author of this book proposes that socialization pressures for females may also act to enhance their emotional expression. However, at an early stage, innate temperamental differences apparently determine individual differences in sending ability.

A rather different contribution has been made by Allen Dittmann in his recent book, *Interpersonal Messages of Emotion* (1972). Dittmann has developed a theory of emotional interaction based on the mathematical theory of communication (Shannon, 1948; Shannon and Weaver, 1949). By taking this point of view, Dittmann looks at many neglected areas of emotional communication. He considers individual and cultural differences in choice of channels for emotional messages, so, for example, some people and cultures may favor the voice rather than the face. He also thinks that channels change as a function of the age and depth of a social relationship. Two strangers may communicate in the most universally understood channels: words, stereotyped facial expressions, and gestures. As the two get to know each other better, they use more subtle gradations of expressions and rely more on subcultural variations common to both or decoded by each member. Dittmann observes, "Many 'family resemblances,' by which we ordinarily mean genetic similarities of facial features or body build, are probably really based on family codes of expression" (Dittmann, 1972, p. 141). Dittmann also considers the effects of noise on emotional communication. "Noise" in communications theory refers to any interfering stimuli which are received along with the message. Noise can be random or nonrandom; interference between channels is a related problem. Any code of emotional communication has to provide for a filtering mechanism to deal with such noise. One critical problem would be to discriminate emotional from similar nonemotional messages. Thus Dittmann (p. **169,** this book) found that some body movements seem to be a function of the speech encoding process, which is primarily cognitive, not affective. Individual differences in sensitivity to others' emotions may be a function of the success of decoding mechanisms in dealing with such noise. Haggard and Isaacs (1966), for example, showed that very small changes in facial expression, occurring within a fraction of a second (termed micromomentary expressions), are a characteristic of some facial displays and these might be detected by some observers but not by others. Dittmann's contribution, then, is one of providing an innovative framework for looking at problems of emotional communication. It should be interesting to see the sorts of research stimulated by this approach.

Visual interaction

Eye contact is one of the most direct and powerful forms of nonverbal communication. Authority relationships and sexual encounters are examples of interactions which are often initiated and maintained through visual communication. Exline has written a very fine review of research in this area, which we reprint (p. **65**). He describes his own program of research, which demonstrates a dual role for eye contact in maintaining both power and affiliative relationships. Argyle and Dean (1965) also report on a program of visual research, concentrating on the affiliative function. They suggest that eye contact and distance balance each other out, so that approach and avoidance tendencies are equalized at the level of eye contact and distance chosen as "comfortable" by interactants.

Exline's review also cites considerable background work from other areas, including the study of primates, autistic children, and literature. Primates, for example, seem to respond to prolonged eye contact as a threat signal, even if the staring eye is human instead of simian. Vine (1970) provides an excellent integrative review of facial-visual signalling systems in monkeys and man. Autistic children, who are severely withdrawn socially, do not attend to human faces and eyes as do normal children (Hutt and Ounsted, 1966). Exline also presents suggestive research on sex differences in visual interaction, with women engaging in more eye contact than men, which might be a result of greater sensitivity to others' emotional states, as shown by more constant visual monitoring. Finally, Exline reports on the special methods needed to study gaze behavior, that present quite a number of practical problems.

Another review in this area is provided by Ellsworth and Ludwig (1972). Phoebe Ellsworth has been an active and innovative researcher in visual interaction. One study, Ellsworth, Carlsmith, and Henson (1972), found that pedestrians and automobile drivers crossed an intersection faster when stared at than under normal conditions, providing evidence that the stare is a stimulus to flight and a threat display for humans as well as primates. In a later study, Ellsworth and Carlsmith (1973) found that eye contact is often perceived as aversive in potentially aggressive encounters and that one or both members of the dyad take measures to counteract it. Visual interaction is, of course, also a key element in maintaining affiliative relationships, and Rubin (1970) has found that eye contact is correlated with feelings of love in courting couples. It seems that in eye contact, as in life, the line between love and hate is very fine indeed.

In conclusion, we see that research in both facial expression and visual interaction seems to have reached a particularly exciting point, and we may look forward to promising new developments in the years ahead.

REFERENCES

Alloway, T., Krames, L., and Plines, P., eds., *Communication and Affect: A Comparative Approach*, Academic Press, New York, 1972.

Argyle, M., and Dean, J., "Eye contact, distance, and affiliation," *Sociometry*, 1965, 28, 289–304.

Birdwhistell, R. L., *Kinesics and Context*, University of Pennsylvania Press, Philadelphia, 1970.

Blurton-Jones, N., ed., *Ethological Studies of Child Behavior*, Cambridge University Press, Cambridge, 1972.

Buck, R., "Nonverbal communication of affect in children," Report 73-8, 1973, Department of Psychology, Carnegie-Mellon University, Pittsburgh, presented at American Psychological Association meeting, Montreal, September 1973.

Charlesworth, W. R., and Kreutzer, M. A., "Facial expressions of infants and children," in *Darwin and Facial Expression: A Century of Research in Review*, P. Ekman, ed., Academic Press, New York, 1973.

Chevalier-Skolnikoff, S., "Facial expressions of emotion in nonhuman primates," in *Darwin and Facial Expression: A Century of Research in Review*, P. Ekman, ed., Academic Press, New York, 1973.

Darwin, C., *The Expression of the Emotions in Man and Animals*, John Murray, London, 1872 (reprinted 1965, University of Chicago Press).

Dittmann, A. T., *Interpersonal Messages of Emotion*, Springer, New York, 1972.

Ekman, P., "Universals and cultural differences in facial expression of emotion," in *Nebraska Symposium on Motivation, 1971*, J. K. Cole, ed., University of Nebraska Press, Lincoln, 1972, pp. 207–83.

Ekman, P., ed., *Darwin and Facial Expression: A Century of Research in Review*, Academic Press, New York, 1973.

Ekman, P., and Friesen, W. V., "Constants across cultures in the face and emotion," *Journal of Personality and Social Psychology*, 1971, 17, 124–29.

Ekman, P., Friesen, W. V., and Ellsworth, P., *Emotion in the Human Face: Guidelines for Research and an Integration of Findings*, Pergamon Press, New York, 1972.

Ellsworth, P. C., and Carlsmith, J. M., "Eye contact and gaze aversion in an aggressive encounter," *Journal of Personality and Social Psychology*, 1973, 28, 280–92.

Ellsworth, P. C., Carlsmith, J. M., and Henson, A., "The stare as a stimulus to flight in human subjects: a series of field experiments," *Journal of Personality and Social Psychology*, 1972, 21, 302–11.

Ellsworth, P. C., and Ludwig, L. M., "Visual behavior in social interaction," *Journal of Communication*, 1972, 22, 375–403.

Evans, W. F., *Communication in the Animal World*, Crowell, New York, 1968.

Goodall, J. van Lawick, *In the Shadow of Man*, Houghton Mifflin, New York, 1971.

Haggard, E. A., and Isaacs, K. S., "Micromomentary facial expressions as indicators of ego mechanisms in psychotherapy," in *Methods of Research in Psychotherapy*, L. A. Gottschalk and A. H. Auerbach, eds., Appleton-Century-Crofts, New York, 1966.

Hinde, R. A., ed., *Nonverbal Communication*, Cambridge University Press, Cambridge, 1972.

Hutt, C., and Ounsted, C., "The biological significance of gaze aversion with particular reference to the syndrome of infant autism," *Behavioral Science*, 1966, 11, 346–56.

Izard, C. E., *The Face of Emotion*, Appleton-Century-Crofts, New York, 1971.

Klineberg, O., "Emotional expression in Chinese literature," *Journal of Abnormal and Social Psychology*, 1938, 33, 517–20.

Kreutzer, M. A., and Charlesworth, W. R., "Infants' reactions to different expressions of emotions," paper presented at the biennial meeting of the Society for Research in Child Development, Philadelphia, March, 1973.

La Barre, W., "The cultural basis of emotions and gestures," *Journal of Personality*, 1947, 16, 49–68.

Lazetta, J. T., and Kleck, R. E., "Encoding and decoding of nonverbal affect in humans," *Journal of Personality and Social Psychology*, 1970, 16, 12–19.

Lorenz, K., *On Aggression*, Harcourt, Brace and World, New York, 1966.

Montagu, A., ed., *Man and Aggression*, Oxford University Press, New York, 1968.

Rubin, Z., "Measurement of romantic love," *Journal of Personality and Social Psychology*, 1970, 16, 265–73.

Shannon, C. E., "A mathematical theory of communication," *Bell System Technical Journal*, 1948, 27, 379–423, 623–56.

Shannon, C. E., and Weaver, W., *The Mathematical Theory of Communication*, University of Illinois Press, Urbana, 1949.

Tinbergen, N., *The Study of Instinct*, Oxford University Press, London, 1951.

Tinbergen, N., "Ethology," in *Scientific Thought, 1900–1960*, R. Harré, ed., Clarendon Press, Oxford, 1969.

Tomkins, S. S., *Affect, Imagery, Consciousness*, Vol. I, *The Positive Affects*, Springer, New York, 1962.

Tomkins, S. S., *Affect, Imagery, Consciousness*, Vol. II, *The Negative Affects*, Springer, New York, 1963.

Vine, I., "Communication by facial-visual signals," in *Social Behavior in Birds and Mammals*, J. H. Crook, ed., Academic Press, New York, 1970, pp. 279–354.

1

SIMILARITIES AND DIFFERENCES BETWEEN CULTURES IN EXPRESSIVE MOVEMENTS

I. EIBL-EIBESFELDT

Is there a signalling code—a language without words—common to all men? The question has been much discussed and contradictory statements have been published. As long ago as 1872 Charles Darwin pointed out certain similarities in the expressive behaviour of men with different cultural backgrounds. He interpreted these as being due to characteristics inborn in all men, but this opinion has been challenged repeatedly. For instance Birdwhistell (1963, 1967) has advanced the hypothesis that no expressive movement has a universal meaning and that all movements are a product of culture and not biologically inherited or inborn.

Many anthropologists indeed were so struck by the cultural diversity, that they considered the culture-independent invariables to be negligible. Thus Andree (1899) wrote:

One could fill easily a book with the enumeration of the various greeting customs in different nations. The scientific value of such an undertaking how-ever would be trifling. One would encounter an incredible diversity of more or less unexplainable peculiarities and one would wonder about the delicate etiquette of the greeting patterns and the waste of time involved [translation from the German original].

Biologists, biologically-oriented anthropologists and psychologists, on the other hand, have again and again emphasized the basic similarities of human expressive behaviour (e.g. recently, Ekman, Sorenson and Friesen, 1969), but a mutual understanding of the two points of view is still to come. This is partly because human behaviour has, so far, been inadequately documented, as Frijda (1965) has emphasized. Indeed we can search our large film libraries in vain for systematically collected documents on human expressive movements. These libraries contain a rich documentation of cultural activities (baking, weaving, pottery, etc.), but unstaged documents about human social behaviour (greeting, flirting, hugging of children by their mothers and the like) have rarely been collected. There have, however, been some exceptions, such as the films of Sorenson and Gajdussek (1966), Gardner and Heider (1968) and Bateson and Mead (1942). Gardner's film contains a rich documentation of various types of social behaviour, but this is included in a monograph and interspaced with many other scenes. And, to judge from the index, the films published by Sorenson and Gajdussek are similar. However, a person interested in greeting would like to find in one place films dealing solely with the activity he is interested in. This type of film library, containing documents on the social behaviour of man, still does not exist and, worse still, most of the social behaviour patterns have not even been documented cross-culturally. This is to be deplored, since social behaviour leaves no fossil tracks and once we have missed the chance to document the greeting behaviour of a native tribe at its first encounter with people of another civilization, the opportunity may be gone for ever.

This situation encouraged us to start a programme on the cross-cultural documentation of human expressive behaviour (Eibl-Eibesfeldt and Hass, 1967). We work with angle lenses that allow us to film people without their being aware of it. This is a prerequisite for any documentation of natural undisturbed behaviour. Even natives that are not familiar with the technique of filming get restless when a camera is pointed directly at them. But if the camera does not point towards them, they are not bothered by it. Of course, those close to the camera show interest in the proceedings, but this fades after a while and if one stays for a time in a village, one can document the intimate events of family life in people who

would run away if the camera were pointed towards them. The technique works even in Europe and at close distance. People may notice the opening of the angle lens, but the assumption that a camera pointing in one direction is filming in that direction is so strong that very few people realize what is going on. We film most of the events in slow motion (48 frames per second). Sometimes, however, we use the technique of speeding up by filming at 2–7 frames per second.[1] This allows us to record longer-lasting events as a whole, e.g. a ritual, a family resting on the beach, a flirting couple and the like. If the speed of filming is chosen appropriately, the movements of the body, head and limbs can be followed, although the people seem to move very fast to the later observer. Such documents allow us, for example, to count the number and duration of contacts between persons, to measure the distance they move apart and to observe the sequences of patterns involved. It is a valuable technique for collecting data for statistical analysis as well as for documenting the total pattern of an event.

A prerequisite for the later evaluation of the collected film documents is a detailed commentary accompanying every shot and stating in what context each pattern occurred and what the person did before and after the film was taken. Only in this way is an objective motivational analysis possible. It is actually the method ethologists employ when studying animals: that a specific posture signals threat or courtship is after all not assessed only from the posture, but also from its statistically significant recurrence in certain situational and sequential contexts (see Chapters 4 and 8, Hinde, 1972). Data collected in this way reveal upon comparison many detailed similarities between the different cultures, as will be demonstrated in a few examples.[2]

The similarities in expressive movements between cultures lie not only in such basic expressions as smiling, laughing, crying and the facial expressions of anger, but in whole syndromes of behaviour. For example, one of the expressions people of different cultures may produce when angry is characterized by opening the corners of the mouth in a particular way and by frowning, and also by clenching the fists, stamping on the ground and even by hitting at objects. Furthermore, this whole syndrome can even be observed in those born deaf and blind (Eibl-Eibesfeldt, 1970a).

The similarities involve in addition minute details of the behaviour patterns involved. I shall discuss one example at length. When greeting over a distance people smile and nod; and if very friendly they raise their eyebrows with a rapid movement, keeping the eyebrows maximally raised for approximately ⅙th of a second. I have filmed this so far in Europeans, Balinese, Papuans, Samoans, South American Indians (Waika, Quechua) and in Bushmen, and have observed it in a number of other groups (Eibl-Eibesfeldt, 1968, Plate 1a–j). In all these cases the pattern signals readiness for contact, as can be deduced from the contextual and sequential analyses. In Central Europe the eyebrow flash is used mainly as a greeting to good friends and relatives, but if people are reserved they do not use it. This holds true for representatives of primitive cultures as well. In New Guinea I found that Papuans of different tribes initiated a greeting towards me, or responded to my greetings, with an eyebrow flash. In the village Ikumdi of the Kukukuku people,

however, I did not get an eyebrow flash at all. This village was first contacted seven months before my visit and the government patrol at that time ran into trouble. The natives had shot one of their native porters, and in revenge the patrol had burnt some huts and broken the shields and war clubs of the natives. This was apparently the reason for their being reserved towards me, the second visitor. Greeting was restricted to a nod or a nod and smile at the most. However, eyebrow flashes were used when they were greeting each other (Eibl-Eibesfeldt, 1968).

In some cultures the eyebrow flash is suppressed. In Japan, for example, it is considered as indecent. In Samoa, by contrast, it is regularly used in greeting and also as a general sign of approval or agreement, when seeking confirmation, and when beginning a statement in dialogue. We use the signal in approximately the same situations, though we perform it less readily in a greeting encounter. We use it in addition frequently during flirting, when strongly approving, when thanking, and during discussions—for example, when emphasizing a statement and thus calling for attention.

We are normally not aware that we use this signal, but we respond strongly to it in greeting situations. We smile back and often answer with an eyebrow flash. However, if we are not familiar with the person we experience embarrassment. In an experimental set-up subjects addressed with an eyebrow flash then looked away, either by shifting the eyes or even by lowering or turning the head. Only those very familiar with the experimenter returned the eyebrow flash. (Unpublished experiments by Mario von Cranach.)

It is interesting to note that this signal has previously escaped the attentions of scientists. At any rate I have been unable to find any description of it in the literature. And yet, because the eyebrows emphasize this eyebrow flash, women give much attention to this region, often colouring the upper eyelid (in contrast) and thus making the signal more conspicuous.

We mentioned several situations in which eyebrow flashes of approximately the same stereotyped form occur: greeting, flirting, approving ("yes"), seeking (asking) confirmation, thanking, and emphasizing a statement (calling for attention). Can we find a common denominator for all these? In flirting and greeting the initiator certainly asks for contact and signals at the same time readiness to accept contact. When approving, for instance during a conversation, the eyebrow flash again signals acceptance of ideas and suggestions. It is a "yes" to a social interaction, just as in the situations of greeting and flirting. The factual "yes" by eyebrow flashing, as observed in many Polynesians, is probably derived from this. When thanking we again accept not only the present, but also the social bond symbolically initiated by this event. Finally in emphasizing a statement and seeking confirmation we seek contact and approval. So the basic common denominator is a "yes" to social contact, and it is used either for requesting such a contact or for approving a request for contact.

By looking for other contexts in which eyebrow raising occurs we get hints as to its possible phylogenetic origin. People regularly raise their eyebrows during surprise and hold them in this position for a while. The same movement pattern occurs during a conversation when people ask questions, for example: "What did you say?" In both cases people attend, opening their eyes to perceive better: the eyelids are opened and the eyebrows raised in connection with the opening of the eyes. Finally we raise the eyebrows during disapproval, indignation, and when we look at a person in an admonishing way, a pattern reminiscent of the threat stare of a number of infra-human primates. Again this admonishing look at the same time signals attention.

As a hypothesis I would propose that the eyebrow lift of surprise—originally part of the opening of the eye—was the starting point for the ritualization of several "attention" signals. Some of these can be grouped together as the friendly attention signals, as represented by the eyebrow flash, and are mostly given in combination with nodding and smiling. Further evidence that the starting point for the evolution of these friendly attention signals was the surprise reaction is the fact that surprise is often involved in meeting somebody: the utterance "Ah, it's you" when meeting in Central Europe is regularly accompanied by an eyebrow flash.

In its more generalized meaning the movement signals, as stated previously, a "yes" to social contact, either requesting contact or approving a request. Smiling and nodding are added in these situations, whereas the derived factual "yes" does not demand these additions, although they sometimes accompany it, especially the nod. The contact and approval-seeking eyebrow flash, as when emphasizing a statement, can, but need not, be accompanied by nodding and smiling.

The brow-lifting which accompanies indignation can also be derived from the surprise reaction. It can be interpreted as surprise concerning a misbehaving group member. It obviously signals to the group member that he has attracted attention, that he is being looked at but not in a friendly way. There is also a continuous stare emphasized by the eyebrows being held up, which is quite distinct from the eyebrow flash, for in the latter the impression of staring is avoided by the rapid lowering of the eyebrows following their raising. The expressions of disapproval and arrogance are related to indignation, but here the contact is rejected. The brows are kept raised, but

not he is being looked at (von Cranach, in press).

It is of interest to note that very marked lifting of the eyebrows occurs in some kinds of Old World monkeys, notably the macaques, baboons and mangabeys (van Hooff, 1967). In some species the effect is enhanced by a strong colour contrast between the upper eyelids and the surrounding skin. Accentuation may also be achieved by crests of hair (black ape) or eyebrows (patas monkey). This display element

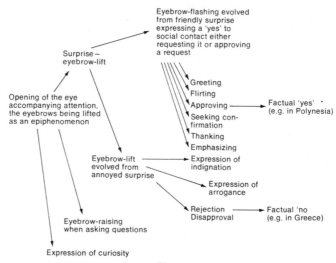

Fig. 1

in addition intention movements of withdrawal are added. The head is lifted in a backward movement and the eyelid is lowered, thus cutting off contact. In some cultures this pattern is used to express a factual "no"—for example in the Greek (p. **25**).

With the exception of the derived expression of arrogance (and "no"), the eyebrow movements signal to another person that he or she is being looked at. This is necessary, since man cannot tell over a distance with certainty from the eye movements alone, whether or

may have been selected as an indicator of visual contact. Depending on possible accompanying expressive elements and situational factors it may be interpreted as a threat or a positive signal.

Figure 1 represents the hypothetical evolution of eyebrow movements into signals in man.

Besides the eyebrow flash, which we have discussed more extensively, a number of other behaviour patterns occurring during greeting are similar in detail in different cultures. In addition to the striking formal similarities, similarities in principle are numerous (Eibl-Eibesfeldt, 1968, 1970b, c) (see p. **28**). Some patterns of greeting, such as embracing and kissing, are apparently very old, since they occur also in chimpanzees (van Lawick-Goodall, 1968). The homologies of our smiling response are discussed by van Hooff (Chapter 8, Hinde, 1972).

Another complex of behaviour patterns which is similar in a diversity of cultures is that of coyness, embarrassment and flirting. One pattern of embarrassment is the hiding of the face or just the mouth behind one hand. I have filmed this in Europeans as well as in Samoans, Balinese, Africans, Papuans and Waika Indians. The pattern seems to be derived from hiding, since in its less ritualised form it can be observed in children. This pattern also occurs in flirting girls. In addition the latter demonstrate ambivalence between flight and approach motivation—for instance by turning away and at the same time looking at the partner. Very often these patterns occur in successive ambivalence: the person looks at the partner, lowers the head, looking away and sometimes turning away, and finally looks back again. Giggling and hiding of the face behind the hand indicate a real conflict. The pattern can express itself in eye language alone: a girl looks at her partner, then lowers the lids thus cutting contact, and looks away.

These patterns of coyness which occur in flirting can be interpreted as ritualised ambivalence between flight and approach tendencies. In addition we can observe patterns inviting contact. Besides turning toward, looking toward, and the already mentioned eyebrow flash, tongue movements can occur. By playing with the tongue, Waika girls flirt with young males, and vice versa. In Central Europe also the

pattern can be observed but it is loaded with sexual meaning and therefore considered as indecent.

So far I have emphasized similarities in human expressive behaviour between cultures. The list could be continued with many other facial expressions and gestures, for instance the patterns expressing grief (sagging of the shoulders, facial expression). But there are also differences to be considered. These may involve not only minor details, but sometimes also the basic patterns. An interesting example is the expression of yes and no. In many cultures people say "yes" by nodding their head and "no" by shaking their head, as Central Europeans do. This is for example the case with the Waika Indians, Samoans, Balinese, and Papuans. The Ceylonese, however, have two ways of saying yes. If one asks a factual question the answer "yes" consists of nodding (example, "Do you drink coffee?"). If, however, agreement to do something is expressed, the Ceylonese sway the head in slow sideways movements. The head is tilted slightly during this movement and it is very different from our no-shaking. This occurs, for example, when I ask the person "Will you join me for a cup of coffee?". "No" in Ceylon is always expressed by headshaking, in the way we do it.

Another example of cultural differences in these basic expressive movements can be observed in Greece. "Yes" is expressed with a nod as we do, but when saying "no" the person jerks his head back, thus lifting the face. Often the eyes are closed and the eyebrows lifted for a while. When the "no" is strongly emphasized one or both hands are lifted up to the shoulders, the palms facing the opponent. They may also say "Okhi" or just click their tongues.

Here we are certainly confronted with cultural ritualizations. Interestingly enough, however, it is not the movement pattern itself which is traditional, but just its use in a particular situation. The movement occurs cross-culturally as a gesture of refusal and disagreement in a social context (see indignation, p. **23**), though not everywhere as the plain statement for "no." It may, however, occur more widely when the "no" is more emotionally loaded. For example, Central Europeans use it when expressing "for heavens sake, no!" Then the head is jerked back, the eyelids are lowered and the hands raised with the palm facing the opponent. The raising of the eyebrows which often occurs with the lowering of the eyelid signals indignation. Furthermore, most of these patterns are part of the gesture of pride, and both have the common origin of being intention movements of withdrawal and refusing social contact. In an interesting parallel, people of some cultures use the eyebrow flash (see above) for expressing "yes" (e.g. the Samoans): as we have seen, this signal occurs cross-culturally and signals readiness for social contact. In each case a signal that had had a more specific function acquired the more general meaning of "yes" or "no." The use of these signals for the plain statement is, however, relatively rare, and nodding and head-shaking are far more widespread in this context. Nodding and eyebrow flashing are often combined, the most common sequence pattern being: lifting the head, eyebrow flashing and nodding.

The origin of headshaking and nodding was discussed by Darwin, who suggested that shaking originated from food refusal. When the baby is satiated it refuses the breast by turning its head away. It could indeed be that this re-fusal gesture becomes ritualized into a "no" by emphasis and rhythmic repetition of the movement. It could, however, also be derived from a shaking-off movement, which is part of the behavioural repertoire of birds and fur-bearing mammals. In man it often accompanies a shiver. Deaf- and blind-born children also refuse by headshaking. Nodding can be interpreted as ritualized submission (Hass, 1968): we nod regularly during conversation as a gesture of reassurance, so to speak, submitting to the ideas of the speaker.

These examples show that cultural variation can result from the use of the available, probably inborn, patterns in slightly different ways. In addition there are numerous gestures which are culturally ritualized both in pattern and meaning—for example the method of saluting by tipping the rim of the hat or by lifting the hat, the latter being said to have originated from the lifting of the helmet as an expression of trust. It is interesting to note that a number of these culturally developed patterns show similarities in principle in different cultures. This suggests that the acquisition of these expressive movements may have sometimes been guided by phylogenetic adaptations involving specific learning dispositions. Whether these are for example "innate releasing mechanisms" biasing the perception of the individual, or drive mechanisms channelling behaviour in particular ways, has yet to be explored (Eibl-Eibesfeldt, 1970*b, c*).

Discussion

There are detailed cross-cultural similarities in both the meaning and the patterning of expressive behaviour. It is highly improbable that these similarities are due to chance. It remains to discuss the various possible ways in which they could have arisen. Many of the expressive behaviour patterns in man are certainly passed on by tradition. This is clear with patterns that are unique to one culture, such as the lifting of the hat. Often the historical origin of such patterns, their spread and the way in which they are learnt during ontogeny, can be followed. However, whether there are universals that are culturally traditional still needs to be explored. Since those behaviour patterns that are culturally learnt vary between cultures (for example, the development of dialects and languages —Erikson, 1966), it seems less probable that expressive patterns which occur as universals are culturally learnt. It is more likely that their universality is due either to common conditions in early upbringing channelling learning in a common manner, or that they are inborn. If Darwin was correct in suggesting that our headshaking as a gesture expressing "no" develops from a sideways turning of the head as a gesture of refusing the breast after satiation, then this could well be an example of how a similar gesture can be learned in so many different cultures independently. In a similar way the refusal gesture of warding off with the open palm might be acquired from the pushing away of unwanted objects. There are many cases, however, where it is difficult to see how a complex pattern, as for example a facial expression, or a whole syndrome of behaviour, could have been acquired in this way.

Recently I have systematically filmed and studied the behaviour of deaf- and blind-born children of different ages. The results show that the basic patterns of facial expression are present in these highly deprived individuals. They laugh, smile, sulk, cry, show surprise,

anger and the like (Eibl-Eibesfeldt, 1970a). The probability that they acquired all these facial and gestural expressions by learning is practically nil. Of course, one could imagine that shaping processes could take place accidentally: a smile, for instance, could be rewarded when it occurred the first time. But it would have to be an orderly pattern and not a mere grimace to release affection. And although shaping could be a faint possibility in the case of smiling, it is difficult to see how an anger syndrome (which would not be rewarded) could possibly be shaped in this way.

Another argument, which I once encountered in discussion, was that the deaf- and blind-born individuals may have acquired information about facial expressions by the sense of touch. However, I know of three deaf- and blind-born who are thalidomide children, born without arms: they cannot acquire information in this way. They nevertheless exhibit the normal repertoire of facial expressions. Finally, I may mention that the typical facial expressions are also shown in those deaf- and blind-born who are so much brain-damaged that even intensive trials to train them to hold and guide a spoon fail. It is difficult to imagine how they could have learned social expressions without any deliberate training. If anyone insists in such cases on the learning theory, the burden of proof for such an improbable hypothesis lies on his side. It seems more reasonable to assume that the neuronal and motor structures underlying these motor patterns developed in a process of self-differentiation by decoding genetically stored information. That would mean that the motor patterns in question are phylogenetic adaptations, which I assume they are. For a detailed theoretical discussion of the concept of phylogenetic adaptations see Lorenz (1965) and Eibl-Eibesfeldt (1970a, b).

The cross-cultural comparison revealed also similarities in principle. These could be explained in several ways. One possibility which has to be taken into consideration is the possible influence of phylogenetically acquired receptor mechanisms (innate releasing mechanisms) on perception. Experiments of Ahrens (1953) and Fantz

independent learning of patterns of shifting the glance, or of cutting off the stare by lowering the lids and briefly looking away, during friendly social contact, without further imitation or advice.[3] The wide-spread use of eye-patterns as protective devices (Koenig, 1970) could also be explained by an in-born perceptual structure.

Another perceptual structure may be responsible for the widespread use of phallic figurines as guards (Wickler,

A   B   C

Fig. 2 Phallic European sculptures: **A.** capital of a column in the cloister of St. Remy, France. The penis of the male figure (standing head-down) has been chiselled away. **B.** 'Gähnteufel' sitting below the pulpit in the Cathedral of Lorch (Germany). **C.** Herme of Siphnos (Greece). (After Eibl-Eibesfeldt, 1970d, and Wickler, 1966.)

(1967) with babies, and of Hess (1965) and Coss (1969) with adults, demonstrate that we react strongly to two horizontally presented dark spots and even more strongly when a central dark spot is surrounded by a brighter iris-like circle. Depending on the size of the dark spot ("pupil") sympathy or antipathy (small circle) is released in adults. People react differentially to these characteristics, without being able to tell what they are responding to (Hess, pers. comm.). If it is true that we respond innately with fear to a stare or to eye-patterns resembling a stare, then this alone could bring about the

1966; Eibl-Eibesfeldt and Wickler, 1968; Eibl-Eibesfeldt, 1970d). These figurines show a male genital display, which is reminiscent of the phallic display of many infra-human primates (Ploog, Blitz and Ploog, 1963; Wickler, 1966). In vervet monkeys, baboons and others, some males sit at the periphery of the group "on guard": with their backs to the group they display their genitals, which are often conspicuously coloured. This display is addressed to members of other groups and serves to aid in spacing. If a member of another group approaches, erections occur in the guards. The display probably derived from a mounting threat (Eibl-Eibesfeldt, 1970*b*) which became ritualized into a postural display. By behaving thus the males become territorial markers.

It is hardly mere coincidence that male phallic displays as well as mounting occur in very different cultures as an aggressive display, though they are sometimes expressed only verbally. Nor

In addition we can be sure that a number of the basic expressive patterns of man are phylogenetically acquired.[4] Many motor patterns develop independently of example. The degree to which such patterns are expressed, either as slight intention movements or in full intensity (or sometimes not at all) may, however, vary between cultures. In the Japanese, for example, the eyebrow

Fig. 3 A. Scarecrow from field in Bali; **B.** phallic scaredevil from Bali (front and side view); **C.** house guardian from Nias. (After Eibl-Eibesfeldt and Wickler, 1968.)

does it seem a mere coincidence that guards, scaredevils and gargoyles in very different cultures are shown in phallic display. We find such figures in Europe, Japan, Africa, New Guinea, Polynesia, Indonesia and ancient South America, to mention just a few examples (Figs. 2, 3, 4 and 5). In modern Japan phallic amulets are used for protection and as good luck charms (Eibl-Eibesfeldt, 1970*d*). These similarities indicate that a perceptual structure, probably of subhuman primate origin, guides man, when he produces such guards.

flash is considered as being indecent and is therefore rarely seen. Here the cultural filter is evidently repressive.

Occasionally the argument has been advanced that the rich variety of our expressive patterns makes it unlikely that they are phylogenetically fixed. A similar argument was once put forward by Schenkel (1947), who studied the expressive behaviour in wolves and was struck by their high variability. Lorenz (1953) in consequence demonstrated that the combination of the intention movements of flight and attack in three different intensities results in nine very characteristic types of expression. The diversity of human expression might well come about by a similar combination of various basic patterns. There are strong suggestions that this is so, although the matter has still to be explored in more detail (see Chapter 8 by van Hooff, Hinde, 1972). The frequent repetition of the statement that all of our expressive patterns are culturally learnt, and that except for a few reflexes of the newborn "nothing" is inborn in man (Montagu, 1968), proves

parisons, and finally on ontogenetic studies. The method of comparison has been discussed elsewhere (Eibl-Eibesfeldt, 1970b) in more detail. In principle we employ the criteria of homology used by morphologists. It might interest the reader to see on what basis the anti-instinct argument—to use an outdated term—is promoted. A well-known publication of La Barre provides an example. He writes in his introduction: "The anthropologist is wary of those who speak of an instinc-

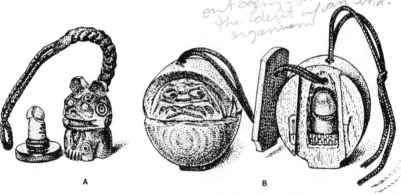

Fig. 4 Japanese amulets: **A.** little plastic bear. The phallus can be screwed into the body of the bear; **B.** front and rear view of an amulet showing a threat face and a penis in a shrine, normally covered by a lid. (From Eibl-Eibesfeldt, 1970d.)

nothing: the authors promoting such views did not even consider the contrary evidence. The study of the deaf- and blind-born at least demonstrates that phylogenetic adaptation partly determines our social behaviour, though the extent of its influence is not yet known. However, the fact that at least some basic modes of communication are inborn to man is of considerable theoretical importance (for a detailed discussion see Eibl-Eibesfeldt, 1970a).

Summing up, we can say that our conclusions are based on the motivational analyses of the observed patterns, on cross-cultural and cross-species com-

tive gesture on the part of a human being" (1947: 49), and then proceeds to enumerate examples of supposed culturally determined expressive movements. This is assumed to be the case wherever people react differently from culture to culture to the same expressive movement, when the same signal is used in different situations, or when different patterns are used to communicate the same message.

"Smiling, indeed," he writes, "I have found may almost be mapped after the fashion of any other culture trait; and laughter is in some senses a geographic variable. On a map of the Southwest

Pacific one could perhaps even draw lines between areas of "Papuan hilarity" and others where a Cobuan, Melanesian dourness reigned. In Africa Gorer noted that laughter is used by the negro to express surprise, wonder, embarrassment and even discomfiture; it is not necessarily, or even often a sign of amusement; the significance given to "black laughter" is due to a mistake of supposing that similar symbols have identical meanings. Thus it is that even if the physiological behaviour

actually laugh. The statistical analysis may well reveal a common denominator.[5] Since such an analysis does not exist, statements asserting different meanings cannot be accepted. La Barre refers in his papers to many other cultural differences, for example in greeting behaviour, but again the comparison remains superficial.[6] The same applies when he discusses cultural differences in situations in which people weep. But La Barre concludes: "So

Fig. 5 A. Papuan from Kogume on the Konca River; **B.** baboon sitting guard; **C.** genital display in a baby squirrel monkey. (After Wickler, 1966, and Ploog et al., 1963.)

be present, its cultural and emotional functions may differ. Indeed, even within the same culture, the laughter of adolescent girls and the laughter of corporation presidents can be functionally different things . . ." (1947: 52).

What La Barre presents as evidence is anecdotal. So far, to my knowledge, no motivational analysis of laughing exists, not even from our own culture (but see van Hooff, Chapter 8, Hinde, 1972). In order to say that laughing in different cultures has a different meaning (or meanings) we need to know in detail and from many examples when people

much for the expression of emotion in one culture, which is open to serious misinterpretation in another: there is no natural language of emotional gesture"(1947: 55).

This is certainly a naive and unscholarly treatment of the subject and must be criticized in face of Darwin's methodological contributions. No doubt, much of our non-verbal communication is learned, and this can be proved by ontogenetic as well as by comparative cross-cultural studies. In order to carry out such research we need *data* and not just superficial verbal descriptions. La Barre states, for example, that sticking out the tongue means different things in different cultures. To which type of tongue-showing does he refer? I have found a variety of forms of tongue-showing, each with a highly specific meaning, e.g. expressing disgust, sexual flirtation, mocking, etc. The subject is certainly not as simple as La Barre likes to present it, especially since additional signals are often added to one expressive movement and this results in a new pattern. Careful analysis is needed and this means adequate documentation. If one wants to argue about the natural or "instinctive" signalling code in man, one should not confuse the meaning of a movement and its pattern, as if they were the same. Both could be inborn but it is not necessarily so. The "meaning" of an inborn motor pattern could be learned even when the motor pattern is a phylogenetically adapted one, and vice versa. A learned motor pattern might be shaped by a perceptual structure and often both are acquired from the culture.

NOTES

1. Among the various advantages of changing the film-speed is that one sees patterns that normally escape attention. The eyebrow flash, to which we respond strongly but automatically without registering the expression consciously, was discovered when we examined slow motion films of greetings.

2. It is our intention to continue in our efforts to collect film documents, especially of populations that had had little contact with Europeans, and to build up a film encyclopaedia which publishes and archives such films. For this purpose the Max-Planck Society has established a research

unit for Human Ethology in Percha, Bavaria.

3. In order not to be mistaken, I want to emphasize that I do not intend to say that this is the case and that the motor patterns are indeed learned. I only point to possibilities.

4. Whether the understanding of these signals is preprogrammed by Innate Releasing Mechanisms, is open to question. Cross-cultural understanding certainly occurs (Ekman *et al.*, 1969).

5. My cross-cultural film documents at least seem to indicate this.

6. The cross-cultural examination of greeting behaviour indeed reveals many basic similarities (Eibl-Eibesfeldt, 1970*b*).

REFERENCES

Ahrens, R. (1953). Beitrag zur Entwicklung des Physiognomie und Mimikerkennens. *Z. Exptl Agnew. Psychol.* 2, 412–54, 599–633.

Andree, R. (1889). *Ethnographische Parallelen und Vergleiche*. Leipzig.

Bateson, G. and Mead, M. (1942). *Balinese Character*. Special Publ. of the New York Academy of Sciences, II.

Birdwhistell, R. L. (1963). The kinesis level in the investigation of the emotions. In *Expressions of the Emotions in Man*. Ed. P. H. Knapp, New York; Int. Univ. Press.

Birdwhistell, R. L. (1967). Communication without words. In *L'Aventure Humaine* (Paris). Ed. P. Alexandre, Société d'Etudes littéraires et Artistiques.

Coss, R. G. (1969). Perceptual aspects of eyespot patterns and their relevance to gaze behaviour. In *Behaviour Studies in Psychiatry*. Ed. S. H. Hutt and C. Hutt, Oxford; Pergamon.

Cranach, M. von (in press). *Über die Signalfunktion des Blickes*, Soziale Theorie und Praxis, Festschrift Baumgarten. Meinsenheim; A. Hain.

Darwin, C. (1872). *The Expression of*

the Emotions in Man and Animals. London; Murray.

Eibl-Eibesfeldt, I. (1968). Zur Ethologie menschlichen Grußverhaltens I. Beobachtungen an Balinesen, Papuas und Samoanern nebst vergleichenden Bemerkungen. *Z. Tierpsychol.* 25, 727–44.

Eibl-Eibesfeldt, I. (1970*a*). The expressive behaviour of the deaf and blind born. In *Non-verbal behaviour and Expressive Movements.* Ed. M. von Cranach and I. Vine, London; Academic Press.

Eibl-Eibesfeldt, I. (1970*b*). *Ethology, The Biology of Behaviour.* New York; Holt Rinehart and Winston.

Eibl-Eibesfeldt, I. (1970*c*). *Liebe und Hass—Zur Naturgeschichte elementarer Verhaltensweisen.* Munich; Piper.

Eibl-Eibesfeldt, I. (1970*d*) Männliche und weibliche Amulette im modernen Japan. *Homo* 20, 175–88.

Eibl-Eibesfeldt, I. and Hass, H. (1967). Neue Wege der Humanethologie. *Homo* 18, 13–23.

Eibl-Eibesfeldt, I. and Wickler, W. (1968). Die ethologische Deutung einiger dämonenabwehrender Figuren von Bali. *Z. Tierpsychol.* 25, 719–26.

Ekman, P., Sorenson, E. R. and Friesen, W. V. (1969). Pan Cultural Elements in the Facial Displays of Emotion. *Science, N.Y.* 164, 86–8.

Erikson, E. H. (1966). Ontogeny of Ritualisation in Man. *Phil. Trans. Roy. Soc.* B 251, 337–49.

Fantz, R. L. (1967). Visual perception and experience in infancy. In *Early Behaviour.* Ed. H. W. Stevenson, New York; Wiley.

Frijda, N. H. (1965). Mimik und Pantomimik. In *Handb. d. Psychol.* 5, 351–421. Ausdruckspsychologie.

Gardner, R. and Heider, K. G. (1968). *Gardens of War.* New York; Random House.

Hass, H. (1968). *Wir Menschen,* Wien; Molden.

Hess, E. H. (1965). Attitude and Pupil Size. *Sci. Amer.* 212, 46–54.

Hinde, R. A., ed. (1972). *Nonverbal Communication,* Cambridge; Cambridge University Press.

Hooff, J. A. R. A. M. van (1967). The facial displays of the catarrhine monkeys and apes. In *Primate Ethology,* 7–68. Ed. D. Morris, London; Weidenfeld and Nicolson.

Koenig, O. (1970). *Kultur und Verhaltensforschung,* München; Deutscher Taschenbuch Verlag.

La Barre, W. (1947). The cultural basis of emotions and gestures. *J. Personality* 16.

Lawick-Goodall, J. van (1968). The behaviour of free-living chimpanzees in the Gombe Stream Reserve. *Anim. Behav. Monogr.* 1(3), 161–311.

Lorenz, K. (1953). Die Entwicklung der vergleichenden Verhaltensforschung in den letzten 12 Jahren. *Zool. Anz. Suppl.* 16, 36–58.

Lorenz, K. (1965). *Evolution and Modification of Behaviour.* Chicago; University of Chicago Press.

Montagu, M. R. A. (1968). *Man and Aggression,* New York; Oxford University Press.

Ploog, D. W., Blitz, J. and Ploog, F. (1963). Studies on Social and Sexual Behaviour of the Squirrel Monkey (*Saimiri sciureus*). *Folia Primat.* 1, 29–66.

Ploog, D. W. and MacLean, P. D. (1963). Display of penile erection in squirrel monkey (*Saimiri sciureus*). *Anim. Behav.* 11, 32–9.

Schenkel, R. (1947). Ausdrucksstudien an Wölfen. *Behaviour,* 1, 81–129.

Sorenson, E. R. and Gajdussek, D. C. (1966). The Study of Child Behaviour and Development in Primitive Cultures. *Pediatrics, Suppl.* 37, 149–243.

Wickler, W. (1966). Ursprung und biologische Deutung des Genitalpresentierens männlicher Primaten. *Z. Tierpsychol.* 23, 422–37.

2

FACIAL AFFECT SCORING TECHNIQUE:
A FIRST VALIDITY STUDY [1]

PAUL EKMAN, WALLACE V. FRIESEN, AND
SILVAN S. TOMKINS

In 1862 Duchenne published his *Mécanisme de la physionomie humaine, ou analyse électro-physiologique de l'expression des passions,* in which he used "the electrical currents for contraction of the muscles of the face to make them speak the language of passions". In this atlas of the anatomy of emotion, Duchenne delineated many of the muscles whose contractions together contributed to the production of each specific emotional expression of the human face. Although Duchenne was the father of modern kinesiology, of whose work Darwin (1872) had written, "no one has more carefully studied the contractions of each separate muscle and the consequent furrows produced on the skin", later investigators virtually ignored his contributions.

Rather than continuing the study of the particular facial muscles which distinguished one from another emotion, the past five decades of psychological research on the face in relation to emotion instead have been devoted primarily to determining what emotion observers can judge from the face (whether their judgments are accurate, what categories of emotion can be judged, etc.). Comparatively few investigators have actually looked at the face itself, applying some measurement procedure to the appearance of the face and determining whether the resulting measurements were related to some index of emotion.

Those few who did measure facial components asked one of two questions, depending upon which index of emotion they employed. (1) Can measurements of the face distinguish among emotions experienced, when the emotional state of the person is defined by his self-report or experimentally varied changes in his environment (Fulcher, 1942; Landis, 1924; Landis and Hunt, 1939; Leventhal and Sharp, 1965; Thompson, 1941; Trujillo and Warthin, 1968)? (2) Can facial measurements predict how observers will judge emotion, or be correlated with observers' judgment of emotion (Frijda and Philipszoon, 1963; Frois-Wittmann, 1930)?

All but one of these studies that did examine the face itself obtained positive results. The only negative answer was from the first study by Landis, but that experiment has been severely criticized on a number of methodological grounds (Arnold, 1960; Coleman, 1949; Davis, 1934; Ekman, Friesen and Ellsworth, 1971; Frois-Wittmann, 1930; Honkavaara, 1961; Murphy, Murphy, and Newcomb, 1937). Although all the other studies did obtain positive results, a comparison of their findings does not yield much evidence about how specific facial behaviors are related to specific emotions. This lack of convergence may be due to limitations in the design of each of these experiments, which could have led to idiosyncratic findings. All of the studies were limited by insufficient sampling of at least one of the following: the number of emotions studied (whether defined by observer judgment or environmental condition); the number of different faces measured; the number of different stimulus persons used; and the number and kind of facial components measured. This last limitation may be due to the atheoretical bias of these investigators, none of whom specified the basis for their choice of facial components or scores. Instead, it would seem that they measured anything that appeared to vary in their set of faces, or that they could reliably measure, or that was salient to them. If they had looked to theory, they would have found only some guidance, primarily from Duchenne (1862) and those who were influenced by him (Darwin, 1872; Plutchik, 1962; Tomkins, 1962, 1963). However, even these theorists about emotion who emphasized the face

failed to describe completely all of the facial configurations they thought relevant to all of the emotions they discussed. And their descriptions were not intended to be a measurement procedure for determining what emotion is shown in a face.

Problem

Our purpose was to develop a tool for the measurement of facial behavior that would be equally applicable to predicting observers' judgments of emotion and to distinguishing emotional state as indicated by environmental condition or self-report. The Facial Affect Scoring Technique (FAST) was to be constructed for use with both still and motion records of the face. A second aim was to provide as complete as possible a description of the facial components that would distinguish among emotions to facilitate further development of theory.

We will report here on the development of FAST and describe a test of its validity in predicting the recognition value of a face. Subsequent reports will deal with other validity questions, such as distinguishing among faces in terms of self-reported or posed emotion, and emotion-arousing circumstances.

FAST's validity in predicting the recognition value of a face was investigated by determining whether FAST scores could distinguish the emotions ascribed to faces by observers. Only faces that had yielded high agreement among observers about the presence of a single emotion were considered. An attempt was made to include faces of as many different stimulus persons as was possible, to evaluate whether the facial scoring technique could cope with physiognomic differences.

Our hypothesis was that FAST scores

would accurately predict the judgments of the specific emotions shown on the stimulus persons' faces.

Method

The development of the facial affect scoring technique (FAST)

Our first decision was to develop FAST in terms of emotion categories (happiness, anger, surprise, etc.) rather than emotion dimensions (pleasantness-unpleasantness, active-passive, etc.). The decision was based on three considerations. First, more past work specifying facial components has utilized emotion categories than dimensions. Second, recent cross-cultural research has suggested that there are a set of facial components that are associated with emotion categories in the same way for all men, since the same faces were found to be judged as showing the same emotions in many cultures (Ekman, 1968; Ekman, Sorenson, and Friesen, 1969; Ekman and Friesen, 1970; Izard, 1968; 1970a, 1970b). Finally, our own theoretical bias was to conceptualize emotions in terms of categories rather than dimensions. The specific categories selected were those that had been consistently found by all the investigators within Western cultures who had attempted to determine how many categories of emotion can be judged from the face, and that had also been found by both Ekman et al., and Izard to be interpreted in the same way across cultures. These six categories of emotion are: happiness, sadness, anger, fear, surprise, and disgust. These six categories do not include ALL of the emotions that have been found to be reliably judged across cultures, but they are a sufficient number to meet our aim of showing that it is possible to

measure the facial behavior that distinguishes one emotion from another.

The next step required a decision about how to describe facial behavior. Initial attempts to describe facial behavior in terms of muscle movements revealed that it was often quite difficult to determine which muscles had moved by looking at the face. A decision was made to describe the appearance of the face primarily in terms of wrinkles, of tension or relaxation in specific features, and of positions of features. These appearance descriptions were made separately for three facial areas: brows-forehead; eyes-lids-bridge of nose; lower face, consisting of cheek-nose-mouth-chin-jaw. There were two reasons for dividing the face into these three areas, rather than into two or four or five areas. First, this division is based upon the anatomical possibilities for independent movement and appearance changes in the face. Within each of the three areas, a movement in one facial part will almost always lead to an observable change in appearance in other parts of that same area. But across areas, movement in one area (e.g., brow-forehead) need not necessarily result in an observable shift in the appearance of another area (e.g., lower face). While the eye area is most subject to reflecting movements from other facial areas, nevertheless, the eye area can shift in appearance without any observable shift in the other two areas.

The second reason for dividing the face into these three areas was our expectation that if scoring of particular facial components was not to be influenced by impressions of the whole face or from one very pronounced component in one part of the face, it would be necessary to limit the scorer to seeing only one area of the face at a

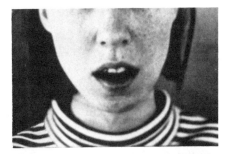

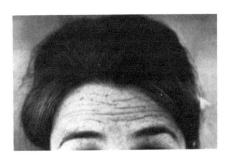

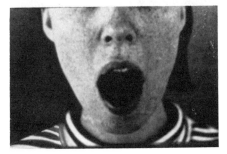

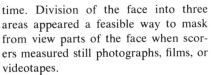

Fig. 1 FAST items for surprise.

time. Division of the face into three areas appeared a feasible way to mask from view parts of the face when scorers measured still photographs, films, or videotapes.

Lists of facial components within each of the three facial areas for each of the six emotions were compiled. These lists were based in part on past literature, including the theoretical writings and empirical studies referred to earlier and other writings (Allport, 1924; Birdwhistell, 1952). To this literature, we added our own combined observations and intuitions. We con-

sidered for each emotion each of the facial areas and the possibilities for muscular movements within each facial area, checking our hypotheses with a mirror and by looking at each other. An attempt was made to include components for slight, moderate, and extreme intensity versions for HAPPINESS, SURPRISE, and DISGUST, and in the case of ANGER, for both controlled and uncontrolled versions.

Specifying the appearance of some of the components within a facial area required such lengthy, awkward descriptions, which sometimes even then were insufficient, that it became obvious that the only way to make clear to scorers just what was being described was to imitate the appearance ourselves or show a photographic sample. For example, there was no obvious way to describe in words the differences in the appearance of the raised lower eye lids when they were raised by muscular tension or by the skin being pushed up from a grin in the lower face. After a year of pilot studies, in which scorers matched verbal descriptions with photographs, the verbal descriptions were abandoned, and in their place a visual-photographic definition of each item was made.

TABLE 1

Number of FAST photographic items for each emotion and facial area

	Brows—forehead	Eyes—lids	Lower face
Happiness	1	4	5
Sadness	8	8	10
Surprise	1	2	4
Anger	1	3	9
Disgust	1	2	11
Fear	1	2	4
	13	21	43

One or two photographic examples were made to define each item within each facial area. Models were told and shown what to do with the face, rather than asked to pose emotions. A model's attention was focused upon producing a particular appearance in a single facial area. More than one model was employed, since no single person was able to show all of the components in all of the facial areas. (We do not know whether this limit in facial performance might be due to differences in physiognomy, musculature, or learned ability

for voluntary control of facial movements.)

FAST consists of three sets of photographs, one set for each facial area, and a few verbal descriptions of head orientation and gaze direction, which, because they were easy to describe verbally, did not require visual definition. Table 1 shows the number of FAST photographs, or items, in each facial area for each emotion. Figure 1 shows, as examples, the brow area, eye area, and lower-face area items for SURPRISE. Table 2 gives the head orientation and gaze direction code. The procedure required the scorer to compare part of the face to be scored, one of the three areas, with the set of FAST photograph-items for that facial area, selecting the FAST item which was the best match to

TABLE 2

FAST: head/eye orientation

HEAD/EYE JUXTAPOSITION

Up—Down

Chin up and eyes fixated ahead
Chin up and eyes down
Chin down and eyes straight or up
Chin down and eyes down
Chin level and eyes down
Chin up or level and eyes up
None of these

Left—Right

Head oriented left or right with eyes opposed
Not relevant

HEAD POSITION ONLY

Head pulled back
Head thrust forward
Neither of these

EYE DEVIATIONS

Wall-eyed
Cross-eyed
Neither of these

the face to be scored. That item then became the score for that facial area. The scoring procedure will be described in more detail below.

Selection of faces to be scored with FAST

Two principles guided selection of the faces to be used to determine whether FAST scores predict how observers judge emotion. Each face should be one which observers agree shows only one emotion, and faces of many different stimulus persons should be included. Other work has shown that faces vary not only in the level of agreement they elicit from observers in judgments of emotion categories, but also in terms of whether they show a single emotion or a blend of two or more emotions (Ekman and Friesen, 1969a, 1969b; Nummenmaa, 1964; Plutchik, 1962; Tomkins and McCarter, 1964). While it would be important to determine whether FAST could differentiate blends from single-emotion faces, and one type of blend from another, this seemed to be a more complex differentiation, which should follow rather than precede determination of whether FAST could distinguish among the emotions conveyed by single-emotion stimuli.

The rationale for using as many different stimulus persons as possible was to test FAST's ability to ignore differences in facial appearance associated with age, sex, and physiognomy, and differences in lighting and contrast that would occur across pictures of different people. Our aim was to obtain 10 pictures of each of the six emotions, using sixty different people. Photographic candidates were selected from the photographs used by past investigators (Ekman and Friesen, 1968; Engen, Levy, and Schlosberg, 1957; Frijda,

1969; Frois-Wittmann, 1930; Izard, 1970a; Nummenmaa, 1964; Tomkins and McCarter, 1964). Any stimulus that had been found to elicit at least seventy percent agreement among observers about the presence of a single emotion was considered a candidate. The norms utilized were published or provided by investigators, including ourselves. The photographic candidates were shown to a new group of judges to replicate the high agreement finding, this time utilizing one judgment task and one group of observers for all stimuli, and to screen the stimuli further with a judgment task more sensitive to discriminating single from blend stimuli.

Pilot studies had revealed that the use of a single choice emotion judgment task could sometimes conceal the presence of a blend. If, for example, a stimulus showed primarily disgust but also signs of anger somewhat less salient, then a single choice judgment task would yield high agreement about only the more salient message, disgust. But, if observers were allowed to indicate a second choice, few would choose disgust only; many would choose disgust as their first choice and anger as their second choice. Such a two-choice judgment task would, of course, isolate stimuli that showed only one affect.

The candidates selected on the basis of previous norms with a single choice judgment task were shown to a group of 82 observers who were given a two-choice judgment task. The judgment task required them to circle the single word that best described the emotion shown in the face and, IF there was a second emotion also shown, to write a number "2" beside a second word. The emotion words listed in the judgment task were Happiness, Sadness, Anger, Fear, Surprise, Disgust, and Contempt.

Utilizing the results from these observers, and screening stimuli so as to select only single emotion photographs, we could not achieve our goal of 10 pictures for each emotion, each shown by a different stimulus person; further, the standards for inclusion in terms of agreement among observers had to be modified for each of the emotion categories. Table 3 shows that three criteria were employed to select single emotion

emotion category or more than once across categories.

Procedure

The photographs were projected life-size by a 2 x 2 slide projector on a back projection screen. The screen was masked so that only one facial area was visible; all pictures were scored on that facial area before the next facial area was presented. Scoring all stimuli on

TABLE 3
Judgment results on photographs selected for FAST validity test

Emotion category	Number of stimuli	Number of different persons within each category	Range of percentages saying only the relevant emotion is present	Range of percentages judging the next most frequent emotion as the only emotion present	Range of percentages judging that both the relevant and the second most frequent emotion were both present
Happiness	10	10	91–97	0–1	0–6
Sadness	10	7	72–90	1–8	1–12
Surprise	10	8	64–84	1–4	1–18
Anger	10	8	50–71	3–13	12–31
Disgust	4	4	56–67	6–10	12–15
Fear	7	7	44–54	0–15	11–38

stimuli, that the level of agreement varied for the different affect categories and that for the last two categories, Disgust and Fear, it was not possible to obtain 10 pictures, even though the standard for inclusion was considerably more lax for these two categories, allowing the possibility of blend stimuli. (Variations in agreement on a single emotion did have a bearing on the accuracy of FAST predictions, as will be discussed later.) In the 51 pictures selected, there were 28 different persons shown, some more than once within an

one facial area at a time was intended to reduce the likelihood that a scorer would be influenced in scoring one part of the face by being able to remember how he had scored another part of that same face. To further impair memory for individual pictures, the 51 selected photographs were grouped with 50 other photographs for scoring. These other photographs were often of some of the same stimulus persons. Thus, all 101 pictures were scored on a single facial area before the next area was shown.

Three scorers were trained for about six hours each. Each FAST item was discussed, the relevant wrinkles or positions of the face in each item were indicated, important discriminations between particular pairs of items were emphasized. Practice photographs were then scored; discrepancies between the scores and those made by two of the authors (Paul Ekman and Wallace V. Friesen) were discussed. Scoring a photograph was found to be a fairly rapid procedure. A scorer usually scored a face on one facial area in less than thirty seconds.

The three scorers worked independently, with the set of FAST photographic items for a particular facial area on a board in front of them, so that all could be seen at once. Their task was to find the FAST item(s) which best matched the appearance of the face to be scored. The scorer had five choices:

1 A single FAST item that best matched the facial area to be scored.
2 Two FAST items, one indicated as a first choice, and another as a second choice, if there were two items that closely approximated the facial area to be scored.
3 Two FAST items, indicated as tied scores for first choice, if there was asymmetry within the facial area to be scored (e.g., the left brow resembled one FAST item, and the right brow resembled another).
4 A NEUTRAL score, if the facial area to be scored appeared to be in a normal or rest position or the wrinkles shown were inferred to be a permanent part of the physiognomy.
5 A NO-SCORE, if there was some movement in the facial area to be scored but no FAST item that approximated its appearance.

As a last step, after all three facial areas were scored by the three scorers, the entire face was shown and scored on the head orientation code.

Facial area score

The three scorers did not always agree. (Reliability is reported later in "RESULTS.") An *a priori* procedure was devised for combining the results of the three independent scorers into a single set of scores for each facial area for each of the 51 faces. Each facial area was assigned nine points, which were to be distributed across the six emotion categories, the neutral category, and the no-score category. Each of the three scorers contributed three out of the nine points to a facial area. If a scorer indicated only one choice for a facial area, that choice received his three points regardless of whether the choice was a FAST item, neutral, or no-score. If a scorer indicated both a first and second choice, the first choice was given two points and the second choice one point. And, if the scorer indicated a tied choice, each item received a point and a half. In assigning points, the FAST items chosen by each scorer were converted into the emotion categories the items represented. If a scorer made two choices but both were items for one emotion category, that category received all three of his points; (Table 1 shows more than one FAST item for certain emotion categories within certain facial areas).

Whole face emotion prediction

The points for each emotion category, and for the neutral and no-score categories were summed across the three facial areas for each of the 51 selected faces, to yield a total of 27 points for each face; (nine points from each of three facial areas). A simple set of *a priori* arbitrary rules was employed for determining from the distribution of points whether there would be no prediction, a single emotion prediction, or a blend prediction.

No prediction was made either if there were fewer than six points accumulated by any one emotion category, or if the no-score category had the highest number of points and the most

Results

Reliability

Table 4 shows two measures of agreement among the scorers. The first measure is quite strict, requiring that the scorers agree exactly on their choices. If, for example, two scorers had given the same first choice for a picture, but one of them had also given a second

TABLE 4

Reliability on FAST scoring

(*percent of the 51 stimuli scored where scorers agreed*)

	EXACT AGREEMENT ON BOTH FIRST AND SECOND CHOICE		FIRST CHOICE OF ONE SCORER IS EITHER FIRST OR SECOND CHOICE OF OTHER SCORERS	
	2 of 3 scorers	*3 of 3 scorers*	*2 of 3 scorers*	*3 of 3 scorers*
Brows-Forehead	80%	31%	98%	69%
Eyes	82%	41%	98%	78%
Lower face	88%	59%	98%	78%

frequent emotion category had accumulated fewer than nine points. A single emotion category was predicted either if a single category had two points more than the next most frequent category and the number of points for the predicted category was more than six, or if the neutral category had the most points, but there was an emotion category that had at least six points. If two categories had at least six points but were tied or within less than two points of each other, the head orientation code was consulted in an attempt to break the tie. If the head orientation score supported only one of the two tied emotion categories, then that was the predicted category. If the head orientation score supported both of the tied categories, or neither, then the blend of the two emotions was predicted.

choice, this was counted as a disagreement. The table shows the percentage of the 51 faces on which two of the three and all three scorers agreed exactly. The second measure was a more generous index of agreement. Disagreement was noted only if one scorer's first choice was not either the first or second choice of another scorer. Again, agreement is shown for two and for all three of the scorers.

The extent of agreement shown in Table 4 suggests there was sufficient reliability among scorers; the only low agreement figures are those measuring exact agreement among all three scorers. Examination of the pattern of agreement did not suggest that any one scorer was generally deviant. Instead, it appeared that, on occasion, any one scorer would fail to grasp all the details in the facial area to be scored, and thus would disagree with the other two scorers. The procedure for deriving affect scores for each facial area allows for such occasional deviance on scoring, since relatively few points are contributed to a prediction by any one scorer if his choices are not replicated by another scorer.

single emotion as were the faces for the other emotion categories. Table 2 showed that when all three criteria utilized in selecting single emotion faces were considered, the FEAR pictures elicited less agreement among observers about that single emotion than did the other emotion category faces.

TABLE 5

FAST prediction about perceived emotion in relation to emotion judged by the majority of observers

Emotion judged by majority of the observers	FAST PREDICTION								
	Hap-piness	Sur-prise	Anger	Sad-ness	Disgust	Fear	Hap-piness Fear	Fear Surprise	Fear Surprise Sad
Happiness	10								
Surprise		10							
Anger			10						
Sadness				9			1		
Disgust				1	3				
Fear			1	1		3		1	1

Validity

Table 5 shows that FAST correctly predicted the emotions judged by the observers for the majority of the faces. With 45 out of 51 faces correctly predicted, there is no need for a statistical test to establish significance. FEAR was the only emotion category for which FAST scores did not succeed with the majority of the faces. Those errors were not totally irrelevant, since two of the four incorrectly predicted FEAR faces were predicted to be blends involving fear.

It may well be that FAST's relatively poor success with FEAR as compared to other emotion category faces was related to the fact that the FEAR faces were not as adequate in showing the

We believe that FAST would succeed as well in predicting FEAR as other emotion categories, if similarly high agreement, single emotion FEAR faces were scored. It might be argued, however, that perhaps such faces cannot occur. Since no such FEAR faces were found among all the faces initially considered, and there were high agreement faces for each of the other emotion categories, perhaps FEAR faces always elicit lower agreement or judgments of blended emotions. Yet, when we posed faces by having untrained persons imitate FAST FEAR items, those faces were judged with as much agreement about a single emotion as is shown in Table 2 for the emotion categories of SADNESS, SURPRISE and ANGER. However, until it can be shown that FAST can correctly predict the majority of some new set of faces which observers agree represent only FEAR, some question will have to remain about whether the FAST fear items are completely adequate for this task. (Our new FEAR faces could not be used for this purpose, since these faces were obtained by having persons imitate FAST photographic items).

Comparison of facial areas

Table 6 shows the percentage of the 51 faces which were correctly predicted when FAST scores were considered for each of the three facial areas separately, as compared with the combined scores which were shown in Table 5 and which are shown again in Table 6. No one facial area provided as many correct predictions as did the combined facial area scores. Certain facial areas

did, however, provide better predictions than other areas for particular emotions; and, for five emotion categories, a particular facial area did yield a prediction as good as or better than the combined facial area score.

These findings contradict most of the results reported by earlier investigators who had attempted to determine whether one facial area was better than another by comparing observers' judgments made from different facial areas (Coleman, 1949; Dunlap, 1927; Hanawalt, 1944; Nummenmaa, 1964; Ruckmick, 1921). But there was little consistency among those investigators, probably because most chose to utilize the facial behavior of but one stimulus person. The data in Table 6 were based on 28 different stimulus persons. It may be that particular people tend to

TABLE 6

Comparison of percent correct predictions from each separate facial area (FAST scores)

EMOTION CATEGORY	FACIAL AREA			
	Brows-forehead	*Eyes*	*Lower face*	*All three facial areas combined (data reported in Table 5)*
Happiness	70	90	100	100
Sadness	70	90	0	90
Surprise	70	90	90	100
Anger	80	50	100	100
Disgust	25	0	75	75
Fear	29	71	29	43
Correct predictions across all emotion categories	49	73	67	88

employ one facial area more than another when attempting to pose a particular emotion. The present data do not allow study of that possibility, since we had selected very few faces from each stimulus person in order to have many different stimulus persons included. Table 6 does suggest that certain facial areas may provide more information for one emotion than for another, and that there might be benefits in weighting scores from particular facial areas for predicting particular emotions. But replication of the differential importance of facial areas for particular emotions with another sample of stimulus persons should be obtained before reaching any such conclusions.

Discussion

These results are very encouraging. It has been possible to specify and measure the particular facial behavior relevant to the recognition of six emotions. The extent of success achieved with this measurement procedure is remarkable, especially since it was based on *a priori* theory and hunches and employed simple, logically based rules for combining scores to yield predictions rather than weighted scores based on empirical results. FAST opens for investigation a large number of research questions previously neglected because of the lack of an adequate method for measuring facial behavior. FAST should serve to legitimate research on the face and emotion, since the stimulus basis for observers' impressions about emotions can now be specified. FAST should encourage studies where the facial behavior itself is the dependent variable, rather than observers' judgments of the face, where measurement of the face can be related to changes in environmental conditions, self-reported emotion, instructional set, etc.

It should be recognized, however, that the present report represents but a first step in establishing the validity of FAST, albeit a promising one. The necessary next steps for establishing validity, a few of the potential problems in this measurement procedure, and experiments we have in progress will now be discussed. The first validity test reported here employed still photographs of posed facial behavior judged as single emotion stimuli. We will first discuss the question of FAST's applicability to spontaneous behavior, to blends, and to motion rather than still records of the face. We will then consider FAST's use in expression rather than recognition studies, the problems of physiognomic variables, and the comprehensiveness of the scoring system.

Some investigators (e.g., Hunt, 1941) have viewed posed facial behavior as a unique set of culturally bound, learned conventions that have little relevance to spontaneous facial behavior. Since FAST succeeded in predicting the recognition of posed faces, that view might suggest that FAST would have little applicability to the study of spontaneous facial behavior. The fact that posed behavior is judged as showing the same emotions across eleven literate cultures and one preliterate culture (Ekman, 1968; Ekman and Friesen, 1970; Ekman, Sorenson, and Friesen, 1969; Izard, 1968, 1970a) argues against the view that posed behavior has no relationship to spontaneous facial behavior, since it is highly improbable that so many different cultures would have developed the same set of learned arbitrary conventions for each emotion. These cross-cultural studies have provided strong evidence of a pan-cultural element in the facial behavior associated with emotion, namely that particular facial behaviors are associated with particular emotions. Significantly, association of the same emotions with the same faces across cultures was established with posed faces. Further, most of the facial stimuli used by Ekman *et al.* in their cross-cultural investigations were included in the FAST study reported here, so that the present results could be extended to show that FAST predicts how most of these faces will be judged by observers from a number of different cultures. In light of this evidence, it seems reasonable to assume that posed behavior differs little from spontaneous facial behavior in form. Ekman, Friesen, and Ellsworth (1971) have suggested that posed differs from spontaneous facial behavior in duration, in the lack of attempt to control or otherwise moderate the behavior, and in the frequency of single emotion faces as compared to blend faces. Direct evidence, however, is required to show that FAST can accurately predict how spontaneous faces are judged by observers. We have such a study in progress, and expect that it will suggest the need to add some items to FAST, since we may well have overlooked certain movements for some of the emotions.

Another validity test in progress is investigating whether FAST can discriminate faces judged as blends from those judged as single emotions, and the particular emotions that compose a blend. Blends can be shown on the face in three different ways: (1) division by facial areas, in which one emotion is shown in one facial area, another emotion shown in another facial area; (e.g., raised brows as in surprise, and pressed lips as in anger); (2) division within a facial area, in which one emotion is shown in one part of that facial area, another in another part of that area; (e.g., one brow raised as in surprise, the other lowered as in anger); (3) the display of a face that does not incorporate the elements of either blended emotion but instead is the product of the simultaneous muscle action relevant to each single emotion. This last type of blend face should not be accurately predicted by FAST, and might suggest the need for additional items. The discrimination of blends from single emotion faces will probably require the development of a more complex set of prediction rules utilizing some weighting of scores for each of the three facial areas rather than the simple summing of points and predicting the majority score that was used in the study reported here.

Another study in progress has been applying FAST to videotape records of facial behavior. FAST seems to be as applicable to such motion records as to still photographs, although the scoring of videotapes is slower. Most of the excess time is required for determining the exact duration of each change in facial appearance, however, rather than determining which FAST item is applicable. The resolution required for FAST scoring of videotapes necessitates filling the videopicture with just the face. In one respect, FAST is easier with motion records than with still photographs. The scorer has no problem deciding whether a particular wrinkle is part of the permanent physiognomy of the person when utilizing motion records, since he has the base-line facial behavior and can discount anything that never changes in appearance.

FAST was designed to be applicable not only in recognition of emotion studies, but also in expression studies, where the aim is to predict the person's self-reported feelings or the conditions under which the facial behavior occurred. One such study is in progress utilizing the videotape records mentioned above. In a comparison of Japanese and U.S. subjects, FAST is being applied to spontaneous facial behavior emitted while the subjects watched stressful and neutral films (Ekman, Lazarus, Friesen, Opton, Averill, and Malmstrom, 1970). FAST seems sufficiently comprehensive to encompass most of the facial behavior shown in these videotapes, although certain facial behaviors, purposefully omitted from FAST because they were not considered emotion-specific, do occur in these records; (e.g., tongue showing, lip biting, cheek biting, etc.). Agreement among scorers is comparable to that reported earlier for the scoring of still photographs. Validity studies in progress will compare FAST scores with self-reported emotions, with psychophysiological measurements, and between the two experimental conditions, watching a neutral or a stress film.

Physiognomic determinants of facial behavior may have two undesired influences on FAST scores. People may differ in the permanent wrinkle patterns that with age become part of their facial appearance, more or less noticeable perhaps depending upon the action of the facial muscles. Some of those permanent wrinkles may resemble FAST items and not be discriminated from wrinkles produced by muscle movement. As mentioned earlier, this problem does not occur if motion records are utilized, so that the scorer can see the base line, unchanging wrinkles. With still photographs, the scorer may not be able to make that differentiation. This would not be a problem in a recognition study, since even permanent wrinkles are part of the stimulus configuration seen by the observer; if the permanent wrinkles are relevant to emotion, they should be scored by FAST. In expression studies, however, where

the aim is to distinguish a transient event, a mood, an environmental change, etc., if FAST scores the permanent wrinkles it is adding information irrelevant to that transient event. This may not be a serious problem, however, since in such expression studies the investigator would rarely decide to utilize a single still photograph as his record, but instead would utilize either multiple sequential stills or a motion record, and the scorer could see the base-line pattern.

A potentially more serious problem may result from individual differences in facial repertoire. Pilot studies requiring individuals to imitate FAST items suggest that there are reliable individual differences in ability to make certain facial movements. The distribution of such differences is not yet known, nor is it known whether they are due to bone structure, facial musculature, fatty deposits, or psychological factors. But if there are such individual lacunae in the repertoire of facial behavior included in FAST, they would weaken FAST predictions for particular people. For example, if a person is unable to produce vertical wrinkles between the brows and a lowering and drawing together of the inner corners of the brow, he cannot be eligible to receive a FAST anger score for the brow-forehead area. We have begun to specify rules that predict the six emotions even when certain elements within particular facial areas are not shown, on the basis of the presence of certain other items. In the example just described, if the lower eye lid movement and the mouth positions listed in FAST for ANGER were shown, but the brow resembled a DIGUST or SADNESS brow (which we have found can occur when some people attempt to imitate FAST's ANGER brow), or a neutral or no-score brow, the prediction would still be ANGER. Utilizing some of these decisions rules based on such physiognomic considerations increased FAST'S success in prediction. There were 49 out of 51 faces correctly predicted, rather than 45 out of 51, as reported earlier when the sum of scores across facial areas had been used. This suggests the value of this approach, but most of the work on determining such individual differences in ability to show the movements depicted in FAST and the development of relevant prediction rules remains to be done.

It is difficult to evaluate whether FAST is too elaborate a system, or too limited in its coverage. Considering only six emotion categories, FAST allows for more than 12,000 combinations of items for the three facial areas. Obviously, some of these must not be anatomically possible. In studying more than 2,000 of the combinations, however, we have not yet found one of the impossible ones. There may well be more items necessary for these six emotions, and this should be discovered in the spontaneous recognition and spontaneous expression studies in progress. FAST will be broadened to cover emotions of INTEREST, CONTEMPT, and SHAME. Other emotions might be considered, depending upon the theoretical orientation of the investigator. We believe that other emotions beyond these mentioned either do not have a distinctive facial appearance or can be conceived as blends of those we have considered, but there is no conclusive research as yet to support that belief.

While FAST presently allows for thousands of facial appearances, it should be remembered that it was designed to describe and measure facial behaviors associated with emotion. Many facial behaviors that we considered as either not emotion-specific or

not relevant to emotion (e.g., tongue showing, lip biting, etc.) are not included in FAST, and presumably these nonemotional facial behaviors far outnumber the facial appearances covered by FAST.

NOTE

1. This research was supported by research grants from the National Institute of Mental Health (MH 11976), and the Advanced Research Projects Agency (AF AFO SR-1229-67), and by a Research Scientist Development Award Type II (5-KO2-MH-06092), and a Research Scientist Award (K5-23, 797) from the Research Fellowships Branch of the National Institute of Mental Health. The authors are grateful to Jerry Boucher, Phoebe Ellsworth Diebold, and Virginia Sullwold for their help in the initial steps of the research, and to Patricia Garlan for her editorial assistance.

REFERENCES

Allport, F. H., 1924 *Social Psychology* (Boston: Houghton Mifflin).

Arnold, M. B., 1960 *Emotion and Personality* (New York: Columbia University Press).

Birdwhistell, R. L., 1952 *Introduction to Kinesics* (Louisville, Ky.: University of Louisville Press).

Coleman, J. C., 1949 "Facial Expressions of Emotion", *Psychological Monograph* 63:296.

Darwin, Charles, 1872 *The Expression of the Emotions in Man and Animals* (London: John Murray).

Davis, R. C., 1934 "The Specificity of Facial Expressions", *Journal of General Psychology* 10, 42–58.

Duchenne, B., 1862 *Mécanisme de la physionomie humaine ou analyse électro-physiologique de l'expression des passions* (Paris: Baillière).

Dunlap, K., 1927 "The Role of Eye-Muscles and Mouth-Muscles in the Expression of the Emotions", *Genetic Psychology Monograph* 2, 199–233.

Ekman, P., 1968 "The Recognition and Display of Facial Behavior in Literate and Non-Literate Cultures", *Proceedings, American Psychological Association Convention* 3, 727.

Ekman, P., and W. V. Friesen, 1968 "Nonverbal Behavior in Psychotherapy Research", *Research in Psychotherapy* 3, ed. by J. Shlien (Washington, D.C.: American Psychological Association), 179–216. 1969a "Nonverbal Leakage and Clues to Deception", *Psychiatry* 32:1, 88–105. 1969b "The Repertoire of Nonverbal Behavior: Categories, Origins, Usage, and Coding", *Semiotica* 1, 49–98. 1970 "Constants across Culture in the Face and Emotion", *Journal of Personality and Social Psychology* (in press).

Ekman, P., W. V. Friesen, and P. Ellsworth, 1971 *The Face and Emotion: Guidelines for Research and an Integration of Findings* (New York: Pergamon).

Ekman, P., R. S. Lazarus, W. V. Friesen, E. T. Opton, J. R. Averill, and E. J. Malmstrom, 1970 "Facial Behavior and Stress in Two Cultures", unpublished manuscript (Langley Porter Neuropsychiatric Institute).

Ekman, P., E. R. Sorensen, and W. V. Friesen, 1969 "Pan-Cultural Elements in Facial Displays of Emotions", *Science* 164, 86–88.

Engen, T., N. Levy, and H. Schlosberg, 1957 "A New Series of Facial Expressions", *American Psychologist* 12, 264–66.

Frijda, N. H., 1969 "Recognition of Emotion", *Advances in Experimental Social Psychology* 4, ed. by L. Berkowitz (New York: Academic Press).

Frijda, N. H., and E. Philipszoon, 1963 "Dimensions of Recognition of Emo-

tion", *Journal of Abnormal Social Psychology* 66:1, 45–51.

Frois-Wittmann, J., 1930 "The Judgment of Facial Expression", *Journal of Experimental Psychology* 13,113–51.

Fulcher, J. S., 1942 " 'Voluntary' Facial Expression in Blind and Seeing Children", *Archives of Psychology* 38:272.

Hanawalt, N. G., 1944 "The Role of the Upper and the Lower Parts of the Face as the Basis for Judging Facial Expressions II: In Posed Expressions and 'Candid Camera' Pictures", *Journal of General Psychology* 31, 23–36.

Honkavaara, S., 1961 "The Psychology of Expression", *The British Journal of Psychology*, Monograph Supplements 23, ed. by R. H. Thouless (New York: Cambridge University Press).

Hunt, W. A., 1941 "Recent Developments in the Field of Emotion", *Psychological Bulletin* 38:5, 249–76.

Izard, C., 1968 "Cross-Cultural Research Findings on Development in Recognition of Facial Behavior", *Proceedings, American Psychological Association Convention* 3, 727. 1970a "The Emotions and Emotion Constructs in Personality and Culture Research", *Handbook of Modern Personality Theory*, ed. by R. B. Cattell (Chicago: Aldine). 1970b "The Emotions as a Culture-Common Framework of Motivational Experiences and Communicative Cues", *The Subjective Culture*, ed. by G. Vassiliou and V. Vassiliou (in press).

Landis, C., 1924 "Studies of Emotional Reactions II: General Behavior and Facial Expression", *Journal of Comparative Psychology* 4, 447–509.

Landis, C., and W. A. Hunt, 1939 *The Startle Pattern* (New York: Farrar).

Leventhal, H., and E. Sharp, 1965 "Facial Expressions as Indicators of Distress", *Affect, Cognition and Personality: Empirical Studies*, ed. by S. S. Tomkins and C. E. Izard (New York: Springer), 296–318.

Murphy, G., L. B. Murphy, and T. M. Newcomb, 1937 *Experimental Social Psychology*, rev. ed. (New York and London: Harper Brothers).

Nummenmaa, T., 1964 *The Language of the Face* (=*Jyväskylä Studies in Education, Psychology, and Social Research*) (Jyväskylä, Finland: Jyväskylän Yliopistoyhdystys).

Plutchik, R., 1962 *The Emotions: Facts, Theories, and a New Model* (New York: Random House).

Ruckmick, C. A., 1921 "A Preliminary Study of the Emotions", *Psychology Monograph* 30:134–39, 30–35.

Thompson, J., 1941 "Development of Facial Expression of Emotion in Blind and Seeing Children", *Archives of Psychology* 37:264.

Tomkins, S. S., 1962 *Affect, Imagery, Consciousness*, Vol. 1: *The Positive Affects* (New York: Springer). 1963 *Affect, Imagery, Consciousness*, Vol. 2: *The Negative Affects* (New York: Springer).

Tomkins, S. S., and R. McCarter, 1964 "What and Where Are the Primary Affects?: Some Evidence for a Theory", *Perceptual and Motor Skills* 18, 119–58.

Trujillo, N. P., and T. A. Warthin, 1968 "The Frowning Sign Multiple Forehead Furrows in Peptic Ulcer", *Journal of the American Medical Association* 205:6, 218.

3

COMMUNICATION OF AFFECT THROUGH FACIAL EXPRESSIONS IN HUMANS [1]

ROSS W. BUCK, VIRGINIA J. SAVIN,
ROBERT E. MILLER, AND WILLIAM F. CAUL

It has long been recognized that, under the right circumstances, emotional states are associated with expressive nonverbal facial expressions and gestures, and many have suspected that a person's ability to accurately "send" and "receive" such nonverbal messages may be an important factor in his ability to communicate with others. Early efforts to experimentally investigate the communicative role of nonverbal behaviors did not yield notable success, perhaps because most of the studies employed static photographs or enactments of posed emotional expressions. During the past few years, there has been a resurgence of interest in this problem, and a number of investigators have begun to direct their efforts toward nonverbal communication. Fortunately, since their research training has encompassed a number of different disciplines, several different approaches to the problem have been attempted and, thus, today there is an extensive literature in the field and a rich diversity of techniques for studying nonverbal phenomena (Duncan, 1969); Ekman, Friesen, & Ellsworth, 1970; Frijda, 1969; Vine, 1970).

The present experiment attempted to study nonverbal communication in man utilizing an adaptation of the "cooperative conditioning" approach which has been developed to study the nonverbal communication of affect in monkeys (Miller, 1967). This laboratory method, as used with animals, involves the presentation of a conditioning stimulus to one of a pair of animals, the "sender," which is not provided with the instrumental devices required to respond appropriately to the stimulus. The second animal of the pair, the "observer," does not receive the stimulus but does have access to the manipulanda essential to the appropriate conditioned response. The face and head of the sender is televised to the observer so that an expressive reaction to the onset of the conditioning stimulus may be perceived by the observer who may, in turn, make the appropriate conditioned response to the conditioning situation. A number

From *Journal of Personality and Social Psychology,* 1972, 23, 362–71. Copyright © 1972 by the American Psychological Association and reprinted by permission.

of experiments have demonstrated that monkeys perform at very high levels of accuracy in the cooperative conditioning situation, that the communication process is accompanied by significant and discriminated physiological responses in both the stimulus and responder animals, and that monkeys which have been subjected to experimental isolation regimens that destroy or impair social behaviors fail to either send or receive adequate nonverbal messages when paired with other monkeys (Miller, 1967; Miller, Caul, & Mirsky, 1967).

The cooperative conditioning method has been successfully applied to humans using electric shocks to produce emotional responses (Gubar, 1966; Lanzetta & Kleck, 1970). These experiments have demonstrated that it is feasible to elicit affective expressions repeatedly during the course of an experimental session and to thus examine the variables affecting nonverbal fluency.

In the present study, emotional responses were produced through the presentation of emotionally loaded visual stimuli. Color slides with varied emotional content were presented to a human sender, while an observer watching the sender's face on closed-circuit television attempted to (a) judge what kind of slide the sender was watching and to (b) rate the sender's emotional reaction. The experiment was designed to investigate whether significant nonverbal communication of affect could be demonstrated in this kind of experimental situation. It also explored the physiological concomitants of the communication process: whether the physiological responses of an observer were influenced by the reception of accurate emotional information from a sender, and whether

"physiologic covariation" between the physiological responses of the sender and observer occurred and were related to the accuracy of communication (cf. Kaplan, Burch, & Bloom, 1964). Finally, the present experiment explored the relationships of sex of subject, personality variables, and physiological responding, with the ability to send and receive emotional information through facial expression.[2]

Method

Subjects

A total of 21 female and 17 male college students were recruited as paid subjects in the experiment. The females were tested in a total of 12 pairings, with 3 of the subjects serving first as senders and subsequently as observers for other subjects. Two of these pairings were dropped from the experiment because of apparatus and procedural flaws. The female pairings received their instructions and preexperimental and postexperimental interviews from a female experimenter. The 17 male subjects were tested in a total of 9 pairings by a male experimenter. One male subject served first as a sender and then as an observer for another subject. Because of the nature of the experiment and the necessity that the sender be unaware that another subject was involved in the procedures, no subject could ever serve as a sender after having been an observer.

Apparatus

Three separate experimental rooms were required for this experiment. The sender subject was placed in one of these rooms that contained an adjustable chair facing a white wooden partition constructed in the shape of a U from three 4 x 8 sheets of plywood.

Fluorescent light fixtures attached to the partition provided sufficient illumination for televising the subject. In the center of the wall facing the subject was a 20.5-centimeter square rear projection screen, a jewel lamp to be used for signals from the experimenter, and two inked scales which were to be used by the subject in rating his own response to the stimulus materials. One of the 9-point scales was defined by the adjectives "strong-weak" and the other by "pleasant-unpleasant." A microphone was positioned on a table near the subject. An automatic slide projector, loudspeaker, and a closed-circuit television camera were concealed behind the partition. The camera was focused on the sender subject's head and face.

The observer subject was placed in another test room located a considerable distance from the sender subject's room. Both the distances involved and three closed doors, one of which was soundproofed, eliminated any transmission of voice or sounds between the two test rooms. The observer subject sat in a comfortable chair facing a television receiver. A jeweled signal lamp was placed on top of the television to provide signals from the experimenter. A telegraph key and a digital display device were placed on a table to the front and right of the observer subject.

The third room was the control room for the experiment, and it contained the trial programmer, timers, and related electronic equipment; tape recorders for presenting instructions and recording verbal responses of the sender subject; and an eight-channel Grass Model 7 polygraph equipped with two 7P1A low level direct current preamplifiers for skin conductance measurement and two 7P5A wide band alternating current electroencephalogram preamplifiers for heart rate measurement. There was also a television monitor in the control room so that the experimenter could observe the facial responses of the sender subject.

Electrodes were attached to both of the subjects for skin conductance and heart rate measures. Zinc electrodes with zinc sulphate electrode paste, prepared and applied according to the suggestions of Lykken (1959) in a unipolar arrangement, were used to monitor skin conductance. The active electrode was placed on the volar surface of the distal phalange of the second finger of the left hand. The inactive electrode was placed on the left forearm after the site was pretreated by rubbing vigorously with facial tissues containing electrode paste. Heart rate was recorded from standard 2 x 4 centimeter electrocardiogram electrodes, with electrode paste, strapped to the underside of each wrist.

Stimuli for the experiment consisted of 25 color slides selected by the experimenters to represent five content categories: sexual, scenic, maternal, disgusting, and unusual or ambiguous. Sexual slides consisted of pictures of nude and seminude males and females; scenic slides were landscapes and street scenes; maternal slides were pictures of mothers and young children in various activities; disgusting slides depicted severe facial injuries and burns; and unusual slides showed strange light effects, double exposures, and art objects.

Procedure

Female subjects responded to a series of personality inventories prior to the experimental session. The tests were administered to groups of 10–30 persons in a context unrelated to the experiment. The personality scales included the following tests: The Eysenck

(1959) Extraversion-Introversion scale, the Janis and Field (1959) Self-Esteem scale, the Byrne (1961) Repression-Sensitization scale, the Alpert and Haber (1960) Test Anxiety Scale, a 20-item form of the Taylor (1953) Manifest Anxiety Scale, and the Marlowe and Crowne (1960) Social Desirability Scale.

The subjects were contacted by telephone at least a week after they had taken the personality scales. They were not selected from the pool of subjects on the basis of any of the test results but simply drawn randomly from the list of women who had been present for the personality tests. Appointments were made so that the first subject of a pair arrived 15 minutes before the second. The first subject to arrive for the experimental session was arbitrarily assigned to the observer role and promptly ushered to the appropriate test room before the sender subject arrived. The nature of the experiment was explained briefly to the observer subject, and the electrodes for monitoring skin conductance and heart rate were then attached.

The second subject of the pair was taken to the sender subject room and was told that the experiment was concerned with the relationship between his physiological response and his "subjective verbal report" of his emotional reaction to different kinds of pictures. The experimenter attached the electrodes for physiological monitoring, briefly explaining the physiological mechanisms involved in the two measures as he did so. The sender subject was seated in the chair facing the rear projection screen. The experimenter explained that the lens of the television camera, which was dimly visible to the sender subject, was a second slide projector used in concept formation experiments and which would not be used in the present session. Interviews and ratings taken after the experiment indicated that this was accepted by virtually all of the subjects. The experimenter then asked the sender subject to sit quietly for 5 minutes in order to establish a physiological base line, and explained that he would give more details about the experiment after the base-line period over a loudspeaker located behind the screen.

While the sender subject waited, the experimenter returned to the observation room to give detailed instructions to the observer subject. The experimenter showed the observer subject two examples of each kind of slide through a projector and demonstrated the prepared rating scales which the observer subject would use. These consisted of descriptions of the five slide categories and three 9-point rating scales which the observer subject was to fill out after each slide presentation. The experimenter told the observer subject to circle the slide category that he believed was most likely presented to the sender subject on each occasion. He was then to fill out three rating scales which indicated (a) how certain he was of his judgment, (b) how strong he thought the sender subject's emotional reaction was along a 9-point strong-weak dimension, and (c) how pleasant he thought the sender subject's emotional reaction was along a 9-point pleasant-unpleasant dimension.

The experimenter explained the sequence of events on each trial as follows:

You won't have any signal when the slide first comes on, so watch his face carefully to catch his first reactions. When the light over the TV and the number in the box come on, the other person will start talking about his emotional reaction to the slide. You won't hear him, but keep watching his face as he talks. Then when the light and number go off, stop looking at the TV and make your ratings. When you finish rating, press the key to signal me that I can present the next slide. After you press the key, start looking at the TV again for the subject's response to the next slide.

After the observer subject indicated that he understood the instructions, the experimenter returned to the control room to await the end of the sender subject's base-line period.

After the 5-minute base-line period had elapsed, the sender subject was given the following tape-recorded instructions over the loudspeaker:

The purpose of this experiment is to compare your physiological reactions with your subjective reactions as you look at a series of pictures. To do this, we will record your heart rate and skin conductance. In addition, we'd like to have your description of your feelings about the pictures. When a picture comes on, just look at it until the light next to it turns on. Then begin describing the emotional reaction you have when you look at the picture. The light will be on for about 20 seconds. You may keep talking all the time the light is on. Try to describe your subjective emotional reaction as accurately as you can. Feel free to say anything you like about your feelings. When the light goes off, you may stop talking. Then tell me your emotional response to the picture, rating from strong to weak and from pleasant to unpleasant, according to the scales in front of you. There will be about 25 slides in all. Do you have any questions?

The first slide was shown 30 seconds after the end of the instructions. Each trial was run as follows: A slide was presented to the sender subject for 10

seconds, with no signal to the observer subject ("slide" period). The signal lights were then activated in both rooms, and a number corresponding to the number of the slide appeared in the observer subject's digital display. The light signaled the sender subject to verbally describe his emotional response to the slide while the observer subject watched ("description" periods). After 20 seconds, the lights, digital display, and slide were simultaneously turned off. This signaled the sender subject to stop talking and to verbally rate the strength and pleasantness of his emotional reaction to the slide according to the two 9-point scales in front of him ("postslide" period). At the same time, the observer subject stopped looking at the sender subject and made his own ratings of the sender subject's responses as he had perceived them. When he completed his ratings, usually within 30 seconds, the observer subject signaled the experimenter by pressing on the telegraph key. The experimenter waited 10–20 seconds and then presented the next slide. In the rare event that the observer subject failed to signal the completion of his ratings within 45 seconds, the next trial was presented. A total of 25 trials were presented.

When the session was over, the experimenter removed the electrodes and gave both subjects a post-experimental questionnaire. The two subjects were then brought together, the experiment was explained in detail, and the experimenter answered any questions that the subjects raised.

Dependent variables

Physiological records are analyzed by dividing each trial into five consecutive 10-second periods: (a) pretrial; (b) slide only; (c) first description period, the first 10 seconds during which the sender subject described his reactions to the picture; (*d*) second description period, the second 10 seconds during which the sender subject talked about his responses to the picture; and (*e*) postslide, or rating, period, during which both subjects made their ratings of the sender subject's reactions. Mean heart rate in beats per minute, number of skin conductance responses exceeding 500 ohms, and the magnitude of the largest skin conductance response in log microhms were obtained for each period on each trial for both sender subject and observer subject.

Nonverbal communication was measured by three behavioral measures: (*a*) the percentage of trials on which the observer subject was able to correctly categorize the type of picture that the sender subject had been shown (categorization index); (*b*) the Pearson product-moment correlation coefficient between the sender subject's and observer subject's ratings of the strength of the sender subject's reactions to the slides over the 25 trials (strength index); and (*c*) the product-moment correlation coefficient between the two subjects' ratings of the pleasantness of the sender subject's reactions to the pictures over

the session (pleasantness index). It was anticipated that these three measures should be sensitive to different aspects of the communication process. Categorization requires the transmission of information about the specific emotional experience of the sender subject, and it also obliges the observer subject to make some inferences about the sender subject's mode of response to the content of the pictures. Thus, if an observer subject detects an expression of revulsion on the face of the sender subject, he is still faced with the problem of deciding whether a disgusting or sexual slide was shown. No such further interpretation is required with the strength or the pleasantness measures. The strength measure presumably reflects the communication of affective intensity, while the pleasantness measure should involve the communication of general affective tone.

Results

Accuracy of communication

The results from the three measures of accuracy of communication are presented in Table 1. In 9 of the 10 female pairs, the observer subject correctly

TABLE 1

Mean values for three indexes of communication accuracy

Index	Female pairs	Male pairs
Categorization (mean percentage of slides correctly identified)	.396 **	.249
Pleasantness (mean correlation index between the sender's and the observer's rating of pleasantness)	.48 **	.22 *
Strength (mean correlation index between the sender's and the observer's rating of strength)	.22 *	.01

* $p < .005$.
** $p < .001$.

identified more than a chance percentage (20%) of the stimulus slides. In 5 of these pairs, chi-square tests revealed that significant levels of communication had been achieved ($p < .05$). In contrast, only 3 of the 9 male pairs correctly identified more than a chance number of slide categories, and in only two of these pairs were the differences significant by the chi-square test. The combined chi-square for all female pairs (McNemar, 1955) also indicated that, as a group, the observer subjects correctly identified the specific category of stimulus pictures shown to the sender subjects at greater than chance levels ($x^2 = 66.16$, $p < .001$). The overall chi-square for male pairings was not significant.

All of the pairings, both male and female, showed positive product-moment correlations between the sender subject's and observer subject's ratings of the pleasantness of the sender subject's emotional responses to the stimuli. Six of the correlation coefficients were significant for female pairs, and three were significant for male pairs ($p < .05$). The individual correlation coefficients were transformed to z scores and averaged to obtain overall correlation indexes (McNemar, 1955). The mean z score was significant for both female pairs ($p < .001$) and male pairs ($p < .005$). The mean z scores were then transformed back to correlations, and these are presented in Table 1.

Nine of the female pairs and five of the male pairs showed positive correlations between the sender subject's and observer subject's ratings of the strength of the sender subject's emotional response. However, since none of the individual correlation coefficients proved to be significantly different from zero, the strength ratings were not considered further.

Physiological responses to the experimental situation

The average physiological responses of the sender subjects are presented on the left side of Figure 1, and the t values of the changes from point to point are

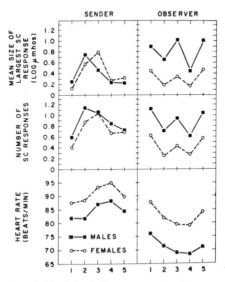

Fig. 1 Physiological response to the experimental situation.

given in Table 2. Both the number and size of skin conductance responses increased when the slide was presented, and then tended to return to base-line levels during the remainder of the stimulation period. There was no significant heart rate response to the slide presentation, but heart rate accelerated during the first description period, perhaps as a function of vocalization (Campos & Johnson, 1966). The cardiac rate dropped back toward base-line levels during the rating, or postslide, period. There were no significant differences between male and female senders on any of these responses.

Observers seemed to have more complex and phasic skin conductance re-

TABLE 2

t *Values of physiological changes*

MEASURE	Pre-slide–slide	Slide–first de-scription	First–second descrip-tion	Second descrip-tion–post-slide
		PERIOD		
			SENDER SUBJECT	
Mean size largest skin conductance response				
Males	4.21 **	−1.94	−5.78 **	.03
Females	2.29 *	1.40	−2.31 *	.79
No. skin conductance responses				
Males	10.81 **	−1.89	−2.38 *	−1.13
Females	4.59 **	3.86 **	−4.43 **	.19
Heart rate				
Males	−.04	4.50 **	1.69	−2.87 *
Females	1.19	5.98 **	2.25	−6.62 **
			OBSERVER SUBJECT	
Mean size largest skin conductance response				
Males	−1.66	1.76	−4.35 **	4.44 **
Females	−3.68 **	1.76	−1.79	2.82 *
No. skin conductance responses				
Males	−4.64 **	2.37 *	−3.47 **	5.06 **
Females	−5.04 **	2.50 *	−1.53	2.98 *
Heart rate				
Males	−2.91	−3.98 **	−1.83	4.44 **
Females	−9.02 **	−2.68 *	−.42	6.69 **

* $p < .05$.
** $p < .01$.

sponses. Both the number and size of skin conductance responses diminished during the period when a stimulus was being presented to the sender subject and increased significantly during the first description period and the rating, or posttrial, interval. These responses were probably due to the signal light which was illuminated at the end of the slide period and extinguished at the end of the second description period. While a similar light was also presented at the same time for senders without, apparently, affecting skin conductance responses in the same way, it is possible that a differential effect of the light as

a function of sender–observer role influenced the results. The heart rate responses of observers were clearly decelerative through the period during which the sender was responding to the stimulus and trended back toward base line only when the observer subject terminated his attention to the sender subject and began filling out the rating form.

The physiological responses of male and female sender subjects and observer subjects during the preslide period were compared to explore sex differences in base-line physiological responding. This analysis indicated that the heart rate of female observer subjects was significantly higher than that of male observer subjects ($p < .01$), and that male observer subjects had more numerous skin conductance responses than female observer subjects ($p < .05$). There were no significant differences between the physiological responses of male and female sender subjects.

Physiological response and communication accuracy

An examination was made of the physiological responses of senders and observers on those trials where correct identification of the slide category was made as opposed to trials where an error was made. There were no differences for either male or female sender subjects or female observer subjects on correct versus incorrect trials. Male observer subjects, however, showed a smaller preslide to slide decrease in the number of skin conductance responses on correct than on incorrect trials ($p < .05$) and a larger mean skin conductance response during the slide period on correct trials ($p < .01$). Thus, male observer subjects displayed more frequent and larger skin conductance responses during the slide period on trials where they accurately detected slide content than they did on incorrect trials.

Product-moment correlations were calculated between each sender's and observer's physiological responses to the slide period over the 25 trials of the session. These correlations presumably reflected the amount of correspondence or "physiological covariation" between the physiological responses of the sender subject and observer subject (cf. Kaplan et al., 1964). The correlations were generally low and nonsignificant, indicating that the physiological responses of the two subjects did not tend to covary during the communication period.

Individual differences in communication ability

Data from the personality scales were available for the female pairs only. Analysis of the relationships between personality factors and the categorization index of communication accuracy revealed significant correlations between extraversion of the sender subject ($r = .62$, $p < .10$); test anxiety (Janis-Field, 1959, scale) of the sender subjects ($r = .85$, $p < .01$); debilitating test anxiety (Albert-Haber, 1960, scale) of the sender subjects ($r = .65$, $p < .05$); and self-esteem of the observer subject ($r = .64$, $p < .10$).

The pleasantness index of communication accuracy was not significantly related to any of the personality measures. It was, however, correlated with the tendency of the sender subject to respond physiologically to the slides. Table 3 gives the product-moment correlations of the accuracy of judgments of pleasantness with (*a*) the changes in the number of skin conductance responses from the preslide to the slide period, (*b*) the median size of the largest skin conductance response during the slide, and (*c*) the heart rate change from the preslide to the first description period.

These analyses reveal that, in general, there was a negative correlation between the sender's physiological response to the slide and the accuracy of the observer's rating of pleasantness. These relationships were particularly strong for female pairings with significant negative relationships between

TABLE 3

Correlations between the pleasantness index of communication accuracy and measures of the sender subject's physiological response to the slides

Pair	Change in no. skin conductance response preslide— slide	Median size of largest skin conduct- ance response slide period	Heart rate change pre- slide—first description
Female	− .91 ***	− .65 **	− .60 **
Male	− .55 *	− .15	.21

* $p < .10$.
** $p < .05$.
*** $p < .01$.

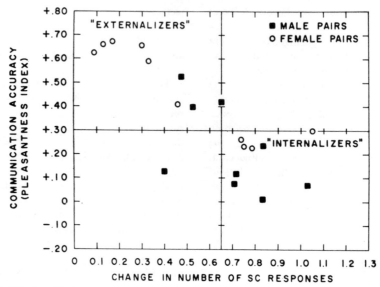

Fig. 2 Relationship between sender's skin conductance responding and accuracy of observer's pleasantness rating.

physiological response and accuracy of communication on both skin conductance and heart rate measures. Male pairings approached significance with respect to the number of skin conductance responses.

The negative relationship between change in the number of skin conductance responses of the sender subject and the accuracy of communication on pleasantness ratings is shown in Figure 2 as a scatterplot. Median splits in each of the variables are superimposed on the figure for the combined sample of female and male pairs. Generally, in those pairs where the sender has few skin conductance responses, the accuracy of communication was above the median, while just the opposite was true of those senders who gave many skin conductance responses. These results appeared to be consistent with Jones's (1960) distinction between overtly expressive but physiologically nonreactive "externalizers" and overtly

nonexpressive but physiologically reactive "internalizers." For illustrative purposes, the appropriate portions of Figure 2 were labeled according to Jones's terminology.

Discussion

It would seem that several rather direct conclusions may be drawn from the results of this complex mass of data. In the first place, it would seem reasonably clear that, at least in the present experimental situation, female pairs were more effective in the transmission and reception of nonverbal emotional cues than were the male pairs. It is undeterminable from the current experiment whether this result was attributable to a more overt and "readable" nonverbal signal from the female senders than from the male senders or to a heightened sensitivity to nonverbal cues by the female observers. It could be that both factors were involved, but until all combinations of mixed male and female pairings are tested, the specific role of sex in the transmission and reception of the nonverbal cues of emotional experience cannot be identified.

It is also clear that both male and female pairs showed negative relationships between the physiological responding of the sender subject and the accuracy of communication. There is a considerable body of evidence which supports this finding that overt expressiveness and autonomic disturbance are negatively related. Jones (1935, 1960), in discussing similar results from his experiments with infants and children, contrasted "internalizers," who show little overt affect but evidence large electrodermal activity and "externalizers," who display affect overtly but have minimal changes in skin potential. Learmonth, Ackerly, and Kaplan (1959) have also reported similar results as a function of personality variables and have traced the evidence supporting this observation back to the early 1920s. Recently, Lanzetta and Kleck (1970), in a study of nonverbal communication using methods similar to those reported here, demonstrated that there were significant negative relationships between skin conductance lability and the expression of affect as measured by the ability of judges to correctly identify from facial expression and trunk posture the presentation of aversive stimuli. Interestingly, Lanzetta and Kleck also reported that the subjects who were relatively inexpressive as senders proved to be unusually sensitive in perceiving affect in others.

The present study indicates that sex may be important in terms of this relationship between physiological responding and communication accuracy. It can be seen from Figure 2 that females tended to be externalizers in this experimental situation, while males tended to be internalizers. This sex difference may be related to the suggestions of both Jones (1960) and Lanzetta and Kleck (1970) that internalizers are persons who have been discouraged from manifesting emotional responses overtly. It would seem to be the case that, in our culture, young boys are systematically taught to inhibit and mask many kinds of emotion to a greater extent than are girls, leading, perhaps, to a greater tendency for adult males to be internalizers of affect.

It is interesting in this regard that males have been shown to have greater skin conductance responding than females in a variety of situations. For example, male observers in the present studies had more numerous base-line skin conductance responses than did females. Craig and Lowrey (1969) found a similar effect in observers watching another person receive shocks, and they also noted that, on more "overt" self-ratings of emotions, males rated themselves as feeling less discomfort than females. Other investigators have found that males show greater skin conductance responding than females in classical conditioning situations involving shock (Graham, Cohen, & Shmavonian, 1966; Shmavonian, Yarmat, & Cohen, 1965). All of these findings could be interpreted as being due to a tendency of males to be internalizers in emotional situations.

The analysis of the physiological concomitants of the communication process did not reveal significant covariation between the physiological responses of the senders and observers. The only finding was that male observers had more frequent and larger skin conductance responses during the slide period on correct than on incorrect trials. The lack of a similar finding among the generally more accurate females suggests that the reception of accurate emotional information from another person did not in itself influence physiological responding. It may be that this effect was observed only in male pairs because the occurrence of interpretable affective cues was more unusual with male senders. This novelty could have been the basis for the greater skin conductance responding for male observers on accurate trials.

Among the three measures of communication attempted in these studies, the pleasantness index showed the most significant results. The categorization index was successful only for the female pairings, and the ratings of strength of the senders' responses did not reflect any significant communication. It is possible that judgments of pleasant-unpleasantness reflect a relatively global, undifferentiated kind of emotional response, which, of the three measures of communication attempted in these studies, requires the fewest inferences about the individual expressing the affect. In order to properly categorize the kind of stimulus that is evoking the expressive response in the sender, the observer has not only to place the expression along the pleasantness—unpleasantness scale but also must make some qualitative judgments regarding the personal characteristics of the expressor. Thus, he might perceive that a sender is smiling during presentation of a stimulus. Does that smile suggest that the sender is amused by a humorous picture, appreciating an attractive sexual slide, or looking at a pleasant landscape? The observer's judgment in this situation may reflect some of his own personality characteristics as well as his attitudes regarding the way that individuals of the sender's

type (age, sex, etc.) are believed to react. Similarly, in order to accurately judge the strength of an emotional response, it may be that the observer must be familiar with the customary levels of response of the individual sender. If this analysis is correct, one would expect that judgments of stimulus category and strength of emotional response would be more effective among familiar rather than unfamiliar pairs. An alternative explanation for the failure of the strength measure is provided by a study by Ekman and Friesen (1967), which suggested that body cues are more important than facial cues in the communication of the intensity, as opposed to the quality, of affect.

It is noteworthy that the categorization judgments for female pairs were significantly related to personality measures of senders and receivers but not to physiological changes, while the pleasantness judgments showed the opposite pattern. Clarification of the meaning of this finding must await further study.

The heart rate deceleration exhibited by the observer while watching the sender is consistent with other studies (Craig & Lowrey, 1969; Craig & Wood, 1969; Sapira & Shapiro, 1966). It may be analogous to the deceleration found by Lacey to occur during "environmental acceptance" tasks in which the subject is required to pay close attention to environmental events (Lacey, Kagan, Lacey, & Moss, 1963). The cardiac responses of the sender were consistent with recent emphasis on the importance of verbalization in driving heart rate acceleration (Campos & Johnson, 1966, 1967; Johnson & Campos, 1967). No consistent heart rate response occurred to the slides, but the description period, when verbalization took place, was associated with acceleration in the sender.

NOTES

1. This research was supported by Grant M-487 from the National Institute of Mental Health, United States Public Health Service, and by the Commonwealth of Pennsylvania.
2. The nature of the present design does not easily allow the study of the specific cues involved in the communication process or the precise point in time in which the communication occurs. Future experiments using videotapes of the sender's facial expressions will be able to address such problems.

REFERENCES

Alpert, R., & Haber, R. Anxiety in academic achievement situations. *Journal of Abnormal and Social Psychology*, 1960, 61, 207–215.

Buck, R., Savin, V. J., Miller, R. E., & Caul, W. F. Nonverbal communication of affect in humans. *Proceedings of the 77th Annual Convention of the American Psychological Association*, 1969, 4, 367–368. (Summary)

Budner, S. Intolerance of ambiguity as a personality variable. *Journal of Personality*, 1962, 30, 29–50.

Byrne, D. The Repression-Sensitization Scale: Rationale, reliability, and validity. *Journal of Personality*, 1961, 29, 334–339.

Campos, J. J., & Johnson, H. J. The effects of verbalization instructions and visual attention on heart rate and skin conductance. *Psychophysiology*, 1966, 2, 305–310.

Campos, J. J., & Johnson, H. J. The effect of affect and verbalization instructions of directional fractionation of autonomic response. *Psychophysiology*, 1967, 3, 245–290.

Craig, K., & Lowrey, H. J. Heart rate components of conditioned vicarious autonomic responses. *Journal of Personality and Social Psychology*, 1969, 11, 381–387.

Craig, K., & Wood, K. Physiological differentiation of direct and vicarious affective arousal. *Canadian Journal of Behavioural Science*, 1969, 1, 98–105.

Crowne, D., & Marlowe, D. A new scale of social desirability independent of psychopathology. *Journal of Consulting Psychology*, 1960, 24, 349–354.

Duncan, S. Nonverbal communication. *Psychological Bulletin*, 1969, 72, 118–137.

Ekman, P., & Friesen, W. V. Head and body cues in the judgment of emotion: A reformulation. *Perceptual and Motor Skills*, 1967, 24, 711–724.

Ekman, P., Friesen, W. V., & Ellsworth, P. The face and emotion: Guidelines for research and a review of findings. In W. Schramm (Ed.), *Handbook of communication*. New York: Rand McNally, 1970.

Eysenck, H. J. *Maudsley Personality Inventory*. San Diego, Calif.: Educational and Industrial Testing Service, 1959.

Frijda, N. H. Recognition of emotion. In L. Berkowitz (Ed.), *Advances in experimental social psychology*. Vol. 4. New York: Academic Press, 1969.

Graham, L., Cohen, S., & Shmavonian, G. Sex differences in autonomic responses during instrumental conditioning. *Psychosomatic Medicine*, 1966, 28, 264–271.

Gubar, G. Recognition of human facial expressions judged live in a laboratory setting. *Journal of Personality and Social Psychology*, 1966, 4, 108–111.

Janis, I., & Field, P. Sex differences and personality factors related to persuasibility. In C. Hovland & I. Janis (Eds.), *Personality and persuasibility*. New Haven, Conn.: Yale University Press, 1959.

Johnson, H. J., & Campos, J. J. The

effect of cognitive tasks and verbalization instructions on heart rate and skin conductance. *Psychophysiology,* 1967, 4, 143–150.

Jones, H. E. The galvanic skin reflex as related to overt emotional expression. *American Journal of Psychology,* 1935, 47, 241–251.

Jones, H. E. The longitudinal method in the study of personality. In I. Iscoe & H. W. Stevenson (Eds.), *Personality development in children.* Austin: University of Texas Press, 1960.

Kaplan, H., Burch, N. R., & Bloom, S. W. Physiological covariation and sociometric relationships in small peer groups. In P. H. Liederman & D. Shapiro (Eds.), *Psychobiological approaches to social behavior.* Stanford, Calif.: Stanford University Press, 1964.

Lacey, J. I., Kagan, J., Lacey, B. C., & Moss, H. A. The visceral level: Situational determinants and behavioral correlates of autonomic response. In P. Knapp (Ed.), *Expression of the emotions in man.* New York: International Universities Press, 1963.

Lanzetta, J. T., & Kleck, R. E. Encoding and decoding of nonverbal affect in humans. *Journal of Personality and Social Psychology,* 1970, 16, 12–19.

Learmonth, G. J., Ackerly, W., & Kaplan, M. Relationships between palmar skin potential during stress and personality variables. *Psychosomatic Medicine,* 1959, 21, 150–157.

Lykken, D. T. Properties of electrodes used in electrodermal measurement. *Journal of Comparative and Physiological Psychology,* 1959, 52, 629–634.

McNemar, Q. *Psychological statistics.* New York: Wiley, 1955.

Miller, R. E. Experimental approaches to the physiological and behavioral concomitants of affective communication in rhesus monkeys. In S. A. Altmann (Ed.), *Social communication among primates.* Chicago: University of Chicago Press, 1967.

Miller, R. E., Caul, W. F., & Mirsky, I. A. Communication of affects between feral and socially isolated monkeys. *Journal of Personality and Social Psychology,* 1967, 7, 231–239.

Sapira, J. D., & Shapiro, A. P. Pulse rates in human volunteers during frustration and the observation of frustration. *Journal of Psychosomatic Research,* 1966, 9, 325–329.

Shmavonian, B., Yarmat, A., & Cohen, S. Relations between the autonomic nervous system and central nervous system in age differences in behavior. In, *Behavior, aging, and the nervous system.* Springfield, Ill.: Charles C Thomas, 1965.

Taylor, J. A personality measure of manifest anxiety. *Journal of Abnormal and Social Psychology,* 1953, 48, 285–290.

Vine, I. Communication by facial-visual signals. In J. H. Crook (Ed.), *Social behavior in birds and mammals.* New York: Academic Press, 1970.

4

VISUAL INTERACTION: THE GLANCES
OF POWER AND PREFERENCE [1]

RALPH V. EXLINE

I first became interested in the study of interpersonal visual behavior rather by accident. Several years ago I composed a number of unisexual groups of five persons each according to their relative ratio of affiliation to achievement need. The purpose of the study was to investigate some hunches as to why women were more capable than men in the assessment of interpersonal preferences within task-oriented discussion groups. The task given the group was a structured discussion task which required that the group members speak in a prearranged order two times around the group. The floor was then thrown open to all, and the discussion generally became a free-for-all.

A curious regularity caught our attention as we observed the groups at their work. Whenever a member of an affiliative group spoke, whether male or female, the speaker would evenly distribute a considerable amount of visual attention around the group. When making a general statement, he or she

would first rest his gaze upon one person, then another, then the third, and fourth, until the whole group had been encompassed in a rather stately progression. Equally striking were the behaviors of the affiliative listeners. They appeared to rivet their visual attention upon the face of the speaker, giving the observer the impression that he was the relatively constant focus of four pairs of orbs.

If, in the general discussion, one affiliator spoke to a point made by another, the two would first engage each other in a mutual glance, usually broken by the speaker to look at the others who sat watching him.

On the other hand, the relatively more achievement-oriented groups provided a marked contrast in visual interaction. The achievement-oriented speaker was more prone to give an initial quick sweep of the group, then focus his attention on notes in hand, or on the middle distance. Occasionally he would sweep the group again before re-

From *Nebraska Symposium on Motivation*, 1971, J. Cole, ed., University of Nebraska Press, Lincoln, 1972, pp. 163–206. Copyright © 1972 by the University of Nebraska Press and reprinted by permission.

turning to his notes or briefly engage one person who may have inadvertently caught his eye. Neither did the achievement-oriented listeners look steadily at the speaker. They too would peruse their notes, look into the distance, or occasionally look at the speaker when his visual attention was elsewhere.

Hastily constructing a crude symbol system to represent one-way glances, mutual glances, encompassing sweeps, and the like, we confirmed that, in the groups needed to complete our original design, affiliative groups were indeed visually more interactive to a statistically significant degree. While we found the phenomenon interesting, we made no mention of it when publishing the results of the study. Our data collection methods were most primitive; a single observer watched five persons and made some hen scratches on a piece of paper. In addition the observer was a research assistant who had participated in our discussions about the phenomena —by no stretch of the imagination could she be said to be blind as to our expectations. Thus we decided to restrain our enthusiasm until more systematic and better controlled studies of the behavior could be accomplished.

Once alerted to the phenomenon, we found references to it cropping up everywhere in nonscientific literature. Poets used it to signify the communication of affective expression: "Lips and eyes, glances and smiles are the major elements in the arsenal of expression," wrote Ogden in 1961. In more florid style, Magnus, in 1885, declared that "though we were as eloquent as Demosthenes or Cicero . . . yet our skills would not equal the bewitching speech of the eyes."

Novelists have made use of visual interaction to portray the feel of a momentary interaction, or to delineate the nature of a more enduring relationship. As an example of the former we have Hermann Broch's description of a nineteenth-century happening:

So they smiled frankly at each other and their souls nodded to each other through the windows of their eyes, just for an instant, like two neighbors who have never greeted each other and now happen to lean out of their windows at the same moment, pleased and embarrassed by this unforeseen and simultaneous greeting. Convention rescued them out of their embarrassment, and lifting his glass Bertrand said: "Prosit Pasenow." [H. Broch, *The Sleepwalkers: A Trilogy*]

For an example of the latter, i.e., the glance that characterizes a relationship, listen to Nagio Marsh: "From the time that they had confronted each other he had looked fully into her eyes. It was not the half-unseeing attention of ordinary courtesy, but an unanswering, fixed regard. He seemed to blink less than most people"; and almost immediately following: "At the same time it seemed to her that he and she acknowledged each other as enemies" (Nagio Marsh, *Spinsters in Jeopardy*).

Others have pointed to the more fearful properties of the look. Elworthy (1895) has documented the opinion that belief in the evil eye is one of the most ancient superstitions of the human race, being referred to in the literature of ancient Egypt, Babylonia, Greece, and Rome. In more recent times, Tomkins (1963) has called our attention to contemporary news reports to the effect that English country folk attribute the wildness of pigs to the evil eye and that an American businessman hired an expert to keep employees at work by "glaring at them."

I found concern with the phenomenon was by no means restricted to poets and novelists. The mutual glance has its practical applications. For example, in the film *Yesterday, Today, and Tomorrow*, Sophia Loren was required to perform a striptease. In order to help her do it in professional style, the management hired the coach of the girls at Le Crazy Horse night club in Paris to work with her. According to Miss Loren, he gave her one tip which she found "extremely decisive." He said that a girl cannot undress with style and be convincing if she does not look straight into the eyes of a man, one man, casually selected among the audience. Let me put it in her own words:

I was very uncomfortable and embarrassed during the shooting of the scene. There was one moment when I thought to drop the stip sequence and beg for something else. Now I can be positive of one thing, if I was able to do successfully the scene it was because I picked one person and performed only for him, looking straight into his eyes. My audience in the film is composed of one lonely spectator, Marcello Mastroianni! [*Life,* April 10, 1964]

Throughout the literature two themes recur—the theme of *preference* and the theme *of power*. Both the sociologist Simmel (1969) and the philosopher Sartre (1957) have stressed the role of mutual glances in the establishment of significant interpersonal bonds. According to Simmel, it is the mutual as distinct from the one-way glance which signifies union—whether we seek or avoid such visual contact depends upon our desire for union with each other. Sartre, on the other hand, stresses the threat to individual autonomy inherent in the mutual glance: "Either the other looks at me and alienates my liberty, or I assimilate and seize the liberty of the other" (Scheutze, 1948).

Farfetched? Perhaps, but listen to Norman Mailer (1968) describe a visual experience he underwent in the back of a truck while waiting to be arraigned for his part in the antiwar march on the Pentagon in the fall of 1967:

They were interrupted by the insertion of the next prisoner . . . , a young man with straight blond hair and a Nazi armband on his sleeve. He was installed in the rear . . . but Mailer was not happy, for his eyes and the Nazi's bounced off each other like two heads colliding . . . . Standing in the truck, a few feet apart from each other, all prisoners regarding one another, the Nazi fixed on Mailer. Their eyes looked like magnets coming into line, and for perhaps twenty seconds they stared at each other. Mailer looked into a pair of yellow eyes so compressed with hate that back of his own eyes he could feel the echo of such hatred ringing. . . . Mailer could feel violence behind violence rocking through his head. If the two of them were ever alone in an alley, one of them might kill the other in a fight—it was not unlike holding an electric wire in the hand. . . .

After the first five seconds of the shock had passed, he realized he might be able to win . . . now he could feel the hint of force ebbing in the other's eyes, and could wonder at his own necessity to win . . . the thought of losing had been intolerable as if he had been obliged not to lose, as if the duty of his life at that particular moment must have been to look into that Nazi's eye, and say with his own, ". . . you know nothing! My eyes encompass yours. My philosophy contains yours. You have met the wrong man." And the Nazi looked away, and was hysterical with fury on the instant. "You Jew bastard," he shouted. "Dirty Jew with kinky hair." [*Armies of the Night,* pp. 160–163]

Mailer's vignette would seem to be the living embodiment of Sartre's position.

"Either the other looks at me and alienates my liberty, . . ." wrote Sartre. "My eyes encompass yours. My philosophy contains yours," exulted Mailer as he sensed the Nazi giving way.

Empirical studies

A questionnaire study of comfort with visual interaction during speech and silence

Several times I have asked classes or audiences to pair up and silently look into each other's eyes for 30 seconds. A few seconds pass and some begin to fidget, others giggle, or unsuccessfully try to suppress laughter. Smiles and nervous grimaces can be observed, and though some pairs sit silently boring deadpan into each other's eyes throughout, many more break contact before the half minute is up. Subjective reports of the feelings engendered by the experience range from a loss of the sense of self to great tension and awareness of the other. "Spooky" and "weird" are terms often used to describe the encounter.

Such behavior and sensations are consistent with the results we obtained when we asked 500 U.S. and British students to indicate on an 8-point scale how comfortable they would be with another who, when speaking, listening, or sharing mutual silence, would look at the respondent 50% of the time, never, or always. For each respondent the imaginary other was further classified as to whether he was older, younger, or a peer of the same or opposite sex as the respondent. Thus any one respondent would provide nine look-speak-listen comfort ratings for only one of six categories of hypothetical other interactants.

The results are comparable for both national samples and clearly show

highly significant effects concerned with the amount of the other's looking, whether the other is speaking, listening, or both are silent, and for the interaction between speech and gaze patterns. Figure I represents the first two effects

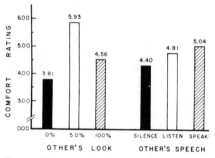

Fig. 1 Mean anticipated comfort ratings made by 360 U.S. students concerning the visual attention or speech behaviors of hypothetical other persons.

and shows that across all speech and silence conditions respondents anticipate the most comfort with the 50% look and least comfort when the other never looks. Similarly, when we ignore the visual conditions, we see that respondents expect to be most comfortable when the other is speaking, and least comfortable when both are silent.

Table I represents the interaction of look and speech conditions, and from it we can see that respondents would find the other's visual attention less aversive when someone is speaking than when both are silent, the reverse being the case for the other's visual avoidance. These relationships are more graphically demonstrated in Figure 2, where it is clearly seen that one expects to be least comfortable when another never looks when one is speaking, or always looks when both are silent. An analysis of written descriptions of the impressions that respondents would form on the basis of such behaviors of another

TABLE I

Mean anticipated comfort ratings made by U.S. men and women of the behavior of hypothetical other persons, categorized by visual attention and speech (N = 360)

| PERCENT LOOK CATEGORY | SPEAKING CATEGORY | | | | | | | |
| | *Other speaks* | | *Other listens* | | *Both silent* | | *Total percent look* | |
	M	S	M	S	M	S	M	S
0	3.76	1.39	3.28	1.33	4.38	1.70	3.81	1.47
50	6.17	.94	6.01	1.44	5.60	1.53	5.93	1.30
100	5.19	1.85	5.14	1.88	3.34	1.89	4.56	1.87
Means: Look t Speaking	5.04	1.39	4.81	1.55	4.40	1.71		

indicates that the modal impression of the nonlooking listener is one of rejection or personal disinterest. The silent starer, one the other hand, is perceived as "queer" or otherwise deviant.

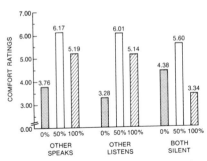

Fig. 2 Mean anticipated comfort ratings made by 360 U.S. students of the visual attention and speech behaviors of hypothetical other persons.

Figure 3 represents a more detailed breakdown of the comfort ratings elicited by one of the most interesting of our interaction conditions, namely that of the 100% look during complete silence. It is apparent that both men and women are less disconcerted by the silent stares of younger persons than by those of peers or older persons. In ad-

dition, while both sexes of respondents would seem to prefer the complete visual attention of a peer of the opposite sex to that of their own, the comfort differential would seem to be much greater for men than for women. Note that men rate their comfort with an attentive male at only 2.70, lowest of all the male comfort ratings. This increases to a rating of 4.27 if the other is a female peer. For women, on the other hand, these same ratings increase from 2.23 to only 3.60. The impact of bedroom eyes would seem to be greater on the male of the species.

The least comfortable lowest mean comfort rating in any of the look-speak-silence conditions for any category of hypothetical other is also to be found in Figure 3. In the American sample this is the situation in which college-age women are the target, in silence, of the complete visual attention of a male of their fathers' generation (M = 2.50).[2] Though the rho correlation between British and U.S. mean comfort ratings for the 12 age-sex categories in this condition is .87, significant beyond the .01 level, the lowest comfort rating in the British sample is found when

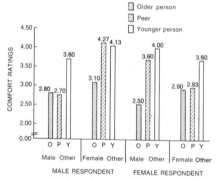

Fig. 3 Mean comfort ratings made by 180 U.S. men and 180 U.S. women of an anticipated 100% look in silence received from hypothetical other persons categorized as to age and sex. (N = 30 per mean)

women anticipate the complete visual attention of a woman of their mothers' generation. While it is tempting to consider these latter data in terms of homo- and heterosexual concerns, we do not intend to claim that these data represent cross-national differences in the sources of sexual anxieties of British and American women. The differences between means of 2.50 (older men) vs. 2.90 (older women) for Americans, and 1.80 (older men) vs. 1.50 (older women) for British, are not statistically significant. Neither do we know whether the feeling of discomfort is rooted in concern over intimacy, the memory of parental disapproval, or a combination of both factors. Figure 3 does, however, demonstrate a complex interplay of visual attention and speech behavior upon the feelings of comfort which characterize the anticipated interaction of young men and women in like-sex or cross-sex pairs.

It is clear from our questionnaire study that we prefer a moderate amount of visual attention from those with whom we interact in face-to-face situations. The study, however, throws

no light upon the reasons for our preferences, nor does it provide us with much direct information about the themes of power and preference to which we earlier referred.

Visual interaction in relation to competition, sex, and need for affiliation

Let us return for a moment to the study first mentioned—the one in which persons with opposite affiliation-to-achievement ratios exhibited such apparently different styles of visual interaction. The study raised questions both methodological and substantive in nature. First, could we record and quantify the phenomena in a way to check upon our impression that the two types of persons showed systematically different visual interaction patterns? Second, assuming that the first question could be answered affirmatively, what might these differences mean for the study of interpersonal processes? Third, if systematic variations in the structure and dynamics of the interaction situation could be shown to have predictable effects upon the visual behavior of the interactants, could systematic variation of the visual behavior of one party to a social interaction predictably effect the response of others? Put another way, can visual behavior as a dependent variable be shown to be an indicator (Ekman, 1965) of mood, state, or orientation toward another? Can it, on the other hand, be an independent variable, driving or shaping the nature of the interaction process? It is to these questions that I will address myself in the remainder of this paper.

When reflecting upon the phenomena, we intuited that the phenomena, if capable of being reliably measured, would be related to questions of power and preference. These two themes would appear to run through the literature I mentioned earlier, but I do not claim that we were familiar with it at that time. We did have evidence that persons characterized by a high affiliation-to-achievement ratio did not raise group-decision issues as soon as did their opposites (Exline, 1962b), and also that the messages they wrote to co-workers in a group-decision task were less indicative of a desire to exert control over others than were those of their opposites (Exline, 1962a). These data may have influenced our thinking.

In any event, our first study was designed to check upon the hypotheses that those high in n-affiliation would be relatively more likely to engage in mutual glances with each other, and that such glances would be inhibited by a situation which required them to compete with one another. We assumed that as n-affiliation theoretically represents a preference for warm, close, intimate personal relations, while n-achievement represents a set of impersonal, task-oriented concerns, persons manifesting a relatively high ratio of affiliative-to-achievement concerns should engage in relatively more mutual glances than would persons characterized by a relatively low ratio of such needs. In addition we hypothesized that the incidence of mutual glances among the relatively more affiliative persons would be attenuated by the power issues inherent in a competitive situation.

I will touch only briefly upon this first study to show how we devised methods to answer the first question and to indicate how the results of our hypothesis testing led to more refined studies of the glances of power and preference.

Experimental arrangements for the observation and recording of eye-contact data

First let us address ourselves to some methodological considerations. Figure 4

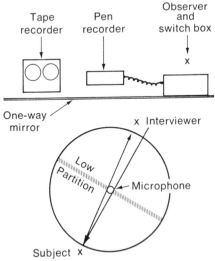

Fig. 4 Schematic representation of arrangements for the observation of visual orientation of subject to interviewer. (Reprinted by permission from R. V. Exline et al., "Visual behavior in a dyad as affected by interview content and sex of respondent," *Journal of Personality and Social Psychology,* 1965, I, 201–209. Copyright © 1965 by the American Psychological Association, Inc.)

constitutes a schematic representation of our usual arrangements for the observation and recording of eye contact. One person, usually a naive subject, sits more or less directly across a small table from another person. The second person is sometimes identified as an interviewer (as depicted in Figure 4), sometimes as an experimenter giving instructions, and sometimes as another student. In the latter case, the second person is sometimes a second naive subject, other times a student acting as a paid confederate of the experimenter. Observers, located almost directly behind the second person, are screened from the subject by a two-way-vision mirror and are positioned to give them almost the same view of the first subject's face as the person sitting in the interviewer's position. Whenever the observer judges that the subject has looked into the eyes of the interviewer, he depresses a noiseless button switch which activates an event recorder. In our early studies the switches were connected to pens of an Esterline-Angus Event Recorder. These pens inked out the patterns of looks and glances during speech and silence as a series of "on-off" events recorded on a moving paper tape, calibrated as to time. More recently we have used a specially constructed electronic apparatus to store and later print out the time units associated with the event patterns the system is instructed to record. Each system enables us to recapture the frequency of single events or combinations of events as well as the duration of each event or combination.

Figure 5 represents two 2-minute segments of actual records taken during one of the studies in which we used the Esterline-Angus Recorder. S's visual behavior is depicted in the left pen tracing in each cluster of three tracings. The middle tracing represents the interviewer's speech behavior, while the right-hand line represents the speech of the subject. In this particular record each deflection of the "Subject look" pen represents a mutual glance because the interviewer was instructed to look steadily at the subject.

From this record we can obtain a great variety of information. For example, we can obtain: (a) the frequency of reciprocated (mutual) and nonreciprocated glances; (b) the duration of each

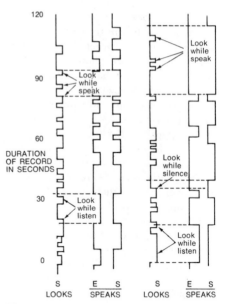

Fig. 5 Two-minute samples of visual interaction between subject and experimenter showing mutual glances during S's speaking and listening behavior, and during mutual silence. (Reprinted by permission from R. V. Exline et al., "Visual behavior in a dyad as affected by interview content and sex of respondent," *Journal of Personality and Social Psychology,* 1965, 1, 201–209. Copyright © 1965 by the American Psychological Association, Inc.)

event in the above two categories; (c) the number of times each person speaks and the number of overlapping speeches; (d) the duration of each speech unit for each person, etc. By combining and recombining the various events we can obtain: (a) the total frequency of glances; (b) the total amount of time each person spends looking at and speaking to others; (c) the total amount of time spent in mutual and one-way glances; (d) the average duration of each speech or glance unit; and (e) the total amount of time and average duration of each time each person looks at the other while speaking, listening, or in total silence.

Data are generally reported either in terms of mean frequencies or mean percentages of visual behavior per unit of time; e.g., total time, listening time, speaking time, or silence.

RELIABILITY AND VALIDITY OF EYE-CONTACT RECORDINGS What is the evidence that the data I have shown you were reliably and validly recorded? Gibson and Pick (1963) have shown that individuals can report with a high degree of accuracy when they are and are not being looked at. We have found that well-trained observers, positioned as I described earlier, report almost identical patterns of eye contacts as does an observer seated across the table from the subject. Ten male and ten female students were interviewed by the author for periods of time ranging from 283 to 384 seconds. Eye contact of subject with interviewer was simultane-

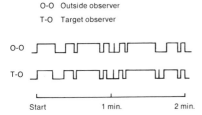

O-O Outside observer

T-O Target observer

Fig. 6 A two-minute reproduction of two observers' recording S's observed eye contact with a target observer (T-O).

ously recorded by the interviewer and by an out-of-the-room observer positioned as depicted in Figure 4. In order to investigate the effect on reliability of measurement of possible distractions associated with beginning and ending the interview, as well as to standardize the periods in which reliability was measured, interobserver reliability measures were derived from the following three time periods: (a) the first 15 seconds after the interviewer was signaled

to start the interview, (b) the 250 seconds immediately following the first 15 seconds, and (c) the last 15 seconds of the interview. Figure 6 represents eye-contact profiles recorded by the two observers during 120 seconds taken from the middle 250 seconds of an actual interview. The measure of reliability was obtained by subtracting number of seconds in which the two profiles did not overlap from the total number of seconds in the time period under consideration. The difference divided by total time (15 or 250 seconds) then gave the percent of interobserver agreement.

The mean percentage of profile agreement was .905, .942, and .916 in the three time periods respectively. The number of subjects for whom the obtained coefficients of agreement amounted to .900 or higher were 14, 18, and 18, in the three time periods respectively. The mean coefficient of agreement for men was not found to differ from that of women. It seems clear that, given the arrangements described in this paper, eye contact of one person with another can be very reliably recorded during the initial and final phases of the interaction as well as throughout the bulk of the interaction.[3]

Although we have relied on Gibson and Pick's study for evidence that eye contact can be validly measured, it is true that their study was not done in the context of a conversation. The reliability study just described above could easily be converted into a validity study by having both parties to the interaction take turn and turn about in recording (a) when they were actually looking the other in the eye and (b) when they thought the other was looking at them. Though we have not carried out such a study, we have data which suggest that individuals think they are being looked in the eye when in actual fact the looker is focused somewhere in a zone marked by the eyebrow and eye pouch above and below the eye, and by the eye corner nearest to the ear on either side of the head. Within this zone a look focused on the root of the nose between the eyes is often interpreted as an eye-to-eye look. It is my belief that the validity problem is not critical, for our observations indicate that most people turn their heads and faces slightly away from the other when they break contact. Even if one looks into a zone of regard rather than at the eye itself, the other reacts as if he were engaged in eye contact.

The arrangements in our first laboratory investigation differed somewhat from those shown in Figure 4, as we used three naive subjects and had three observers recording visual and speech behavior. Thirty-two groups of three like-sex subjects each were studied as they were processed through a discussion task in a $2 \times 2 \times 2$ factorial design. The independent variables were sex of group, affiliation-to-achievement ratio of group members, and the competitiveness of the task situation. The results of this study have been reported elsewhere in detail (Exline, 1963), and Figure 7 represents only the major findings.

These data demonstrate three interesting phenomena. First, mutual glances are relatively rare in task-oriented discussions, occurring, on the average, only during 3% of the total possible interaction time in male groups, and 7½% of the time in female groups. Second, on all indices of visual behavior, mutual or nonreciprocal, women are more active than men. The percents of the total time that women looked at other women in this study

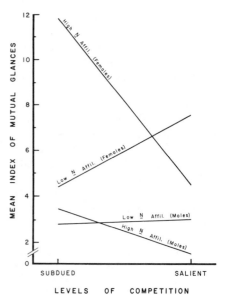

Fig. 7 Mean percentage of time each sex spends in mutual visual interaction for each of two levels of n-affiliation at two levels of competition. (Reprinted, by permission, from R. V. Exline, "Explorations in the process of person perception: Visual interaction in relation to competition, sex, and the need for affiliation," *Journal of Personality,* 1963, 31, 1–20. Copyright © 1963 by the Duke University Press.)

averaged 37.3% as compared to 23.2% for men.[4] Third, there is a significant interaction of affiliation, competitiveness, and sex upon the tendency to engage in mutual glances. Finally, though not shown in this figure, Ss gave significantly more visual attention to another when listening to him than when speaking to him, and rarely engaged in mutual glances in silence. The last finding provides behavioral confirmation for the low comfort ratings given in the questionnaire study to an anticipated 100% look from another in silence.

Let us return for a moment to the interaction effect mentioned above. One possible interpretation of these data is that affiliative persons, especially if they are women, find the power struggle inherent in a competitive situation aversive. Thus a mutual glance in such situations takes on a different meaning from such a glance in less competitive situations. Perhaps the affiliative individual unconsciously indicates his or her desires not to interact with others in such situations by avoiding visual intercourse. Implicit in such an interpretation is the suggestion that those showing extremely low affiliative tendencies tend to orient themselves in more rivalrous ways toward others. One could argue that, in a competitive situation, the intimacy inherent in the mutual glance could be interpreted as the intimacy of combat, an intimacy less repellent to the nonaffiliative person than to his affiliative counterpart, and thus increase his motive to engage the other in a battle of eyeballs. We are reminded of Norman Mailer's description of his encounter with the American Nazi.

Studies of attraction and aversion

The next two figures suggest that, irrespective of one's own degree of affiliation motive, aversiveness and attractiveness of other persons are correlated with willingness to share a mutual glance with them.

Figure 8 demonstrates the effect of derogatory and complimentary feedback upon an *S*'s willingness to engage in eye contact with an interviewer. Eye contact was measured before and after the feedback session, and it is clear that only derisory feedback is followed by diminished eye contact in the second period. *S*s in the complimentary and control conditions were unaffected by feedback. All 12 *S*s in the derogatory condition reduced their eye contact with the interviewer, while there was a seven to three and a four to three in-

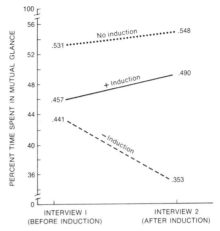

Fig. 8 Percent time spent in mutual glances by experimental and control *S*s in two interview periods (before and after affect induction). (Reprinted, by permission, from R. V. Exline and L. Winters, "Affective relations and mutual glances in dyads," in S. Tomkins and C. Izard [Eds.], *Affect, cognition, and personality.* Copyright © 1965 by the Springer Publishing Co.)

crease-to-decrease ratio in complimentary and control conditions respectively. *S*s in the complimentary condition also evaluated the interviewer significantly more positively than did those in the derogatory condition.

Figure 9 depicts the results obtained when we measured the visual attention given to two interviewers of the *S*s' own sex, both before and after *S*s were removed from the presence of the interviewers and asked to state which one they found more attractive. It is clear that both sexes increased eye contact with the preferred interviewer and decreased it with the other. The slight crossover noted for females in the control group reflects the fact that control females developed a preference for one of the two interviewers whereas males would admit to no such preference.

The studies mentioned to date pro-

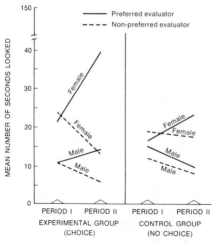

Fig. 9 Increments and decrements in the number of seconds *Ss* looked at evaluators while speaking to them. (Reprinted, by permission, from R. V. Exline and L. Winters, "Affective relations and mutual glances in dyads," in S. Tomkins and C. Izard [Eds.], *Affect, cognition, and personality*. Copyright © 1965 by the Springer Publishing Co.)

vide rather good evidence that persons are more prone to engage in mutual glances when they find the relationship with another attractive rather than aversive. The relationship between considerations of interpersonal power and visual interaction, however, was only indirectly touched upon in the study of affiliation and competitiveness. I will now describe a study in which we measured the effect of power and influence on visual interaction by creating actual power differences between two persons.

Visual interaction and power differences in legitimate and illegitimate hierarchies [5]

Thibaut and Kelley (1959) define social power as the control one person has over another's outcomes. Assuming that individuals are aware of the difference in power which defines their role

relationship, we would expect that in a face-to-face interaction in which outcomes are in question, the person in the less powerful position would have a greater need to monitor the expressive behavior of the other. Such monitoring would serve two purposes: (a) it would provide the low power person (LP) with information concerning the reaction of the other to LP's efforts, information which LP could use to adjust his own behavior; (b) it enables the LP person to indicate that he is attentive to the higher power person (HP), thus serving as a signal that he accepts his role, or at least is behaving in a manner appropriate to his position.

Accordingly our first hypothesis was that *in a dyad marked by different power positions, the less powerful person would, everything else being equal, look more into the line of regard of the other.*

Implicit in the statement of the above hypothesis is the assumption that the LP person accepts the legitimacy of the power difference. If he does not, he should neither wish to obtain expressive feedback to adjust his behavior vis-à-vis HP's reactions, nor indicate acceptance of a subordinate role by giving the other his visual attention. Thus we proposed a second hypothesis as a qualification of our original hypothesis, namely that *the more legitimate the perception of the power hierarchy, the more will the less powerful person look into the line of regard of the other.*

Forty pairs of male *Ss* were required, through discussion, to arrive at an agreed upon solution to each of three problems. None of the problems had an obviously correct solution, solutions being a question of opinion or judgment difficult to verify. The study was presented as an investigation into the processes of group decision making.

Upon arriving at the laboratory, Ss were shown to separate rooms where they filled out a personality inventory, then were given the instructions designed to create differential power positions. Outcome control was established by instructing the person assigned the LP position that "the other person is going to divide the chips, giving you however much he wants to." On the other hand, the person assigned the HP position was instructed to divide a 10-chip reward for work on each task according to the following schedule: HP was to give LP 3 of the 10 chips after the first problem and 4 of 10 chips after each of the second and third problems. Thus the outcomes were controlled by the HP person, and the LP person always received a lower outcome. It was assumed that LP's lower reward would emphasize the power differences—especially after the 7-to-3 split following the first task. Both persons were told that chips would be exchanged for money at the end of the experiment.

The power induction was rationalized to both persons by pointing out that, in real-life groups, one person often had the power to determine the rewards and privileges of others. It should be noted that the HP person was to a degree a confederate of the experimenter. He was asked not to reveal that the division of chips was predetermined, and was assured that this aspect of the experiment would be explained to the other person upon completion of the experiment. After the instructions were completed, the LP person was taken to the work room where the HP person was already seated at a table facing the door.

The perception of the relative legitimacy of the power hierarchy was manipulated by selecting pairs in such fashion as to encourage the perception of legitimacy on the one hand and nonlegitimacy on the other. All 20 pairs in the legitimacy category were composed of one ROTC cadet officer and one ROTC basic (comparable to an enlisted man). Both men were in uniform and were taken from a drill class to participate in the study. Pairs in the illegitimate power condition were composed of two strangers released from a large gym class. Pairs of acquaintances were eliminated and replaced with strangers.

The problems consisted of one probability judgment, one human relations problem involving leadership in an industrial setting, and the development of a story from a TAT card. The problems were designed to provoke discussion and a certain amount of disagreement. In no case was there an obviously correct solution.

Subjects first read the problem and were allowed to take notes. After a specified time the experimenter collected the description of the problem and left the room. A buzzer signaled both the beginning and end of the discussion period. The problem period was terminated after 3 minutes, or after 10 seconds of silence following a quicker decision.

After completion of the third task the LP person was taken from the room and both Ss filled out a questionnaire which enabled us to validate the effectiveness of the inductions and assess the degree of acquaintance.

In addition to the face validity of the power difference inherent in the assignment of control over the distribution of chips to one person, effectiveness of the power induction was inferred from the S's preference for his own or the other's job. The HP person preferred his job to a significantly greater degree than did the LP person. The latter preferred the HP position to his own.

The effectiveness of the legitimacy induction was demonstrated by the following ratings: (a) the less powerful ROTC person reported that the HP person was within his rights in dividing the chips the way he did to a greater degree than did the LP gym person; (b) less powerful ROTC Ss would like to work again with the HP person more than would LP gym Ss; (c) less powerful ROTC more so than LP gym Ss would like to have the HP position; (d) the ROTC pairs reported that they wanted to and tried to influence the other more than did the gym pairs. All of the above differences were significant beyond the .05 or .01 probability levels.

Figure 10 shows the effect of the

power and legitimacy conditions upon the extent to which Ss in the HP and LP positions visually monitored each other. It is clear that, over all periods and experimental conditions, the less powerful person looked more at the powerful person than vice versa. The trend was established in the first trial and reached significance in the second and third trials. This was the case for looking while listening and tended to be the case for looking while speaking.

One could argue that these results may merely reflect the tendency for visual monitoring to match the amount which the other spoke. Thus if the HP person spoke more, this would indicate that our induction influenced speech and that our results would be better explained in terms of a politeness convention which requires a listener to give visual attention to a speaker. Three pieces of evidence argue against this explanation, for the HP person did not consistently control the floor; speech increased in the second trial and decreased in the third, whereas the reverse was true for looking; and, finally, a subsidiary analysis showed significant differences in the extent to which the looking behavior of HP and LP persons matched that of their opposites. HPs' looking while listening matched LPs' looking while speaking, but LP's looking while listening overrode HPs' looking while speaking by some 10 seconds per minute on each trial.

What about the effect of the perceived legitimacy of the power hierarchy? Figure 10 shows that from the very first problem, the relative differences between HP and LP persons were greater in the legitimate than in the illegitimate condition; that the mean level of visual monitoring was significantly higher in the legitimate condition; and, bearing most directly upon

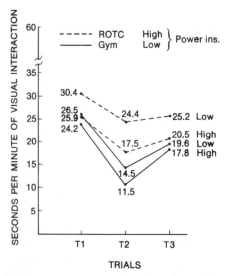

Fig. 10 Mean seconds per minute of visual interaction of high and low power members of gym and ROTC dyads during three decision-discussion trials ($N = 20$ per mean).

our second hypothesis, that the LP person in the illegitimate (gym) as compared to the legitimate (ROTC) hierarchy tended to look less at HP in the first trial, and did look significantly less at him in the second and third.

While the data concerning the visual behavior of the LP person in a hierarchy would clearly seem to support the hypothesis that he who sees a power difference as illegitimate will be visually less attentive to the more powerful person, we cannot yet say that we have eliminated all alternative explanations for this phenomenon. We cannot yet say, that is, whether the reduced attentiveness was due to (a) negative affect felt toward one who would take advantage of his position to apparently violate a norm of fair play, (b) a desire to avoid any suggestion that one accepted a subordinate role felt to be illegitimate, or (c) a combination of both of the above explanations. A further study would seem to be required—one in which negative feeling toward the occupant of a power position perceived to be illegitimate is held constant.

Neither can we eliminate the possibility that the lower visual activity of the occupants of the HP position was due only to the power inherent in the position. It is possible that a feeling of guilt engendered by the power induction may have caused our HP subject to have avoided looking at the other. Ellsworth and Carlsmith (1968) have shown that we do not like those who watch us while they criticize us. We feel that they enjoy our discomfort. Perhaps an intuitive awareness of such feelings prevented the HP subjects from looking at those they felt they were required to take advantage of. Both of the above considerations can be eliminated by removing the inequities involved in the distribution of the re-

wards, and such a study is now underway. Until the results are in we can only say that the data of the study just described provide tentative but not definitive support for our theory concerning the effects of power considerations on visual interaction with another.

Perception of another's potency as a function of the personality of a speaker and the visual behavior of a listener [6]

We have also approached the study of power considerations in interpersonal visual behavior by identifying those persons who exhibit a need to exert control over their interpersonal environment. In the study which I will next describe, we identified such persons and then developed a situation in which visual behavior was manipulated as an independent variable.

Twenty male undergraduates of Oxford University were given Schutz FIRO B scale (1958), on the basis of which they were designated as being high or low in their orientation toward controlling others in their environment. Those assigned to the high-control category described themselves as wishing to control others more than they wanted others to control themselves, whereas the reverse was true of those assigned to the low-control category. A student confederate, seated across a table some 3 feet distant from S, then engaged each S in a 5-minute discussion of travel interests. During the conversation the confederate looked at all Ss approximately 50% of the time when he (the confederate) spoke, but systematically varied his visual attention when the S spoke. One half of the Ss in each control category received the undivided visual attention of the listening confederate (100% glance). When the remainder of the Ss spoke, the confederate never looked at them, but swept the air above their heads as he listened (zero glance).

The visual behavior of Ss was recorded as they spoke and listened to the confederate. Following the interview, Ss' impressions of the confederate were obtained by means of Osgood's semantic differential technique (Osgood, Suci & Tannenbaum, 1957).

Since the visual behavior of the confederate was the major independent variable in this study, we were interested to learn whether or not Ss with the greater control orientation would respond more steadily to the steady glance of the listener. In view of the folklore which equates "outstaring" another with dominance, we speculated that control-oriented persons in the 100% look-listen condition would be more likely to look into the eyes of our confederate both when speaking and listening to him than would the less control-oriented Ss.

Data in Table 2 show that the high-control-oriented person does indeed look more at the confederate than does the low-control-oriented person when both speaking and listening to him. These differences approach, but do not reach, significance. When a separate analysis is carried out for looking while speaking and looking while listening, however, we find a significant interaction between the look received from the confederate and the control orientation of the subject, in its effect upon the visual attention a subject gives to the confederate while listening to him. The high-control-oriented S does not differ in the amount of visual attention he gives to the confederate, regardless of the amount of visual attention he receives from the confederate. However, the less controlling S gives significantly more visual attention to the confederate if the confederate has withheld his gaze from him. This is a complicated set of relationships, especially since the reverse of this interaction approached

TABLE 2

Mean percent looking at confederate by British Ss,
categorized as to own control orientation and speech role,
and by visual attention of confederate

		Ss' CONTROL ORIENTATION					
Confederate's visual attention	Ss' speech role	High control		Low control		Total	
		M	s	M	s	M	s
Zero	Speaker	47.4	17.9	63.4	16.8	55.4	17.1
	Listener	73.6	11.9	86.8	11.0	80.2	12.9
	Total	60.5	19.9	75.1	16.8	67.8	19.4
100%	Speaker	67.8	23.2	54.0	14.4	60.9	19.6
	Listener	76.4	18.1	63.4	16.8	69.9	17.8
	Total	72.1	20.1	58.7	15.6	65.4	18.8
Speech Role	Speak	57.6	22.3	58.7	13.9	58.2	18.1
	Listen	75.0	14.5	75.1	18.2	75.0	16.0
	Total	66.3	20.4	66.9	17.9		

significance when the looking-while-speaking data were analyzed. The relationships are more clearly depicted in Figure 11.

the reinforcing listener, and the less controlling Ss to the nonreinforcing listener. The pattern was almost identical to that shown in Figure 11.

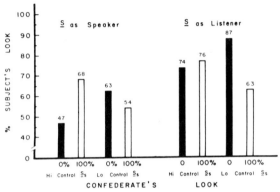

Fig. 11 Mean percent looking at confederate by British Ss categorized as to own control orientation and speech role, and by visual attention from confederate ($N = 5$ per mean).

What is most clear is that Ss, taken as a group, give a visually attentive confederate about the same amount of attention whether he speaks or listens to them, but give a visually inattentive speaker significantly more attention when listening than when talking to him. Previous research has shown that Ss generally look more when listening than when speaking (Kendon, 1967; Exline, Gray, & Schuette, 1965). Our data suggest that there may be something unsettling in receiving the 100% look of a listening other—especially for the less control-oriented Ss.

The visual behavior of the speaking Ss is reminiscent of the results I reported in a study with David Messick (1967). In that study we found that controlling and less controlling Ss showed very similar patterns of visual attention when they were speaking to a listener who provided them with very much or very little in the way of verbal social reinforcement. The control-oriented Ss, gave much more attention to

Some light may be thrown on the above findings by the ratings our subjects gave the confederate on the semantic differential. This consisted of 12 opposed adjective pairs, 4 pairs being very highly loaded on the potency factor, 4 on activity, and 4 on evaluation. Though the instrument was given as a heuristic device, we rather hoped that our two experimental looking conditions would each have a different impact upon our subjects. You will remember that in the questionnaire study described earlier, to receive no visual attention from a listener was rated as one of the two most uncomfortable interaction situations of those presented.

No differences between control types or across the confederate looking inductions were found for the evaluation factor, but there was an interesting and unexpected interaction between the independent variables with respect to the potency factor. As is indicated in Figure 12, control-oriented Ss, rated the confederate who never looked while

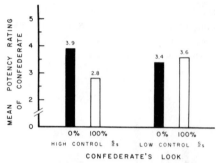

Fig. 12 Mean potency rating of confederate by British Ss categorized as to own control orientation and visual attention from confederate.

listening as being significantly more potent than those who received his undivided visual attention. Control-oriented Ss also rated the nonlooking confederate as more potent than did the less controlling subjects. Thus those who like to control others would seem to find those whose visual attention they cannot capture more powerful than those whose they can. Shades of Jean Paul Sartre—"I assimilate and seize the liberty of the other"—but only if I can capture his eyes.

Perhaps the potency impressions help to explain the rather complicated set of interactions shown in Figure 11. If one has control needs and wishes to retain the floor, it would behoove him not to look too much at one he feels has the capacity to wrest it from him, should he catch his eye. On the other hand, if the confederate looks steadily without attempting to speak, he may be seen as weak, which would enable one to look more steadily at him with impunity. The reverse could be true for the less controlling subject. The data show, though the interaction was not significant, that the the control-oriented subjects did look less steadily at the nonlooking than at the looking listener, while the reverse tended to be true for

the less controlling subject. To look or not to look, that is the question. The answer, for those who need to control, may lie in the perceived force of the other.

Much of what I have reported in these studies of visual behavior and interpersonal power problems seems to be concerned with the avoidance of eye contact. Powerful people do not monitor less powerful people. Those who feel that another's power is illegitimate avoid potential eye contact with the usurper. Dominant men seem more impressed with the personal force of one who listens without looking and also seem more reluctant to look at those whom they perceive to be forceful. Why so much avoidance?

Eye contact as a sign between man and monkey

The literature on primates provides one compelling suggestion as to why men may be loath to look at one another. Over and over the ethologists have reported that the mutual glance between male primates initiates mutual threat displays which reaffirm or reorder one's place in the dominance hierarchy. The phenomenon has been reported for baboons (Hall & Devore, 1965), rhesus and bonnet macaques (Hinde & Rowell, 1962), langurs (Jay, 1965), and the mountain gorilla (Shaller, 1963). Van Lawick-Goodall (1967) did not specifically mention this phenomenon in her field studies of chimpanzees, but she did mention that they did not like to be "stared at." Many of these studies also identify the averted gaze as a sign of submission.

Diebold (1968) has suggested that such behaviors are part of a shared primate ethogram, and I would like to conclude my presentation of our empirical studies by briefly reporting some work in which we demonstrated that humans can elicit and inhibit threatening displays of rhesus macaques merely by initiating and breaking off mutual eye contact (Exline & Yellin, 1969).

Four male rhesus macaques, of Indian origin and approximately 18 months old, were stimulated in their cages by male experimenters who stood directly in front of each monkey's cage and stared fixedly at the eyes of the monkey. An observer, located out of the monkey's line of sight, recorded the reaction to each eye engagement.

Figure 13 shows the experimental arrangements.

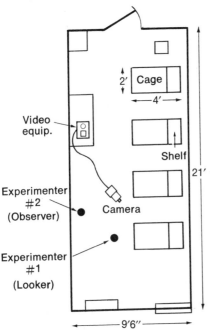

Fig. 13 Schematic representation of arrangements used to signal, and observe monkeys' responses to eye engagement.

The challenging look required the stimulator to stare without expression at the face of the monkey until he caught the monkey's full-faced visual attention. Once eye contact was achieved, the looker continued his stare until the monkey either moved or broke visual contact. Three blocks of 10 stimulus looks each were recorded on different days by each of the stimulators. All stimulus periods were scheduled during a period of generally high activity.

In the deferent stimulus look condition, the experimenter first established eye contact with the monkey, then immediately lowered his gaze by dropping his head and eyes.

There was no difficulty in establishing that the looker had caught the monkey's attention. The monkey would suddenly pull himself together into a tight crouch, his head pulled down between his shoulders. For a second or two he would sit immobile, staring intently into the eyes of the looker. The look has been described as "hard" and certainly gives one the impression of menace, the brows generally being drawn into a V-shaped, frowning look. This concentrated look, which we used as the sign that eye engagement had been achieved, has been described (by Eimerl and DeVore, 1965) as the first and mildest stage of the macaque threat display. (See Figure 14.)

Beginning with the "hard stare" (our sign of eye engagement), the macaque display progresses through a stare accompanied by an open mouth and bared teeth, to darting the head forward and pulling it back in a quick bobbing movement. If the opponent does not submit after the display reaches the third stage, the monkey will either attack or flee.

Preliminary observation showed that our caged monkeys manifested all of the above aggressive behaviors observed in field studies, plus such variations as pulling the head back but not

Fig. 14 The "hard stare" of the rhesus macaque—
first stage of the threat display.

Fig. 15 Three examples of *Macaca mulatta*'s response to eye engagement;
left to right: avoidance, anger threat, and attack (leaping).

darting it forward, or leaping in attack but falling short of the door of the cage. On the basis of these observations we developed an 8-point scale anchored by the avoidance of eye engagement at one extreme and by a direct leap at the face of the looker at the other. Summed over trials, readings of this scale enabled us to obtain an average aggressiveness response score for each monkey.

We also categorized the responses more simply under three headings: "avoidance" (breaking eye contact with no forward movement), "attack" (leaping at the experimenter), and "threat" (all intermediate responses, mouth open, head bob, etc.).

Figure 15 shows examples of avoidance, threat, and attack behaviors.

Table 3 shows the mean changes in aggressiveness of response to the challenging and deferent looks over the three trial blocks. A 4 x 2 x 2 x 2 x 3 fixed effects analysis of variance showed significant effects for monkeys, looks, trial blocks, and monkeys by looks interactions. The Neuman-Keuls test demonstrated that the first monkey responded less aggressively and the third monkey more aggressively than the others. The Neuman-Keuls test also indicated that differences between trial blocks occurred between the first and second trials, and that two of the monkeys responded with significantly more aggression to the challenging as compared to the deferent look, while the other two only tended to do so.

The analysis of the categorization of responses by avoidance, threat, and attack showed similar results. In fact, when χ^2 was computed for each monkey in regard to the frequency of response in each aggressiveness category over the two looks, the null hypothesis was rejected at better than the .01 level

TABLE 3

Mean aggressiveness response (0–7) by four monkeys to dominance and deference signs over three trial blocks of ten blocks each

| | | STIMULUS LOOK | | |
| | | Direct challenging look M | Downcast deferent look M | Response per monkey M |
Monkey number	Trial block			
I	I	3.20	.75	1.58
	2	2.40	1.20	
	3	.75	1.20	
	Total	2.12	1.05	
2	I	3.60	2.80	2.39
	2	2.70	1.50	
	3	2.40	1.35	
	Total	2.90	1.88	
3	I	6.90	4.15	5.10
	2	6.85	3.60	
	3	6.05	3.05	
	Total	6.60	3.60	
4	I	3.65	2.10	2.39
	2	2.70	1.90	
	3	2.25	1.75	
	Total	2.87	1.91	
stimulus look × trial block				response per trial block
	I	4.33	2.45	3.39
	2	3.66	2.05	2.86
	3	2.86	1.83	2.34
response per sign		3.62	2.11	

for each monkey. Examination of the data shows attack and threat behavior to be more frequently elicited by the challenging glance while nonaggressive responses are more likely to be elicited by the deferent downcast glance. These relationships are shown in Table 4.

We believe our data support the conclusion that maintenance of eye engagement (the mutual glance) serves as a dominance challenge to the rhesus macaque whether the contender is another rhesus as observed by the ethologists, or a human being, a member of

TABLE 4

Percent responses to challenging (direct) and deferent (down) eye engagements, coded as attacking, threatening, or nonaggressive (n = 60 per stimulus look per monkey)

		RESPONSE CATEGORY		
Monkey number	*Stimulus look*	*Attack*	*Threaten*	*Nonaggressive*
I	Direct (Challenge)	35	15	50
	Down (Deferent)	18	4	78
2	Direct	25	48	27
	Down	22	20	58
3	Direct	97	0	3
	Down	54	0	46
4	Direct	23	55	22
	Down	25	25	50
total response	Direct	47	29	24
× look	Down	28	12	60

another primate genus. Similarly, aversion of the gaze, once established, serves to inhibit the threat display of the rhesus regardless whether the looker is of the same or another primate genus.

We believe that eye engagement is a necessary feature of the stimulus complex which elicits the threat display, for when we assumed our stimulus posture with closed eyes our monkeys rarely if ever responded with a threat display. We do not claim it is a sufficient condition, however, for we attempted no variations such as smiling, grimacing, vocalizing, or moving the head while staring at the monkeys. Neither did we mask the face, leaving only the eyes active, nor did we provide an inanimate model, or picture of a human head with eyes open or closed.

Subsequent work has shown that posture is not a releaser, for the same intensity of response was elicited with both an erect and a stooped, crouching posture. Neither does movement alone serve to elicit aggressive displays, for though a darting human head will catch the monkey's attention, it is only when the eyes are in mutual contact that the threat or attack display is elicited. The features of a face do seem to play some part, however; for a while a head completely covered with a stocking mask elicits no response, adding eye holes and open eyes elicits only a small insignificant increase in threatening displays.

While more work remains before we can precisely characterize the context in which open eyes are sufficient to elicit threat, we do believe that an affirmative answer to Diebold's question is possible. We believe, that is, that eye engagement does serve an interpersonal-regulatory function in a shared primate ethogram. Perhaps men are generally predisposed to avoid visual engagement with another (especially in silence) to reduce the probability of getting caught up in disturbing dominance struggles.

Discussion

The empirical studies just described have been based on the assumption that eye contact is one of the nonverbal processes we use to establish a relationship with another. We have focused mainly upon affiliative and dominance relationships, using what Mehrabian (1969) has called encoding and decoding methodologies to study the communication or indication of the relationships. Examples of the encoding method, in which the manipulation of the experimental situation is designed to elicit attitudes which can be inferred from postures, positions, or eye engagements concomitant to the induced attitude, are the studies of affiliation and competition, of preference and eye engagement, and of legitimate and illegitimate power hierarchies. Decoding methodology, in which subjects are presented with prepared stimuli and asked to infer feelings and attitudes of the stimulator, is represented by the study of the responses of British and American students to the visually attentive and avoidant listener.[7] In an unreported study, a speaker instructed to look was perceived as much more favorable and confident than when he delivered the identical message but avoided eye engagement (Exline & Eldridge, 1967). Thus both encoding and decoding methodologies can be used to study the role played by visual behavior in the establishment of affiliative or dominance relationships.

Other investigators provide valuable insights concerning relationships between eye engagements and affiliation or dominance. In regard to affiliation, Phoebe Ellsworth (Ellsworth & Carlsmith, 1968) has shown that those who look while telling us good things about ourselves are preferred to those who look when criticizing us; Efran and Broughton (1966) have shown that one looks more at a friendly familiar person than at one who is a stranger; Mehrabian (1968a, 1968b) has shown that eye contact shows an increasing but curvilinear relationship to liking for an addressee; and Rubin (1970) has found love to be significantly and positively related to mutual glances. Strongman and Champness (1968) have shown a positive relationship between dominance and "winning" a staring contest, as have Thayer (1969), and Edelman, Omark, and Freedman (1971, personal communication).

Argyle (1969) has pointed out that eye engagement serves an important function in processes other than those of establishing and defining the particular nature of the relationship. He suggests that it is also important in obtaining feedback about the reactions of others, in controlling the communication channel, and (through avoidance) in reducing the distracting effect of incoming information. With respect to channel control, Kendon (1967) has shown that patterned eye contact figures as a signal in turning over the floor to another during conversation. One looks away a few seconds before ceasing to speak and looks back at the listener just as he ceases speaking. Champness (personal communication) carried out an interesting study in which two people found themselves looking each other in the eyes as a curtain rose to signal the start of a conversation. Champness found that *dominant* Ss were the first to break the gaze. They looked away and immediately began speaking. Perhaps, as is suggested by Kendon's work, they realized that to sit looking at the other in silence was a cue for the other to speak, and what dominant person wants to cede the floor to another?

With respect to general gaze aversion, Exline and Winters (1965) demonstrated that systematic variation in the cognitive difficulty of a conversation topic decreased the amount of time a speaker looked at his listener in direct relation to the difficulty of the topic. Incidentally, personality variables served to moderate visual behavior in the above study. Personality considerations have also been shown to affect visual behavior by Lefcourt (Lefcourt & Wine, 1969), who categorized Ss by inner and outer locus of control, by Champness (personal communication), who grouped them by dominance-submission, and by our own group (Exline, Thibaut, Hickey, & Gumpert, 1970), which has made extensive use of Christie and Geis's Machiavellianism scale, Schutz's FIRO B (1958) and various measures of n-affiliation.

As was indicated earlier, it seems clear that eye engagement alone is not sufficient to indicate the nature of the relationship or the specific roles played by the interactants. Information relevant to the interaction context, facial displays, postural and spatial arrangements, and verbal themes are undoubtedly necessary to the specification of relationship and role. Eye engagement then is but one indicator variable, and the work of Wiener and Mehrabian (1968), Mehrabian (1968a, 1968b), Ekman and his colleagues (1965, 1967, 1969), Scheflen (1964), Birdwhistell (1970), Hall (1966), Duncan (1969), Sommer (1969), Argyle et al. (1970), and others, have thrown valuable light upon the operation of other nonverbal factors in the processes of interpersonal communication.

Notwithstanding the complex inter-relations of gaze direction and other variables, we plan to continue our investigation of these phenomena. We are presently concerned with eye engagement, or the lack of it, as an indication of the authenticity of a spoken communication. We have data to suggest that, for women at least, eye conatct is less when reporting false as opposed to true impressions of another person to the person in question.[8] The synchrony of eye engagements with other nonverbal expressive processes intrigues us. We have tentative evidence that the affect state of persons whose postural inclination toward or away from another matches the amount of their eye engagement with a listener can be judged more easily from silent films than can the affect states of those who lean forward and look little (or who lean back and look much).

We also wish to explore more thoroughly the implications of the specific planes or directions used by one who breaks or avoids eye contact with another. Would one who listens with downcast or sideways gaze impress a control-oriented speaker in the same fashion as did our upward-sweeping confederate? We doubt it, and suggest that specific affective impressions may be decoded from specific gaze directions.

Research concerning the development of eye engagement tendencies in children would seem to offer promise for understanding the development of affiliative and dominance tendencies. There are some suggestions that response to eye contact may be innate (Argyle, 1969) and that the orienting response leads to attending to the mother, especially if there is eye contact (Walters & Parke, 1965; Ambrose, 1961).

Hutt and Ounsted (1966) have observed that autistic children avoid looking at human faces and eyes. Rimland (1962) has reported that parents of autistic children are cold and withdrawn, while Singer and Wynne (1963) describe such parents as showing apathy about interaction and as manifesting an intellectualized distance from people. Taken together, the above reports suggest that the visual interaction of mother and child in the first year of life may be a critical factor in the healthy socialization of the child. Longitudinal studies in which the visual interaction of mother and child could be compared with other developmental indices, if possible to carry out, would be very interesting indeed. One wonders, also, if it would be possible to establish meaningful relationships with hostile and withdrawn children by using behavior modification techniques to shape mutual glance behavior with a therapist.

Earlier, I mentioned that our studies of young adults showed women to be much more visually interactive than men. I recently learned of a Ph.D. dissertation carried out by Nancy Russo (personal communication). Russo found that sex differences in visual interaction did not appear until around the fourth grade. It would be interesting to explore the concomitants of this apparently age-related divergence. Is it due to social pressures toward the taking of sex roles, roles which require different emphases on dependency and autonomy behaviors? Is it related to increasing concerns with dominance hierarchies and the threat displays which seem to be triggered by extended mutual glances between primate males? Is the mutual glance somehow cortically arousing (Wada, 1961), and are males "wired up" so that such arousal becomes more intense and disturbing as

they physically develop than is the case for females?

I have no answers to the above questions, neither do I know if they are the best ones to pose. Nevertheless, systematic study of age-related sex differences in willingness to engage in mutual glances strikes me as worth pursuing.

Finally there is the question of cultural relativity of eye engagement. Our studies have been limited to British and American middle-class men and women. Russo studied only American children. There are undoubtedly cultural and subcultural norms concerning the appropriateness of the extent to which we engage in mutual and even one-way glances. No doubt there are also different codes concerning the inferences to be drawn from the adherence to, and violation of, such norms. We are presently moving to investigate black-white differences among college students in the use of the line of regard, but such a study merely scratches the surface of cultural comparisons.

We have found this work fascinating and stimulating, as well as occasionally perplexing. I hope I have managed to convey to you some of the excitement we have enjoyed in our research. If some of you, after reading this paper, are motivated to improve upon our efforts, what more can an investigator ask?

NOTES

1. Studies reported in this paper were supported by funds from Contracts Nonr 2285 (02) and Nonr 2285 (07), Office of Naval Research.
2. Contrast this to the mean rating of 6.73 recorded by women who anticipate listening to a male peer who looks 50% of the time.

3. The author wishes to express his appreciation to Miss Bja Fehr, who was responsible for developing and carrying out the methodological study reported here.
4. We have consistently observed this sex difference in visual attentiveness in all studies in which sex has been a variable.
5. Exline, R. V., and Long, B., unpublished MS, 1971.
6. Exline, R. V., Fairweather, H., Hine, J., and Argyle, M., unpublished MS, 1971.
7. Exline, R. V., and Snadowski, A., unpublished MS, 1971.
8. Exline, R. V., and Greenberg, E., unpublished MS, 1971; see also Exline, R. V., Thibaut, J., Hickey, C. B., and Gumpert, P., 1970.

REFERENCES

Ambrose, J. A. The development of the smiling response in early infancy. In B. M. Foss (Ed.), *Determinants of infant behavior.* Vol. I. London: Methuen, 1961.

Argyle, M. *Social interaction.* New York: Atherton Press, 1969.

Argyle, M., et al. The communication of inferior and superior attitudes by verbal and non-verbal signals. *British Journal of Social and Clinical Psychology,* 1970, 9, 222–231.

Birdwhistell, R. L. *Kinesics and context.* Philadelphia: University of Pennsylvania Press, 1970.

Broch, H. *The Sleepwalkers: A Trilogy.* New York: Pantheon Books, 1964.

Diebold, A. R. Anthropology and the comparative psychology of communicative behavior. In T. A. Sebeok (Ed.), *Animal communication: Techniques of study and results of Research.* Bloomington: Indiana University Press, 1968. pp. 525–571.

Duncan, S. Nonverbal communication. *Psychological Bulletin,* 1969, 72, 118–137.

Edelman, M. S., Omark, D. R., &

Freedman, D. G. Dominance hierarchies in children. Unpublished manuscript, *Committee on Human Development,* University of Chicago, 1971.

Efran, J. S., & Broughton, A. Effect of expectancies for social approval on visual behavior. *Journal of Personality and Social Psychology,* 1966, 4, 103–107.

Eimerl, S., & Devore, I. *The primates.* New York: Time, Inc., 1965.

Ekman, P. Communication through nonverbal behavior: A source of information about an interpersonal relationship. In S. S. Tomkins and C. E. Izard, *Affect, cognition, and personality.* New York: Springer, 1965 p. 390–442.

Ekman, P., & Friesen, W. V. Head and body cues in the judgment of emotions: A reformulation. *Perceptual and Motor Skills,* 1967, 24, 711–724.

Ekman, P., & Friesen, W. V. The repertoire of nonverbal behavior: Categories, origins, usage, and coding. *Semiotica,* 1969, I, (I), 49–98.

Ellsworth, P. C., & Carlsmith, J. M. Effects of eye contact and verbal content on affective response to a dyadic interaction. *Journal of Personality and Social Psychology,* 1968, 10, 15–20.

Elworthy, F. T. *The evil eye: The origins and practices of superstition.* London: John Murray, 1895.

Exline, R. V. Effects of need for affiliation, sex, and the sight of others upon initial communications in problem-solving groups, *Journal of Personality,* 1962, 30, 541–556. (a)

Exline, R. V. Need affiliation and initial communication behavior in task-oriented groups characterized by low interpersonal visibility. *Psychological Reports,* 1962, 10, 78–89.(b)

Exline, R. V. Explorations in the process of person perception: Visual interaction in relation to competition, sex, and the need for affiliation. *Journal of Personality,* 1963, 31, 1–20.

Exline, R.V., & Eldridge, C. Effects of two patterns of a speaker's visual behavior on the perception of the authenticity of his verbal message. Paper presented at the meeting of the Eastern Psychological Association, Boston, 1967.

Exline, R.V., Fairweather, H., Hine, J., & Argyle, M. Impressions of a listener as affected by his direction of gaze during conversation. Unpublished manuscript, University of Delaware, 1971.

Exline, R., Gray, D., & Schuette, D. Visual behavior in a dyad as affected by interview content and sex of respondent. *Journal of Personality and Social Psychology*, 1965, 1, 201–209.

Exline, R. V., & Greenberg, E. Visual behavior in relation to the authenticity of a message in a dyad. Unpublished manuscript, University of Delaware, 1971.

Exline, R. V., & Long, B. Visual behavior in relation to power of position in legitimate and illegitimate power hierarchies. Unpublished manuscript, University of Delaware, 1971.

Exline, R. V., & Messick, D. The effects of dependency and social reinforcement upon visual behavior during an interview. *British Journal of Social and Clinical Psychology*, 1967, 6, 256–266.

Exline, R. V., & Snadowsky, A. Anticipations of comfort with various age and sex partners according to visual behavior during speech and silence. Unpublished manuscript, University of Delaware, 1971.

Exline, R. V., Thibaut, J., Hickey, C. B., & Gumpert, P. Visual interaction in relation to Machiavellianism and an unethical act. In R. Christie & F. Geis. *Studies in Machiavellianism*. New York: Academic Press, 1970. Pp. 53–75.

Exline, R. V., & Winters, L. C. Affective relations and mutual glances in dyads. In S. S. Tomkins and C. E Izard (Eds.), *Affect, cognition, and personality*. New York: Springer, 1965. (a)

Exline, R. V., & Winters, L. C. Effects of cognitive difficulty and cognitive style upon eye to eye contact in interviews. Paper read at Eastern Psychological Association Meetings, 1965. Pp. 319–350.

Exline, R. V., & Yellin, A. Eye contact as a sign between man and monkey. Symposium on non-verbal communication, Nineteenth International Congress of Psychology, London, 1969.

Gibson, J. J., & Pick, A. D. Perception of another person's looking behavior. *American Journal of Psychology*, 1963, 76, 86–94.

Hall, E. T. *The hidden dimension*. New York: Doubleday, 1966.

Hall, K. R. L., & Devore, I. Baboon social behavior. In I. Devore (Ed.), *Primate behavior:Field studies of monkeys and apes*. New York: Holt, Rinehart & Winston, 1965. Pp. 53–110.

Hinde, R. A., & Rowell, T. E. Communication by posture and facial expressions in the rhesus monkey (Macaca mulatta), *Proceedings of the Zoological Society of London*, 1962, 138, 1–21.

Hutt, C., and Ounsted, C. The biological significance of gaze aversion with particular reference to the syndrome of infantile autism. *Behavioral Science.* 1966, 11, 346–356.

Jay, Phyllis. Field studies. In A. Schrier, H. F. Harlow, & F. Stollnitz (Eds.), *Behavior of nonhuman primates: Modern research trends*. New York: Academic Press, 1965. Pp. 525–592.

Kendon, A. Some functions of gaze-direction in social interaction. *Acta Psychologica*, 1967, 26, 22–63.

Lefcourt, H. M., & Wine, J. Internal versus external control of reinforcement and the deployment of attention in experimental situations. *Canadian Journal of Behavioral Science*, 1969, 1, 167–181.

Magnus, H. *Die Sprache der Augen*. Wiesbaden : 1885.

Mailer, N. *The armies of the night*. New York: Signet Books, 1968.

Marsh, Nagio. *Spinsters in jeopardy.* Boston: Little, Brown, 1953.

Mehrabian, A. Inference of attitude from the posture, orientation, and distance of a communicator. *Journal of Consulting and Clinical Psychology,* 1968, 32, 296–308. (a)

Mehrabian, A. Relationship of attitude to seat posture, orientation, and distance. *Journal of Personality and Social Psychology,* 1968, 10, 26–33. (b)

Mehrabian, A. Significance of posture and position in the communication of attitude and status relationships. *Psychological Bulletin,* 1969, 71, 359–372.

Ogden, A. Looks and glances. *Harper's Bazaar,* 1961, 84, 109–110.

Osgood, C., Suci, G. J., & Tannenbaum, P. H. *The measurement of meaning.* Urbana: University of Illinois Press, 1957.

Rimland, B. *Infantile autism.* London: Methuen, 1962.

Rubin, Z. Measurement of romantic love. *Journal of Personality and Social Psychology,* 1970, 16, 265–273.

Sartre, J. P. *Being and nothingness.* London: Methuen, 1957.

Schaller, G. *The mountain gorilla: Ecology and behavior.* Chicago: University of Chicago Press, 1963.

Scheflen, A. E. The significance of posture in communication systems. *Psychiatry,* 1964, 27, 316–333.

Scheutze, A. Sartre's theory of the alter ego. *Philosophical and Phenomenological Research,* 1948, 9, 181–199.

Schutz, W.C. FIRO: *A three-dimensional theory of interpersonal behavior.* New York: Holt, Rinehart & Winston, 1958.

Simmel, G. Sociology of the senses: Visual interaction. In R. E. Park & E. W. Burgess (Eds.), *Introduction to the science of sociology.* (Rev. ed.) Chicago: University of Chicago Press, 1969. Pp. 356–361.

Singer, M. T. & Wynne, L. C. Differential characteristics of childhood schizophrenics. *American Journal of Psychiatry,* 1963, 120, 234–243.

Sommer, R. *Personal space: The behavioral basis of design.* Englewood Cliffs, N. J.: Prentice-Hall, 1969.

Strongman, K. T., & Champness, B. G. Dominance hierarchies and conflict in eye contact. *Acta Psychologica,* 1968, 28, 376–386.

Thayer, S. The effect of interpersonal looking duration on dominance judgments. *Journal of Social Psychology,* 1969, 79, 285–286.

Thibaut, J. W., & Kelley, H. H. *The social psychology of groups.* New York: Wiley, 1959.

Tomkins, S. S. *Affect, imagery, consciousness: the negative affects,* Vol. 2. New York: Springer, 1963.

Van Lawick-Goodall, J. *My friends the wild chimpanzees.* Washington, D.C.: National Geographic Society, 1967.

Wada, J. A. Modification of cortically induced responses in brain stem of shift of attention in monkeys. *Science,* 1961, 133, 40–42.

Walters, R. H., & Parke, R. D. The role of the distance receptors in the development of social responsiveness. In L. P. Lipsitt & C. C. Spiker (Eds.), *Advances in child development and behavior.* New York: Academic Press, 1965. Pp. 59–96.

Wiener, M., & Mehrabian, A. *Language within Language: Immediacy, a channel in verbal communication.* New York: Appleton-Century-Crofts, 1968.

two

PARALANGUAGE

Psychology has recently rediscovered the importance of language in understanding human behavior, a fact long known to philosophy and literature. The emergence of the field of psycholinguistics as an important focus of study has marked this trend. The acquisition and structure of language as indicators of the structure of mind have been emphasized by psycholinguists. The development of transformational grammar by Noam Chomsky and his followers has brought new excitement to the study of language, promising linkages with more general theories of cognitive processes. Developmental psychologists have found the study of the child's acquisition of language to be a valuable area of concern (Brown, 1973).

The social function of language has not been forgotten, nor has its affective content. The field of sociolinguistics has emerged to consider such issues as dialects, accents, and the relationship of language to social class, role relationships, personality, and the regulation of interaction (see Robinson, 1972 for a recent overview of the field). An important contribution has been made by Wiener and Mehrabian (1968) in their discussion of immediacy. They contend that the choice of words in an interaction is an indication of the closeness of the relationship of the two interactants, as well as of the speaker to the subject discussed. Thus, in any discourse, there exists a large number of potential choices of words, and the choice among these alternatives is thought to be a nonrandom event, determined by some special psychological determinants. For example, in referring to a party attended by myself and another person, I could say: *"I met John* at *Tom's* party last night" (most immediate), or *"John and I* met at *that* party last night" (less immediate, with words scored indicated by italics). Wiener and Mehrabian (1968) present a scoring scheme for verbal interactions and report some studies validating their concept of immediacy, but the research has not been picked up in the literature as much as it might have been.

We have slowly moved away from the strictly linguistic and cognitive analysis of language exemplified by the psycholinguists and have gone on to the social context of language usage considered by the sociolinguists. Allied with the sociolinguists are the paralinguists, the subject of our present chapter. What differentiates the psycholinguists and sociolinguists from the paralinguists is that the first two are concerned with the semantic aspects of speech, the words themselves, while the paralinguists are happy with the "leavings" of the psycho- and sociolinguists—the nonsemantic aspects of speech, everything *but* the words themselves. At first glance, it may seem that they have cornered themselves out of a field, for what else is left after the words are gone? Quite a bit, it seems. Paralinguists set great store on *how* something is said, not on *what* is said. The tone of voice, pacing of speech, and extralinguistic sounds (such as sighs) make up their area of concern. Trager (1958) defined the limits of the field and provided the basis for further research. Luckily, the paralinguists have linked their concern with the general field of nonverbal communication, feeling that there is a common focus of interest, generally centering on the communication of affective information.

The field of paralinguistics has developed in two major directions: voice as indicator of personality and voice as indicator of the state of the interaction. Prominent in the first tradition have been the voice and personality studies, which have generally shown that raters have stereotyped conceptions of which vocal qualities indicate which personality traits. The studies also show, but not as strongly, that there exists a link between the traits and vocal qualities themselves (see Kramer, 1963 for an overview of the area, and Scherer, 1972 for a more recent study). Kasl and Mahl (1965) have contributed to the paralinguistic literature by distinguishing eight categories of speech disturbance, such as "ahs," stutters, and repetitions as indicators of emotional state, particularly anxiety in patients in psychotherapy. Pacing in speech, especially the hesitation pause, has also been linked to grammatical encoding processes (Boomer, 1965; Boomer and Dittmann, 1962, 1964).

Our concern here is more with the second trend of paralinguistic research: voice as indicator of the state of the interaction. This field was given impetus by two developments: one methodological, the other conceptual. The discovery of content-free speech as a research tool provided a methodology for the field (Starkweather, 1956) and the centering of attention on the experimenter effect, stimulated by Rosenthal's (1966, 1967) research provided a problem area for which paralinguistics promised a partial answer.

Various types of content-free methods for isolating the paralinguistic level of speech from the semantic content have been developed. The first two selections in this chapter present different methods for such treatment. Davitz and

Davitz (p. **99**, this book) indicate that reading the alphabet can carry affective meaning when Ss are instructed to instill such meaning into their reading (see also Davitz, 1964). Sophisticated filtering techniques have been developed to mask the meaningfulness of actual speech to see if affective tone is preserved. Starkweather (1956) describes the result as "a kind of mumble as though heard through a wall." Rogers, Scherer, and Rosenthal (1971) describe a simple electronic system for effecting such content filtering of natural speech. Scherer (1971) has also developed a simpler technique of masking speech content: randomized splicing, in which tape is cut up and spliced back together in random sections. Although the full range of pitch is preserved in this method, the continuity and rhythm are destroyed, cues one might think important to the transmission of emotional information. Scherer, Koivumaki, and Rosenthal (1972) do show evidence, however, that even randomized spliced speech retains its affective tone, a high testimonial to the strength of paralinguistic cues. Scherer's latest work, presented in this volume (p. **105**) indicates that entirely artificial tone sequences can also be discriminated on an affective dimension. The profound ability of music to inspire feelings is, of course, a result of this effect, a generalization from paralinguistic research to a more abstract sphere.

The study of the experimenter effect gave a focus to study of human interaction and provided a special role for paralinguistic variables. Rosenthal's (1966) research indicated that something special was going on in the experimenter-subject interaction. Along with the overt process of instruction-giving and direction, there was a covert communications system that was subtly influencing the performance of the subject by transmitting the experimenter's expectations to him. Subjects then responded to the expectations by behaving in accordance with them and with other demand characteristics of the situation, acting as "good subjects" (Orne, 1962). A critical series of experiments by Rosenthal and his associates demonstrated that by instilling different expectations in experimenters, subjects' performance could be altered in accordance with these expectations, even though the overt behavior of experimenters did not obviously seem to differ between the two sets of experimenters. The site of the hidden communications system seemed to be the paralinguistic and nonverbal channels. Indeed, in a follow-up series of experiments, subtle alterations of vocal emphasis in instructions were found to affect experimental outcomes in the expected directions (Duncan, Rosenberg, and Finkelstein, 1969; Scherer, Rosenthal, and Koivumaki, 1972).

Rosenthal's group is currently developing and testing a measure of nonverbal sensitivity to various channels, called the PONS test (Profile of Nonverbal Sensitivity). The S sees 220 short film clips of a stimulus person enacting various emotions, with the clips representing the facial, bodily, and vocal channels singly and in various combinations. The S is to guess which of two situations is being enacted in each clip (for example, expressing jealous anger versus talking to a lost child). From these scores, a Profile of Nonverbal Sensitivity is computed, assessing the *S* on overall, separate, and combined channel scores. Sensitivity to positive-negative and dominant-submissive emotions can be measured separately by this technique. The test has been given to over a hundred samples all over the world, and factors such as sex, age, social class, and personality have been studied (Rosenthal, 1973).

The interest in the specialized world of the experimenter-subject interaction soon spread to the study of other dyads, more common in everyday life. The two studies presented here by Milmoe and her associates, center on two important, affect-laden interactions, the doctor-patient and mother-child dyads. In the first study, "The Doctor's Voice," doctors whose voices were rated as less angry and more anxious were more successful in referring alcoholic patients for further treatment (see p. **112**). The second study, "The Mother's Voice," indicated that mothers whose voices were rated high on dimensions of anxiety and anger had children who showed "various signs of irritability," such as crying and upset at separation (see p. **122**).

Other important interactions have also come under paralinguistic scrutiny. Duncan, Rice, and Butler (1968) found definite vocal factors associated with peak and poor performances of clinicians in therapy hours. Weitz (1972) looked at interracial interaction and found that rated friendliness of voice tone of whites was significantly related to friendliness of behavior toward blacks in a simulated interaction, whereas overt verbal attitude was negatively related to behavior. In such situations, where whites are often conflicted in their relationship toward blacks, the paralinguistic channel may carry more accurate information than the more socially controlled verbal channel. Indeed, informal discussions with blacks have confirmed the observation that tone is often closely attended to as being a reliable indication of attitude, be it hostile, patronizing, or genuinely friendly. Cross-sex interactions may also rely heavily on the paralinguistic channel (Weitz, 1973). Sachs, Lieberman, and Erickson (1973) provide evidence that children may shape their voices to sound like the adult version of their sex, since anatomical differences between male and female larynxes at early ages are insufficient to account for the degree of sex typing in voices found in prepubertal children. Lieberman (1967) reports on a series of studies on vocal intonation, emphasizing physiologic, acoustic, and perceptual data.

It seems clear that all interactions operate on various levels, sending messages differing in complexity and validity. When the content of verbal messages is constrained by normative forces, paralinguistic and nonverbal channels may be relied on for more valid information, as in interracial interaction. It is likely that there is individual variation in sensitivity to such channels, with the more dependent member of the dyad having the most to gain by being attuned to the other's emotional state and to the affective tone of the interaction. Thus, the author's observation that women seem to be more sensitive to such cues than men, and blacks more so than whites.

Actors have long known the nuances of vocal tone and pacing; psychologists are just adding this cue to their understanding of the theater of social interaction.

REFERENCES

Brown, R., *A First Language: The Early Stages,* Harvard University Press, Cambridge, 1973.

Boomer, D. S., "Hesitation and grammatical encoding," *Language and Speech,* 1965, 8, 148–58.

Boomer, D. S., and Dittmann, A. T., "Hesitation pauses and juncture pauses in speech," *Language and Speech,* 1962, 5, 215–20.

Boomer, D. S., and Dittmann, A. T., "Speech rate, filled pause, and body movements in interviews," *Journal of Nervous and Mental Disease,* 1964, 139, 324–27.

Davitz, J. R., *The Communication of Emotional Meaning,* McGraw-Hill, New York, 1964.

Duncan, S., Rice, L. N., and Butler, J. M., "Therapists' paralanguage in peak and poor psychotherapy hours," *Journal of Abnormal Psychology,* 1968, 73, 566–70.

Duncan, S., Rosenberg, M. J., and Finkelstein, J., "The paralanguage of experimenter bias," *Sociometry,* 1969, 32, 207–19.

Kasl, S. V., and Mahl, G. F., "The relationship of disturbances and hesitations in spontaneous speech to anxiety," *Journal of Personality and Social Psychology,* 1965, 1, 425–33.

Kramer, E., "The judgment of personal characteristics and emotions from nonverbal properties of speech," *Psychological Bulletin,* 1963, 60, 408–20.

Lieberman, P., *Intonation, Perception and Language,* MIT Press, Cambridge, 1967.

Orne, M. T., "On the social psychology of the psychological experiment; with particular reference to demand characteristics and their implications," *American Psychologist,* 1962, 17, 776–83.

Robinson, W. P., *Language and Social Behavior,* Penguin, Baltimore, 1972.

Rogers, P. L., Scherer, K. R., and Rosenthal, R., "Content filtering human speech: a simple electronic system," *Behavioral Research Methods and Instruments,* 1971, 3, 16–18.

Rosenthal, R., *Experimenter Effects in Behavioral Research,* Appleton-Century-Crofts, New York, 1966.

Rosenthal, R., "Covert communication in the psychological experiment," *Psychological Bulletin,* 1967, 67, 356–67.

Rosenthal, R., "The use of film in assessing sensitivity to nonverbal communication: the PONS test," paper presented at the 81st annual convention, American Psychological Association, Montreal, August 1973.

Sachs, J., Lieberman, P., and Erickson, D., "Anatomical and cultural determinants of male and female speech," in *Language Attitudes: Current Trends and Prospects,* R. W. Shuy and R. W. Fasold, eds., Georgetown University Press, Washington, D.C., 1973, pp. 74–84.

Scherer, K. R., "Randomized splicing: a note on a simple technique for masking speech content," *Journal of Experimental Research in Personality,* 1971, 5, 155–59.

Scherer, K. R., "Judging personality from voice: a cross-cultural approach to an old issue in interpersonal perception," *Journal of Personality,* 1972, 40, 191–210.

Scherer, K. R., Koivumaki, J., and Rosenthal, R., "Minimal cues in the vocal communication of affect: judging emotions from content-masked speech,"

Journal of Psycholinguistic Research, 1972, 1, 269–85.

Scherer, K. R., Rosenthal, R., and Koivumaki, J., "Mediating interpersonal expectancies via vocal cues: differential speech intensity as a means of social influence," *European Journal of Social Psychology,* 1972, 2, 163–76.

Starkweather, J., "Content-free speech as a source of information about the speaker," *Journal of Abnormal and Social Psychology,* 1956, 52, 394–402.

Trager, G., "Paralanguage: a first approximation," *Studies in Linguistics,* 1958, 13, 1–12.

Weitz, S., "Attitude, voice, and behavior: a repressed affect model of interracial interaction," *Journal of Personality and Social Psychology,* 1972, 24, 14–21.

Weitz, S., "Sex differences in nonverbal communication," 1973, several studies in progress.

Wiener, M., and Mehrabian, A., *Language within Language: Immediacy, A Channel in Verbal Communication,* Appleton-Century-Crofts, New York, 1968.

THE COMMUNICATION OF FEELINGS
BY CONTENT-FREE SPEECH

JOEL R. DAVITZ AND LOIS JEAN DAVITZ

The purpose of this research was to investigate the communication of feelings by content-free speech. Specifically, this study was designed (1) to test the hypothesis that feelings can be communicated reliably by content-free speech and (2) to discover relevant problems for future research about the vocal communication of feelings.

This research began with a consideration of Suzanne Langer's theory of symbols and communication.[1,2] Miss Langer suggests that symbols may be either discursive or nondiscursive. Discursive symbols correlate names or concepts and things, are verifiable, duplicable, and have a defined syntax and order. Nondiscursive symbols, on the other hand, depend on personal perceptions, on intuition, and on direct insight for understanding. They cannot be verified or duplicated, do not have "dictionary meanings," and do not have a socially defined syntax and order.

Miss Langer interprets art as communication in the nondiscursive mode. The artist is concerned with the expression of feeling; specifically, he creates forms symbolic of human feeling. Communication in the arts depends primarily upon form rather than content, for it is the form of the communication which carries the feeling value of the artist's expression.

Generalizing Miss Langer's thesis to the vocal communication of feelings in everyday life suggests that feelings are communicated in the nondiscursive mode and, therefore, are communicated vocally primarily by the form of the message, or by how the message is spoken. However, generalization of Miss Langer's theory of the expression of feelings in art to the problem of communication of feelings in everyday speech seems to require some qualification. First, some feelings undoubtedly are communicated by the content of a spoken message. Although the way a phrase such as "I am happy" is spoken determines, to a large degree, the feeling expressed, the content of the message "I am happy" also may influence the feeling communicated. Secondly, if

From *Journal of Communication*, 1959, 9, 6–13. Copyright © 1959 by the International Communication Association and reprinted by permission.

feelings are communicated in everyday speech with even a moderate degree of efficiency, it seems unlikely that understanding the feelings expressed by another person depends entirely on unique, personal, nonverifiable, and nonduplicable perceptions. Rather, it seems reasonable to assume that within any given speech community there are more or less stereotyped formal aspects of speech associated with the expression of particular feelings. Although there is no dictionary of these forms, to the degree that members of a speech community can communicate feelings to one another with at least moderate effectiveness, the definitions correlating form and feeling are shared and verifiable. No doubt individual differences exist in any given group, but, in general, one would expect members of a group to share at least some consistent correlations between forms of speech and feelings expressed.

If feelings are communicated, at least in part, by the form of a spoken message and if there are relatively stereotyped form-feeling correlations within a speech community, it is reasonable to predict that feelings can be reliably communicated by content-free speech. The present research was designed to test this prediction.

Procedure

The research procedure involved two steps: (1) recording expressions of feeling by persons reciting parts of the alphabet; (2) identification by judges of the feelings expressed.

Expression of feeling

Each of eight subjects, four males and four females, expressed ten feelings by reciting parts of the alphabet. Subjects were white, native American speakers of English; they were undergraduate and graduate students and college faculty members in New York City. One subject, speaker B indicated in Table 2, was a professional actress and singer; however, none of the other subjects had ever received either vocal or dramatic training. The subjects were given the following instructions:

GENERAL INSTRUCTIONS In this study you will be asked to express various feelings through speech. But this speech will consist only of letters, not words. In each case, you will be asked to express a particular feeling simply by saying the alphabet, using your voice to express a *feeling* rather than any special content. You can stop at any point, repeat or omit letters. The important point to remember is to try to express a particular feeling without using words.

WARM-UP In this study it is important that you feel as free and uninhibited as possible. As a first step, would you please say the alphabet a few times just to warm up. Try to let yourself go, loosen up, get the feel of using letters as if they were words, and expressing some feeling through the use of only letters. Take as much time as you like to warm up. Then turn to the next card.

After the warm-up period, the subjects were given the first card, which asked them to recite the alphabet as if it were "normal conversation." They then were given ten cards, each of which contained the name of one feeling and a brief description of a situation in which the feeling might be expressed. For example, the feeling called "Anger" was accompanied by the following instructions:

Anger: Another person has taken your copy of an important term paper that has to be handed in today. He's just told you he has lost it through carelessness, and he doesn't seem to be concerned about it. You're infuriated. You've lost your temper and you're expressing your ANGER.

Another feeling was "Fear," which had the following instructions:

Fear: You're just about to undergo an extremely dangerous operation. You've just discovered that there may be great pain involved and that your chance of recovering is slim. Extremely afraid, you are talking to a friend, expressing your great FEAR.

The ten feelings expressed by each subject were: (1) anger, (2) fear, (3) happiness, (4) jealousy, (5) love, (6) nervousness, (7) pride, (8) sadness, (9) satisfaction, and (10) sympathy. The order of presentation was random and different for each subject. The expression of normal conversation and the ten feelings were tape-recorded and then presented to judges for identification of feelings expressed.

Identification of feelings

Thirty judges, graduate students enrolled at Teachers College, Columbia University, attempted to identify the feelings expressed. Each judge was given a list of the feelings expressed and the following information: (1) the recording to be played consisted of eight different speakers, each reciting the alphabet eleven times; (2) in the case of each speaker, the first time he or she recited the alphabet would represent normal conversation, and each of the following ten recitations of the alphabet would represent the expression of one of the feelings listed; (3) each speaker might express a particular feeling any number of times. Each judge then heard the recordings of each of the eight subjects; since each subject expressed ten feelings, every judge made eighty judgments.

Results

The results were analyzed in three related ways: (1) the number of times each feeling was correctly identified; (2) the accuracy of judges in identifying feelings; and (3) the accuracy with which each of the eight speakers expressed the ten feelings.

Analysis of feelings expressed

Table 1 indicates the number of times each feeling was correctly identified. The total number of judgments was 240 (thirty raters, each hearing eight speakers). Since ten different feelings were expressed, chance expectancy for the correct identification of each feeling is one in ten. In other words, if the feelings were judged merely on the basis of chance, twenty-four correct

TABLE 1
Number of correct identifications of each feeling

Feeling expressed	Number of correct identifications
Anger	156
Fear	60
Happiness	104
Jealousy	59
Love	60
Nervousness	130
Pride	50
Sadness	118
Satisfaction	74
Sympathy	93

identifications would occur for each feeling. The probability of obtaining as many correct identifications of each feeling as listed in Table 1 was estimated by the normal approximation of the binomial distribution, where p is .1,

q is .9, and M is 24. For each of the ten feelings, the probability of obtaining by chance as many correct identifications as listed in Table 1 is less than one in a hundred. Therefore, the hypothesis that feelings can be communicated reliably by content-free speech is supported by this analysis of the data.

Analysis of judges' accuracy

A related analysis of the data concerns the accuracy with which each feeling was identified by the thirty judges. Each person made a total of eighty judgments—ten judgments for each of the eight speakers. By chance, one judgment in ten, or eight for each judge, would be correct. The mean number of correct responses for the thirty judges is 29.4 with a range from 16 to 39 and a standard deviation of 5.7. Once again estimating the probability of obtaining these results by chance, using the normal approximation of the binomial distribution, the probability of obtaining by chance as many correct responses as those made by the judges in this study is less than one in a hundred.

Accuracy of speakers

The data also were analyzed in terms of the accuracy with which each speaker communicated the ten feelings. Each speaker expressed ten feelings, and each feeling was judged thirty times for a total of 300 judgments about each speaker. The data for the eight speakers are summarized in Table 2. Chance would produce thirty correct communications for each speaker. In each of the eight cases, the probability of obtaining as many correct communications as those listed in Table 2 is less than one in a hundred.

TABLE 2

Number of correct judgments about each speaker

Speaker	Number of correct judgments
A	70
B	161
C	125
D	96
E	150
F	122
G	78
H	128

Discussion

The three analyses of the data are not independent; they merely view the data from three perspectives. Obviously, an analysis from any one of these viewpoints provides a test of the hypothesis. However, considering the data from these three points of view does provide a basis for formulating various kinds of problems for further research. First, considering the feelings expressed, it is apparent that there are differences in the number of correct identifications among the ten feelings. For example, anger was correctly identified 156 times, but pride was identified correctly only 50 times. The differential accuracy with which various feelings are identified may bear important implications for understanding the vocal communication of feeling, and an estimate of the accuracy with which a wider range of feelings are expressed would seem to be an important problem for future research. In addition, it would seem important to discover the particular dimensions or characteristics of various feelings associated with the differential accuracy of communicating these feelings. Such characteristics, for example, may involve either subjective aspects of the feeling itself or objective factors, such as changes in the tone of voice during the expression of the emotion.

Further examination of the data reveals that some feelings are mistaken for others well beyond chance expectancy. For example, although fear was correctly identified 60 times, it was mistakenly identified as nervousness 41 times and as sadness 48 times. Similarly, love was correctly identified 60 times, but mistakenly identified as sadness 54 times and as sympathy 47 times. Pride was correctly identified 50 times, but mistakenly identified as satisfaction 48 times and as happiness 37 times. In short, there appear to be more or less consistent patterns of errors in the identification of feelings, and an important problem for further research is the identification of these patterns or clusters.

Finally, from the point of view of feelings expressed, the results of this study support the theoretical assumption that there are form-feeling correlations shared by members of a speech community. The expression of some feelings may involve chiefly changes in tone, but the presentation of others may be accomplished primarily by changes in volume or rate. Discrimination among various emotions may involve subtle and complex differences in the patterns of physical characteristics involved in the communications. A significant problem, therefore, is the rigorous clarification of the form-feeling correlations in terms of the physical characteristics of speech, such as tone, volume, and rhythm, associated with the expression of various feelings. Other aspects of form, such as the characteristic structure of the language associated with particular feelings, also

may prove to be an important problem for investigation.

In respect to the speakers and judges, it is apparent that there are wide individual differences in the accuracy with which persons express and judge feelings. In the present study, the most effective speaker communicated the feelings accurately a total of 161 times; the least effective speaker communicated accurately only 70 times. Similarly, the most accurate judge made 39 correct identifications; the least accurate judge made only 16 correct identifications. One might investigate, for example, the relationship between an individual's ability to express and judge vocal communications of feeling. Is there a general sensitivity, awareness, or ability underlying both of these aspects of the communication process, or are these abilities relatively independent? Is the ability to express or judge feelings communicated vocally related to abilities to express ar judge feelings in other modes of communication? If the ability to either express or judge feelings is a generalized, stable dimension of behavior, is it related to other dimensions of personality, such as introversion-extraversion or other measures of interpersonal sensitivity? The relationship between speaker and judge would seem to be another important problem. In the present study, both speakers and judges were American, native-born speakers of English. Thus, they were members of a fairly large speech community. But if there are individual differences in form-feeling correlates, one would expect the familiarity of the judge with the speaker to be positively related to the accuracy of communication. For example, it seems likely that husband and wife can communicate feeling to each other more accurately than can one stranger to another. In general, accuracy of communication seems likely to be positively related to the familiarity or social distance of the persons involved in the communication.

Only a few of the more obvious problems suggested by the present research have been indicated; however, even these seem to be important questions for investigation. Furthermore, the general methodology of the present study appears to offer one useful way of attacking these problems. Although the present stage of research permits little or no generalization to practical problems, it does not seem unreasonable to anticipate that further work in this area, perhaps along some of the lines suggested by the present study, may eventuate in useful information applicable to a wide range of problems involving the vocal communication of feelings. These may include areas as diverse as the teaching of poetry and the practice of psychotherapy. In both cases, sensitivity to feelings expressed is of primary importance, and knowledge which might serve as a basis for increasing this sensitivity could be of great value. But probably more important than practical implications is the possibility that research in this area may contribute to a general theory of communication. It is conceivable, for example, that just as grammars and dictionaries concerned with communication in the discursive mode have been developed, an approximation of the more-or-less generally shared form-feeling correlations of everyday speech could be established. Therefore, while the data support the prediction which initiated the research, perhaps the most important value of the present study is the stimulation of further research in this area.

Summary

This study was designed (1) to test the hypothesis that feelings can be communicated reliably by content-free speech and (2) to discover relevant problems for future research about the vocal communication of feeling. Eight speakers each expressed ten different feelings by reciting the alphabet, and thirty judges identified these communications. The data were analyzed from three related points of view, and the hypothesis was supported in all instances. This paper closed by suggesting problems for further research concerning the feelings expressed, the speakers, and the judges.

NOTES

1. S. K. Langer, *Philosophy in a New Key* (Cambridge: Harvard University Press, 1942).
2. S. K. Langer, *Feeling and Form* (New York: Scribners, 1953).

ACOUSTIC CONCOMITANTS OF EMOTIONAL DIMENSIONS: JUDGING AFFECT FROM SYNTHESIZED TONE SEQUENCES [1]

KLAUS R. SCHERER

PROBLEM The ability of naive listener-judges to recognize the affective state of a speaker on the basis of nonlinguistic auditory cues independent of the verbal content of an utterance has been well established by a large number of studies, summarized by Kramer (1963), Davitz (1964), Vetter (1969), and Scherer (1970). Results of a recent study by Scherer, Rosenthal, and Koivumaki (1971), using content-masking by random splicing (Scherer, 1971), electronic content filtering (Rogers, Scherer, and Rosenthal, 1971) and their combinations, suggest that a minimal set of vocal cues consisting of pitch level and variation, amplitude level and variation, and rate of articulation or tempo may be sufficient to communicate the evaluation, potency, and activity dimensions of emotional meaning.

In order to assess more precisely the way in which inferences of emotional content are based on specific acoustic cues and their combinations, one would want to be able to manipulate these cues experimentally. Since, in spite of recent advances in the area of speech synthesis, this is rather difficult to achieve with actual speech signals, the present study has used artificial stimuli produced by a Moog synthesizer to vary pitch level and variation, amplitude level and variation, and signal duration and speed (tempo) systematically in a factorial design.

Study I

STIMULI A simple tone sequence modeled after the intonation contour of a short sentence, consisting of eight sine wave tones of differential pitch and duration, were synthesized repeatedly on a Moog electronic synthesizer with sequencing unit. Five parameters of the sequence were varied independently in a 4x2x2x2x2 factorial design with the following levels on each parameter: pitch variation—moderate, extreme, up contour, down contour; amplitude variation—moderate, extreme; pitch level-high, low; amplitude level-low,

Paper presented at Eastern Psychological Association meeting, Boston, April 1972, and new postscript, June 1973. Reprinted by permission of the author.

high; tempo—slow, fast. The resulting 64 stimuli, rendered two times each, were edited in random order on to a demonstration tape.

RATERS Ten undergraduates, six male and four female, were used as raters. They were recruited by sign-up sheets and were paid.

PROCEDURE The raters heard the tape-recorded stimuli in random order and were asked to rate each sample on ten-point scales of pleasantness, evaluation, activity, and potency as well as to indicate whether the sample to be rated could or could not be an expression of the following emotions: interest, sadness, fear, happiness, disgust, anger, surprise, elation, boredom.

RESULTS Table 1 shows F-ratios, significance levels, and the direction of the effect for main effects and two-way interactions with $p < .01$ yielded by a five-way analysis of variance with repeated measures. The parameters that seem to have had the most influence on the judges' ratings are tempo and pitch variation. Moderate pitch variation leads to ratings of generally unpleasant emotions, like sadness, fear, disgust, and boredom, showing little activity or potency. Extreme pitch variation and up contours produce ratings of highly pleasant,[2] active, and potent emotions such as happiness, interest, surprise, and also fear. Down contours have similar effects but do not seem to contain elements of surprise or uncertainty. Fast tempo leads to an attribution of high activity and potency as in the emotions of interest, fear, happiness, anger, and surprise. Slow tempo is seen as indicative of sadness, disgust, and boredom.

Extreme amplitude variation is seen as active and potent, mostly indicative of the emotions of fear and anger, whereas moderate amplitude variation is seen as happiness or disgust. High pitch level yields happiness and surprise, low pitch level, on the other hand, leads to ratings of disgust and boredom. High amplitude level leads to ratings of potency.

There is some evidence for differential acoustic manifestations of different types of specific emotions. For example, whereas anger is generally characterized by extreme amplitude variation and fast tempo, which may represent "hot" anger, a significant interaction effect shows that moderate pitch variation and moderate amplitude variation interact to produce higher ratings on anger, possibly indicative of "cool" anger. Another interesting interaction effect, that leads to consistently higher ratings on activity and surprise, usually associated with up contours, occurs between down contour and high pitch level which may represent a special type of novel situation.

Study II

STIMULI 16 of the 64 stimuli used in Study I were chosen to represent happiness, fear, anger, and sadness.

RATERS 166 undergraduates, 69 male and 97 female, rated the stimuli during a demonstration in class.

PROCEDURE The raters were asked to choose between a pair of alternative labels for each of the 16 stimuli. The "correct" label was determined by the highest mean rating of the respective stimulus in Study I.

TABLE I

F-ratios, significance levels, and direction of means [a]

	ACOUSTIC PARAMETER					
Emotion	*PV*	*AV*	*PL*	*AL*	*TE*	*Interaction*
Pleasantness	5.33 ** Ex,down	1.81	<1	<1	2.05	11.26 ** LoAL+HiPL HiAL+LoPL
Activity	9.94 *** Ex,up, down	5.98 ** Ex	4.23	8.73 * Hi	35.48 *** Fast	9.21 ** MoPV+LoPL DoPV+HiPL
Potency	23.46 *** Ex,up, down	22.03 ** Ex	1.14	10.44 * Hi	5.48 * Fast	
Interest	4.72 ** Ex,up, down	<1	2.45	4.95	23.63 *** Fast	
Sadness	4.27 ** Mo	2.82	3.19	3.49	115.20 *** Slow	13.97 ** MoAV+HiPL ExAV+LoPL
Fear	3.71 * Mo,ex,up	6.32 * Ex	<1	1.12	11.05 ** Fast	
Happiness	8.26 *** Ex,up, down	7.17 * Mo	9.38 * Hi	<1	33.30 *** Fast	5.12 ** ExUpPV+ Fast TE
Disgust	5.62 *** Mo	22.50 ** Mo	6.43 * Lo	<1	6.37 * Slow	
Anger	1.22	6.70 * Ex	<1	3.84	7.43 * Fast	4.83 ** MoPV+ MoAV
Surprise	9.81 *** Ex,up	1.77	12.62 ** Hi	2.72	45.20 *** Fast	7.38 *** ExDoPV+ HiPL
Elation	2.49	1.87	2.60	<1	3.16	
Boredom	5.59 ** Mo	<1	5.50 * Lo	<1	60.19 *** Slow	

[a] Higher ratings were found for the level of each parameter shown in the cell.

ABBREVIATIONS:
PV=pitch variation, AV=amplitude variation, PL=pitch level, AL=amplitude level, TE=tempo, Mo=moderate, Ex=extreme.

* $p<.05$.
** $p<.01$.
*** $p<.001$.

RESULTS The frequency distribution of the raters over the number of correct choices is shown in the following table:

Number of correct choices	1–7	8	9	10	11	12	13	14	15	16	*Total*
Number of raters	0	3	8	15	21	35	39	36	8	1	166

There were no significant differences in accuracy between male and female raters. The degree of accuracy shown by the judges is far above of what may be expected by chance (p<.001).[3] Furthermore, most of the errors made are due to inaccurate choices on 4 of the 16 stimuli,[4] the error distribution being significantly different from chance (p<.001).[5]

CONCLUSION These results support the contention that the attribution of emotional meaning from auditory stimuli is based on characteristic patterns of acoustic cues. Specifically, there is evidence for earlier suggestions (Scherer, 1971; Scherer, Rosenthal, and Koivumaki, 1971) that specific cues or cue combinations communicate the major dimensions of emotional meaning. Relationships have been found between amplitude level and the potency dimension, between variation of pitch and amplitude as well as tempo and the activity and potency dimensions, and between pitch level and variation and the evaluative dimension.

The present approach suggests a rapprochement between studies on emotional expression in speech and the psychological investigation of emotion in music, with interesting implications concerning speculations on the common origin of music and speech in primitive emotional displays of our prehistoric ancestors (Langer, 1942). Pertinent studies on the cross-cultural universality of the vocal expression of emotion as well as on the development of the ability to recognize emotions from vocal or musical material in young children seem promising and have yet to be done. Judging from recent evidence (Ekman and Friesen, 1971) supporting Darwin's theory of innate mechanisms in emotional expression (Darwin, 1887), one may be justified in speculating about the existence of unlearned neural programs for the vocal expression and recognition of emotion, especially given the strong correspondences between respiratory phenomena and physiological correlates of affective state. This line of reasoning might eventually lead to a comparative analysis of the vocal expression of emotion in humans and auditory signals found in primate communication.

Postscript

The study reported above was recently replicated in an extended format with a large number of listener judges (Scherer and Oshinsky, in preparation). In the replication seven acoustic parameters (with two levels each) were manipulated: Amplitude variation (moderate, extreme), pitch variation (moderate, extreme), pitch contour (down, up), pitch level (low, high), tempo (slow, fast), duration/shape of the signal ("round" vs. "sharp" attack and decay of the signal), filtration or lack of overtones (moderate, extreme).

The listener judges' ratings of emotional content, which were found to be highly reliable across raters, strongly supported the earlier findings and

TABLE 2

Concomitants of acoustical dimensions

AMPLITUDE VARIATION	Moderate	Pleasantness, Activity, Happiness
	Extreme	Fear
PITCH VARIATION	Moderate	Anger, Boredom, Disgust, Fear
	Extreme	Pleasantness, Activity, Happiness, Surprise
PITCH CONTOUR	Down	Pleasantness, Boredom, Sadness
	Up	Potency, Anger, Fear, Surprise
PITCH LEVEL	Low	Pleasantness, Boredom, Sadness
	High	Activity, Potency, Anger, Fear, Surprise
TEMPO	Slow	Boredom, Disgust, Sadness
	Fast	Pleasantness, Activity, Potency, Anger, Fear, Happiness, Surprise
DURATION (SHAPE)	Round	Potency, Boredom, Disgust, Fear, Sadness
	Sharp	Pleasantness, Activity, Happiness, Surprise
FILTRATION (LACK OF OVERTONES)	Low	Sadness
	Moderate	Pleasantness, Boredom, Happiness
		Potency, Activity
	Extreme	Anger, Disgust, Fear, Surprise
TONALITY	Atonal	Disgust
	Tonal-Minor	Anger
	Tonal-Major	Pleasantness, Happiness
RHYTHM	Not rhythmic	Boredom
	Rhythmic	Activity, Fear, Surprise

showed highly significant effects for the two parameters added in the replication, duration and filtration. In a second part of the study, for a small subset of the standard stimuli and for a short simple melody by Beethoven, the parameters of tonality and rhythm were manipulated in addition to attempt a first extension into the area of the psychology of musical expression. Table 2 shows a qualitative summary of the results by presenting for each level of the acoustic parameter the emotion for which a significant effect was found. A regression analysis of the results showed that the independently varied acoustic parameters on the average accounted for three fourths of the variance in the ratings of the listener judges.

A pilot study with 2nd graders, 6th graders and adults on the correct recognition of emotional content universally attributed to some stimuli by the original raters, showed that age differences were much less pronounced than the differences in the recognizability of different emotions, anger being most difficult.

These results strongly encourage further research into the inference / attribution structures from standard acoustic parameters to emotional expression especially in terms of cross-cultural and developmental research approaches.

NOTES

1. The author expresses his gratitude to Martin Yaffee and Paul Leiman for help in the preparation of the synthesized stimuli. The data analysis was partially supported by a research grant (GS-2654) to Robert Rosenthal (Harvard University) who has contributed helpful comments. The study has been supported by an NSF institutional grant to the author's institution.

2. After the present study was completed, the author was made aware of an experiment showing that pleasantness ratings of tone sequences bear a curvilinear relationship to the amount of stimulus variation, with moderate variation being perceived as most pleasant. (P. C. Vitz. Affect as a function of stimulus variation. *Journal of Experimental Psychology,* 1966, *71,* 74–79). It is likely that extreme pitch variation in the present study corresponds to moderate variation in the former.

3. Chi square test of goodness of fit to normal distribution.

4. The reason for the much more frequent errors on these stimuli can be found in the fact that the mean difference in the ratings for both alternatives in Study I are much lower than for the rest of the stimuli. A correlation between number of errors and mean difference between alternatives for each stimulus yielded $r = .40$, $p < .10$, $N = 16$, one-tailed.

5. Kolmogorov-Smirnov test of goodness of fit.

REFERENCES

Darwin, Ch. *The expression of the emotions in man and animals.* London, 1872.

Davitz, J. R. (Ed.) *The communication of emotional meaning.* New York, 1964.

Ekman, P. and Friesen, W. V. Constants across cultures in the face and emotion. *Journal of Personality and Social Psychology,* 1971, 17, 124–129.

Kramer, E. The judgment of personal characteristics and emotions from nonverbal properties of speech. *Psychological Bulletin,* 1963, 60, 408–420.

Langer, S. *Philosophy in a new key.* Cambridge, Mass., 1942.

Rogers, P. L., Scherer, K. R., and Rosenthal, R. Content-filtering human speech. *Behavioral Research Methods and Instrumentation,* 1971, 3, 16–18.

Scherer, K. R. *Non-verbale Kommunikation.* Hamburg, 1970.

Scherer, K. R. Randomized-splicing: A note on a simple technique for masking speech content. *Journal of Experimental Research in Personality,* 1971, 5, 155–159.

Scherer, K. R., Rosenthal, R., and Koivumaki, J. Minimal cues in the vocal communication of affect: Judging emotions from content-masked speech. Unpublished manuscript, Harvard University, 1971.

Vetter, H. J. *Language Behavior and Communication.* Itasca, Ill., 1969.

7

THE DOCTOR'S VOICE: POSTDICTOR OF
SUCCESSFUL REFERRAL OF ALCOHOLIC PATIENTS [1]

SUSAN MILMOE, ROBERT ROSENTHAL,
HOWARD T. BLANE, MORRIS E. CHAFETZ
AND IRVING WOLF

"It wasn't what he said; it was the way he said it." Investigators are paying increased attention to the intuitively long-recognized ability of people to pick up and utilize what Kauffman (1954) referred to as "expressive" cues in the language of others, and to the importance of these expressive cues as clues to personality and feeling states. The literature on nonverbal communication in speech has been reviewed by Kramer (1963), Mahl and Schulze (1964), and Starkweather (1961). For example, speech disruptions have been related to situational anxiety (e.g., Dibner, 1956; Eldred & Price, 1958; Feldstein, Brenner, & Jaffe, 1963; Kasl & Mahl, 1958; Mahl, 1956), and reliable "global" judgments have been related to emotions in speech (e.g., Davitz, 1964; Davitz & Davitz, 1959a, 1959b).

An important area for research has been emotion judged from "content-filtered" speech, in which a tape is rerecorded through a low-pass filter to remove high-frequency sounds and thus render the words themselves unrecog-

nizable. Starkweather (1956) found that content-filtered voices of hypertensives were judged to be higher on dominance than similarly presented voices of nonhypertensives. Kramer (1964), however, has observed that one of the problems in most studies which correlate paralinguistic ratings with independent variables is the weakness of the latter. Another difficulty is that studies of emotion in speech have primarily utilized speech elicited in an experimental situation in which the speaker is asked to "act out" the emotion in one way or another. An unpublished study by Starkweather (cited by Kramer, 1963), in which 12 clinical psychologists rated excerpts from the Army-McCarthy hearings, seems to be one of the first in which emotional content was rated globally in completely spontaneously elicited speech. Soskin and Kauffman (1961) demonstrated that listeners could agree to a significant extent about the emotional content of content-filtered spontaneously elicited speech samples gathered in a variety of

From *Journal of Abnormal Psychology*, 1967, 72, 78–84. Copyright © 1967 by the American Psychological Association and reprinted by permission.

situations—but they had no indepen-dent variables to which the ratings were related.

The purpose of the present study was to relate emotion communicated in spontaneous speech to a clearly defined independent variable. Global ratings of emotion in the voices of physicians (presented under three conditions— normal tape recording, filtered tape re-cording, and transcript) were used to postdict their success in referring alco-holic patients newly arrived on the Emergency Service of a large general hospital for further treatment at the Al-coholic Clinic of the hospital. The in-fluence of the initial contact with the alcoholic on the course of subsequent treatment has been stressed by Chafetz, Blane, Abram, Golner, Lacy, McCourt, Clark, and Meyers (1962). Sensitized to rejection, the alcoholic has been said to be especially aware of the subtle, unin-tended cues conveyed by the doctor, be they those of sympathy and acceptance or those of anger and disgust. Gotts-chalk and his co-workers (1961) and Pittenger, Hockett, and Danehy (1960) have in their separate work on lan-guage in psychotherapy interviews demonstrated a relationship between speech and the dynamics of an inter-personal situation. The interpersonal situation of a loosely structured inter-view about doctors' experiences in the hospital in general and with alcoholic patients in particular, is here seen as having elicited a variety of emotional responses as assessed in the speech of the doctors. These responses may be tentatively supposed to have also been elicited to some degree by the actual confrontation with the alcoholic pa-tient, and to have affected the outcome of that confrontation.

Method

BACKGROUND   Massachusetts General Hospital in 1959 inaugurated an exper-imental program of "massive attention" for selected alcoholics, described more fully elsewhere (Chafetz et al., 1962); the first 20 patients diagnosed as alco-holic on the Emergency Service at the beginning of each month were alter-nately assigned to an experimental group or to a control group, the former receiving special care, the latter receiv-ing the standard Emergency Service treatment. Like other patients, the alco-holic was presented to the Chief Medi-cal Officer (C.M.O.) on duty for diag-nosis and disposition. The C.M.O. was nominally required to offer the services of the hospital Alcoholic Clinic to each diagnosed alcoholic; however, prior to the inauguration of the experimental program, very few alcoholics took ad-vantage of this opportunity. The exper-imental group alcoholic was immedi-ately seen by a psychiatric resident on 24-hour call who thereupon became "his" doctor: the patient was thus able to avoid the necessity of assuming com-plete initiative for seeking treatment and coping with a whole series of inter-mediate steps (calling up, making an appointment with the social worker, etc.). The control-group alcoholic's major contact with the hospital was, as had been true for all alcoholics in the past, his confrontation with the C.M.O. It appeared reasonable to suppose that the manner of the latter's presentation and the quality of his concern was re-lated to the decision of the control-group alcoholic to seek further treat-ment.

Resident physicians at Massachusetts General Hospital during the time of the project rotated in 12-hour shifts as C.M.O.s on the Emergency Service. In the course of the program, 15 residents were so rotated, of whom 9 are represented in the material used in this study. Records were kept of the number of alcoholics, out of the total number diagnosed by each doctor during the experimental period, who sought subsequent treatment, both those assigned to the experimental group and those assigned to the control group. In the case of each group, the C.M.O. was the first link in the chain, but since his influence in the experimental group was immediately superseded by that of the psychiatrist on call, only the percentage of control-group alcoholics who sought further treatment (defined as making and keeping at least one appointment at the Alcoholic Clinic) served as the criterion of a doctor's success at referral. Other studies of these physicians trace a relationship between their conscious, socially held attitudes toward alcoholism and their diagnosis or non-diagnosis of alcoholic patients (Blane, Overton, & Chafetz, 1963; Wolf, Chafetz, Blane, & Hill, 1965). The study reported here attempts to trace a relationship between doctors' feelings reflected in their speech and their success in referring alcoholic patients for continued treatment.

INTERVIEW MATERIAL Approximately a year after the completion of the program for alcoholics, each doctor who had served as C.M.O. during that program participated in a loosely structured, open-ended, tape-recorded interview about his experiences during the residency in general and with alcoholic patients in particular. From the full tapes available for nine of the doctors were excerpted their replies to the question, "What has been your experience with alcoholics?" or to whichever question in the individual interview that most closely approximated that question. The replies varied in length from 79 to 390 words (mean number of words = 177.4 and mean length of reply = about 1.5 minutes. The tape on which the interview segments were recorded was then passed through a filter modifier, passing only frequencies below the range of 410–450 cycles per second, with an attenuation of 60 decibels per octave.[2] This procedure resulted in a content-filtered recording. With the high-frequency sounds filtered out, the doctors' voices sounded as though they were heard through a closed door— variations in pitch and volume were still discernible, but it was not possible to ascertain what was being said. Verbatim typed transcripts of each of the segments were also made. Thus there were three stimulus conditions: unfiltered tape (normal), filtered tape (tone-only), and transcript (content-only).

JUDGES Thirty undergraduate and graduate students at Harvard-Radcliffe (29) and M.I.T. (1), 15 men and 15 women, ranging in age from 18 to 27, served as raters and were paid for their participation in the study. Ten judges (five men and five women) rated the unfiltered tape, 10 rated the filtered tape, and 10 rated the transcript.

RATINGS The method of rating was essentially the same for all three conditions. In the case of the normal and tone-only groups, the judges were told that they would be listening to excerpts from interviews with doctors who would be discussing their experiences with alcoholics, and that the study was concerned with the ability of people to infer feelings and attitudes from the voices of other people. In addition, the nature and purpose of the content filter was explained to those who rated the tape recording under this condition. They were asked to rate each of the segments on four dimensions— Anger-Irritation, Sympathy-Kindness, Anxiety-Nervousness, and Matter-of-factness–Professionalism—along a 6-point scale (1 = none, 6 = quite a lot). The dimensions were not defined further. Each segment was played once and judges were given as much time as they needed after each. (In no case was more than 3 minutes required.) There was evidence of involvement in the task from all the raters. In the case of the content-only group, the judges were handed each transcript in turn and told to read it and rate it. They were required to return one before receiving another. They also were told that they were participating in a study of the ability of people to infer feelings and attitudes from the verbal productions of other people, and they were informed as well that other judges had rated the tape recordings of the interview segments. Two additional variables were included in the content-only condition: Sophistication about Alcoholism and Psychological Mindedness. The combined rating score for each of the nine doctors on each dimension and under each condition was then correlated (Pearson r) with the percentage of control-group alcoholics seeking further treatment out of the total number of control-group alcoholics seen by each doctor.

Results and Discussion

An overview of the results shows that the doctor's speech and tone of voice were related to his success in referring

TABLE 1
Intercorrelations among postdictive variables (df = 7)

Judges	Ang.-Symp.	Ang.-Anx.	Ang.-Matt.	Symp.-Anx.	Symp.-Matt.	Anx.-Matt.	Soph.-Psych.
Normal channel							
Male	−.11	+.27	−.54	−.09	−.06	−.56	
Female	−.49	−.19	−.62 *	−.52	.27	.04	
Total	−.46	−.03	−.58 *	−.40	.24	−.38	
Tone only channel							
Male	−.75 **	−.00	.07	−.30	−.38	−.09	
Female	−.72 **	.65 *	−.22	−.66 *	.24	−.67 **	
Total	−.77 **	.44	−.02	−.58 *	.05	−.67 **	
Content only channel							
Male	−.21	−.06	.00	.38	−.07	−.57	.79 **
Female	−.48	.05	+.04	−.24	.25	−.79 **	.70 **
Total	−.46	.01	.03	+.04	.27	−.75 **	.78 **

Note   Abbreviations: Ang. = Anger; Symp. = Sympathy; Anx. = Anxiety; Matt. = Matter-of-factness; Soph. = Sophistication about alcoholism; Psych. = Psychological mindedness.
* $p \leq .10$.
** $p \leq .05$.

his alcoholic patients for additional treatment. Before giving the details of these findings, however, it will be useful to consider (1) the relationships among the variables employed in postdicting success in referral, (2) the correlations among channels of information, (3) the agreement among individual judges in rating vocal and verbal behavior, and (4) the agreement in judgment between the average male and average female judge.

Table 1 shows the correlations among the postdictor variables for male, female, and all judges under each information channel or condition of observation. In the tone-only condition, anger was negatively related to sympathy ($p < .05$) and anxiety was negatively related to matter-of-factness ($p < .05$). In the content-only condition, anxiety was also related negatively to matter-of-factness ($p < .05$), and sophistication about alcoholism was positively related to psychological mindedness ($p < .05$). Both the latter variables were significantly related to sympathy ($r \geq .80$, $p < .01$).

Table 2 shows the correlations between mean ratings of the doctors' speech in each channel of information with the mean ratings made in the other channels. Inspection suggests that while ratings made in the different channels tended to be positively correlated, each was tapping quite different sources of variance. The median r's for the three sets of intercorrelations, combining male, female, and total r's, were .39, .49, and .21, respectively, for normal-tone-only, normal-content-only, and tone-only-content-only. The highest median correlation was the one between normal ratings and content-only ratings, although Starkweather (1956) reported that, for the two variables he employed in a somewhat similar design

TABLE 2

Media intercorrelations (df = 7)

Variable	Normal tone-only	Normal content-only	Tone only content-only
Male judge			
Anger	.33	.38	.22
Sympathy	.60 *	−.45	−.27
Anxiety	.13	.34	.55
Matter-of-factness	.04	.88 ***	.38
Female judge			
Anger	.45	.52	.53
Sympathy	.49	.68 **	−.06
Anxiety	.46	.52	.18
Matter-of-factness	−.07	.40	−.11
Total judge			
Anger	.53	.49	.43
Sympathy	.69 **	.08	−.29
Anxiety	.33	.48	.36
Matter-of-factness	.27	.72 **	.19
Median	.39	.49	.21

* $p \leq .10$.
** $p \leq .05$.
*** $p \leq .005$.

(aggression and pleasure), the highest correlations were between normal and tone-only ratings (for aggression and pleasure, respectively, r's were normal-tone-only .79, .59; normal-content-only .22, .20; tone-only-content-only .17, .05). This work was, however, done with speakers who were *acting out* a situation in which only one dominant emotion was to be conveyed, presumably more by voice quality than by content. Also, an examination of the results for the one variable that approximates his "aggression" (anger-irritation) reveals a somewhat similar pattern of correlation (for total raters, normal-tone-only $r = .53$, normal-content-only $r = .49$, tone-only-content-only $r = .43$). Kramer (1964) reports similar results in his work with judgments of emotion (by English-speaking raters) in normal English speech, tone-only speech, and Japanese speech; the correlation he obtained between ratings of the filtered presentation and ratings of the unfiltered presentation in English was only .16, lower than the obtained correlation (.34) between ratings of the content-filtered presentation and ratings of the Japanese presentation. He concluded that the ability to judge emotion from speech presented under "strange" or "unusual" conditions may be different from the ability to judge emotions in ordinary unfiltered speech.

Table 3 shows the interrater reliabilities which were estimated by computing Kendall's Coefficient of Concordance (W) for each variable within each of the three conditions. With the exception of matter-of-factness-professionalism in all conditions, and anger-irritation and sympathy-kindness in the content-only condition, interjudge reliabilities were significant at or below the .05 level.[3]

The amount of agreement on the rat-

TABLE 3
Table of reliabilities: Kendall W (df = 8)

	MALE JUDGE		FEMALE JUDGE		TOTAL JUDGE	
	W	x^2	W	x^2	W	x^2
Normal						
Anger	.625 **	25.00	.555 **	22.19	.302 **	24.15
Sympathy	.457 *	18.29	.512 **	20.50	.242 *	19.33
Anxiety	.449 *	17.97	.491 *	19.66	.318 **	25.01
Matter-of-factness	.674 ***	26.96	.384	15.36	.345 ***	27.59
Tone-only						
Anger	.413 *	16.55	.631 **	25.26	.278 **	22.27
Sympathy	.493 *	19.75	.557 **	22.31	.323 **	25.88
Anxiety	.395 *	15.91	.502 **	20.08	.303 **	24.28
Matter-of-factness	.126	5.03	.319	13.78	.065	5.24
Content-only						
Anger	.256	10.25	.329	13.77	.212 *	16.93
Sympathy	.492 *	18.55	.417 *	16.69	.106	8.51
Anxiety	.493 *	19.71	.719 ***	28.79	.481 ***	38.52
Matter-of-factness	.282	11.29	.509 **	20.36	.188	15.10
Sophistication	.688 ***	27.54	.694 ***	27.77	.369 ***	29.53
Psychological mindedness	.438 *	17.52	.541 **	21.63	.348 ***	27.83

* $p \leq .05$.
** $p \leq .01$.
*** $p \leq .001$.

ings generally is surprising when one recalls that the doctors whose voices were being rated had not been instructed to act out any emotion, that they were not in situations which might be expected to produce any specific emotions, and that the judges had been given neither training nor even explicit definitions of the attributes to be rated. It should be noted that in most comparable studies the investigators have predetermined which speech sample was to be considered "angry" and which "sympathetic," etc. The results seem to show, most strongly in the case of the tone-only ratings, that some definite impression of a person's feeling state and underlying attitudes may be gathered from listening to his voice over a very short period of time. These findings bear out those of Soskin and Kauffman (1961). The agreement on the transcript ratings suggests that in the interview situation enough emotional cues of one sort or another were escaping into the semantic channel of the doctors' speech to permit judgment.

Table 4 shows the agreement between the average male and average female judges. Correlations were remarkably variable ranging from − .07 to + .98 (median $r = .69$, $p < .05$). For at least some of the variables rated under some conditions of observation, the value of keeping tabulations separately for male and female judges is evident (Carlson & Carlson, 1960; Kagan & Moss, 1962).

Postdiction of referral effectiveness

As predicted, the control group of alcoholics which had not received the intensive-care routine of the experimental group was the only one in which significant relationships emerged between speech ratings and doctors' success in getting patients to seek treatment.

TABLE 4

Agreement between male and female judges (df = 7)

CHANNEL

Variable	Normal	Tone-only	Content-only
Anger-irritation	.78 *	.42	.97 ***
Sympathy-kindness	.42	.61	.06
Anxiety-nervousness	.81 **	.84 **	.98 ***
Matter-of-factness—Professionalism	.71 *	− .07	.66
Median	.74 *	.52	.82 **

* $p \le .05$.
** $p \le .01$.
*** $p \le .001$.

NORMAL SPEECH As shown in Table 5, the only significant relationship between speech ratings and doctors' success rates was that involving anxiety-nervousness. The ratings of anxiety by the male judges were positively correlated with effectiveness: the more anxious a doctor's voice was rated to be, the more successful the referrals he made ($r = .75$, $p \le .02$). The ratings of anxiety by female judges were similarly positively correlated with effectiveness, though the relationship here failed to reach statistical significance ($r = .49$). For the total group of judges, male and female combined, $r = .62$, $p < .08$. Male judges' ratings of matter-of-factness–professionalism tended to be negatively associated with effectiveness ($r = − .54$) though this tendency was not significant at the .05 level. Neither ratings of anger nor rat-

TABLE 5

Relationship of speech ratings to referral effectiveness (df = 7)

Channel	Anger	Sympathy	Anxiety	Matter-of-factness	Sophistication	Psychological mindedness
Male judge						
Normal	− .00	− .13	.75 **	− .54		
Tone-only	− .67 **	.37	− .25	.13		
Content-only	− .42	− .49	.05	− .50	− .43	− .52
Female judge						
Normal	− .37	− .27	.49	− .27		
Tone-only	− .49	.13	− .26	− .10		
Content-only	− .36	− .34	.04	− .14	− .40	− .45
Total judge						
Normal	− .24	− .25	.62 *	− .45		
Tone-only	− .65 *	.27	− .27	.06		
Content-only	− .38	− .57	.05	− .31	− .48	− .50

* $p \leq .10$.

** $p \leq .05$.

ings of sympathy in the normal condition postdicted effectiveness.

TONE-ONLY There was a significant negative relationship between male judges' ratings of anger in the tone-only condition and effectiveness with alcoholic patients ($r = − .67$, $p < .05$, for female judges, $r = − .49$, $p > .10$, and for the total group of judges, $r = − .65$, $p = .06$). Other variables were unrelated to effectiveness.

CONTENT-ONLY No significant relationships emerged between the transcript ratings and success rates. There was a rather puzzling tendency for ratings of "psychological mindedness," "sophisticated about alcoholism" (variables introduced only in the content-only condition), and sympathy-kindness to be correlated negatively with success rates and highly intercorrelated (mean intercorrelation = + .80). This cluster of "sophisticated-sympathetic" behavior may have given the alcoholic patient a

feeling of insincerity. This interpretation seems supported by the fact that when greater sympathy was shown in the tone-only channel, alcoholic patients were more successfully influenced to seek treatment though the correlation was not significant statistically. There is a hint here that sympathetic content may be "invalidated" by an accompanying lack of sympathy in the tone of voice.

Considering the small sample of doctors for whom interview data were available, the small sample of alcoholics, and the many possible contaminating factors in the doctor-patient situation (contact with nurses, clerks, and other subsidiary ward personnel, for example), the relationships between the speech ratings and effectiveness with alcoholic patients reported above may be viewed as surprising and encouraging. The need for more systematic research is evident. The relationship between an "angry" tone of voice and lack of effectiveness with alcoholic patients who may be especially sensitized to rejection accords with clinical and anecdotal accounts of doctor-alcoholic patient encounters. The positive relationship between inferred anxiety in the "normal" (unfiltered) voice and effectiveness with alcoholic patients may relate to the notion that an effectively functioning healer whose manner of speech is perceived by others to have an anxious, nervous quality may be seen by the patient as showing greater concern. The literature on the relationship between speech disruptions and anxiety suggests one reason for the emergence of the correlation as significant for the normal ratings but not significant for the tone-only ratings. In the filtered tape recordings, words are not distinguishable, and it is not possible to tell speech disruptions from speech per se. The correlation of Speech Disruption Ratios for each segment with global ratings of anxiety is in progress.

Interestingly, for most, though by no means all, variables in the three conditions, male judges' ratings of voice qualities and attitudes were better postdictors of success than were female judges' ratings. Heinberg (1961) found that females were superior to males in guessing the situation and the emotion being acted out in ambiguous but non-content-filtered dialogues involving either a man and a woman or two women. Perhaps nuances of feeling are recognized with greater ease and accuracy in the voices of members of one's own sex. A similar study involving female doctors or nurses would be of interest.

NOTES

1. This study was supported by National Science Foundation Grants G S-177 and G S-714, by Mental Health Grant O M-210, National Institute of Mental Health, United States Public Health Service, and by the Division of Alcoholism, Massachusetts Department of Public Health. The first author was a participant in the National Science Foundation Program in Undergraduate Research during the period in which the data were being collected.

2. The filtering procedure was carried out by Audio Labs, 16 Eliot Street, Cambridge, Massachusetts.

3. It should be noted that Matter-of-factness—Professionalism was a relatively nondiscriminating dimension, since almost every judge in every condition rated all the doctors extremely high on it. Perhaps the knowledge that the speakers were doctors biased the rating, since most people may think of (and want to think of) doctors as being extremely matter-of-fact and professional in their attitudes.

REFERENCES

Blane, H., Overton, W., & Chafetz, M. Social factors in the diagnosis of alcoholism. 1. Characteristics of the patient. *Quarterly Journal of Studies on Alcohol*, 1963, 24, 640–663.

Carlson, E. R., & Carlson, R. Male and female subjects in personality research. *Journal of Abnormal and Social Psychology*, 1960, 61, 482–483.

Chafetz, M., Blane, H., Abram, H., Golner, J., Lacy, E., McCourt, W., Clark, E., & Meyers, W. Establishing treatment relations with alcoholics. *Journal of Nervous and Mental Disease*, 1962, 134, 395–409.

Davitz, J. (Ed.) *The communication of emotional meaning.* New York: McGraw-Hill, 1964.

Davitz, J., & Davitz, L. The communication of feelings by content-free speech. *Journal of Communication*, 1959, 9, 6–13. (a)

Davitz, J., & Davitz, L. Correlates of accuracy in the communication of feelings. *Journal of Communication*, 1959, 9, 110–117. (b)

Dibner, A. S. Cue counting: A measure of anxiety in interviews. *Journal of Consulting Psychology*, 1956, 20, 475–478.

Eldred, S. H., & Price, D. B. A. linguistic evaluation of feeling states in psychotherapy. *Psychiatry*, 1958, 21, 115–121.

Feldstein, S., Brenner, M. S., & Jaffe, J. The effect of subject sex, verbal interaction, and topical focus on speech disruption. *Language and Speech*, 1963, 6, 229–239.

Gottschalk, L. (Ed.) *Comparative psycholinguistic analysis of two psychotherapy interviews*. New York: International Universities Press, 1961.

Heinberg, P. Factors related to an individual's ability to perceive implications of dialogues. *Speech Monographs*, 1961, 28, 274–283.

Kagan, J., & Moss, H. *Birth to maturity*. New York: Wiley, 1962.

Kasl, S., & Mahl, G. Experimentally induced anxiety and speech disturbances. *American Psychologist*, 1958, 13, 349. (Abstract)

Kauffman, P. An investigation of some psychological stimulus properties of speech behavior. Unpublished doctoral dissertation, University of Chicago, 1954.

Kramer, E. Judgment of personal characteristics and emotions from nonverbal properties of speech. *Psychological Bulletin*, 1963, 60, 408–420.

Kramer, E. Elimination of verbal cues in judgments of emotion from voice. *Journal of Abnormal and Social Psychology*, 1964, 68, 390–396.

Mahl, G. Disturbances and silences in the patient's speech in psychotherapy. *Journal of Abnormal and Social Psychology*, 1956, 53, 1–15.

Mahl, G., & Schultze, G. Psychological research in the extralinguistic area. In T. A. Sebeok, A. S. Hayes, & M. C. Bateson (Eds.), *Approaches to semiotics*. London: Mouton, 1964. Pp. 51–124.

Pittenger, R., Hockett, C., & Danehy, H. *The first five minutes*. Ithaca: Paul Martineau, 1960.

Soskin, W. F., & Kauffman, P. E. Judgment of emotion in word-free voice samples. *Journal of Communication*, 1961, 11, 73–80.

Starkweather, J. Content-free speech as a source of information about the speaker. *Journal of Abnormal and Social Psychology*, 1956, 52, 394–402.

Starkweather, J. Vocal communication of personality and human feelings. *Journal of Communication*, 1961, 11, 63–72.

Wolf, I., Chafetz, M., Blane, H., & Hill, M. Social factors in the diagnosis of alcoholism in social and nonsocial situations. *Quarterly Journal of Studies on Alcohol*, 1965, 26, 72–79.

THE MOTHER'S VOICE: POSTDICTOR OF
ASPECTS OF HER BABY'S BEHAVIOR [1]

SUSAN MILMOE, MICHAEL S. NOVEY,
JEROME KAGAN, AND ROBERT ROSENTHAL

That the semantic content of human speech is the top part of an iceberg is coming to be recognized: interest in "paralinguistic" communication is burgeoning. It is known that people can reliably identify emotions in "content-filtered" spontaneous speech (e.g., Milmoe, 1965; Milmoe, Rosenthal, Blane, Chafetz, & Wolf, 1967; Soskin & Kauffman, 1961), but the *validation* of their identifications has been a problem. Allport and Cantril (1934) thought that shared stereotypes of "anger," etc., inflated agreement about emotion in voices, and certainly these and other judge-intrinsic factors account for some variance (cf. Lambert, 1967; Milmoe, 1965). Nevertheless, Starkweather (1956) found that ratings of emotion in content-filtered speech were correlated with degree of hypertension, Milmoe (1965), that they were somewhat related to personality-test scores, and Milmoe et al. (1967), that they postdicted doctors' performance with alcoholic patients.

The pilot study here reported represents a very preliminary attempt to extend the validity of ratings of content-filtered speech in a direction which is of considerable clinical relevance. The quality of communication between mother and child has been thought to be of great importance in the growth and development of personality (cf. Sullivan, 1953). Disturbances in communication, particularly "affective" and "semantic" channel discrepancies (cf. Soskin & Kauffman, 1961), have been hypothesized to result in psychopathology (cf. Bateson, Jackson, Haley, & Weakland, 1956). An effort was made, thus, to relate ratings of emotion in mothers' voices to measures of their children's behavior made over a period of almost 2 years.

Method

*Subjects and measurements
of children's behavior*

Eighteen mothers and their children (nine boys, nine girls) were *S*s, all par-

From *Proceedings,* 76th annual convention, American Psychological Association, 1968, 463–64. Copyright © 1968 by the American Psychological Association and reprinted by permission.

ticipants in the ongoing Harvard Infant Study (for details, see Kagan, 1967; Reppucci, 1968). Mothers varied in education and children in ordinal position. Children were seen in a laboratory at 4, 8, 13, and 27 months. Observations included perceptual sessions, free-play sessions (8, 13, 27), and discrimination tasks (27 only). In the perceptual sessions, the child was presented with a series of visual stimuli, representing a human face or body and distorted transformations of them, and with tape-recorded passages consisting of normal sentences and nonsense phrases (high and low meaning) read by a male speaker with high and low inflection (8, 13). Fixation times (to the visual stimuli), smiling, vocalization, heart-rate deceleration, and orientation to speaker (during the auditory episode) were measured.

Preparation of tape recording

Brief interviews with the mothers immediately following the 27-mo. experimental session were tape-recorded. The first sustained "meaningful unit" of speech of up to 15 sec. in reply to the first "neutral" question and up to 30 sec. in reply to each of three others, designed to elicit a range of positive and negative emotion, were rerecorded onto a master tape (mean total speaking time = 51 sec., $SD = 11.1$ sec.). The master tape was copied through an electronic crossover set at 400 cps with an LC low-pass filter in series, resulting in sounds resembling unintelligible speech heard through a wall.

Judges and rating procedure

Twenty-nine Harvard-Radcliffe undergraduates (13 men, 16 women) rated the filtered tape, and 32 (16 men, 16 women) rated the unfiltered one on five dimensions: anger-irritation, anxiety-

nervousness, warmth, pleasantness, and emotional involvement (of mother in what was being said). Discrepancy scores were computed for each mother on each dimension by subtracting total judges' ratings in the normal condition from total judges' ratings in the filtered condition.

Results and discussion

Reliability

Kendall coefficients of concordance (Ws) were computed for male judges, female judges, and total judges. They support the findings of previous studies that judges can agree significantly about their identifications of emotion in content-filtered as well as in unfiltered spontaneous speech, though agreement was slightly better, overall, in the unfiltered condition.

Dimension and modality intercorrelations

As in previous studies, ratings of different emotions were by no means independent (median absolute r's = .41 and .40 for filtered and unfiltered ratings, respectively). Ratings of emotion in filtered and unfiltered voices were in closer agreement for mothers of boys than for mothers of girls (median r's = .49 and .31, respectively). The intercorrelations were more or less comparable to those reported in previous studies; evidently, the two conditions tap somewhat different sources of variance.

Relationship of voice ratings and measures of children's behavior

Data were analyzed separately for mothers of girls and mothers of boys, since previous work (Kagan, 1967) showed very different patterning of behavior in the various experimental situations for the two sexes. (Indeed, different relationships in many instances were found.)

The small sample size (and perhaps also the non-normality of the distributions of the measurements of the children's behavior) should be borne in mind when interpreting the p values referred to below. Scatterplots were examined to eliminate from consideration those correlations inflated by a single anomalous S.

Belief in the validity of the voice ratings was strengthened by the many large correlations between them and the measures of the children's behavior. Space permits the reporting of only a few of the most representative and seemingly meaningful of these.[2] It should be noted that, overall, filtered ratings were at least as postdictive as unfiltered ones; in some instances, they were more so.

Ratings of anxiety and anger in both conditions were associated with various signs of irritability and insecurity in the children, such as fretting and crying at 4 mo. (for boys: r's $= .36$; $.56$; for girls: r's $= .46$; $.80$, $p < .01$), early upset following separation from mother by a barrier at 13 mo. (for boys only: r's $= -.50$, $-.86$, $p < .05$), and physical closeness to mother during the first 5 min. in the playroom at 27 mo. (for boys: r's $= 69$; $.61$; for girls: r's $= .70$; 60). Discrepancies in anxiety (more filtered, less unfiltered) were related to lack of expression of positive affect in boys at three different ages (for 8, 13, and 27 mo.: r's $= -.67$; $p < .05$; $-.33$; and $-.60$, respectively).

Daughters of mothers with "anxious" voices tended to be more attentive and "cautious" in several different test situations at three ages. They fixated longer on human faces at 8 mo. (r's $= .66$, $.81$) and on human figures at

13 mo. (r's $= .70$, $.78$, $p < .05$). At 27 mo., they showed inhibition when faced with response uncertainty (r's $= .59$, $.74$) and had longer sustained periods of attention in play (r's $= .91$, $p < .01$; $.28$).

Ratings of warmth and pleasantness in the filtered condition (but not in the unfiltered one) were related to various indexes of attention to a human voice at 13 mo. Daughters of mothers with "warm," "pleasant" voices vocalized less after the "strange" low-meaning low-inflection auditory presentations (r's $= -.72$, $p < .05$; $-.83$, $p < .05$ for warmth and pleasantness, respectively) and spent more time looking at the speaker during the "normal" high-meaning high-inflection ones ($r = .61$ for warmth only). Sons of such mothers showed greater heart-rate deceleration to voices generally (ranges of r's $= .35 - .75$, $p < .05$; $.36 - .66$ for warmth and pleasantness, respectively). The larger the discrepancies between filtered and unfiltered warmth and pleasantness (more filtered, less unfiltered), the more time boys spent looking at the speaker during the normal presentation (r's $= .68$, $p < .05$; $.72$, $p < .05$ for warmth and pleasantness, respectively).

There are several possible explanations (which are by no means mutually exclusive) for the apparent relationships between the voice ratings and the measurements of the children's behavior. They may be caused by a condition relatively external to both mother and child. While education of parents and ordinal position of child did account for some variance (e.g., mothers of later-born boys were rated to be angrier than mothers of firstborns [r's $= .55$, $.75$][2] and mothers of later-born girls, less anxious [r's $= -.69$, $-.77$]), in many instances voice ratings were much more postdictive.

The ratings may reflect the transitory situational emotional state of the mother, and when her voice was recorded this state may have been to a great extent determined by her evaluation of her child's performance in the just-completed experimental session. Such an explanation would not, of course, wholly account for the relationships between voice ratings and measurements made 23 months previously. The child's independent characteristics manifested over a period of 2 years may, however, have affected the mother's emotional reactions in more long-lasting ways. A child who, for whatever reason, rarely smiled, for example, might well generate feelings of inadequacy and anxiety in his mother which would be reflected in her voice as she talked about him.

Both the ratings and the children's behavior may be directly influenced by aspects of the mother's personality. Finally, and most speculatively, there may be inherent qualities of voice to which infants directly respond regardless of firm associations between these qualities and anything else. Effects of this kind probably do exist, but it is unclear what predictions should be made.

Some fragmentary clinical observations further substantiate the validity of the ratings. Of the 180 children in the entire longitudinal sample, one boy and one girl, at all four ages, consistently impressed the project staff as being very different from the others. Their mothers' voices were, luckily, among the 18 rated. Both voices were given extreme scores by almost all the judges: the mother of the girl, in particular, was rated most extreme or second most extreme on 16 out of 20 possible dimensions (Emotion $\times$ Condition $\times$ Men and Women Judges).

In toto, the pilot study here reported is felt to indicate that people's evaluations of others' voices do have objective correlates, to hint provocatively that reactions to voice quality may begin early in life and have important effects, and to provide encouragement for the use of ratings of content-filtered speech in clinical research.

NOTES

1. This research was supported by funds from United States Public Health Service Research Grant MH 8792, for which the third author is principal investigator, and by funds from the National Science Foundation given by the Laboratory of Social Relations of Harvard University to the first author. Interviewing was done by Judith Jordan.

2. Degrees of freedom, because of occasional missing observations, vary; hence, reported p values of the same r may differ. Filtered r's follow normal r's in all parenthetical listings; all r's represent correlations with ratings of the total group of judges.

REFERENCES

Allport, G., & Cantril, H. Judging personality from voice. *Journal of Social Psychology*, 1934, 5, 37–55.

Bateson, G., Jackson, D. D., Haley, J., & Weakland, J. H. Toward a theory of schizophrenia. *Behavioral Science*, 1956, 1, 251–264.

Kagan, J. Passivity and styles of thought in children. (Progress rep., Res. Grant MH-8792) Unpublished manuscript, Harvard University, 1967.

Lambert, W. E. A social psychology of bilingualism. *Journal of Social Issues*, 1967, 23, 91–109.

Milmoe, S. Characteristics of speakers and listeners as factors in non-verbal communication. Unpublished senior honors thesis, Harvard University, Department of Social Relations, 1965.

Milmoe, S., Rosenthal, R., Blane, H., Chafetz, M., & Wolf, I. The doctor's voice: Postdictor of successful referral of alcoholic patients. *Journal of Abnormal Psychology*, 1967, 72, 78–84.

Reppucci, N. D. Antecedents of conceptual tempo in the two-year-old child. Unpublished doctoral dissertation, Harvard University, 1968.

Soskin, W. F., & Kauffman, P. E. Judgment of emotion in word-free voice samples. *Journal of Communication*, 1961, 11, 73–80.

Starkweather, J. Content-free speech as a source of information about the speaker. *Journal of Abnormal and Social Psychology*, 1956, 52, 394–402.

Sullivan, H. S. *The interpersonal theory of psychiatry*. New York: Norton, 1953.

three

BODY MOVEMENT AND GESTURES

The most popularized aspect of nonverbal communication is undoubtedly the area of body movement and gestures. Books like Julius Fast's (1970) *Body Language* promise the reader that he can "penetrate the personal secrets, both of intimates and total strangers" by reading key body signs. Advice on love and business encounters is especially well covered. Nierenberg and Calero's (1971) *How to Read A Person Like A Book* tries to apply body movement research to business success. Fast (1970) does a competent job of summing up research in nonverbal communication for the layman, though one suspects his conclusions will be taken a bit too uncritically by the average reader.

The scientific literature on body movement and gestures is quite extensive. Davis (1972) has compiled a very helpful annotated bibliography of over 900 books, monographs, and articles in the area (including studies on facial expression). A historical review of some very early work can be found in Critchley (1939, reprinted 1970). Writings on gestures in oratory, mime, and dance have been found to date back to early Greece and Rome. In modern times, Rudolf Laban (1956, 1960, 1963, 1966) has developed a notational system for the dance, called Labanotation and a theory of movement to support it. He later developed (Laban and Lawrence, 1947; Dell, 1970) the effort-shape concept as a means of studying emotional and personality patterns. In this system, the flow and concentration of effort through space is studied to determine patterns of flow within a three-dimensional system. Dance therapy is partially based on some of these ideas. Bartienieff and Davis (1965) have described "movement case studies" of psychiatric patients and psychotherapy sessions (which is reminiscent of Scheflen's courtship movement analogy, shown in his paper in this section as well as Kendon's work on synchrony, also included here). Kestenberg (Kestenberg, Marcus, Robbins, Berlowe, and Buelte, 1971), another worker in the effort-shape tradition, has turned to the Freudian developmental sequence (oral, anal, phallic) as a frame of analysis for movement pattern changes in children. For example, the "anal body ego" is characterized by resistance and erectness in body movement. Alan Lomax (1973) and others have applied Labanotation to the cross-cultural analysis of movement. On the whole, the Laban system has not had a very wide-spread influence on body movement research, but the presence of an organized notational system (widely used by choreographers) and a rudimentary psychological theory to accompany it promises future development in this area.

The most often cited work in the recent past history of body movement is Efron's (1941) *Gesture and Environment*. This work is basically a descriptive study of the gestural system of first and second generation Eastern European Jews and Southern Italians in New York City, indicating the effects of assimilation on nonverbal behavior. Probably the most significant contribution of this work was to isolate the field of gesture as worthy of study and to indicate the effects of the social process of assimilation on the intimate psychological world of gesture. Although an innovative recording system was used, no personality-oriented theoretical basis was provided, as Efron's primary interest was anthropological, not psychological. There were no direct follow-ups on Efron's work.

A few years later, Charlotte Wolff's (1945) *A Psychology of Gesture* appeared. She tied in her observations of children and mental patients to a general theory of emotional expression. Workers in the Labanotation tradition often cite her work, but it seems to have had little influence outside of that circle. More recently, Ekman and Friesen (1969) have put forth a classification system for nonverbal behavior, including gestures.

Historically, the entry of Ray Birdwhistell and Paul Ekman to the study of body movement signaled the beginning of two important research traditions. Birdwhistell's tradition is more heavily represented in this section, with Scheflen, Dittmann, and Kendon having the same general view. Ekman is represented by contributions in two other sections, with articles on facial expression and deception. Both have shaped different research traditions in nonverbal communication in general, and body movement in particular. Duncan (1969) makes a similar distinction between the structural and the external variable approach.

Ray Birdwhistell first began his research in 1952, with the publication of *Introduction to Kinesics* and has continued for the ensuing twenty-odd years to be an active proponent and pioneer in body movement research. His 1970 book, *Kinesics and Context,* is a collection of his essays (of which, two are presented here, p. **134** and p. **144**) and presents his point of view quite directly and persuasively. Adam Kendon (1972) has written a very fine book review of *Kinesics and Context* which may well serve as an introduction to Birdwhistell's work. (See also Dittmann, 1971.) An anthropologist by professional affiliation, Birdwhistell's influence has been felt most heavily in the nonexperimental areas of psychiatry and communications research. He favors a contextual approach to studying the entire communications situation and vigorously opposes the isolation and manipulation of variables favored by Ekman's group. Birdwhistell characteristically does an extremely detailed analysis of short film segments of interactive behavior, taken in naturalistic settings. One famous film clip, "The Cigarette Scene," about a woman having her cigarette lighted by a man, takes eighteen seconds of film time, but considerably longer than that to read the finely honed analysis of verbal and nonverbal components. Birdwhistell's method of analysis is based on the descriptive linguistic model. Kinemes are relatively large units of body movement, such as lateral head sweeps and eye lid closure. Kinemes combine to form kinemorphs, then kinemorphemic classes, complex kinemorphs, and complex kinemorphic constructions. Birdwhistell has isolated body, facial, and head kinemes and is also interested in integrating kinesic behavior into the general communicative stream, including verbal behavior. In fact, he does not see the verbal-nonverbal dichotomy as a valid one and is reported by Knapp (1972) to have said that "studying nonverbal communication is like studying noncardiac physiology"; the distinction simply does not exist in his system.

Kendon's work on synchrony, presented in this chapter (p. **150**) flows very nicely from this holistic tradition. The verbal and nonverbal components intertwine into an interactive dance of great elegance and rhythm. Kendon demonstrates that "the flow of movement in the listener may be rhythmically coordinated with the speech and movements of the speaker," thus indicating that the inseparability of verbal and nonverbal components is maintained across an interaction as the unit of analysis, and not only within individual interactants. Condon and Ogston (1967) first described this phenomenon, as well as self-synchrony, between individual movement and speech patterns. Kendon (1972) reports on a recent update of his work, and more recently Condon (1973) has turned up an intriguing case of synchrony, in which the body movements of very young infants (from less than one day to fourteen days old) are seen to be synchronized with adult speech occurring in the same room! Thus, sound segments in adult speech were coordinated with points of change in infant movement, in much the same way adult synchrony occurs. Other investigators have looked at the temporal patterning of speech during dyadic interviews (Matarazzo, Wiens, and Saslow, 1965; Jaffe and Feldstein, 1970; Feldstein, 1972; Webb, 1972). Our major concern here, of course, is with the relationship between speech and body motion.

Dittmann's work, also included in this chapter (p. **169**) deals in a cognitive way with the issue of verbal-nonverbal congruence. According to Dittmann, body movements occur at times of nonfluency in verbal interaction and may possibly accompany the speech encoding process within the individual.

Scheflen provides a metaphorical model for human communication: that of the courtship ritual. His article (p. **182**) analyzes the flow of verbal and nonverbal communication as twin characteristics of this process. The example here is that of psychotherapy, but more recently Scheflen (1972) has said that "the quasi-courting reciprocal is used in establishing rapport in *any* kind of relationship." In this book, Scheflen takes the position that body language acts as a control mechanism, monitoring the interaction and interactants within it. He punctuates his arguments with a persuasive group of photographs illustrating his points in natural communications settings.

The Birdwhistell holistic, nonexperimental tradition has its drawbacks as well as its virtues. On the negative side, kinesic analysis is very much like literary analysis, one can impose one's own structure on the material and never really be certain that this is the best fitting model or the "correct" one. Experiments can, of course, be stacked in favor of a model, though we are slower to acknowledge the existence of this sort of bias than the other. On the more practical side, Birdwhistell's mode of analysis is extremely time-consuming and difficult for one not carefully trained and experienced in the notational system. The sampling of situations often seems haphazard and is limited to few cases. However, since Birdwhistell is working within the linguistic model, he feels that there is a universal grammar of kinesics, as in language, so that any kinesic sample, like any speech sample, can provide reliable information about the deep structure of the language. On the positive side, Birdwhistell's insistence on a holistic approach to communications has much to offer psychology, a field already riddled by atomism. At some point, we will have to fit all the verbal and nonverbal pieces together, and it makes sense to have a gadfly to continually remind us of our ultimate aim.

Another group of nonverbal communications researchers, a group which is proud of the designation "nonverbal," has been extremely active. Paul Ekman is probably the best known of this group. He wrote two early articles (Ekman, 1965; Ekman and Friesen, 1968) which helped to bring nonverbal behavior to the attention of experimental social psychologists and psychotherapists. More recently he has concentrated his energies almost exclusively on facial expression (Ekman, Friesen, and Ellsworth, 1972; Ekman, 1973), and we deal more extensively with this aspect of his work in the chapter on that topic. His earlier work on body movement was premised on the view that information about a subject's affective state could be reliably obtained from nonverbal materials, even when he sought to deceive the investigator (see p. **269**, this book). As such, it was seen as a valuable tool for psychiatric interviewing. Mahl (1968) has also developed this application of nonverbal research. Freud, of course, came to the same conclusion:

When I set myself the task of bringing to light what human beings keep hidden within them, not by the compelling power of hypnosis, but by observing what they say and what they show, I thought the task was a harder one than it really is. He that has eyes to see and ears to hear may convince himself that no mortal can keep a secret. If the lips are silent, he chatters with his finger tips; betrayal oozes out of him at every pore. And thus the task of making conscious the most hidden recesses of the mind is one which it is quite possible to accomplish. (Freud, 1905, pp. 77–78).

Ekman, then, is not trying to establish a grammar of body language, or even to study the communication process per se, as Birdwhistell is. Rather, his concern is the relationship of nonverbal behavior to inner feeling states and to the decoding of these states by others. His more recent work on facial expression is clearly in this area. Ekman also does not integrate the verbal and nonverbal spheres, a primary goal of the Birdwhistell school. Ekman is concerned with the psychological problem of communication of emotional state, rather than the structural one of the nature of the communications system itself. Recently, Wiener has challenged the view that all nonverbal behavior is by definition communicative of emotional state (Wiener, Devoe, Rubinow, and Geller, 1972). Dittmann's work, reprinted in this section, also seems to support the idea that body movement may have other functions (as an accompaniment to speech encoding, for example).

Other work that is somewhat similar in orientation to Ekman's has been done by Mehrabian (1972) and his associates. Mehrabian's work is characterized by the manipulation of nonverbal, psychological, and environmental variables in the style that has come to be identified with experimental social psychology. Since his mode of analysis involves a number of different nonverbal variables, we will wait to discuss his work in the final section on multichannel communication.

A final promising direction in the analysis of movement behavior might be mentioned. Freedman (1972) has completed a number of studies on the relationship between psychological differentiation and kinetic behavior (Freedman, O'Hanlon, Oltman, and Witkin, 1972; Freedman, Blass, Rifkin, and Quitkin, 1973). This research relies on Witkin et al.'s (1962) distinction between field independence and field dependence as distinctive cognitive styles. These differences are predicted to affect kinetic behavior, as well, with object-focused movements (away from the body and related to speech) characteristic of field-independent, highly differentiated individuals with a complex language structure and body-focused movements (oriented to the body, and not related to speech) characteristic of field-dependent, less differentiated individuals with a less complex language structure. The orientation is somewhat like Birdwhistell's approach, yet the effort to link body movement to psychological state is reminiscent of Ekman. In this case, however, the psychological state is primarily a cognitive one, although generalization to emotional tone is suggested. Some support for Freedman's view has been found. The interested reader is referred to an article by Freedman (1972) detailing the body-object focus distinction and to a recent study of body movements and the verbal encoding of aggressive affect (Freedman, Blass, Rifkin, and Quitkin, 1973).

In conclusion, then, we have considered several promising approaches to the study of body movement, an area which continues to fascinate both scientist and layman alike.

REFERENCES

Bartienieff, I., and Davis, M., "Effort shape analysis of movement: the unity of expression and function," unpublished monograph; Albert Einstein College of Medicine, New York, 1965 (available from Dance Notation Bureau, 8 E. 12 St., New York, New York 10003).

Birdwhistell, R. L., *Introduction to Kinesics.* University of Louisville Press, Louisville, 1952 (available on microfilm from University Microfilms, Inc., Ann Arbor, Michigan).

Birdwhistell, R. L., *Kinesics and Context,* University of Pennsylvania Press, Philadelphia, 1970.

Condon, W. S., "Movement of awake-active neonate demonstrated to synchronize with adult speech," paper presented at biennial meeting of the Society for Research in Child Development, March 1973, Philadelphia.

Condon, W. S., and Ogston, W. D., "A segmentation of behavior," *Journal of Psychiatric Research,* 1967, 5, 221–35.

Critchley, M., *The Language of Gesture,* Edward Arnold, London, 1939 (reprinted 1970, Haskell House Publishers).

Davis, M., *Understanding Body Movement: An Annotated Bibliography,* Arno Press, New York, 1972.

Dell, C., *A Primer for Movement Description Using Effort-Shape and Supplementary Concepts,* Dance Notation Bureau, New York, 1970 (available from Dance Notation Bureau, 8 E. 12 St., New York, New York 10003).

Dittmann, A. T., Review of *Kinesics and Context* by Ray L. Birdwhistell, *Psychiatry,* 1971, 34, 334–42.

Duncan, S., "Nonverbal communication," *Psychological Bulletin,* 1969, 72, 118–37.

Efron, D., *Gesture and Environment,* King's Crown Press, New York, 1941.

Ekman, P., "Communication through nonverbal behavior: a source of information about an interpersonal relationship," in *Affect, Cognition and Personality,* S.S. Tomkins and C. E. Izard, eds., Springer, New York, 1965, pp. 390–442.

Ekman, P., ed., *Darwin and Facial Expression: A Century of Research in Review,* Academic Press, New York, 1973.

Ekman, P., and Friesen, W. V., "Nonverbal behavior in psychotherapy research," in *Research in Psychotherapy,* Vol. III, J. M. Shlien, ed., American Psychological Association, Washington, D.C., 1968, pp. 179–216.

Ekman, P., and Friesen, W. V., "The repertoire of nonverbal behavior: categories, origins, usage, and coding," *Semiotica,* 1969, 1, 49–98.

Ekman, P., Friesen, W. V., and Ellsworth, P., *Emotion in the Human Face,* Pergamon Press, New York, 1972.

Fast, J., *Body Language,* M. Evans & Co., New York, 1970.

Feldstein, S., "Temporal patterns of dialogue: basic research and reconsiderations," in *Studies in Dyadic Communication,* A. W. Siegman and B. Pope, eds., Pergamon Press, New York, 1972, pp. 91–113.

Freedman, N., "The analysis of movement behavior during the clinical interview," in *Studies in Dyadic Communication*, A. W. Siegman and B. Pope, eds., Pergamon Press, New York, 1972, pp. 153–75.

Freedman, N., Blass, J., Rifkin, A., and Quitkin, F., "Body movements and the verbal encoding of aggressive affect," *Journal of Personality and Social Psychology*, 1973, 26, 72–85.

Freedman, N., O'Hanlon, J., Oltman, P., and Witkin, H. A., "The imprint of psychological differentiation on kinetic behavior in varying communicative contexts," *Journal of Abnormal Psychology*, 1972, 79, 239–58.

Freud, S., "Fragments of an analysis of a case of hysteria," 1905, in *The Standard Edition of the Complete Psychological Works of Sigmund Freud*, Vol. 7, Hogarth, London, 1953.

Jaffe, J., and Feldstein, S., *Rhythms of Dialogue*, Academic Press, New York, 1970.

Kendon, S., Review of *Kinesics and Context* by Ray L. Birdwhistell, *American Journal of Psychology*, 1972, 85, 441–53.

Kendon, A., "Some relationships between body motion and speech: an analysis of an example," in *Studies in Dyadic Communication*, A. W. Siegman and B. Pope, eds., Pergamon Press, New York, 1972, pp. 177–210.

Kestenberg, J. S., Marcus, H., Robbins, E., Berlowe, J., and Buelte, A., "Development of the young child as expressed through bodily movement I," *Journal of the American Psychoanalytic Association*, 1971, 19, 746–64.

Knapp, M. L., *Nonverbal Communication in Human Interaction*, Holt, Rinehart and Winston, New York, 1972.

Laban, R., *Principles of Dance and Movement Notation*, Macdonald & Evans, London, 1956.

Laban, R., *The Mastery of Movement*, L. Ullmann, ed., 2nd ed., Macdonald & Evans, London, 1960.

Laban, R., *Modern Educational Dance*, 2nd ed., rev. by L. Ullmann, Macdonald & Evans, London, 1963.

Laban, R., *Choreutics*, L. Ullmann, ed., Macdonald & Evans, London, 1966.

Laban, R., and Lawrence, F. C., *Effort*, Macdonald & Evans, London, 1947.

Lomax, A., "Cultural differences in movement style," 1973 (literature available from Dance Notation Bureau, 8 E. 12 St., New York, New York 10003).

Mahl, G. F., "Gestures and body movements in interviews," in *Research in Psychotherapy*, Vol. III, J. M. Shlien, ed., American Psychological Association, Washington, D.C., 1968, pp. 295–346.

Matarazzo, J. D., Wiens, A. N., and Saslow, G., "Studies in interview speech behavior," in *Research in Behavior Modification: New Developments and their Clinical Implications*, L. Krasner and L. P. Ullmann, eds., Holt, Rinehart and Winston, New York, 1965.

Mehrabian, A., *Nonverbal Communication*, Aldine, Chicago, 1972.

Nierenberg, G. I., and Calero, H. H., *How to Read a Person Like a Book*, Hawthorn, New York, 1971.

Scheflen, A. E., *Body Language and the Social Order*, Prentice-Hall, Englewood Cliffs, 1972.

Webb, J. T., "Interview synchrony: an investigation of two speech rate measures in an automated standardized interview," in *Studies in Dyadic Communication*, A. W. Siegman and B. Pope, eds., Pergamon Press, New York, pp. 115–33.

Wiener, M., Devoe, S., Rubinow, S., and Geller, J., "Nonverbal behavior and nonverbal communication," *Psychological Review*, 1972, 79, 185–214.

Witkin, H. A., Dyk, R. B., Faterson, H. F., Goodenough, D. R., and Karp, S. A., *Psychological Differentiation*, Wiley, New York, 1962.

Wolff, C., *A Psychology of Gesture*, A. Tennant, transl., Methuen & Co., London, 1945.

TOWARD ANALYZING AMERICAN MOVEMENT [1]

RAY L. BIRDWHISTELL

It would be wonderful but premature to report that we have completed the kinological analysis of the American movement system. A number and, hopefully, the majority of American kinemes (see Birdwhistell, 1970) have been abstracted and withstood the test of contrast analysis. It seems safe now to predict that the kinemic catalog will probably contain between fifty and sixty items. At the risk of being dully repetitive, it must be reiterated that these are building blocks with *structural meaning*. As these units are combined into orderly structures of behavior in the interactive sequence they contribute to social meaning.

For purposes of demonstration, it seems useful to list the kinemes found in the face area of the American system. Two warnings must be included. First, these vary "dialectically." In America, there exist body motion areas with locally special variations of movement as distinctive as the variations to be heard in the varied speech communities. Second, tentative and preliminary research upon French, German, and English movers suggests that the body motion languages vary comparably to the range of difference heard between these in their spoken language. However, this remains suggestive rather than definitive. Only when full kinesic analyses exist from each of these cultural communities can we speak of national kinesic systems with any confidence.

American kinemes

Physiologists have estimated that the facial musculature is such that over twenty thousand different facial expressions are somatically possible. At the present stage of investigation, we have been able to isolate thirty-two kinemes in the face and head area. (I am reasonably confident that this is accurate within two or three units.) There are three kinemes of head nod: the "one nod," the "two nod," and the "three nod;" two kinemes of lateral head sweeps, the "one sweep" and the "two sweep;" one of "head cock" and one of "head tilt." There are three junctural, that is connective, kinemes which use the entire head (but with allokines from the head and brow regions), one of "head raise and hold," one of "head lower and hold" and a third of "head position hold." All of these full head kinemes have allokines of intensity, extent, and duration.

We have thus far isolated four kinemes of brow behavior: "lifted brow," "lowered brows," "knit brow," and, finally, "single brow movement."

Extensive and technically difficult research reveals that there are four significant degrees of lid closure: "overopen," "slit," "closed," and "squeezed." There are besides these a series of circumorbital kinic complexes that have resisted analysis. For instance, contraction of the distal aspects of the circumorbital area gives us the familiar "laugh lines." We have not yet been able to determine whether this distal crinkling has kinemic status. It is clear that its absence significantly varies the "meaning" of a smile or laugh, but until we can demonstrate that it is not merely an allokine of lid closure, we must withhold its assignment. Less difficult is the order of problem occasioned by lower lid activity. Extensive research has revealed that its usage in the United States seems to be reserved to certain ethnic groups originating in Eastern and Southeastern Europe. If so, it would have only diakinesic significance in the American movement system. That is, the lower lids seem to be of no more (or less) significance than the absence or presence of the /η/ phoneme in the repertoire of New York City speakers.

The nose is the anatomic locus for four significant behaviors: "wrinkle-nose," "compressed nostrils," "bilateral nostril flare," and "unilateral nostril flare or closure."

The mouth has been very difficult to delineate. The seven kinemes which make up the present circumoral complex are tentative. Only continued research will give us confidence that these represent complete assessment and that the list is composed of equivalent categories. The list includes "compressed lips," "protruded lips," "retracted lips," "apically withdrawn lips," "snarl," "lax open mouth," and "mouth overopen." I am particularly doubtful about the first two of these. Both may belong to some general midface category which we have thus far been unable to isolate.

To this list must also be added "anterior chin thrust," "lateral chin thrust," "puffed cheeks," and "sucked cheeks." "Chin drop" may gain kinemic status but at present is seen as part of the behavioral complex discussed under parakinesics below.

Kinemorphology

These kinemes combine to form *kinemorphs*, which are further analyzable into *kinemorphemic* classes which behave like linguistic morphemes. These, analyzed, abstracted, and combined in the full body behavioral stream, prove to form *complex kinemorphs* which may be analogically related to words. Finally, these are combined by syntactic arrangements, still only partially understood, into extended linked behavioral organizations, the *complex kinemorphic constructions,* which have many of the properties of the spoken syntactic sentence. Only extensive further research is going to give us full understanding of the formal structuring of kinesics. This summary, admittedly skeletal, is presented only to amplify the larger problem undertaken in this chapter.

Much of the research that went into the initial isolation of the microkinesic structure was done on behavior captured on film for slow-motion projection and study. As each new unit was abstracted, it was tested both in multiple universes provided by thousands of feet of interactional film and in the direct observational situation. Whenever possible, each generalization was tested by the employment of live actors in a test situation.

For the purposes of the present chapter, the most significant finding was that these complex microkinesic behaviors could take place without obvious accommodation to the presence or absence of a vocalic accompaniment. Furthermore, while increased velocity of interpersonal vocalic activity *usually* led to increased kinesic behavior at *this* level, increased kinesic activity did not seem nearly as likely to occasion increased vocalic activity. The reader is warned that this may be the result of the choice of the familial and the psychiatric interview contexts as test situations; in more impersonal encounters, the conversational etiquette may impose a different interactional style.

The slow-motion film analyzer provided us not only with a method whereby we could repeat and test our descriptive abstraction but with a method whereby fleeting movements could be detected and timed. In terms of duration, kines have been recorded in sequences that ranged from $1/50$ of a second (significant lid, finger, hand, lip, and head movements faster than this *seem* to be allokinic within a range from as fast as $1/100$ of a second to as long as a full second) to over 3 seconds. These extended performances seem rare, usually such a held position has a double utility: on the one hand, a kine, say a "head cock," serves as a kineme in a series of kinemorphemes *within* the complex kinemorphic construction; on the other it has a suprasegmental and syntactic function as a transsequence juncture which ties together a stream of behavior into a single extended behavioral unit.

Speech-related body motion

As indicated above, the descriptive structure methodology takes the exhaustion of the data stream as a cardinal rule. In a sense, we peel off layers of data. More accurately, we lift out layers of structure. Since the behavior can have multilevel functions, as in the "head cock" mentioned above, we are not merely cutting out and discarding pieces of anatomy as inconsequential to further analysis. As analysis proceeded on particular interactional sequences and the micro-kinesic elements abstracted, once again we had the experience of discovering that we amplified more data in the residual corpus than we had eliminated. Microkinesic analysis left us with two orders of data of differing size: the first of these data were of relatively short duration and were characterized by the fact that they were normally associated with a vocalic stream. At first we dismissed them as "fall-out behavior," the effects of the effort involved in speaking. As their regularity became more manifest, we recognized that we move as well as speak American English. Immediately, a tantalizing problem which had been with us since the inception of kinesic research became illuminated, if not solved.

Just after World War II, I had had access to newsreel film files and had found there strips of film depicting that beloved New York politician, Fiorello La Guardia. La Guardia spoke Italian, Yiddish, and American English. As a public speaker, he was fluent and effective. To me, at that time, the astonishing thing was that even with the sound removed, any observer who knew the three cultures could immediately detect whether he was speaking English, Yiddish, or Italian. The significance of this phenomenon was buried under the deceptive generalization: "La Guardia is a great actor: he knows how to *look* Italian, Jewish, or middle class American." Nor did the point become apparent when George Trager and I working with one of his Taos (Amerind) informants, found an equally manifest shift in the behavior of the informant when speaking Taos and English. Later, I had an opportunity to study in a preliminary fashion a Lebanese who was similarly transformed when switching from English to Arabic and from Arabic to Parisian French. The partial error I made was to subsume all such ethnically and linguistically tied behavior under a broad parakinesic description (discussed below). Accumulated research is convincing that, while ethnic groups do display differential parakinesic behavior, there is, besides this (at least for Western European languages), a set of necessary and formal body motion behaviors which are tied directly to linguistic structure. The old joke, "She couldn't talk at all if you made her hold her body still," seems to be literally true.

Kinesic markers

Two orders of kinesic behavior interdependent with speech have been isolated for American talkers. The first of these are the *markers,* which are particular movements that occur regularly in association with or in substitution for certain syntactic arrangements in American English speech.[2]

Conventions such as these seem to extend with minor variations, say, in body part reference, to the Romance and Germanic languages. Many African, Asian, and Amerind groups, on the other hand, find these confusing, incomprehensible, or insulting when used in combination with their own language.

Kinesic stress

During the same period that research was delineating these semantically bound markers, systematic observation revealed that a second series of behaviors, previously dismissed as speech effort behavior, were regular and orderly. Slight head nods and sweeps, eye blinks, small lip movements, chin thrusts, shoulder nods and sweeps, thorax thrusts, hand and finger movements, as well as leg and foot shifts proved to be allokines of a quadripartite kinesic *stress* system. These formed suprasegmental kinemorphemes which, when associated with speech, served a syntactic function by marking special combinations of adjectivals plus nominals, adverbials plus action words, and, furthermore, assisted in the organization of clauses, phrases, and finally, connected specially related clauses in extended and complex syntactic sentences. The four stresses include:

Primary stress	V	A relatively strong movement normally concurrent with loudest linguistic stress. One occurrence for each spoken American English sentence. In contrast with
Secondary stress	∧	a relatively weaker movement occurs in association with the Primary in certain spoken American English sentences. In contrast with
Unstressed	—	the normal flow of movement associated with speech may occur either before or after Primary and before or after and between Secondary.
Destressed	o	Involves reduction of activity below normal over portions of a syntactic sentence. (Sometimes confused as "dead pan" or "poker face" which are maintained kinemorphs which extend over one or more syntactic sentence; destressed normally occurs over phrases and clauses.)

To illustrate these stresses, two sentences are presented in contrasting form below.

In spoken English we detect a loudness contrast between the adjective plus noun in the form "hot *dog*" (heated canine) and the name form for a popular American sausage, the "hot dog." Conventions of writing in English, whereby we can capitalize and/or omit the space between "hot" and "dog" to indicate the close relationship between the subforms, reduce the ambiguity in such forms just as does capitalization of the noun in German or the special article forms for French. Rulon Wells (1945) brilliantly demonstrated that spoken English utilizes four phonemically significant degrees of loudness to assist the communicant in making these same distinctions.

The appropriate response to the question, "What is the term for that sandwich?" is:

That + is + a + hótdòg

(Primary plus tertiary stress)

The appropriate response to the question, "Is that a *cold* dog?"

(No) that + is + a + hót + dôg

(Primary plus secondary stress)

The appropriate response to the question, "Is that a *cold cat?*" is:

(No) that + is + a + hót # dóg

(Primary plus terminal juncture plus primary)

In each of these cases we have abstracted partial sentences from the full stream of behavior to demonstrate the stress point. Using a different set of words, perhaps, we can demonstrate how the kinesic stress system operates to make a comparable point. Let us suppose that we have an uninformed speaker of English who does not know that Americans use the form "hot dog" to indicate a wiener or frankfurter. Sent for a "hot dog" by his hungry employer, he returns with a poodle and says, "I've found a dog for you, but we'll have to exercise him for a few minutes to make him warm." The employer laughs and says:

I + want + a + hotdog

not + a + hot + dog #

Kinesic stress analysis and function can be demonstrated by depicting the kinesic activity which occurs regularly at three levels of analysis; first, the articulatory or anatomic activity level; second, the kinemic level; third, the kinemorphemic level.

cidentally, when spoken, (A) and (B) will also stand in linguistic pitch and stress contrast. In spoken (B) after a

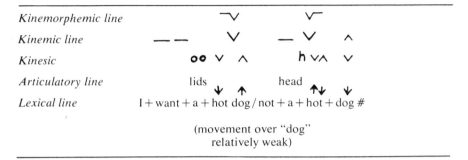

Kinemorphemic line		
Kinemic line		
Kinesic		
Articulatory line	lids	head
Lexical line	I + want + a + hot dog / not + a + hot + dog #	

(movement over "dog"
relatively weak)

Kinesically, at still the next higher level of organization, the complex kinemorphic construction level, we derive data which can then be used to describe kinesic-linguistic sentence types and to compare such types for the assessment of the universe of discourse. The sequence above contains no *destress*. The following sentence will demonstrate an order of context in which it does appear. In case (A) which follows, the context describes Jones, the president of a scientific society, as a leader in the scientific community. This stands in contrast with the second context (B) in which Jones is described, while admittedly functional as president of the society, as leaving something to be desired as a leader of science or of the community.

primary linguistic stress on "Jones," "as a president" will be marked by an even and relatively unvarying stress and pitch profile while (A) is marked by the pitch and stress expectable for a more statistically normal spoken English sentence. While this example is fresh in the reader's mind, let us review an analytic point. In the discussion of kinesic stress above, it was pointed out that the inexperienced kinesicist may confuse a destressed passage with one which is accompanied by "poker-faced" behavior. An informant can produce this sentence with an accompanying kinemorphic construction of "poker face" which involves perceptible reduction of facial activity. The actor still must move the necessary kinesic stresses. Informants have no difficulty with the

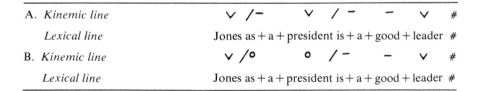

A. Kinemic line		
Lexical line	Jones as + a + president is + a + good + leader #	
B. Kinemic line		
Lexical line	Jones as + a + president is + a + good + leader #	

The use of kinesic destress / 00/ in the included phrase in (B) calls attention to the special emphasis on this phrase. In-

contrast between (B) above and (C) below, which puts special emphasis on the included phrase of (B) *within* a sequence of "dead pan or poker face." Thus:

show how kinesics at this level of analysis can operate in a redundancy role."

C. *Kinemorphic construction*	Face+O TZ	K/T+O . . . . K/TZ . . . . K #
Kinesic stress	∨	○ ○ _ _ ∧ _
Lexical	Jones /	the president / is + a + good + leader #

The frozen body (T +) over "the president" is a clear example of the use of various parts of the body to code separate pieces of information for the communication. While the face is immobilized to form the complex kinemorph $\left(\begin{array}{c} H + O \\ \text{Face} + O \end{array}\right)$ the (TZ) in hands, fingers, shoulders, and so forth can produce the stress markers. One warning must be given to those who would quickly jump to assuming that destress has a *particular* meaning. In this special case, taken from an observed interaction, the context was one in which the actor-speaker was casting doubt on the ability of Dr. Jones. Destressed clauses, depending upon the larger context, have wide ranges of social meaning. Destress over a vocalized stretch has a *syntactic* function and indicates some order of *inclusion*. In contexts other than the one discussed above, such an inclusion could serve to draw attention to the unusually *high* esteem in which the referent is held rather than to his deficiencies.

Multichannel redundancy

The reader may very well, at this point, exhausted by the technical and unfamiliar gymnastics of these paragraphs, ask if one point being made here is the conventional one: communication is, by nature, redundant. The answer to this is, "Yes, we have been trying to

However, I would immediately reject the suggestion that multichannel reinforcement of structure is *merely* redundant. Part of the objection would be to the implication that a reinforced message has the same content as a simple message; *there is no reason to assume that nature is haphazard in the selection of certain messages for emphasis and reinforcement.* All of the available data, derived from extended observations, indicate that apparent redundancy is often an agent of reinforcement which serves, at one level, to tie together stretches of discourse and interaction that are longer than sentence length. Of equal importance is the fact that behavior which appears merely repetitive at one level of analysis demands further analysis. Such behavior always seems to be of very special social and cultural significance at other levels.

In the larger evolutionary sense, the possession of physiological equipment which permits multichannel redundancy increases man's adaptive potential. Multichannel reinforcement is positively adaptive, if for no other reason than it provides a far wider range of possibility for the utilization of individual variation within a population. Human beings do not all mature at the same rate and at maturity they are not sensorily equal. Redundancy of the type described above makes the contents of messages available to a greater portion of the population than would be possible if only one modality were utilized to teach, learn, store, transmit, or structure experience. Multichannel reinforcement makes it possible for a far wider range within the population to become part of and to contribute to the conventional understandings of the community than if we were a species with only a single-channel lexical storehouse. We must not allow the fact that it seems easier to recover the data stored in words and sentences to blind us to the vast storehouse of conventional usages, to the multiple arenas of exploration that are the heritage of a multisensory species. We are aware of this with relation to music, graphic art, and the dance. We need to recognize that these art forms are special derivations of deeper and more basic human mechanisms.

Speaking of language in its broadest sense, Margaret Mead has written:

. . . all natural languages that survive are sufficiently redundant that they can be learned by the members of any *Homo sapiens* group.
. . . we would say that any language developed by a human society can be learned by the members of another human society, and that this learning is possible both because of the redundancy, which provides for a whole range of individual differences in sensory modalities, memory and intelligence, and because language has been conceptualized the world over as a part of culture that can be learned by members of different cultures.[3]

No society has a monopoly on observation, reflection, or invention. Transmission of experience from society to society multiplies the opportunity for experimentation, for innovation and development. And, since societies place differential stress on sensory reliability,

a multichannel system maximizes the opportunities for transmission between unlike societies. Multisensory redundancy and channel reinforcement thus not only increase the social viability and potential contribution, both to innovation or conservation, of a wider range of individuals within a specific society, but contribute to intersociety communication and, thus, to the opportunities for viability of the species.

Paralanguage

The abstraction of the microkinesic structure and the circumverbal kinesic material does not exhaust the body motion behavior observable in any interactional sequence. Complex kinemorphic constructions are seldom more than 4 or 5 seconds in duration. The markers, even when complexly bound in "syntactic" sequence, are only, at the most, slightly longer than the vocalized sentences they accompany. The suprasegmental morphemes of kinesic stress are usually of clause length. Besides these, there occurs body motion behavior which can be almost instantaneous in appearance or can extend for minutes, hours, or, perhaps even for portions of a lifetime. Obviously, further investigations will reveal portions of this behavior which properly belong in the microkinesic structure. At the present writing, however, most of it defies microkinesic analysis. I am here referring to that behavior which is covered by categories like *stance, posture,* and *style.* Such matters of muscular and skin action as *flaccidity, rigidity,* and *tone,* because they shift contextually in what seems to be a regular manner, belong here, too. Visibly variable *vascularity* and the *oiliness* and *dryness* of the skin seem, under observation, to have communicative consequence, and this kind of learned activity should be scrutinized for more formal properties. General categories of behavior like *appearance, self-presentation, beauty* and *ugliness, gracefulness* and *clumsiness,* seem likely to have regular, abstractable qualities. (These latter, usually only considered as normative categories, gained communication analysis status when the examination of extended stretches of interaction—an hour or more—showed these to be far more transitory and regular than we had formerly assumed.)

Because this behavior, when parallel research was undertaken with descriptive linguists, was revealed to be so similar in occurrence to behavior on the vocal level, we have described it as *parakinesic* to maintain the terminological parallel with the earlier linguistic concept of *paralinguistics.* Such terminological borrowing seems increasingly appropriate as we move from the study of the communicational subsystems of linguistics and kinesics to the analysis of the communicational system itself. Thus far, because of the time and labor involved, only a limited number of long interactional sequences have been exhaustively studied. However, such body motion and vocalic behaviors seem so intimately and systematically interdependent that they can only be heuristically separated. Present evidence is convincing that while canons of descriptive care must be adhered to, in the recording of each modality, parakinesics and paralinguistics may be comprehended as a single system, *paralanguage.* And I have no reason to believe that paralanguage will be fully understood until the other channels of communication—tactile, olfactory, gustatory, and proprioceptive are analyzed and comprehended. Furthermore, I feel most of the communicational data sketched by Hall (1959, 1966) and Wescott (1966) ultimately will be structured somewhere in the complex paralanguage area.

Fifteen years of extended and increasingly systematic observation is persuasive that paralanguage is too gross a category to be final. It, too, theoretically should emerge as a structure composed of a series of ordered levels of communicational behavior. It seems likely that as we discover how sentences are linked together to make up discourse, as we, following Scheflen's lead (1965c), delineate the conventionalized structures which order two- and three-member and group discussions, that as we decode the signals that compose a system whereby we can leave and return to topics in an interaction without strain, that as we learn how humans can separate and return to each other to maintain continuous interaction, we will absorb into structural categories much of the material now preanalytically assigned to paralanguage.

NOTES

1. Adapted from "Communication without Words," in *Encyclopédie des Sciences de l'Homme,* Vol. 5 (Geneva, Editions Kister, 1968), pp. 157–166.
2. The discussion omitted here covers the material treated at length in the next selection (see Birdwhistell, 1970, Chapter 17).
3. Margaret Mead, *Continuities in Cultural Evolution,* Terry Lectures (New Haven, Yale University Press, 1964), p. 45.

REFERENCES

Birdwhistell, R. L., *Kinesics and Context,* University of Pennsylvania Press, Philadelphia, 1970.

Hall, E. T., *The Silent Language*, Doubleday, New York, 1959.

Hall, E. T., *The Hidden Dimension*, Doubleday, New York, 1966.

Scheflen, A. E., *Stream and Structure of Communicational Behavior: Content Analysis of a Psychotherapy Session*, Behavioral Monograph Press, No. 2, Eastern Pennsylvania Psychiatric Institute, 1965.

Wells, R. S., "The pitch phonemes of English," *Language*, 1945, 21, 17–39.

Wescott, R. W., "Introducing coenetics," *American Scholar*, 1966, 35, 342–356.

10

MASCULINITY AND FEMININITY AS DISPLAY [1]

RAY L. BIRDWHISTELL

Zoologists and biologists have over the years accumulated archives of data which attest to the complex ordering of animal gender display, courtship, and mating behavior. Until recently, the implications of much of this data have been obscured by the governing assumption that this behavior was, while intricate and obviously patterned, essentially a mechanical and instinctual response to a genetically based program. There has been, however, an increasing realization that intragender and intergender behavior throughout the animal kingdom is not simply a response to instinctual mechanisms but is shaped, structured, and released both by the ontogenetic experiences of the participating organisms and by the patterned circumstances of the relevant environment. Behavioral scientists focusing upon human behavior have been forced to relinquish the ethnocentric assumption that human gender and sexual behavior is qualitatively different from that of other animals. Many have

conceded that culture, a human invention, is not interpreted profitably as a device for curbing and ordering "animalistic," "brutal," "bestial," or instinctual appetites. The elaborate regulation of fish, bird, and mammalian courtship and mating behavior has been of particular interest to sociologists and anthropologists. That this interest has not been more productive seems to me to be occasioned by confusion in the ordering of gender-centered behavior. In the discussion to follow, which utilizes certain insights derived from analysis of communication, I wish to focus upon one aspect of gender-related interactional behavior—that of gender identification and response.

Biologists have long been aware that the clear demarcation between the production of ova and spermatazoa in organisms of a bisexual species is not necessarily accompanied by any comparable bifurcation in the distribution of secondary sexual characteristics. In some species there is such extreme gender-linked dimorphism that only the specialist in the particular species can recognize that males and females are conspecial. At the other extreme, some species are so unimorphic that near-surgical techniques are required to determine the gender of isolated individuals. By and large, researchers concerned with human behavior have assumed that in relatively unimorphic species there were subtle differences in the perceptible taxonomy of males and females which were easily recognizable by conspecifics even if they were difficult to detect by humans. However, it would be difficult for any reader conversant with Konrad Lorenz' (1957) description of the difficulties involved in the mating of graylag geese to maintain the fiction that gender differences are always apparent to the membership of a unimorphic species. There is humor and a certain pathos in the situation when two graylag males meet and each acts as though the other were a member of the opposite sex. Only the reproductive rate of graylags gives us confidence that even a goose can solve such a problem.

The social biologist Peter Klopfer has pointed out that even with the incomplete evidence now at hand, it would be possible to establish a spectrum of species rated by the extent of their sexual dimorphism.[2] Insofar as I have been able to determine, no such list has been prepared. However, by establishing an ideal typical gamut with an unimorphic species at one end and an extreme of dimorphy at the other, it has been possible to tentatively locate *Homo sapiens* on this scale. Obviously, the position of any particular species on this scale is a function of both the number of species chosen and the special characteristics of the selected species. When, however, the secondary

sexual characteristics themselves are stressed (whether visibly, audibly or, olfactorily perceptible), man seems far closer to the unimorphic end of the spectrum than he might like to believe.

Physical anthropologists have long pointed out that if such anatomical markers as differential bone structure or the distribution of body hair are used, the measurement of human population reveals no bimodal curve in the distribution of secondary sexual characteristics. Most authorities agree that instead of a single curve shaped $\sim\!\!\wedge$, we find two overlapping bell curves: $\sim\!\!\!\wedge$. Masculine and feminine traits in aural sound production seem to be distributed in a similar manner following puberty. There is as yet no definitive evidence that there is a significant difference in the odor-producing chemicals released by human males and females. This may be due to the crudity of our available measuring instruments, but at the present, odor does not seem to function as a constant gender marker for humans.

The case for the relative unimorphy or the weak dimorphy of man should not be overstressed for the purposes of this argument. The upright position of humans obviously makes for clear visibility of differential mammary development and for the easy display of the genitalia. These may provide sufficient signals in themselves. However, certain pieces of data permit us to discount these as definitive of gender in and of themselves. First, we have long been aware that children do not, even in societies as preoccupied with these organs as ours, immediately note the gender-defining qualities of either the external genitalia or the differential mammary development. I doubt seriously that this represents some psychological denial function in the child's perception of his universe. The near universality of the G-string or other clothing protecting, obscuring, or hiding the genital region, even in societies with minimal shame or embarrassment about genital display, does not seem sufficient evidence for the final importance of genitalia display for gender identification. Furthermore, the fact that the more prominent breasts of females or the less prominent breasts of males do not seem to have universal sexual stimulus value would seem to support our de-emphasis upon mammary dimorphism as gender identifiers. Needless to say, however, until we have more systematic knowledge about clothing and other cosmetological devices, we are not going to be able to settle this particular question. There is no reason to make the *a priori* assumption that uncovered breasts are more or less obvious than covered ones (except of course, to those trained to make these distinctions). It seems permissible to proceed in our discussion while holding this aspect of human dimorphy open for future investigation.

My work in kinesics leads me to postulate that man and probably a number of other weakly dimorphic species necessarily organize much of gender display and recognition at the level of position, movement, and expression. It seems methodologically useful to me to distinguish between *primary* sexual characteristics which relate to the physiology of the production of fertile ova or spermatazoa, the *secondary* sexual characteristics which are anatomical in nature, and the *tertiary* sexual characteristics which are patterned social-behavioral in form. These latter are learned and are situationally produced.

Let me hasten to add that the terms "primary," "secondary," and "tertiary" imply no functional priorities. There seems plenty of reason to believe that

these levels are mutually interinfluential. Patterned social behavior seems to be required to permit the necessary physiological functioning requisite for successful and fertile mating. And, we have at least anecdotal evidence and clinical reports that certain of the secondary sexual characteristics respond to both the physiological substratum and the particular social-behavioral context. I hope that premature "explanation" which accounts for this behavior in simplistic psychological or cultural terms does not preclude investigation on other levels.

I have worked with informants from seven different societies. It has been clear from their responses that not only could native informants distinguish male movement from female movement (and the items of what was regarded as "masculine" and "feminine" varied from society to society) but they easily detected different degrees of accentuation or diminution of such movement, depending upon the stuation. In all of these societies (Chinese, middle- and upper-class London British, Kutenai, Shushwap, Hopi, Parisian French, and American) both male and female informants distinguished not only typically male communicational behavior from typically female communicational behavior but, when the opportunity presented itself, distinguished "feminine" males and "masculine" females. This does not imply that any informant could make a complete and explicit list of "masculine" or "feminine" behavior. However, each culture did have stereotypes which could be acted out or roughly described. That the behavior described by the informants did not always coincide with the general range of scientifically abstractable gender-identifying behavior should not come as a surprise to any field worker who has tried to elicit microcultural behavior from native informants. One comment should be included here before we turn for examples to the body motion communicational system most intensively studied, the American. Informants from all of these societies either volunteered or without hesitation responded that young children matured into these behaviors and that as people got older they gave up or matured out of them. As might be expected, both the propedeutic period and the duration of the active gender display varied from society to society. Furthermore, while most informants agreed that in their particular society some individuals learned how to accentuate or obscure these signals, informants from all of these societies interpreted the differences as instinctually and biologically based.

I have no data which would permit me to assess the relative emphasis American culture places upon gender display and recognition as compared to other societies. However, it is quite clear that within American society, class and regional variations occur— not so much in the signals themselves as in the age at which such messages are learned, the length of time and situations in which they are used, and the emphasis placed on them in contrast to other identification signals.

As an illustration, I will describe a few of the most easily recognizable American gender identification signals. Two are derived from the analysis of posture, one from "facial expression." The male-female differences in intrafemoral angle and arm body angle are subject to exact measurement. American females, when sending gender signals and/or as a reciprocal to male gender signals, bring the legs together, at times to the point that the upper legs

cross, either in a full leg *cross with feet still together,* the lateral aspects of the two feet parallel to each other, or in standing knee over knee. In contrast, the American male position is one in which the intrafemoral index ranges up to a 10- or 15-degree angle. Comparably, the American female gender presentation arm position involves the proximation of the upper arms to the trunk while the male in gender presentation moves the arms some 5 to 10 degrees away from the body. In movement, the female may present the entire body from neck to ankles as a moving whole, whereas the male moves the arms independent of the trunk. The male may subtly wag his hips with a slight right and left presentation with a movement which involves a twist at the base of the thoracic cage and at the ankles.

Another body position involved in gender presentation is made possible by the flexibility of the pelvic spinal complex. In gender identification the American male tends to carry his pelvis rolled slightly back as contrasted with the female anterior roll. If the range of pelvic positioning is depicted as $\smile$, the female position can be depicted as $\smile$; the male as $\smile\times$. As males and females grow older or, because of pathology, over- or underemphasize gender messages, the male and female position can become almost indistinguishable, or become bizarrely inappropriate.

One more example may be sufficient for our point. Informants often describe particular lid and eye behavior as masculine or feminine. However, only careful observation and measurement reveal that the structual components of circumorbital behavior are related, in closure of the lid in males, to prohibiting movement of the eyeballs while the lids are closed. Comparably, the communicative convention prescribes that unless accompanying signals indicate sleepiness or distress, males should close and open their lids in a relatively continuous movement. Let me stress again that these positions, movements, and expressions are culturally coded— that what is viewed as masculine in one culture may be regarded as feminine in another.

I have presented these examples with a hesitation occasioned by past experience. Inevitably, such examples have been interpreted as the messages males and females send to each other when they wish consciously or unconsciously to invite coitus. However, I must emphasize that *no position, expression, or movement ever carries meaning in and of itself.* It is true that in certain contexts gender display, appropriately responded to, is an essential element in the complex interchange between humans preliminary to courtship, to coitus, and, even, to mating. However, the identical behavior inappropriately presented may have the opposite function; it may prevent the development of the interaction that might culminate in a more intimate interpersonal exchange. For example, a prematurely presenting male may define a situation in such a manner that the female cannot respond without considerable role sacrifice. Thus, the male can prevent coitus and even courtship from occurring by presenting in a manner which defines his action as insufficiently directed to the receiving female. The so-called "sexy" female can by inappropriate gender display effectively protect herself against intimate heterosexual involvement. The male who sends "feminine" or pubescent and awkward "masculine" display signals may in one context be signaling to a

male; in another he degenderizes his female respondent by returning a message more appropriate to a female-female interaction than a male-female interaction. Furthermore, while it is not at all difficult to detect in context the message sent by either a male or a female which reads, "I wish to be considered a homosexual," we have been able to isolate no message, masculine or feminine, which is in itself an indicant of homosexuality or heterosexuality when such sexuality is measured by active genital participation.

For the sociologist and the anthropologist, a more important aspect of the possibility of decoding a given society's gender display and recognition system is that such a code provides him with a tool for more adequately studying the division of labor in the day-to-day life of a community. Social role and status theory have been very useful at one level of social investigation. However, when the researcher seeks to relate such theory to problems of social learning, to personality and character development, or to the solution of individual and social problems, he all too often is prevented from testing high-level generalizations in the crucible of behavior. Gender identity and relationship is only one of several nodal points coded into a society's communicational system. Kinesic and linguistic research has demonstrated, at least for American society, that such nodal behavior never stands alone—it is always modified by other identification signals and by the structure of the context in which the behavior occurs. In these complex but decodable behaviors lies the proof that gender behavior is not limited to a sexual response and that sexual behavior is not always *either* genital or uncompleted genital behavior.

In the discussion so far an attempt

has been made to demonstrate the methodological correctness and convenience of ordering gender-related phenomena into primary, secondary, and tertiary characteristics. Tertiary sexual behavior has been described as learned and patterned communicative behavior which in the American body motion communication system acts to identify both the gender of a person and the social expectancies of that gender. It has been presented with the fiat that gender display or response is not necessarily sexually provocative or responsive and is probably never exclusively genital in nature.

The paper was introduced with a discussion of the relatively weak dimorphy in the structure of human secondary sexual characteristics. Until more animal societies are studied as societies and until the nature and range of the possibilities for the division of labor have been investigated in these animal societies, we cannot make any final appraisal of unimorphy or dimorphy as base lines for social interaction. However, we are in a position to postulate that for human society at least, weak dimorphy creates an opportunity for the development of intricate and flexible tertiary sexual characteristics which can be variably exploited in the division of labor.

Finally, in a society like ours, with its complex division of labor and with the rapid change in social role as related to gender, we should not be surprised to find that the young have considerable difficulty in learning ap-propriate intra- and intergender messages. Nor should we be surprised to find that in such a society messages about sex and gender can become a preoccupation. Children who become confused about the meaning of gender messages can become adults who have difficulty comprehending the relationship between male and female roles in a changing society. Only the fact that children can learn in spite of parental teaching protects us from a situation in which accumulating discrepancy could destroy the necessary conditions for appropriate mating. There is no evidence for the popular statement that men in western European society are becoming "weaker" or that women are becoming "stronger"—there is considerable evidence that both are confused in their communication with each other about such matters.

NOTES

1. Presented to the American Association for the Advancement of Science, in December 1964 under the title "The Tertiary Sexual Characteristics of Man: A Fundamental in Human Communication."
2. Personal communication.

REFERENCE

Lorenz, K., "The role of aggression in group formation," in *Group Processes,* B. Schaffner, ed., Transactions of the 4th Conference of the Josiah Macy, Jr. Foundation, 1957, pp. 181 ff.

MOVEMENT COORDINATION IN SOCIAL INTERACTION: SOME EXAMPLES DESCRIBED [1]

ADAM KENDON

If we are to understand more fully the conditions in which effective and efficient social performance may occur, it will be important to examine in detail the behavior of listeners, and how this is related to the behavior of speakers. As a speaker, we are never indifferent to what the listener is doing. If he drums his fingers, if he frequently shifts in his chair, or looks about the room, or nods his head in an unusual pattern, he may convey the impression that he is bored, improperly attentive or inattentive, or that he is preoccupied. Sometimes this may throw us off balance to the extent that our flow of talk is brought to a stammering halt. More often, perhaps, we leave the encounter with a feeling of discomfort, with a feeling that there was no "rapport". However, we are usually unable to say what it is about our listener's behavior that gave us this feeling. Evidently we may be influenced by quite subtle features of his behavior.

There is a limited amount of work which illuminates some features of the effect of listeners upon speakers. Many studies, for example those reviewed by Greenspoon (1962), have shown that the vocal actions of a listener may "shape" aspects of the speaker's performance. A few studies have demonstrated the influence of such items as nodding, and smiling (Wickes, 1956; Gross, 1959; Matarazzo et al., 1964), and there is one study that shows that the posture of the listener, and the patterning of his facial displays, have an important influence upon how the speaker will respond to the listener's vocal actions (Reece and Whitman, 1962). In all of these cases, however, the investigator has studied only those features of the listener's behavior he has determined on in advance. The listener is always giving a controlled performance, where what he does and when he does it has been decided upon beforehand, as part of the experimental design. We know remarkably little, in a systematic way, about what it is that listeners ordinarily do, and how what they do is related to what speakers do.

It is the aim of this paper to throw some light on this matter.

In this paper some detailed descriptions of the interrelations of the movements of speakers and listeners will be given. These descriptions will provide some further examples of the phenomenon of interactional synchrony, first described by Condon and Ogston (1966, 1967), in which it is found that the flow of movement in the listener may be rhythmically coordinated with the flow of speech in the speaker. We shall also show how the *way* in which individuals may be in synchrony with one another can vary, and that these variations are related to their respective roles in the interaction.

Interactional synchrony

The findings presented by Condon and Ogston are derived from a very close study of sound film records of people in interaction. The film is examined by means of a time-motion analyzer, a projector in which the film can be moved back and forth by hand at any speed. Small sequences may be examined repeatedly, and then compared with immediately adjacent sequences. In analyzing movement, each body part is focused on separately, and a mark is made on a time chart at the point at which there is a minimally perceptible change in the direction of movement of the body part. Each division on the time chart corresponds to a frame on the film. With a film shot at the rate of twenty-four frames per second (the standard rate for film), measurements of time intervals are thus possible to the nearest twenty-fourth of a second. The result of such a plot is a flow chart showing the points at which changes in the direction of movement occur, in each body part examined. A phonetic segmentation of the speech sounds is then undertaken, and this is written in on the time chart so that the relationship between the speech and body motion may be examined.

If this procedure is followed for a stretch of behavior, it is found that the points of change in the movement for the separate body parts coincide. That is to say, the body parts change and sustain direction of movement together. This does not mean that all the parts of the body are moving in the same way. As the arms are lowered, the head may turn to the right, the trunk may bow forward, the eyes shift left, the mouth open, the brows lift, the fingers flex, the feet flex from the ankles, and so on. It is further found that some body parts may sustain a given direction of movement over several changes in other body parts. What emerges from this analysis, thus, is a description of the flow of movement as a series of contrasting waves of movement, where within the larger waves, smaller waves may be contained.

Such a description will apply whenever the individual is in motion. When, in a speaker, the body motion co-occurring with his speech is examined, it is found that the points of change in the flow of sound coincide with the points of change in body movement. But what is found here is that the larger movement waves fit over larger segments of speech, such as words or phrases, the smaller movement waves, contained within the larger, fit over the smaller segments, such as the syllables and the sub-syllabic changes. A fuller account of features of this organization of body motion in its relation to speech may be found in Kendon (1970).

When the behavior of the listener is examined in the same fashion, Condon and Ogston find that while the speaker is speaking and moving, the listener is moving as well. He may be sitting relatively still, not making any specifically gestural movements, but yet moving his hands or head, moving his eyes, or blinking. Where *interactional synchrony* is occurring it is found that the boundaries of the movement waves of the listener coincide with boundaries of the movement waves in the speaker. For synchrony to occur, in this sense, it is only this coincidence of boundaries that must obtain. The listener may otherwise be moving in quite a different fashion, and he usually is.

Condon finds that, as a rule, speaker and listener are in synchrony up to the word level. That is, we observe changes in the listener's movement configurations that coincide with the boundaries of the speaker's movement changes at the phonic, syllabic and word levels of his speech. The larger waves of the listener's movement, however, do not necessarily coincide with the larger waves of the speaker's behavior, though they may do so on occasion. Thus, if speaker and listener are in synchrony, and the listener lifts a cigarette to his lips, draws on it, and lowers the cigarette again, the boundaries of the major components of this action will coincide with boundaries in the behavior flow of the speaker, but these boundaries will not necessarily also be boundaries of larger waves of behavior in the speaker, for instance the boundaries of his phrases, although they may be, as we will see later.

Condon and Ogston have described examples of interactional synchrony in a number of short samples of filmed interaction. However, they have not as yet dealt with the contexts in which this phenomenon may be observed, nor have they described the nature of the patterning of the listener's movements.

In this paper we shall attempt to say something about the context of the examples to be described, and we shall also attempt to describe the patterns of movement in listeners who are directly addressed by a speaker as compared to those who, though yet members of the same encounter, are listening to an interchange they are not directly involved in. In this way we hope to be able to say something about the functions, for the interaction, of the various patterns of behavior that may be observed.

Materials and method

The material from which most of the examples to be analyzed has been drawn is an eighty minute 16 mm black and white sound film of a gathering in a private lounge of a middle class London hotel.[2] The chairs were arranged in a rough circle in the room, and the camera, lighting and sound recording equipment were set up to one side (see fig. 1). Customers at the bar

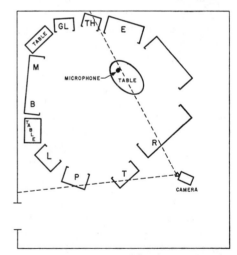

Fig. 1 Arrangement of furniture and positions of the participants (indicated by letters) in the T-extract. Area enclosed by dotted lines indicates the approximate field of view of the camera.

were encouraged to come in and sit down with their drinks. During some parts of the film, discussion was stimulated by the film maker. For much of the time, however, talk was exchanged in smaller groups around the room. Such an occasion is not, of course, typical of anything that normally occurs in a London pub. However, our interest is not in analyzing the character of the social occasion. Instead, the film has been used as a source for examples of those smaller events, such as the exchange of role of speaker, or the behavior of different listeners in relation to the speaker, which occur in all focused gatherings.[3]

The method of analysis employed in this study was as follows: the film was looked at many times on a sound projector, running it at normal speed, and at a slower speed of 16 frames per second. Specific extracts were then selected that were both of good technical quality and that comprised some natural unit of interaction, for instance a question-answer exchange. These extracts were studied in detail with a Bell and Howell time motion analyzer. The movement of the body parts were plotted out on a chart on which the intervals represented the successive frames of the film. The movement of any body part was segmented in the same manner that has been described by Condon and Ogston. Divisions within a line representing a body part are made when there is a change in the direction of movement of the body part. The segments of the line thus divided are then labeled, using a set of terms modified from those proposed by the American College of Surgeons, for describing the functions of the joints (Boyd and Banks, 1965). In this way a kind of flow chart of the movement is laid out. The technique is, thus, to scan the film

in small segments, with the aim of picking out those successive groups of frames over which a single direction of movement in a given body part is sustained.

In the present study we have concentrated primarily upon the movements of the head, trunk, arms and hands. Facial changes, and details such as eye movements have, for the most part, had to be omitted, since the quality of the film did not permit their accurate transcription.

A magnetic tape recording made from the original sound track of the film was used to make the orthographic and phonetic transcript of the speech. The sound was then read from the film, using an optical sound reader, matched with a properly calibrated frame counter, and frame numbers could thus be placed against the phonetic transcription.

Some examples analyzed

Introduction

In this section a detailed analysis of a short extract from the pub film will be presented, with briefer references to a number of other extracts. The piece to be most thoroughly analyzed will be referred to as the T-extract. It comprises TRD 099.2.87591-88221.[4] This extract was selected because it comes from a section of the film in which the interactional structure of the gathering is much simpler than it is in other parts, and also the soundtrack is more intelligible here than elsewhere.

Of the persons present, whose locations may be seen in fig. 1, B is the film-maker and L is a psychiatrist, present at B's invitation. All the other men present are customers at the hotel. They are middle class in background, and range between thirty and fifty years in age. M is a young woman in her mid-twenties, present because of her acquaintance with the manageress.

In the part of the film from which the T-extract was taken, B is acting as a kind of discussion leader, or chairman. By questions and reflections he evoked first from one participant, then from another, opinions and feeling about British customs, particularly in respect to the relationship between parents and children and between siblings. In the T-extract itself, B asks T a question, he replies to this with a speech about thirty seconds long; B puts a further question to T, to which he gives a very short reply; B acknowledges this, and then turns to question another participant. A transcript of the words spoken in the extract is given in fig. 2. In

some of the components of movement, and how this is related in time to the accompanying speech and movement of each interactant. The movement components in these diagrams are labeled by letter, and they will be referred to in the text by a letter in parentheses, following a description of the movement.

T and B description

When B puts his first question to T, he faces him and points at him with an extended arm. As will be seen from the diagram (fig. 3), B turns his head to look at T, and swings his arm round to point at him (B), before his question is uttered in its complete form. That is, he first turns to face T, and to point at him, and then he puts his question. T is

---

B: yeah (20) and then (10) and then what T: (10) well (12) uh (8)

T: (cont.) ca (6) as the years went by (5) and he became more (5)

T: (cont.) shall we say mellowed and matured or possibly (14) less

T: (cont.) (16) to some extent less interested in children (9)

T: (cont.) ten years later (11) twelve years later (3) other children

T: (cont.) arrived (9) then (16) possibly he couldn't be bothered (6)

T: (cont.) but (7) at (3) the same time (12) he was (30) more used

T: (cont.) to children and prepared to give and take B: well now did

B: (cont.) you become the did you become then the part of the

B: (cont.) disciplinarian in the family T: (15) well I tried to

---

Fig. 2 Transcript of the words uttered in the T-extract. Numbers in brackets within the transcript indicate the lengths of pauses to the nearest twenty-fourth of a second.

the account to follow, we shall first concentrate on the relationship between the behavior of T and B, and then we shall look at the behavior of some of the other participants, during the same exchange. Some of the descriptions are accompanied by diagrams which show

sitting forward in his chair (see fig. 4). Just at the beginning of the last syllable of B's question, at 645, T begins to lean back in his chair (b) and it is only after his back is fully in contact with the back of his chair that he begins his utterance, though during this shift in

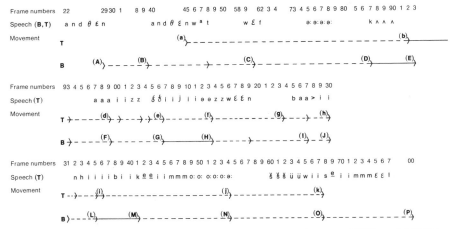

Fig. 3 Diagram to show speech and movement components between 87622 and 87777 in the T-extract from TRD 009. Movement components are labeled by letter and are described in the text.

posture he emits three short vocalizations. These are high pitched, cut off short, almost glottalized. The first two, [wɛɬ] and [ə:], are best described as "ready" signals, but the third, [kʌ], is probably the first part of an unfinished word. The posture that T moves into here (the movement lasts from 645 to 691), is the one that he maintains for the rest of his utterance. His shift in posture, initiated before any vocaliza-

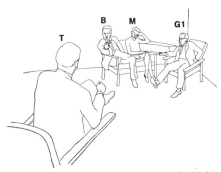

Fig. 4 Tracing from frame no. 87640 in the T-extract showing T in 'forward position', B pointing at T, and M and G1, R, P, L, and Th who are all partly visible in this frame have been omitted from the tracing for the sake of clarity.

tion, is his first response to B's question, and it may be said to mark the change in his position in the interaction from that of a listener, to that of a discourser.[5]

Concurrently with T's change in posture, B also moves. He leans back slightly and lifts his head, and at the same time he lowers his forearm and rotates it inwards, while flexing his elbow and wrist slightly, so that he is no longer pointing directly at T, though his arm is still extended (D). At 688, however, B becomes quite still, and he remains still until 693 (E), when T begins to move his left arm in preparation for speaking (d). It is to be noted that the point where B ceases to move is also the point where T releases the vowel of [kʌ]. It may be that B here ceases to move because he holds himself ready for the onset of T's utterance, the imminence of which is announced by [kʌ] and by the virtual completion of his posture shift.

From 693-706 B bends his trunk forward (F, G) and then, at 713, he begins to move his hand and arm to the right, coming to point directly at T again at 727 (I). His hand is then moved slightly to the left again (J) and then, after a brief period of immobility he cocks his head to the right (N). T's movements during this same period are as follows: Over the first phrase of his utterance, he moves his left arm first out to the left (d), then following some small movements in the hand, it is moved right and lowered to his lap (f). Then it is raised again, and again moved out to his left (g). Then, over the first part of the second phrase of his speech he cocks his head to the right (j). B, as we saw, begins to move his right arm to the right at 713. This is at just the same moment as T begins the second of his leftward movements of his left arm. And then, B's head-cock, though it begins after the beginning of T's head movement, it begins at a boundary in T's arm and hand movements (i), and in his speech, and it ends precisely as T ends the syllable 'more', at 754. After this, B changes to a new posture (P), and he remains relatively still for most of the rest of T's discourse.

During the section we have just described it will be seen that, when B is moving, his movements are coordinated with T's movements and speech, and that in their form these movements amount in part to a "mirror image" of T's movements: As T leans back in his chair, B leans back and lifts his head; then B moves his right arm to the right, just as T moves his left arm to the left, and he follows this with a headcock to the right, just as T cocks his head to the left. We might say that here B dances T's dance. .

This period during which B partly mirrors T's movements lasts for about five seconds. At 768 he begins to move into a new posture, as already mentioned. Here he sits still with his pipe in his mouth, which he holds with his right hand, and he remains still, except for movements in the eyes, mouth, and fingers of the right hand. This position B maintains until 068 and, apart from the minor movements mentioned, he produces one complex head nod, which comes at the end of T's sixth phrase. There are two observations to be made here. First, it is to be noted that compared to the first phase we have described, there is now a relative absence of movement in B, in spite of the fact that T continues to engage in considerable movement and B continues to look at him. However, such movements as he does make, the eye blinks, eye-shifts, and mouth movements, so far as we were able to establish their boundaries, appeared to be coordinated with the patterning of T's speech. For instance, from 810 to 815 B lowers his fingers over the bowl of his pipe. This movement coincides exactly with the middle syllable of "possibly" in T's speech. Again, B moves his eyes off T to his right from 867–875. At the moment T utters the stressed syllable of "interested" however, B moves his eyes to look back at T. This is in contrast to what happens during the multiple head-nod. Here the individual up and down components of the headnod do not appear to be in synchrony with T's speech. This is of interest in that it perhaps suggests that where the listener ceases to receive what the speaker is saying, but initiates a response to it, he then organizes his behavior in his own time, not that of the speaker.

B remains in this relatively quiescent "listening" position for most of the rest of T's discourse. Then, at 068, and for the remaining part of T's discourse, he behaves in a markedly different fashion. This last part of T's discourse consists in the two final phrases of T's speech. They are introduced by the connective "but" which, in the stress it receives, and in its position between two pauses, and in the way it contrasts in pitch with the exaggerated fall in pitch over the word which terminates the preceding phrase, appears to signal that the speech that is to follow is to bring the discourse to an end. T also marks this connective kinesically, for associated with it there is a marked change in the position of his head (see fig. 5).

mate phrase, "at the same time . . ." and this, it is to be noted, is accompanied by a forward and rightward movement of the head. This movement brings T's head into a position that mirrors that of B.

What we see here appears to be the reverse of what we saw at the outset of T's discourse. There B appeared to first pause in his movements, and then mirror the movements T was already making. Here he initiates a movement, a left and forward tilt of the head, in time with a change in movement in T,

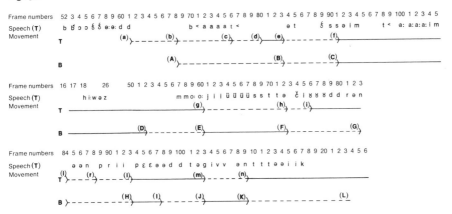

Fig. 5 Diagram to show speech and movement components between 88052 and 88224 in the T-extract of TRD 009. Explanation in text.

He tilts his head back (b) and then, as he ennunciates the "but," he tilts his head markedly left (c), and this is then followed by a forward head tilt, combined with a movement to the right, this movement being associated with the first part of the following phrase (f). At o68, which is the point at which T begins the head movement to the left that is associated with "but," B drops his eyelids over his eyes, and tilts his head markedly forward and to the left (B). He follows this at o84 with a further forward tilt of the head. This is the point at which T begins his penulti-

and this movement T then comes to mirror. At the outset, B picked up T's dance. Here, T picks up B's dance.

For the rest of the discourse B now moves his head and though, as may be seen clearly from the chart his movement components are quite synchronous with components of T's behavior, we do not now see mirroring. Instead, it is as if B is acting out a kinetic representation of certain features of T's speech. Thus, he holds still over the pauses and over T's "he was," but then lowers his head in association with "more" (E), holds still over "used to"

(F), and then tilts his head forward very markedly over "children," where T lowers the pitch of his voice (G). He then lifts his head up high over "an pre-" (H)—as if to meet the high pitch level in T's voice here—he then holds (I), then lowers his head (J), as T produces the last part of this phrase and then, at the boundary between "and" and "take" he initiates a wholly new movement pattern—head goes up, back and to the right, left hand moves out left—which is associated with the question he now puts to T (L). Note how the movements associated with asking the question begin before any vocalization, and it begins just at the point at which it becomes clear how T is going to finish.

Shortly following this question of B, T replies with a short phrase: "well I tried to," with the primary stress brought out strongly on "tried." As T gives this reply, B lowers his head and then turns it to face another participant with whom he will shortly engage. This head movement is timed to take exactly as long as T's reply. It is lowered slowly over "well I," more rapidly over "tried," and the turn to the right begins immediately afterward, and ends as T's utterance ends. Here, evidently, in one movement, B signals his disengagement with T but, as he does so, because of the way his movement is timed and shaped, he also acknowledges his receipt of T's reply.

T and B: discussion

To begin with, we have seen that the listener, B, is in synchrony, in Condon's sense, with T. Our initial aim, to describe another instance of interactional synchrony, has thus been accomplished. Secondly, however, different phases in B's movements could be observed. First B "mirrored" the move-ments of T, then he became quiescent, and then, over the last two phrases of T's speech B again moved conspicuously. Here, however, he did not pick up the movements of T. It appeared that he raised and lowered his head in relation to the rise and fall of the pitch of T's voice, and it was T who brought his head into alignment with B's head, rather than the other way around.

The phenomenon of movement mirroring, which has been observed in a number of instances in TRD 009,[6] appears to occur only between the speaker and the person he directly addresses. As in the T extract, so in the other instances examined, it occurs most conspicuously at the very beginning of an interchange. Other participants may move concurrently with the movements of speaker and listener, as the axis of interaction between them is set up, but their movements are either of quite a different form from those of the direct addressee, or else they have a different timing. By mirroring the movement of the speaker, the person directly addressed thus at once differentiates himself from the others present, and at the same time he heightens the bond that is being established between him and the speaker. For the speaker it can serve as visual confirmation that his speech is properly directed, and for the others present it can serve to clarify the way in which participant activities are being patterned.

Mirroring of movement is not continuous in conversational interaction. As we saw, B soon moved into a new position in which his movements were much reduced, though there was no change in the amplitude of T's movements. Similarly, in other examples we have looked at, the listener will shift synchronously with the speaker into a position which mirrors his initial head position, but he thereafter remains relatively still. Nonetheless we may see movement mirroring intermittently within an ongoing interchange. Thus when, in an interchange, speaker and listener mirror one another's postures, if there is a change in posture which does not reflect a change in the relationship in the interchange, such posture shifts often occur synchronously, and in these instances we may again get movement mirroring.[7] This is in contrast to those occasions when there is a change in the relationship between the participants in the interchange, for instance where one starts to ask the other questions. We may then see synchronous posture shifts, or head position shifts, but the movements are differentiated, not mirrored. An example of this occurs in TRD 009.1.24849–24941, which is described later (see p. **162**).

In the third phase of B's behavior that we distinguished, we observed that here B initiated movement, which T then came to follow. We also observed that these movements appeared to be related to the variations in pitch level of T's speech. It seems probable that these movements serve to give advanced warning that B wants to speak when T is finished and further, it may be that in overtly "beating time" to T's speech, he may thereby facilitate the precise timing of his own entry as a speaker, much as a musician may begin to move conspicuously with the music, as he readies himself to enter with his part at the right moment.

The other participants

We have described T and B as together forming an axis of interaction within an ongoing encounter. The others present are not direct participants in this axis, though they all of them are in a position to become actively involved at any time, as indeed they do. Relative to the interactional axis between T and B, these others may be referred to as the non-axial participants. It is of some interest to look at their behavior during the interchange between T and B. As we shall see, in several cases this is related to the behavior of these two, though in form it is sharply differentiated from it.

M can be dealt with quite briefly. Her posture (which may be seen in figs. 4 and 6) is maintained throughout T's discourse. She does not move, she does not nod her head or show any of the kinds of reaction we noted in B, but she looks continuously at T. This is a very typical configuration for those who are attending closely to an interchange. Examples can very easily be found, for instance in TRD 009, 1.23507–23728, where E and G1 are oriented to the axis between Th and H, they both display behavior very similar to that of M here. They sustain a particular posture with the minimum of movement, and they maintain an almost constant line of visual orientation.

G1, however, in the T-extract, does show considerable movement and this may now be compared to the behavior of T and B. When the extract begins, G1's head is sunk on his chest, with no rotation, and his right forearm lies along the arm of his chair, the hand hanging free from the wrist. The left hand is placed deep in his left jacket pocket (see fig. 4). A minor movement of his fingers of the right hand is observed concurrent with B's "yeah" and then, at 629, he turns his head right, to look at B. This head turn begins one frame after B's first "and then" has ended. G1's head remains oriented to B until 678, when he turns to look at T, and this turn begins immediately after

T's third brief vocalization [kʌ]. He then begins the first of two major shifts at 704. Here he lifts his left hand from his jacket pocket and moves it to the right, close to his body. He then moves it to the left again, to place it in his trouser pocket. At the same time, he bends his right arm at the elbow to bring his right hand, held as a loose fist, into contact with his right ear. He reaches this position at 730, coincidentally with a boundary in the behavior of both T and B. This shift, thus, fits over T's opening phrase in somewhat the same way as B's movements do but in form it is quite different from B's movements and, further, its segments do not have quite the same precise relation to T's speech as do the components of B's movements. G1 remains virtually still until 739, when his head begins to move preparatory to his second major shift. This has two segments: In the first, ending at 759, he moves his right hand down from his ear to his chin. This movement co-occurs with T and B's movement over "more" and the subsequent pause. This is maintained with some minor movements, until 766 and at 767, coincident with B's shift to his "listening" position, G1 shifts his head slightly and moves his arm away from his chin, by extension from his elbow (which rests on the arm of the chair) to a point where it is held at approximately 80° to the arm of the chair, the fingers held in a loose fist. He reaches this position at 793. close to the same point at which B reaches his listening posture. Apart from some minor movements G1 now holds this position for the rest of T's discourse (fig 6). Perhaps it is worth remarking that this position is somewhat analogous to B's position. One could imagine how G1 is holding onto the bowl of a pipe with a very long stem.

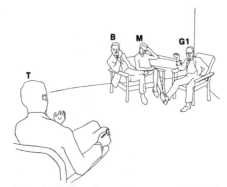

Fig. 6 Tracing from frame no. 87977 of the T-extract showing T in 'back position' and talking, B in 'listening position' and M and G1. Other participants have been omitted for the sake of clarity.

It is possible that in adopting an analogous posture G1 thus shows that he is sharing B's role as listener.[8]

Sometimes a non-axial participant will be smoking or drinking. It is of interest to observe how the movements involved may be closely coordinated with the behavior of the speaker. An example which illustrates this clearly can be found in TRD 009.1.32427, et seq. The participants are X, a donnish Lancashireman who talks at length on regional variations in the British ethos. He has an argument with N, a stocky traveling salesman with a sharp tongue and a London accent. Between these two sits an elegant and attractive girl, G, who works as a lingerie model for a London firm. G and X spend a good deal of time in close tête-à-tête, much to the apparent disgust of N, who is drawn to G. The argument between X and N is quite bitter and it is concerned with whether the British are "self-conscious" or not. It perhaps derives much of its animus from the rivalry between X and N for the attentions of G. Needless to say, it is X, with his superior airs and sophisticated Oxford talk, who wins out, and later on in the evening he and G withdraw together.

The piece dealt with here comes at the very beginning of this argument. It covers N's first entrance into discussion with X, and X's immediate reply. X has just been asked to repeat a large part of his argument for the benefit of someone on the other side of the room who has been drawn into the discussion by B. He says: "In fact we've got to go way back to the conversation in the bar, because this is what it was built up on." A slight pause follows and then he says 'um' but N enters with "self-consciousness wasn't it?" X replies: "Not entirely, it goes way back to the type of investigation our friend here is carrying out." The relations between X's speech and G's movements here are given in fig. 7. Three movement lines are used here: line 1 for the left index finger, line 2 for the left limb, and line 3 for the trunk. Segments of the diagram referred to in the following description will be specified by the line number and letter.

During the early part of X's first sentence from this stretch, G is drinking, she leans forward and places her glass on the table, just at the point where N begins "self-consciousness . . ." She remains still, hand on her glass, during this utterance (2a) but just as it finishes she withdraws her hand and moves it over to her right hand which is holding her cigarette (2b). She takes her cigarette between first and second fingers of her left hand (2c), and lifts it away from her right hand just as X begins "it goes . . ." (2d). She extends her left hand, and leans forward to position her cigarette over an ashtray which is on the table in front of her (2e, 3a). She lifts her index finger (1a), holds it momentarily (1b), raises it further (1c), brings it down sharply on the cigarette to knock off the ash (1d), holds it down on the cigarette (1e), and raises it again (1f) and then leans back in her chair again (3c, 3d). It is to be noted how the index finger is raised at the boundary between "type" and "of," how it is lowered onto the ciga-

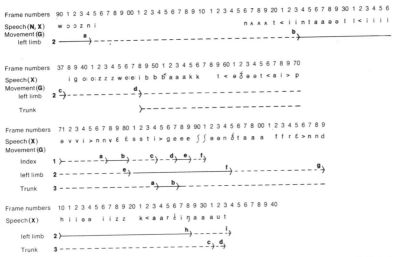

Fig. 7 Diagram to show speech of N and X and movement components of G between 32590 and 32740 from reel 1 of TRD 009. Explanation in text.

rette precisely as X utters the stressed syllable of "investigation," and how she reaches her chair again at precisely the moment he concludes with the word "out." The whole action, leaning over to tamp ash off the cigarette and leaning back again, in itself an action that has no direct social pertinence,[9] is yet done in time to the rhythm of X's speech. Subsequently, she sits, left finger touching the back of her right hand, looking at N, who now demands a definition of "self-consciousness." X then tries to answer him, in a series of measured phrases, and it is noteworthy how, at the end of each of these phrases G changes her pose somewhat. Earlier, during the first part of X's discourse we can observe her doing the same thing. She shifts her position slightly from time to time, as she sits quietly and listens to X. But these shifts in position occur at boundaries in X's speech-flow, not at random, or according to some rhythm of her own. Thus G, though not directly addressed, moves in time with the rhythm of X's behavior. These movements have no clear signal-quality, and they are quite different from the kind of movements she makes when she is turned toward S, listening to him appreciatively as he talks to her.[10]

In contrast to these instances, where the movements of the non-axial participants are clearly differentiated from those of the speaker, as well as from those of the active recipients, we may observe how, in his movement, the non-axial participant appears to be taking the part of the speaker. Thus, in TRD 009.1.24849–24941. GI and M are talking together. P is sitting next to M in a forward posture, closely attentive to their discussion. They are discussing the place of women in bars and M has been saying that she would never go into a bar on her own. GI says: "Why is this?" cocking his head sharply to his left as he does so. Concurrently, M rotates her head to her right, and down, away from GI, turning away as she formulates her answer. P, however, moves his trunk slightly to the right and forward, a trunk movement which is analogous to GI's head movement. Other examples have been noted in RFP 001.61. This is a psychotherapy film in which there are three participants, the patient (a male), the therapist and the patient's (male) nurse. On several occasions when the therapist questions the patient, concurrent movement may be seen in the nurse. For example at 01140 et seq., E (the therapist) is trying to get the patient to remember how many times they have met, and he counts out the occasions on his fingers. Concurrently the nurse moves his fingers in a way which looks very like a highly abbreviated version of the therapist's movements.

In both of these instances, there is a sharp differentiation in the roles of the speaker and active recipient. The relationship is interrogatory. In many situations, of course, the identity of the non-axial participant with the speaker's role is much more conspicuous, indeed it may be formulated in seating positions, clothing, and in the explicit ritual of the occasion as in interviewing committees or committees of inquiry where there is one witness and many questioners. Here we often find one individual who is said to speak for all of the others, while the others sit beside the speaker sharing, sometimes in a more restrained fashion, his postures and demeanor.

To return, once again, to the T extract, it is worth looking, briefly, at the behavior of P and L. These two differ from the others present, in that for

much of the T-extract they are not attending to the prevailing interactional
axis, but are engaged in a little interchange of their own. In this interchange, L offers a cigar to P. which P
takes, and L then lights P's cigar, then
his own, and they they both turn their
attention to T. Of interest here is the
way P and L's behavior is coordinated
first with one another in a reciprocal
fashion and then with T.

We do not see the beginning of this
interchange between P and L. At 591,
when the T-extract opens, L is already
fumbling in his jacket pocket for his ci-
gars, and P is fully turned to L. P follows with his eyes the progress of the
cigar box as L opens it and moves it
over to P to offer him one. P takes a
cigar, and as he does so, L withdraws
the cigar box to take one himself. P
then holds his cigar, eyes still on L,
and does not move to put it in his
mouth until L does so—an interesting
instance of how two people in interaction will keep their actions in pace with
one another, even where such a temporal coordination is not essential for
the maintenance of the interchange. L
then moves over with a flame to light
P's cigar, and P's movement is nicely
coordinated here with L's movement as
he brings the flame. P then draws on
his cigar as L is lighting his own, and
blows smoke from his mouth. He then
turns to L who, having got his cigar
going now turns his attention to T. P
then also turns to T, and it is noteworthy that as he does so he changes
his posture somewhat, coming to rest
his head on his fist. What is of particular interest here, however, is that the
movements of P and L, though now
not reciprocal and quite different in
form, nonetheless are synchronous—
boundaries of their components coincide, that is. It is as if they are both

dancing to the same beat, though the
movements they make are quite different. This analogy is not too far fetched.
They are now both attending to T and,
in doing so they both move synchronously with him and hence synchronously with each other.

In the behavior of P and L, thus, we
can observe a variety of the ways in
which two people may interrelate their
activities, which are different from
those we have already considered. Thus
P's movements are synchronous with
those of L as he follows or tracks L's
movements. P and L move in a reciprocal coordination, as when L moves
the cigar box over to P, and P moves
over to take a cigar; or when L moves
over with a lighter, and P leans forward to meet the flame. P waits for L
to begin carrying his cigar to his
mouth, before putting his own in, so
keeping pace with L. Finally, at the
end, P and L's movements are synchronized not through their attention to
each other, but through their common
attention to a single focus.

It may be worth noting that the interchange between P and L is initiated
in association with the beginning of a
unit of interaction, the T-B axis. This
is but one instance of a phenomenon
that is recurrent in this film, and which
is probably characteristic of the behaviour of non-axial participants generally.
That is, gross posture shifts, and actions pertaining to sub-involvements
such as drinking or smoking, tend to
occur in association with points of
change in the interactional structure of
the gathering. Typically, when someone
stops speaking and another begins, if
this is in the same axis, we see orientation changes in several of the others. In
addition, sips of drinks are taken, if
glasses are already in hand, and puffs
on cigarettes are taken, if these have al-

ready been lit. Where there is a change in who is talking with whom, a change in the interchange or interactional axis, that is, or where the whole direction of the interaction changes, we see larger changes in the participants. Gross shifts of posture occur, cigarettes or pipes are lighted, or glasses are drained or put down, or glasses are picked up. Often such actions by non-axial participants are not simultaneous, but they occur in sequence, as if each triggers the next. This seems to occur in particular where only some of the non-axial participants are attending to an axis which changes, while others are attending elsewhere. In this case, the gross posture shift, or drink or smoke of one, will be picked up by another, and then another, and we see a series of such actions going round the circle.

A number of examples of this phenomenon have been collected, but a more thorough analysis will be reserved for another report. Gatherings vary in the degree to which the attentional foci of those present are coordinated and it may be that the level of joint involvement in a gathering may be gauged by the tightness of clustering of posture shifts, and actions related to sub-involvements like drinking or smoking. Where there is tight clustering, the attentional involvements of the participants are probably more closely coordinated, than where it is loose. In this case the occasion would be said to be more diffuse. Furthermore, for any given individual his degree of "presence" in the gathering may perhaps be gauged by the degree to which his posture shifts, and other actions, are coordinated with those that occur in others present.

Conclusions

In this paper an attempt has been made to give detailed descriptions of the way in which the behavior of speakers and listeners are interrelated. We have had three aims. First we wanted to describe some further instances of the phenomenon of interactional synchrony, as this has been described by Condon. Secondly, we wanted to see if there was any patterning in the listener's flow of movements that could be described in terms of the way it is related to the speaker's movements. Thirdly, we have attempted to contrast the behavior of the listener who is directly addressed by a speaker, with the behavior of those who are participants, but who are not directly involved in the interchange.

In the examples described we have illustrated interactional synchrony, and we have seen that it may occur, even when the individuals who are 'synchronous' with one another are not looking at each other. This suggests that the coordination of the listener's movements with the behavior of the speaker is brought about through the listener's response to the stream of speech. Where, as we saw in the behavior of B, the listener imposes an organization on his movements which 'fit' with those of the speaker, visual input is clearly being used, but for interactional synchrony to arise it is evidently sufficient for the listener to hear the speech of the speaker.

The precision with which the listener's movements are synchronized with the speaker's speech means that the listener is in some way able to anticipate what the speaker is going to say, as indeed current work on speech perception leads us to expect.[11] This work tends to support the analysis-by-synthesis theory of speech perception. On this theory, it is supposed that the listener samples input from the speaker intermittently and then, on the basis of these samples, constructs a version of the message which he then checks against later inputs. He can be said to construct a running hypothesis about what the speaker will be saying a moment hence. In this way, if his construction of what the speaker is saying is correct, his present understanding of the speaker can coincide precisely with what the speaker is saying, as in a tracking task, where precise tracking is possible only if the tracker is able to make predictions about the course the target will take (Poulton, 1957). If we allow that cognitive processes and bodily movement are interrelated, we may expect that the processes involved in the processing of speech by a listener may affect his movements or even be marked in movement. This seems especially likely here where there is such a close relationship between movement and speech production, and where, in listening, so many of the same mechanisms are probably involved.

It is to be noted that the analysis-by-synthesis theory of speech perception allows for flexibility in the size of the speech unit that is processed. The listener can synthesize expected units of speech in terms of syllables, phrases, or larger semantic units. It seems probable, indeed, that this process of synthesis goes on at several of these levels at once. It would be interesting to know if the listener marks in movement differentially the size of the unit of speech he is processing. If this were so it might be possible to gather from his patterning of movements his level of comprehension of the speech.

There is much more about interactional synchrony we would like to know, as need hardly be said. For example, we know nothing about the conditions in which it does not arise. Clearly, for it to arise the listener must pay some degree of attention to the speech, but it would be important to know what degree this must be. We may presume that it will be that level that is required for comprehension of the speech, perhaps as much as is needed for someone to "shadow" the speech. This will also mean that we may not find interactional synchrony where the rhythmical features of the speech are unfamiliar to the listener, or where he cannot understand the words, either because of their unfamiliarity, or because of a high noise level. Questions of this sort are clearly open to experimental exploration.

The other main question of interest, of course, and the one that has chiefly informed the present inquiry, is the possible function of interactional synchrony in the process of interaction itself. Much of the listener's movement may be perceived by the speaker and it may, just insofar as it is a symptom of the listener's comprehension, form an important source of feedback for him. There are additional possibilities, however. In an experiment by Argyle et al. (1968) it was found, among other things, that an interactant A, would feel more uncomfortable in an interaction the less easily he could see his partner, only in the condition where his partner at all times could easily see him. If he could not be seen by his partner, the ease with which he could see his partner made no difference to his comfort. A possible interpretation of this finding is that a speaker needs information about his listener to enable him to regulate those aspects of his behavior that are visible to his partner. In other words, where vision can be used in interaction it becomes important to the interactants that there is a mutual regulation of movement, as well as a pacing of utterances. It seems probable that the synchronization of movements in interaction is important because this is one of the means by which is achieved that delicate coordination of expectancies among participants, so essential to the smooth running of an encounter.[12] This becomes particularly important at those points where an interchange is being established, and where it is to be disbanded, and it is perhaps for this reason that we found that shared rhythmicity in movement was most conspicuous at the beginning and at the end of the interchange. To *move* with another is to show that one is "with" him in one's attentions and expectancies. Coordination of movement in interaction may thus be of great importance since it provides one of the ways in which two people signal that they are "open" to one another, and not to others.

NOTES

1. The work described in this paper was done in 1967 while I was a Visiting Research Fellow at the Western Psychiatric Institute and Clinic, Pittsburgh, Pennsylvania. I am very grateful to Dr. Henry W. Brosin, who made this visit possible, and to Dr. William S. Condon, who gave me a thorough introduction to his discoveries and methods of analysis. I am also indebted to Dr. Ray L. Birdwhistell for some valuable discussions, and to Dr. Albert E. Scheflen for his help and encouragement. Prof. J. J. Gibson and U. Neisser offered useful comments on an earlier draft of this paper. Valuable comments were also made by Dr. Aviva Menkes.

2. The film used is known as TRD 009, English pub scene. It was made in London by Dr. Ray L. Birdwhistell and Mr. Jacques van Vlack, and produced by the Commonwealth of Pennsylvania with the assistance of the Institute of Intercultural Studies. Copies are de-

posited at the film library at Studies in Human Communication, Eastern Pennsylvania Psychiatric Institute, Philadelphia, where they may be viewed by interested persons. Dr. Birdwhistell very kindly provided me with background information about the filming and the persons observed in the film.

3. This term is taken from Goffman (1963). Goffman's ideas have been made use of in many places in this paper, too many places for it to be possible to make specific acknowledgement.

4. Each frame of the film is numbered. Sequences from films will be referred to by reference number or title of film, followed by the reel number (where appropriate), followed by the frame numbers. When frame numbers are referred to in the course of a discussion of a specific sequence, only the last three digits are given.

5. Scheflen (1964) was the first to point out that when an interactant changes his mode of participation in an interaction, he generally alters his posture in a fairly substantial fashion at the boundary of this change. In T's case, there are other examples in TRD 009 in which he changes from "sitting forward" to "sitting back," in both cases prior to taking the floor as a "discourser." For an account of another example of this, see Kendon (1969).

6. Instances of movement mirroring associated with the establishment of an axis of interaction have been observed, for example, in TRD 009.2.23507 et seq., TRD 009.1. 24577 et seq., and GB-SU-008 (the Doris-therapist film).

7. A good example can be observed in TRD 009.2.71810-71970 where G and Th, who have constituted an axis for some time and who maintain postural congruence throughout, readjust their postures simultaneously, still keeping con-

gruence. This occurs at what is certainly a point of change in the axis, but it occurs within the axis, not at its boundaries.

8. Compare Scheflen's (1964) observations on the significance of postural parallelism.

9. It is sometimes argued that all behavior in the presence of others is "socially pertinent" to the extent that it provides information to others. This is, of course, true. Nevertheless one must distinguish between behavior which is specialized for social interaction, such as talking, gesticulating, and certain kinds of postural adjustment, and behavior which is non-specialized for interaction, of which smoking is an example. Such interactively non-specialized behavior may, of course, be coordinated into the interaction, as in the example described here, and in this way it may come to have some interactional *function*. This should, however, be kept distinct from whether the behavior is also specialized for that function.

10. This may be observed through much of reel 2 of TRD 009.

11. A useful, if somewhat brief survey of the work in speech perception is to be found in Neisser (1967). A very clear exposition of the analysis-by-synthesis model for speech perception is also to be found in this book.

12. See for example, Goffman (1957, 1961).

REFERENCES

Argyle, M., M. Lalljee and M. Cook, 1968. The effect of visibility on interaction in a dyad. *Hum. Relat.* 21, 3–17.

Bateson, G., GB-SU-008 'Doris therapy film', 16 mm black and white. In: Studies in Human Communication Film Library, Philadelphia: Eastern Pennsylvania Psychiatric Institute.

Birdwhistell, R. L. and J. van Vlack, 1964. TRD 009 'English pub scene', 16 mm black and white. Commonwealth of Pennsylvania and Institute of Intercultural Studies. In: Studies in Human Communication Film Library, Philadelphia, Pa.: Eastern Pennsylvania Psychiatric Institute.

Boyd, H. B. and S. W. Banks, 1965. *An outline of the treatment of fractures.* American College of Surgeons, 8th ed. Philadelphia: W. B. Saunders Co.

Condon, W. S. and W. D. Ogston, 1966. Sound film analysis of normal and pathological behavior patterns. *J. Nerv. Ment. Dis.* 143, 338–347.

————and————, 1967. A segmentation of behavior. *J. Psychiat. Res.* 5, 221–235.

Goffman, E., 1961. *Encounters: two studies in the sociology of interaction.* Indianapolis: Bobbs-Merril.

————, 1957. Alienation from interaction. *Hum. Relat.* 10, 47–60.

————, 1963. *Behavior in public places.* New York: The Free Press of Glencoe.

Greenspoon, J., 1962. Verbal conditioning and clinical psychology. In: A. Bachrach (ed.), *Experimental foundations of clinical psychology.* New York: Basic Books.

Gross, L. E., 1959. Effects of verbal and non-verbal reinforcement in the Rorschach. *J. Consult. Psychol.* 23, 66–68.

Kendon, A., 1970. Some relationships between body motion and speech: an analysis of an example. In: A. Siegman and B. Pope (eds.), *Studies in dyadic communication.* New York: Pergamon Press.

Matarazzo, J. D., G. Saslow, A. N. Wiens, M. Weitman and B. V. Allen, 1964. Interviewer headnodding and interviewee speech durations. *Psychother. Res. Theory* 1, 54–63.

Neisser, U., 1967. *Cognitive psychology*. New York: Appleton-Century-Crofts.

Poulton, E. C., 1957. On prediction in skilled movements. *Psychol. Bull.* 54, 467–478.

Reece, M. M. and N. R. Whitman, 1962. Expressive movement, warmth and verbal reinforcement. *J. Abnorm. Soc. Psychol.* 64, 234–236.

Scheflen, A. E., 1964. The significance of posture in communication systems. *Psychiatry* 27, 316–321.

———, R. L. Birdwhistell and J. van Vlack, 1961. RFP 001–61, Research in Filmed Psychotherapy Series, Philadelphia, Pa.: Eastern Pennsylvania Psychiatric Institute.

Wickes, T. A., 1956. Examiner influence in a testing situation. *J. Consult. Psychol.* 20, 23–25.

12

THE BODY MOVEMENT-SPEECH RHYTHM
RELATIONSHIP AS A CUE TO SPEECH ENCODING

ALLEN T. DITTMANN

We have by now a good many data on when people move with respect to the rhythmical stream of speech—certainly more than originally anticipated. The implications of what we have learned have relevance to two areas of investigation which do not seem on the surface to be very closely related: the first is emotional expression and the second is psycholinguistics. Emotional expression has been my research interest for some time, and most of my empirical work on body movements has been done in the context of research on interview behavior. The method of studying these movements has been to count their frequency rather than to try to determine their individual meanings. The work can thus most properly be referred to as research in nervousness or fidgetiness. D.S. Boomer of our laboratory has been the local expert in psycholinguistics. He is one of the handful of psychologists in the field who has learned something about linguistics and, more importantly in the context of this report, about speech and its production. But psycholinguistics has lured many workers away from their accustomed paths and this chapter is mainly concerned with work I have done in that field.

The trouble with counting little nervous movements in interviews is that the people are talking while they are fidgeting, and talking casts a shadow over everything else a person does at the same time. Everybody knows this at some level, so it is not a point worth belaboring. What is not known is how much this shadow affects different activities—fidgeting in this case—and this is what we started out to learn. Maybe these little movements are so bound up with the act of talking that there is no point to trying to use them as measures to get at other things, like changing emotional states. In brief, the answer is that by our methods of measurement there is a statistically significant, but not very close relationship between speech and body movement

From *Studies in Dyadic Communication*, A. W. Siegman and B. Pope, eds., Pergamon Press, New York, 1972, pp. 135–51. Copyright © 1972 by Pergamon Press, Inc., and reprinted by permission.

—not close enough to preclude the study of each independently in interview research. In the course of finding this answer, something new was learned about the relationship: that studying movements in detail could throw some light on the act of speaking, or on how speakers get their ideas into words and listeners get those words back into ideas. This is the psycholinguistic aspect of the work.

Movement and speech output

Let us begin with a brief review of how the answer summarized above was found, then go on to what has been done since we found it. The aspect of speech we have been working on is its rhythmical characteristic, its prosodic nature. This does not mean the tone of voice, which would be very useful to get at more precisely, but the repetitive alteration of features like stress and endings by which the stream of speech is divided up into neat little packages. One such package, which we feel is the least common denominator of rhythm in talking, is known as the phonemic clause, originally described by Trager and Smith in 1951. We believe that it is important to have such a handle on speech rhythm because of our conceptualization of the twin tasks of encoding by the speaker and decoding by the listener. We reason that rhythm is produced by the speaker as a by-product of his ongoing task of casting his thoughts into speech and that it provides important clues to the listener in his ongoing task of understanding— perhaps even hearing—what the speaker has said. I shall refer only briefly to studies of the listener and speech rhythm in this report, and focus on what has been found out about the speaker.

The body movement and the speech studies in our laboratory went their separate ways for some time, because while it was suspected that there might be some relationships between the two, we had no easy methodological bridges between them. Boomer forced the issue in 1963 by finding that certain speech characteristics derived from Mahl's work were correlated with body movement frequencies in interview passages chosen (Dittmann, 1962) to represent different feeling states or moods. This sent us down statistical and experimental paths (Boomer and Dittmann, 1964) to determine the nature of the relationship and led us to conclude that speech and body movement were not correlated except when there was parallel variation in feeling state. But there was doubt about this conclusion because of the common knowledge that people move when they speak.

It seemed, then, that we were involved in a paradox. On the one hand, there was experimental evidence that speech and movement are not related in the absence of differences in feeling state. On the other hand, we knew that speech is accompanied by movements, a fact which every layman recognizes and some professionals have studied. Laymen have made up sayings about it in the course of making passing, usually ethnocentric remarks, such as that Neapolitans can be made mute by tying their hands behind their backs. The professionals who have tried studying these phenomena are Renneker (1963), Ekman, (1965, 1968), Condon and Ogston (1966, 1967), Freedman and Hoffman (1967), and now Kendon of this conference, in order of their appearance. The seeming paradox to be faced, our experimental evidence versus common sense and professional opinion, had this in common with most other paradoxes: the two propositions were based on different ways of looking at the same material. In this experiment, and in Boomer's work which led us to do the experiment, the units of analysis were quite long, one and one-half minutes in the original study, and three minutes in the experiment. Units as long as these mask the detailed interplay among factors within the units. The figures we were putting into our analyses were total occurrences of movements and of words or other speech characteristics for the entire duration of each unit. The very length of the units made us miss the ebb and flow of movements which seem to accompany speech.

Hesitations and speech rhythm

A very different approach was provided by Boomer's (1965) study of the relationship between a much smaller unit and hesitation forms in speech, the first study relating to speech encoding in our laboratory. Here the unit of analysis was the phonemic clause, and the basic data for the study took the form of the order of events within that unit. In the passage below are four phonemic clauses, one per line, which include all of the characteristics necessary to illustrate the unit. The subject, a college student, is talking about his high school newspaper days and, in the course of this passage, he has divided his speech into four neat little packages. Pauses are non-phonations of 200 ms or more, measured on an oscillographic record of the speech. We chose 200 ms on rational grounds, dictated by the results of an earlier experiment (Boomer and Dittmann, 1962). There we found by standard psychophysical methods that the threshold for discriminating hesitation pauses, that is, pauses separating

forms within a phonemic clause, was about 200 ms. Juncture pauses, non-phonations between clauses, have much higher thresholds and the 200 ms definition of pause will, of course, also include them. There are hesitation pauses in all but the third clause in the passage below, and juncture pauses between the first and second and between the second and third. It is important to note, incidentally, that marking pauses by listening to the tape will miss many hesitation pauses close to threshold and many more juncture pauses of comparable length , according to our results.

and ah (pause) we would print
(pause) ah (pause) by the offset process
(pause) which isn't with a press
it's a (pause) photographic process

We call a "fluent clause" one which has no non-fluencies within it. Juncture pauses are not counted as non-fluencies, so the third clause in our example is the only fluent one. Hesitation pauses, the ones other than juncture pauses, both filled and unfilled, are considered non-fluencies. A filled pause is usually an "ah," and it may be accompanied by additional non-phonation, as they are in our first two clauses above. Other non-fluencies are false starts, retraces and the like, but hesitation pauses are by far the most frequent.

Boomer found that if you look at hesitations from the vantage point of the phonemic clause, you see that they tend to bunch up toward the beginnings of the clauses. The most frequent location for a pause, in fact, is after the first word, as it is in the first clause in this example. In Figure 1 their distribution is plotted against a chance curve. This latter is simply the proportion of possible places between words in phonemic clauses where a pause might occur. It is a decreasing function, be-

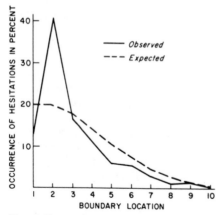

Fig. 1 Comparison of percentages of hesitations occurring at successive boundary locations with those expected by chance. (After Boomer, 1965.)

cause every clause in the sample has at least two words (one-word clauses, an infrequent occurrence, were excluded) and thus two possible places for a pause, while only longer clauses had later word boundary positions. The modal clause in this sample, incidentally, had five words. The difference between these curves is quite large—the Chi Square is well over 300. It is made up mostly of that obvious peak at the second position, which contributes three quarters of the total Chi Square.

Movement and speech rhythm

Boomer's study, then, showed that speakers hesitate toward the beginnings of the little packages in which they divide up their speech. Later, we will return to what this has to do with speech encoding, but only after an explanation of how Llewellyn and I (1969) used this study as a model for investigating movements during speech. The speech sample Boomer used came from the sixteen subjects in the experiment done earlier to prove that speech and movement were unrelated. The method of

tabulating the data from different sources in the experiment was to enter everything on a master typescript of the speech. Movies were made of the sessions with our subjects, and the first part of every session was a base-line condition in which the subject gave a three-minute monologue about hobbies, sports, or anything else that interested him. We looked at these movies and entered the discrete body movements onto the typescript at the words where they occurred. The speech sample was also segmented into phonemic clauses during the data analysis phase of the experiment—it was this segmentation which Boomer used later in his study of hesitations.

A look at the clauses with the movements entered indicated a trend toward bunching reminiscent of that for hesitations, a trend at least worth looking at further. There seemed to be a difference in the bunching, though: movements were not concentrated simply at the beginnings of clauses, but rather at the beginnings of fluent speech, be this when the speaker gets started on a clause or when he gets started after some non-fluency within the clause. Our same four clauses with the movements entered show these relationships.

And ah (pause) we would print
Foot   Head   Foot
              Hand

(pause) ah (pause) by the offset process
                        Head
                        Hand

(pause) which isn't with a press
              Head

It's a (pause) photographic process
              Head   Head
              Hand   Foot

Notice that in the third clause, the one fluent example, there is a head movement at the first word. In the second clause there are head and hand movements on the first word after the hesitation. These were called 'Start Positions." We also included the pauses themselves under this rubric—there are movements at Start Positions, then, in all four of these clauses. Non-Start Positions provided comparative data. There are two Non-Start Positions in the first clause, at "would" and at "print," and there is a movement on one of these. It is clear from this illustration that we could count Start Positions and Non-Start Positions for each subject, then tabulate the number of movements at each and do some statistical analysis. The results were quite clear-cut: while about 40 percent of the possible positions were Start Positions, 54 percent of the movements occurred there.

Two more studies were done following up on these results: first, because it was felt that more precise instrumentation was called for to eliminate possible bias in the data gathering and second, because we wanted to know if these trends would hold up within individuals over a number of sessions spanning several weeks. Our instrumentation also enabled us to obtain considerably longer speech samples per subject and thus to extend the generality of the results. We conducted two fifteen-minute conversational interviews with each of a dozen subjects for the first follow-up, and a dozen such sessions covering eight weeks with each of two subjects for the second. The instrumentation left little chance for our wishes or hopes to influence the recording of speech rhythms and movement; movements were sensed by accelerometers and written out by event markers on a strip chart alongside an oscillogram of the concurrent speech. The results of the

follow-up were in the same direction as in the original study and a bit more pronounced: the proportion of Start Positions in the speech should have led us to expect 41 percent of the movements to be Start movements; we obtained 59 percent. The Chi Square was over 1200—but then our total N was over 8700 movements and Chi Square is notoriously related to N. To find out how much difference all this made, we converted the movement data to rates and did analyses of variance. The effect of location within clause was highly significant, of course, but for both the original study and the first follow-up it accounted for only about seven percent of the movement variance. Individual differences among subjects was the largest single source of variance— larger than all of the sundry error terms combined. The range shows how wide these differences were: one subject recorded only 40 movements on our apparatus, while another moved 1934 times! But no matter how few or how many movements a subject produced, the location of the movements was the same for every subject: significantly more frequent at Start Positions than might be expected from the structure of their speech. The same was true of the longer period of time within subjects represented in the second follow-up study.

These relationships may be seen in Figure 2 in the same terms of the earlier graph of Boomer's findings. This and the next one are based on a random sample of only 200 clauses, so the curves are not as smooth as the ones from Boomer's study—he used almost four times as many clauses. Here we see how the 117 fluent clauses look, that is, more than expected at the Start Positions, juncture pause, and first word, and fewer or about the same at

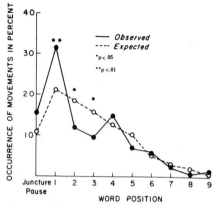

Fig. 2 Percentage of movements in fluent phonemic clauses at successive word positions compared with those expected by chance. (After Dittmann and Llewellyn, 1969.)

the subsequent ones. The 83 non-fluent clauses are shown in Figure 3. Again the same patterns obtain, but the only significant difference for this small sample is at the first word following the non-fluency.

Speech encoding and decoding

All of the research discussed so far may be summarized by stating, as I did at the beginning, that there is a "significant" but not very close relationship between speech rhythm and body movement. Both hesitations in speech and body movements tend to appear early in phonemic clauses and, in addition, movements tend to follow hesitations wherever they may appear in clauses. Now, what about encoding? Boomer's study of hesitations arose from a happy serendipity while he was looking for some unit larger than the word to use in analyzing conversational speech. The word is very neat and handy in written language, but often seems not to exist when you listen to people talk. Boomer had a new typescript made of some speech which had already been segmented into phonemic clauses. The form of the new typing was the one seen in our first illustrative passage—one clause per line. It was obvious on looking at the first page of this revised typescript that the pauses could be found mainly along the left-hand margin. A number of things seemed suddenly to add up, such as Lounsbury's (1954) hypothesis that hesitation is a sign that the speaker is having encoding problems, either in mak-

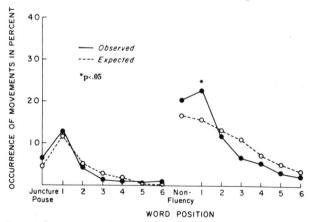

Fig. 3 Percentages of movements in nonfluent phonemic clauses at successive word positions compared with those expected by chance. (After Dittmann and Llewellyn, 1969.)

ing a lexical choice or in casting it into the right syntactic form—or both, since the two are intimately tied together. The lexical item, the word with the highest information value in the clause, ordinarily falls at the end, and the function words, the low-information ones which serve as glue to the successive high-information words, precede it. The lexical word is the one which has the strongest stress in the clause, overriding the syllable stress within words. Looking back at the first clause in the four-clause speech sample, we see that it has one unusual word, "print." It was stressed as this student was talking. The other words are common ones, that is, common to many clauses, and serve to cast "print" into the proper syntactic relationship to the next lexical item, "offset process." Incidentally, "Offset process" is a good example of how the word is a written phenomenon, not a spoken one. It is one of those adjective-noun pairs which go together as one thing, or piece of meaning. Some of these are written as one word, like "gearbox" and "flywheel." Others are written separately, like "transmission housing" and "offset process." And still others have to be looked up in the dictionary to find the current convention on whether they are supposed to be *one word* or not.

This is what is meant, then, by a unit larger than the word: a unit which contains both meaning and syntax. Boomer argued that it may well be the fundamental chunk which people use to cast ideas into words. The unit has a certain functional unity to it, too, the most thoroughly investigated evidence for which is Boomer and Laver's (1968) work on tongue slips. These are not only the Freudian slips, but also the many misarticulations where the

speaker simply gets his sounds out of order. For the most part they are not noticed by either speaker or listener, both of whom do a sort of continuous editing job as they are conversing. Slips turn out to have a good deal of lawfulness about them, and the main laws are about how the form of the slips fits in with the structure of the phonemic clause. First, the interfering element is almost always the main lexical item in the clause, the stressed word. Second, the phonetic interaction which gives rise to tongue slips usually involves the primary-stressed word and another word in the same clause. In the exceptions—something less than a tenth of all instances—the interaction is between the primary-stressed words of contiguous clauses. This last finding, rare as its examples may be, points out that the phonemic clause is not the only encoding unit. There are undoubtedly larger groupings of clauses or of somethings, otherwise we should only be able to talk very haltingly, if at all. People are constantly planning ahead as they speak and they seem to plan ahead in terms of chunks which include both lexical and syntactic material. The phonemic clause is the smallest chunk which can include both.

Our work on decoding indicates that the same unit is used by listeners as they translate back from speech. In one study (Dittmann and Llewellyn, 1967), it was found that listeners inserted both the familiar "Mm-hmmm," and also more extended comments almost exclusively (about 10:1) between phonemic clauses. The large majority of listener responses occurred at pauses and of these, an even larger proportion (about 20:1) were at juncture pauses as compared with hesitation pauses. In a subsequent study (Dittmann and Llewellyn, 1968) which included another listener response, the head nod, the total response rate at junctures as compared with other locations was about 15:1, while that of head nods alone was surprisingly over 50:1! Thus the listener apparently waits until the end of the clause before acknowledging that he has understood or even that he has been listening to what the speaker has had to say. It should be noted in passing that the phonemic clause has not found its way as a unit of speech into a large body of research, possibly because of doubts on the part of investigators about its reliability. These results should be reassuring on this score: a large number of subjects with no formal linguistic training have shown in these two studies that they are able to identify the unit with considerable accuracy.[1]

A further analysis

Let us return now to the significant but not close relationship between these rhythmical units of speech and concurrent movements. The point of getting all these facts about the relationship was to find out how counts of nervous, fidgety movements might be affected. To say that they won't be affected very much is comforting, but the details are of interest in themselves from a psycholinguistic standpoint. Even though the relationship is not close, the production of movements is not random over time in the stream of speech. Movements are thus not, in communication terms, a constant information source. Rather, the information value of any movement depends partly upon the amount of movement which the individual produces over the long run and partly upon what has happened just before it. In our latest look at the data, we have tried to determine how much information about movements is wasted

in redundancy at different points in the phonemic clause. To do this, we have studied the sequential probabilities of the movements as they relate to the rhythmical structure of the clause. Refer back once again to the four clauses we have been using as an example for an explanation of how this is done. In the first clause, the first movement is the foot movement which, so far as the rhythm of the clause is concerned, occurs at the time of the first word. From the standpoint of that movement, the next one occurs—or, in this case, the next ones occur—at the time of the filled pause following the first word. From the standpoint of these movements, in turn, the next one is on the word "would," the material following the non-fluency, and so on. Note that movements of all body areas are included indiscriminately in this analysis because, in the earlier study, we found only very small differences among body areas in the movement-rhythm relationship. Note, too, that in this sequential analysis only one-step sequences are considered: given the location of one movement, what is the location of the next movement following it? Considering three at a time, that is, seeing where the third movement would fall given the location of the first two, leads to a much more complicated analysis but one which could conceivably be done with a larger body of data.

The terms of the analysis are those of the rhythmical components of the phonemic clause. Since the rhythm is interrupted by non-fluencies, these components must be listed separately for fluent and non-fluent clauses. Fluent clauses have only three components which are relevant to rhythm: the juncture pause (if any), the main body of the clause, and the last part of the clause which has to do with the stressed word and the juncture. About four-fifths of stressed words are located just before the juncture (Dittmann and Llewellyn, 1969), so the stress and end of the clause are considered a single component of rhythm in this analysis. In non-fluent clauses a similar breakdown yields five rhythmical components: again the juncture pause (if any), the material preceding the non-fluency, the non-fluency itself, the material following the non-fluency, and the stress or end. These are not necessarily mutually exclusive categories in the real world—the stressed word, for example, is occasionally the only material following the non-fluency—but while coding we must act as if they were. Code numbers were assigned to movements as they were located at these different rhythmical components, 1, 2, and 3, to those of the fluent clauses and 4 through 8, to those of the non-fluent clauses. The number 9 was assigned to the end-of-clause marker, the juncture. A computer was instructed to take the movements in successive overlapping pairs, make several decisions about them and enter them into the necessary tables for further work. Given a first movement at a juncture pause preceding a fluent clause and a second one in the main body of the same clause, for example, the computer made a tally in the appropriate cell of the table. The possible locations for a second movement were the various rhythmical components of the same clause, those of the next following clause and a general category called "later." This last category was included because preliminary work indicated that very few second movements fell beyond the following clause and breaking these down into rhythmical components would produce numbers too small to be stable even with large total *Ns*.

The material analyzed in this way consisted of the two fifteen-minute interviews from each of twelve college students from the Dittmann and Llewellyn (1969) study, plus the first two interviews of the two longer-term students, some data from which were included in that same report. The material thus comprises seven hours of talking, all in a deliberately relaxed conversational atmosphere. For this analysis, all movements were coded from a total of 8526 phonemic clauses, of which 5547 were fluent and 2979 were non-fluent by our definition. As we might expect from the earlier analysis, there are only half as many movements in fluent clauses as there are in non-fluent ones: .79 movements per fluent as compared with 1.59 movements per non-fluent clause.

The most striking result of the sequential analysis of these movements is the way movements tend to bunch up in non-fluent clauses and to be spread out in fluent ones. Given a first movement in a fluent clause, the next movement following it is about as likely to be in the same clause as in any of the ones succeeding it. Not so in the case of non-fluent clauses. Where the first movement occurs in one of those clauses, the second is about twice as likely to appear within the same clause. The results are shown in Figure 4. We see the movements in fluent clauses are followed by next movements as a decreasing function of the passage of time, a seemingly linear function as graphed, although, of course, the abscissa is not by any means an interval scale of time. Non-fluent clauses, on the other hand, show a quite different set of relationships between first and second movements, with a large proportion of second movements falling in the same clause at the expense of both

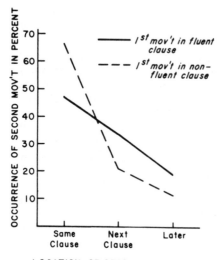

Fig. 4 Sequential probabilities of pairs of successive movements beginning in fluent and non-fluent phonemic clauses.

the next clause and all subsequent locations. In terms of amount of information bound up in the relationship between speech and movement, there is very little in fluent clauses and considerably more in non-fluent ones. The proportions of second movements in the different locations in Figure 4 yield figures of 5.3 percent redundancy for fluent clauses, and 21.9 percent for non-fluent ones.

One might argue that these findings are artifacts of the length of the clauses. Fluent clauses must by definition be shorter, since they contain none of the time-consuming non-fluencies, especially pauses, which characterize non-fluent clauses. Thus there would be more time for second movements to occur within non-fluent clauses. Indeed there is a significant and sizeable difference in length between the two types of clause. The average fluent clause takes about 1.2 seconds to say, while non-fluent clauses average about 2.0 sec-

onds, a difference large enough to lend credence to the artifact hypothesis but not to account fully for the results depicted in Figure 4. If we examine the various rhythmical positions within the clauses, we see that the rapid succession of movements centers around the non-fluency iteslf. Consider for this purpose only those pairs of movements which are confined to the same clause. If the first movement occurs before the non-fluency, the next movement will follow in 73 percent of cases, either also before the non-fluency or during the non-fluency. Among movement pairs where the first movement coincides with the non-fluency, 54 percent of second movements appear at the same non-fluent part of the clause. These percentages of second movements at the non-fluency must be evaluated in the light of the amount of time taken up by the non-fluency in the clause; it averages 31 percent of the total clause time. Thus movements are concentrated at the non-fluency to a greater extent than should be expected, and it is for this reason that second movements are more likely to be confined to the same clause: where the first movement occurs just before or at the same time as the non-fluency, the next movement is very likely to appear in the same clause—84 and 80 percent of the time, respectively, with redundancies of 50.2 and 41.5 percent.

In those cases where the first movement follows the non-fluency, the pattern of the second movement almost reverts to that of the fluent clause: 60 percent of second movements fall in the same clause (14.5 percent redundancy), as compared with 56 percent of those following first movements in the main body of the fluent clause (10.9 percent redundancy). This small but significant difference indicates that the non-fluency still holds some sway over the movement pattern even after the speaker has got started to finish the rest of the clause.

The little movements which our accelerometers can detect, then, appear to be a constant source of information at some times during speech and not at others, and this depends on what is happening to the speech. Non-fluencies interrupt not only the speech itself, but also the person's characteristic production of movements. In the search for methods of counting fidgety movements, we may conclude that movements which immediately accompany non-fluencies of speech must not be counted as ordinary fidgetiness. Movements which come at other times can be regarded as movements produced by a constant information source, and it is up to some other kind of research to determine what sort of information that source conveys.

Thoughts about the encoding process

In the meantime, let us do some speculating about speech encoding and what the bunching up of movements around non-fluencies may mean to it. Most non-fluencies are hesitations by our definition: for the average speaker almost 95 percent are either filled or unfilled pauses. Most workers agree that the speaker hesitates at times of decision-making as he is trying to get out into words, that thought on the tip of the tongue. Both lexical and syntactic choices must be made, and the phonemic clause is the smallest package where we can see the marriage of these two types of choice. Remember that the clause contains both the lexical item whose information concerns the topic of conversation and also the various function words whose information is of

relationships, of how the lexical items are connected and intended to be understood. The requirements for these choices are quite different; the one oriented outward toward the conversation and "meanings of words;" the other oriented inward toward structure. These tasks have been formulated by Lashley (1951) as quite separate: first, activation of the elements of an action, and second, their temporal organization, using language as his primary example. He concluded "that elements of the sentence are readied or partially activated before the order is imposed upon them in expression (p. 130)." Ordinarily, the two tasks have been performed in that sequence before the overt action, before the speaker utters the sounds of speech, and errors in performance indicate that the organization task, the syntax of speech, functions as an inhibitor to the spilling-out of elements which have been overactivated. Lashley uses slips of the fingers in typing and Spoonerisms in speech to illustrate this process. Later writers, such as Lenneberg (1967, Chap. 4), and Boomer and Laver (1968), have followed his formulation.

It is thus apparent that a good deal of energy is involved in these two tasks, that a delicate balance must be maintained between facilitatory and inhibitory commands to the vocal apparatus. We do not yet know the neurological specifics of these forces, but my belief is that the non-fluency is a sign of their continuous interplay and that the movements which surround the non-fluency are motor manifestations of this balancing act. Also, because of this they are qualitatively different from other movements which make up what we call "fidgetiness." We have seen that individual differences in total movement output are very large, but where these movements occur in the rhythmical pattern of speech is not a function of total number of movements. To be sure, there are significant differences—but again very small ones—in how closely the movements adhere to the speech rhythm. Whether these differences are determined by culture patterns or idiosyncrasies we do not know, but an empirical test of these possibilities is being conducted now by applying the same techniques to speech samples from Sicily. The fact remains, however, that a significant proportion of the movements of everyone studied so far are tied to speech rhythm and thus, inferentially, to the speech encoding process.

If our interest is in fidgetiness as an expression of emotional states, as it originally was and still is, then we should develop some way of eliminating those encoding-related movements from further consideration, for they contribute too much redundancy to the measurement system. This would be easy to do by hand, using the findings presented here as a guide, but such a procedure would be so tedious that no one would be willing to do it for a representative amount of interview material. We fare better in using the findings to alter our system of automation: in future studies of frequencies of body movements, we shall be feeding the outputs of the accelerometers into counters for machine processing. We can capitalize on our knowledge that pauses make up the largest category of non-fluencies by detecting pauses and gating the counters to omit those movements which occur at the same time as the pauses, or just following them. Then we can learn if this extended excursion into psycholinguistics has produced practical as well as theoretical gain.

NOTE

1. There are differences in response among types of juncture which may terminate a phonemic clause which make it look as if two sizes of unit are involved. The extreme accuracy of response noted above may obtain more in the case of the larger unit —but the point that everyone seems to be able to recognize rhythmical units of speech is still a valid one.

REFERENCES

Boomer, D. S. Speech disturbance and body movement in interviews. *J Nerv. Ment. Dis.*, 1963, 136, 263–6.

Boomer, D. S. Hesitation and grammatical encoding. *Language and Speech*, 1965, 8, 148–58.

Boomer, D. S. and Dittmann, A. T. Hesitation pauses and juncture pauses in speech. *Language and Speech*, 1962, 5, 215–20.

Boomer, D. S. and Dittmann, A. T. Speech rate, filled pause, and body movement in interviews. *J. Nerv. Ment. Dis.*, 1964, 139, 324–7.

Boomer, D. S. and Laver, J. D. M. Slips of the tongue. *Br. J. Disord. Commun.*, 1968, 3, 2–12.

Condon, W. S. and Ogston, W. D. Sound film analysis of normal and pathological behavior patterns. *J. Nerv. Ment. Dis*, 1966, 143, 338–47.

Condon, W. S. and Ogston, W. D. A segmentation of behavior. *J. Psychiat. Res.*, 1967, 5, 221–35.

Dittmann, A. T. The relationship between body movements and moods in interviews. *J. Consult. Psychol.*, 1962, 26, 480.

Dittmann, A. T. and Llewellyn, L. G. The phonemic clause as a unit of speech decoding. *J. Personal. Soc. Psychol.*, 1967, 6, 341–9.

Dittmann, A. T. and Llewllyn, L. G. Relationship between vocalization and head nods as listener responses. *J. Personal. Soc. Psychol.*, 1968, 9, 79–84.

Dittmann, A. T. and Llewellyn, L. G. Body movement and speech rhythm in social conversation. *J. Personal. Soc. Psychol.*, 1969, 11, 98–106.

Ekman, P. Communication through nonverbal behavior: A source of information about an interpersonal relationship. In S. Tomkins and C. Izard (Eds.), *Affect, Cognition, and Personality*. Springer, New York, 1965. Pp. 390–442.

Ekman, P. and Friesen, W. V. Nonverbal behavior in psychotherapy research. In J. M. Shlein (Ed.), *Research in Psychotherapy, Volume III*. American Psychological Association, Washington, D.C., 1968. Pp. 179–216.

Freedman, N. and Hoffman, S. P. Kinetic behavior in altered clinical states: Approach to objective analysis of motor behavior during clinical interviews. *Perceptual and Motor Skills*, 1967, 24, 527–39.

Lashley, K. S. The problem of serial order in behavior. In L. A. Jeffress (Ed.), *Cerebral Mechanisms in Behavior*. Wiley, New York, 1951. Pp. 112–36.

Lenneberg, E. H. *Biological Foundations of Language*. Wiley, New York, 1967.

Lounsbury, F. G. Transitional probability, linguistic structure, and systems of habit-family hierarchies. In C. E. Osgood and T. A. Sebeok (Eds.), *Psycholinguistics: A Survey of Theory and Research Problems*. Waverly Press, Baltimore, 1954. Pp. 93–101.

Renneker, R. Kinesic research and therapeutic processes: Further discussion. In P. H. Knapp (Ed.), *Expression of the Emotions in Man*. International Universities Press, New York, 1963. Pp. 147–60.

Trager, G. L. and Smith, H. L., Jr. *An Outline of English Structure*. (*Studies in Linguistics: Occasional Papers, 3*). Battenberg Press, Norman, Okla., 1951. (Republished, American Council of Learned Societies, New York, 1965.)

13

QUASI-COURTSHIP BEHAVIOR
IN PSYCHOTHERAPY [1]

ALBERT E. SCHEFLEN

For nearly a decade our research group [2] has been making a comparative study of different methods of psychotherapy. We started out, as so many psychotherapy researchers do, looking only at the techniques of the therapist, by which we meant his verbalizations. But we were forced progressively to widen the field of our observations. We began to see that how the participants looked, sat, moved, and dressed was as important as what they said, and we also came to see very clearly that we could make little sense out of a therapist's action except in reference to what the patient did, to the relationship between the therapist and the patient, and to the established traditions of psychotherapy and of the culture in general.

Within this larger view, we discovered that certain interchanges were performed in a startlingly similar fashion or form, whether the therapist was an active interventionist or an orthodox psychoanalytic listener. For instance, the structure we clinically know as rap-

port shows the same basic elements of posture, voice, and movement, regardless of who the participants are. In other words, we came to recognize that human behavior is patterned and systematic. It is made up of regular, standard gestalten or units which are arranged in lawful configurations.

One of these regular structures that invariably appeared in psychotherapy included behaviors like those found in American courtship. The ethics of psychotherapy have traditionally proscribed sexual behavior, and most of the therapists we studied were unaware that they behaved in ways which could be identified as sexual in therapy sessions. When we interviewed them about it, they spoke defensively, saying that if indeed they showed such actions they did not intend to; they must have unresolved personal problems or untoward countertransference reactions. So at first we thought that these little-known elements of courtshiplike behavior were undesirable contaminants of psychotherapy. But there were reasons to as-

From *Psychiatry*, 1965, 28, 245–57. Copyright © 1965 by The William Alanson White Psychiatric Foundation, Inc., and reprinted by special permission.

sume that this was not the case. First of all, some few therapists were quite aware of such behaviors and considered them a necessary part of their technique. Second, we saw these behaviors in all the psychotherapies we examined and in nearly all other interactions as well. Behavior this universal could not be written off as untoward or incidental.

So it seemed likely that our subject-therapists were mistaken in their surmises that courtinglike activities were merely undisciplined evidences of acting-out. We have found in talking to subjects about other covert kinesic activities that they do not know they are performing them, or they have culture-bound myths about the meaning of such activities. And we also know from experience that psychotherapists' conceptions of what they do are very different from those of research observers who study what they do.[3] The point is evident. If we are to study poorly known and poorly understood human behaviors, we are going to have to be dissatisfied with preconceptions and free associations about their meanings and instead observe them systematically in the contexts in which they occur in order to derive their actual functions in an interaction.

The method of research

Recent developments in the behavioral and biological sciences have provided a method for doing this. From general systems theory[4] we have gotten a model for conceptualizing the organization of living systems. Components are organized into units which, in turn, are part of larger systems. Even more recently it has become evident that behavior is integrated analogously; that is, standard units are integrated into larger units which, in turn, make up still larger units.

Such an arrangement of behavioral units in a hierarchy of levels has been applied to animal behavior by the ethologists.[5] It has long been held by gestalt theorists that human behavior is perceived in gestalten.[6] In the last generation methods have been worked out in structural linguistics for determining the units of speech behavior and their arrangement in larger units,[7] analogous to the hierarchies of levels of material systems. And in both the American[8] and British[9] schools of anthropology the realization has been growing that *all behavior—not only speech—is patterned this way.* So we now know why the gestalt theorists could find that people perceive units, not merely qualities of behavior; for these units are coded in a cultural and institutional tradition, and each generation learns them by conscious and unconscious processes.

These strands of development were formalized as a method of research at Palo Alto in 1956 by Gregory Bateson, Ray Birdwhistell, Henry Brosin, Frieda Fromm-Reichmann, Charles Hockett, and Norman McQuown, and since then have been developed further by Ray Birdwhistell and the author. This approach to human behavior is known as "context analysis." Its principles and procedures have been described in other publications by Birdwhistell[10] and myself.[11] While I shall not detail the approach in this paper, it is this method that I applied to understanding the quasi-courting behaviors to be described here.

Briefly, the many elements of behavior are examined to find their structural configurations as they appear in a stream of behavior. (This practice is very different from the usual approach in the psychological sciences, where this or that a priori decision is made about what elements of behavior will be selected or which qualities will be abstracted for study as variables.) Then, when a unit has been identified, each recurrence of it is examined in the contexts in which it occurs. By contrasting what happens when it does and does not occur, its function in the larger systems—and, therefore, its significance or meaning—is derived. This method differs from the practice of using free associations or judges to determine by intuition the meaning of the various behaviors in an interaction. It should be noted that I did not successfully derive the meanings of the sexual-like activities by asking psychotherapists why they perform them. As it happened, they did not know why, and when they speculated as to the reasons, their speculations did not fit the observable findings. It should also be noted that I did not count these behaviors or measure them. For I am interested in their meaning, and the rule of levels is that the meaning of an event is in its relationship to the larger picture, not in the qualities of the event itself. Finally, I did not correlate these activities with other activities, for it would not be sufficiently informative to know merely that two events occurred simultaneously. I must know, to derive meaning, exactly how each behavioral unit fits in relation to the others in the larger system. So I shall not present charts and statistics, but only simple descriptions, and later abstractions not unlike those that every clinician makes. The advantage is that I can retrace my steps and tell exactly how each is derived. In other words, context analysis makes explicit (and precise) processes that are implicit in intuitive clinical observations.

Component elements in courtship behavior and their qualifiers

Once we had, through some observations of American courtship, become conscious of courting and courtinglike elements in kinesic behavior, we were surprised to see them in any interaction we observed. They appeared not only among lovers, but in psychotherapy sessions, business meetings, parties, conferences, and so on. Certainly all of these interactions were not supposed to end in sexual consummation. It seemed that either Americans court whenever they come together, regardless of what they are doing, or else these subtle sexual behaviors had some qualifying signals that modified their function. This latter possibility is the one I am going to develop. I shall begin by describing the basic courtship elements as they appear in interactions, and then describe the qualifiers that are combined with them in those situations that are not to be taken as seductive or sexual.

Basic elements of courtship

Some of the common activities of early courtship in America are courtship readiness, positioning for courtship, and actions of appeal or invitation.

COURTSHIP READINESS Courtship behaviors occur after a participant has come into a specific state of readiness. People in high courtship readiness are often unaware of it and, conversely, subjects who think they "feel" very sexually active often do not evidence courtship readiness at all. Courtship readiness is most clearly evidenced by a state of high muscle tonus. Sagging disappears, jowling and bagginess around the eyes decrease, the torso becomes more erect, and pot-bellied slumping disappears or decreases. The legs are brought into tighter tonus, a condition seen in "cheesecake" and associated with the professional model or athlete. The eyes seem to be brighter. Some women believe their hair changes. Skin color varies from flush to pallor—possibly depending upon the degree of anxiety. It is possible that changes in water retention and odor occur.

Preening often accompanies these organismic changes, sometimes only as token behaviors. Women may stroke their hair, or glance at their makeup in the mirror, or sketchily rearrange their clothing. Men usually comb or stroke their hair, button and readjust their coats, or pull up their socks. Some preening behaviors which have been observed in psychotherapy sessions are shown in Figure 1.

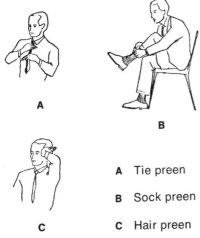

A Tie preen

B Sock preen

C Hair preen

Fig. 1 Some preening behavior of male psychotherapists.

POSITIONING FOR COURTSHIP Courtship, after the earliest steps, occurs in the assumption by the courting partners of postures which have a standard relationship. The partners turn their bodies and heads so as to face each other in a vis-à-vis or tête-à-tête configuration. They tend to lean toward each other and place their chairs or extremities in such a way as to block off others.[12] Figure 2 shows the vis-à-vis positioning

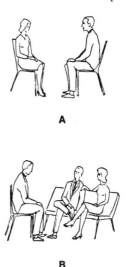

A With two people

B With third party present

Fig. 2 Positioning for courtship.

used in courtship. It also depicts the courtship position which is used when the parties open the position of the upper half of their bodies to include a third person, but form a closed circle with their legs. When courting partners orient themselves vis-à-vis and come into closer physical proximity, they usually adopt an intimate mode of conversation.

ACTIONS OF APPEAL OR INVITATION The assumption of one participant of a vis-à-vis orientation with courtship readiness may be considered an invitation to courtship or to related activities. Other activities also appear to invite reciprocation in courtship. In addition to complementary or invitational statements and soft or drawling paralanguage, characteristic bodily motions are seen. Flirtatious glances, gaze-holding, demure gestures, head-cocking, rolling of the pelvis, and other motions are well known. In women, crossing the legs, slightly exposing the thigh, placing a hand on the hip, and exhibiting the wrist or palm are also invitational. Protruding the breast and slow stroking motions of the fingers on the thigh or wrist also are common. Some of these activities, seen in psychotherapy sessions, are illustrated in Figure 3.

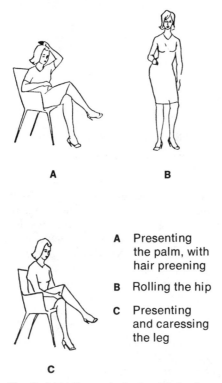

A   Presenting the palm, with hair preening

B   Rolling the hip

C   Presenting and caressing the leg

Fig. 3 Appealing or invitational behaviors of women patients.

Qualifiers of courting behavior

Two boys are wrestling. They may be fighting for domination or to defeat each other; but they also may have a quite different purpose. Their wrestling may not, even over years of repetition, progress to victory for either boy. Neither is hurt or humiliated. Instead of showing anger, both may laugh and show evidence of considerable pleasure. None of the spectators even thinks of intervening. They seem to know from the beginning that injury and victory are not the aims of this interaction. Or two men approach each other in a barroom. They call each other the vilest names, exchange punches, then embrace and buy each other drinks. Animals also show such mock fighting.[13] Two dogs may rush at each other with such a show of ferocity that a spectator would expect them to tear each other apart: instead they romp off gayly together in play.

In such situations, two sets of behavior seem to be alike, but some signal occurs which lets those who know the rules distinguish between them. Some indication occurs that the activity is not a real fight; it is not to be taken literally. Bateson calls such a signal a "metacommunication," [14] that is, a communication about a communication.

Characteristic signals that the sexual elements of behavior which I have described are not to be taken literally as courtship include the following.

REFERENCES TO THE INAPPROPRIATE CONTEXT Partners in a quasi-courtship may make references to the inappropriateness of the situation for sexuality by reminding each other that other people are present or by reminders of taboos or ethical considerations. They may also remind each other that they are together to conduct the business at hand. In psychotherapy, the patient may be encouraged to feel her sexual feelings fully, yet be cautioned, by reference to the context, not to act them out. More often than not, such references are nonverbal. A gesture or movement of the eyes or head toward the setting or toward others is as effective as any verbal statement of inappropriateness.

INCOMPLETE POSTURAL-KINESIC INVOLVEMENT After the earliest steps in a courtship the partners move into vis-à-vis relationship of posture and adopt an intimate mode of conversation, excluding others from their relationship. In quasi-courtship this relationship of postures is incomplete. The participants may face each other, but turn their bodies so that they face partly away from each other, or they may extend their arms so as to encompass others. Or they may cast about the room with their eyes or project their voices so as to be clearly audible to third parties. When no third parties are present, quasi-courting people may face, look at, or project to unseen third parties. This story of divided loyalties is told in Figure 4. In Figure 4A the woman, in vis-à-vis positioning with a man, turns in search behavior to another man passing by. In Figure 4B, the couple on the right are in a semiclosed tête-à-tête position, but the girl is touching the other man with her ankle. This kind of division of the body in multiple simultaneous relationships we have called splitting.[15]

OMISSION OR INCOMPLETENESS OF KEY COURTING BEHAVIORS The behaviors may be modified so as to leave out characteristic courting elements. This is

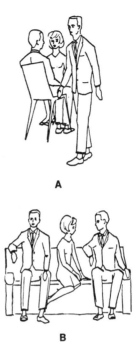

Fig. 4 Multiple postural relationships in quasi-courting.

done by failing to complete typical courting actions or by conducting them only in certain communicative modalities so that the gestalt required for a courting unit is not completed. For example, in courtship a man may lean forward, touch his partner, soften his facial expression, and, in soft paralanguage, verbalize his love. In quasi-courting he may say the words while leaning slightly away from her, smile only by retracting the corners of his lips without crinkling his eyes, and use a matter-of-fact tone of voice.

DISCLAIMERS Participants in quasi-courting may try to reduce ambiguity and indicate noncourtship by lexical disclaimers. They may reassure the partners and others that their interest is not sexual. They may seem to court while talking about their love for another partner, or they may intellectualize the flirtation in a discussion of great books.

BIZARRENESS OF PERFORMANCE OF THE COURTSHIP ELEMENTS Sometimes in an interaction where seduction is inappropriate, the courtship elements appear without the above qualifiers. But instead, the elements are performed in a bizarre, histrionic manner, which seems improper to middle-class eyes, and which can appear to be a burlesque of courtship. When I first saw this in schizophrenic patients I thought such actions were psychotic. But broader observation shows this variant to be characteristic of teen-agers and men and women of the lower social class. The bizarre pattern is used by those who do not use the other qualifiers. If, indeed, this is a class difference, then my choice of the word "bizarre" represents a middle-class value judgment. It is logical that quasi-courting forms might differ between the classes, since their dating and courtship patterns are known to differ markedly.[16]

The quasi-courting complex as an entity

In the tradition-bound performances in a culture a relatively few elemental units of behavior serve as basic building blocks for constructing complex and variegated patterns. An integration as complex as a language, for example, is based upon a relatively small number of standard phonemes. In English, only 43 such elements make up the thousands of morphemes (similar to words) which in turn are formed into such complex structures as sentences, conversation, and literature. In an analogous way, a few elements of courting behavior are put together in the complex pattern of courtship; these same elements, arranged in a different way and combined with "qualifiers," make up integrations that resemble courtship but have a quite different significance in an interaction.[17]

Quasi-courting is one such complex of behaviors. It can be distinguished from actual courtship by three major characteristics: (1) The *integration of components*. With elements of courtship are included the qualifiers that state, in essence, "This activity is not to be taken literally as seduction." (2) The *contexts of appearance*. Quasi-courting is identified also by the fact that it occurs in contexts in which courting or sexual behavior is inappropriate. (3) The *progression*. The ultimate progression in the interactional sequences determines whether the pattern is one of courtship or quasi-courtship. The quasi-courting pattern does not proceed to sexual consummation even in the later history of a given relationship.[18]

It is possible to postulate a state of quasi-courting readiness which includes a few aspects of courtship readiness but is observably different. For example, women may imitate the appearance of high tonus of courtship readiness by wearing nylon hose and high-heeled shoes which throw the foot into flexion and tighten the hamstrings, and may adopt a particular type of provocative, slightly bizarre attire and cosmetics that give the impression of "sexiness." Such devices appear to solicit quasi-courting rather than courting, and experienced men recognize that "sexy" women are not necessarily sexual, and are perhaps even likely to be frigid.

Quasi-courting occurs in nearly any situation—at least among the middle class—in which the members know each other and are engaged in a common objective. The sequence can be observed in the classroom, dining room, and meeting hall, and between parent and children, hosts and guests, teachers and students, doctors and patients. It occurs between men and women and between members of the same gender. The intensity and duration vary from the briefest of kinesic interchanges (in formal activities such as psychotherapy) to the most elaborate, continuous, and intense rituals in situations such as the cocktail party. In the upper middle-class social context, in fact, quasi-courting takes on the quality of a deliberate game for enhancing attractiveness and social interest. Quasi-courting across marital lines is common. It does not produce signs of anxiety or force interruption so long as certain rules are observed.[19]

Often a quasi-courting relationship is at some point converted into an actual courtship. I have no observational data on this eventuality, but I would guess that some special signals or statements would be required to indicate the transition. On the other hand, a courtship may at some point be converted into a quasi-courtship. This would be indicated by the addition of the qualifiers. But by and large, in a quasi-courting sequence, *the qualifiers are enacted from the beginning.*

The occurrence of any deviance highlights and clarifies the lawfulness of the normal structure. For instance, an interactant may perform courting when it is inappropriate to do so, or perform overly intense quasi-courting as a means of forcing another participant to withdraw from relationship. Or the qualifiers may be deliberately kept unclear in order to produce an ambiguity between courtship and quasi-courtship, thereby confusing the other participant or forcing him to declare his intentions.

Quasi-courting sequences in psychotherapy

Quasi-courting has occurred in all the psychotherapies we have observed, from psychoanalytic to active interventionalistic—in family, group, and individual types. In the more psychoanalytic or more conventional psychotherapies the quasi-courting is covert —that is, merely postural and kinesic. The fact that it is nonlexical probably reflects the tendency of such therapists to be unaware of its use. This covert, automatic type of quasi-courting is like that found in any American interaction and functions to maintain the integration of the group—a point which I shall discuss later. Some psychotherapists, however, use quasi-courting openly and explicitly to bring the patient to face certain conflicts and to make special definitions of the relationship conscious. In these cases the quasi-courting is overt, with lexical and tactile components. The illustrations in Figures 5, 6, and 7 from psychotherapy sessions are of the covert type usual in America.[20] I shall return to the overt uses at the end of the paper.

Figure 5 shows a sequence which occurred at the very beginning of a ninth session in which two male therapists were treating a young schizophrenic girl.

At the beginning of the sequence (5A) the therapist on the viewer's left turns to watch an attractive research technician walk across the room. The patient begins to preen (5B). The therapist turns back to the patient and also preens (5C, 5D), but he then disclaims courtship by an ostentatious look of boredom and a yawn (5E). Immediately afterward, the patient tells him she is interested in an attractive male aide.

The sequence depicted in Figure 6

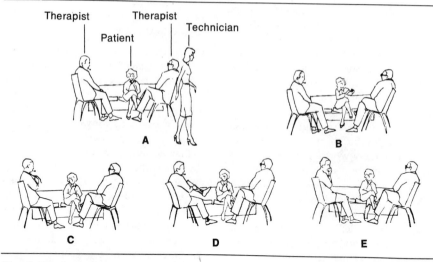

Fig. 5 Quasi-courting sequence that reestablished an interrupted doctor-patient relationship.

occurred in an initial interview conducted by a British family therapist with a British family. The situation at the beginning of the sequence is shown in 6A. Next to the therapist are the patient (a young schizophrenic), her mother, her mother's mother, and her father. Whenever—and this occurs many times during the session—the therapist is in a conversation with either the daughter or the grandmother, the mother moves into courtship readiness and begins coquettish expressions and movements. She crosses her legs and extends them, places her hand on her hip, and leans forward (6B). Invariably the therapist responds by preening and turning to the mother, asking her a question (6C). Both of the other women immediately place a leg across

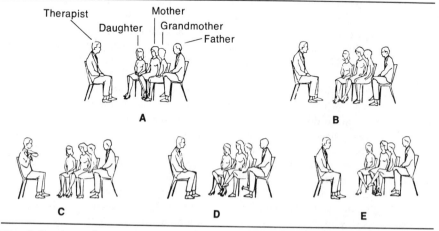

Fig. 6 Quasi-courting sequence that ended in a realignment of relationships.

the space between the mother and therapist, "boxing in" the mother (6D). The mother than "decourts";[21] she goes out of courting tonus, sits back, and stops her coquettish behavior (6E). The daughter and grandmother "box in" the flirtatious mother after a signal (foot-waving) from the father (6D).[22]

The next example occurred in a first session of family therapy. The situation was as follows: The young daughter had at the beginning of the session shown very high courtship readiness toward the therapist. But when he avoided glancing at or speaking to her, she gradually lost tonus and came to appear disinterested and remote. As the therapist continued to focus his attention upon the parents, two of the other children, who seemed always to take their cues from their sister, also began to show signs of losing interest. It seemed at this point that the key to avoiding losing three of the family members called for tactical inclusion of this girl. But the father was holding the therapist in a compelling monologue which allowed no interruption. It was at this point that the therapist began the quasi-courting sequence, which is shown in Figure 7.

In 7A the quasi-sexual sequence between the therapist and the daughter begins with their holding gazes. In 7B the gaze-holding continues while they drag on their cigarettes in perfect synchrony. In 7C the daughter pulls away from the therapist's gaze and sharply turns her head to her left, placing her arm across her lap as a barrier. In 7B she continues to avoid his gaze and begins to decourt. As she does so, she turns to her mother (7E), moving into synchronous smoking with her instead of with the therapist. She also from then on sits in the same posture as her mother. Thus, she ends the quasi-court-

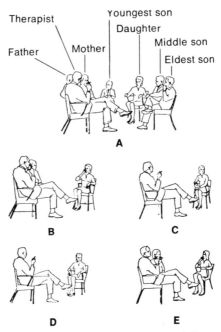

Fig. 7 Another type of realignment following a quasi-courting sequence.

ing, moving into a relationship with her mother—not with the therapist. But she does not, from this point on, any longer dissociate herself from the group.

Quasi-courting as a systems-maintaining device

How meaning or function is derived with new research methods such as context analysis has been described at the beginning of this paper. As I have suggested, the meaning of a unit is found in its relations to other units in the larger context or system. Ordinarily in context analysis it is necessary to define the units level by level in order to derive such relations, but, for my purposes here, there is a simpler way of conveying the idea. One can ask: *In what situations does quasi-courting ap-*

pear? and *What does it do in the interaction whenever it appears?*

In what situations does quasi-courting appear?

We discerned, testing by our methods, two contexts in which quasi-courting regularly appears: Where there is withdrawal by or exclusion of one participant and where there is gender confusion.

WITHDRAWAL OR EXCLUSION In the examples taken from the psychotherapy sessions, a certain context was evident at each appearance of quasi-courting: Some member of the group had withdrawn or had been excluded.

This happened in many other quasi-courting sequences that we have observed, both in psychotherapy and in other interactions. I think that the following generalizations are justified. In a twosome, quasi-courting is likely whenever one or the other of the participants turns away, withdraws, or appears preoccupied. In a larger group (such as a family in therapy, a party, or a meeting), quasi-courting appears in these same situations, and also when some member of the group has been ignored or excluded by others. If any group is to be maintained, a participant who is excluded or who dissociates himself is likely to be called back into relationship by the others. Quasi-courting appears to be one mechanism for soliciting such return to participation or for ending an exclusion. At the social level, then, quasi-courting is one kind of system-maintaining mechanism.[23] But it is only one such device. A withdrawing member might be called back with admonition, exhortation, tactile contact, and a host of other mechanisms. Shortly I shall discuss what specific conditions elicit quasi-courting

rather than one of the other mechanisms.

GENDER CONFUSION Ambiguity arises when some participant behaves in a way that is inappropriate to his gender —for instance, when a woman acts very aggressive and domineering or a man behaves passively and femininely. Ambiguity can also arise about gender identification when the situation is such that some group member is placed in a position usually occupied by a member of the opposite sex—for instance, when two males are alone together at an intimate table in a nightclub. In such situations quasi-courting may appear. Here it seems to be a way of affirming gender or determining which member will fill some generally feminine or masculine role in the relationship. The quasi-sexual behavior generally leads to heightening the signals of gender identification.

What Does Quasi-Courting Do in Interaction?

A person is said to be attractive when he has a compelling effect upon the behavior of a partner or group. Certainly everyone has experienced the effect of the arrival of an attractive person at a dull business meeting. Attractiveness is elicited in others, and the resulting interactions build up to provide an increased attentiveness and readiness to relate by the whole group.[24] Thus a group can become animated and cohesive enough to work together to complete a dull or tedious task.

I am suggesting that a great many different designations have been previously applied to what is a single basic state of a human organism. This state is necessary to group cohesion and the completion of tasks that are not im-

mediately gratifying. Some of the different terms used to describe this state are attractiveness, attentiveness, sociability, readiness to relate, and quasi-courtship. I shall also suggest that this favorable state is in some way a derivative of sexualness—whatever that may be physiologically and psychologically—and indicative of some optimal state between immediate sexual preoccupation and marked sexual inhibition.

I presume that this is what is meant by the psychoanalytic concept of genitality [25]—a personality state that is considered a sublimation of sexual interest and characterized by such qualities as cooperativeness, creativity, and the like. Conversely, in psychoanalytic theory, pregenitality—in many respects comparable to our definition of decourting—is associated with withdrawal, narcissism, suspiciousness, and other qualities inimical to group interests.

It is postulated, then, that quasi-courting is that set of system-maintaining devices that is used when the insufficiency in sociability or attentiveness is due to some inhibition of this sexually-derived state.[26]

The foregoing postulation can be supported by observing the contexts in which decourting occurs—that is, the contexts in which existing states of courtship or courtship readiness disappear into dissociation, unattractiveness, and loss of attentiveness. There are five contexts in which I have often seen this occur: (1) When gender confusion persists. For example, a woman engages a man with preening and other quasi-courting behavior, but he responds with high-pitched voice, cocked head, and eye flutter. The woman may decourt if he persists in refusing her signals of gender identification. (2) When there is ambiguity about whether the situation is one of courtship or quasi-courtship.

For example, a man moves actively toward and into vis-à-vis with a woman without clear qualifiers. She may decourt until he moves partly out of vis-à-vis and adds other disclaimers. (3) When the other person quasi-courts too intensely. The duration and frequency of courtship elements may approach some disruptive level, or the context may be inappropriate even for evident, clearly signaled quasi-courting. (4) When the group is already in a high state of alertness or quasi-sexual tension and can tolerate no more. If the quasi-courting member persists in his behavior, despite monitoring and disapproval of the group, the other members may have to decourt to drop the level of tension. (5) When other group members actively interfere with quasi-courting. For example, in a family session whenever the daughter showed appealing behaviors, the mother engaged in monitoring activities until the girl finally gave up and decourted.

Such contexts lead to an extinguishing of quasi-courtship readiness, and a decrease of attentiveness, relatedness, and other qualities necessary to sustain group participation. These unfavorable states are correctable by proper quasi-courting sequences.

If it is true that quasi-courting is introduced and accepted in a group in which there is a lack of alertness and interpersonal relatedness, and is not accepted in a group in which these qualities are already high, then one can surmise that for any group, at any point in an interaction, there is an optimal range of relatedness, alertness, and quasi-courting states. It can further be postulated, in the manner that is characteristic for describing stable systems, that reductions below the allowable minimum induce more quasi-courting, and that any threatened increase above some allowable maximum reduces it. The idea is thus derived that quasi-courting functions as a cybernetic type of governor for maintaining a favorable range of relatedness.

In the field of psychotherapy technique, this is not a new idea—in individual-centered terms, at least. Psychotherapists think of patients as having optimal states of transference or of sexual and dependent involvement. If they become too remote from the therapist, or so over-involved as to impair their lives outside the sessions, the therapist must exert an influence to remedy this. Traditionally psychotherapists have devices, so far not clearly described, for further engaging a patient or for cooling him off, to keep him within this favorable range. It appears that quasi-courting is one such device.

The principle holds in other interactions as well. In a group, the completion of tasks requires optimum degrees of involvement. It becomes evident when for some member or for the group as a whole the pendulum swings too far toward over-involvement or toward underinvolvement. Quasi-courting and decourting seem to be operants that can be introduced to govern these swings.

Miscommunication and pathology in quasi-courting

While the function of quasi-courting may be derived from observing it in context, it may also be derived from a study of its failures. Whenever a program of interaction has mixed components and multiple aspects, there is much occasion for ambiguity. Deviant members of an ingroup may mislearn the routines and omit the proper qualifiers; or an observer may misinterpret the behaviors of quasi-courting, even though they are performed properly. In any case, courting and quasi-courting are easily confused. It obviously requires a good deal of learning, much of which is out of consciousness, for a member of any culture to perform and to interpret correctly in such complex interactions, in which crucial differences are determined by fleeting and subtle qualifiers.

A simple classification of disorders in performing quasi-courting can be derived from the essential aspects of the structure of quasi-courting. Quasi-courting, it will be recalled, consists of, first, a set of sexual or courting behaviors, and, second, a set of qualifying signals and contexts. The necessary comprehension—conscious or unconscious—demands that both sets or aspects be considered or apprehended as gestalten. Deviance results if *either* aspect alone is performed or perceived at the expense of the other.

Although we have not studied systematically all areas of quasi-courting aberration, we do know enough to state that one type of pathological behavior appears in persons who can only court, whatever the situation. Others can only quasi-court; and still others may court at a professional meeting, then quasi-court in the bedroom. Hysterics and certain schizophrenics appear to show this confusion regularly. They are unable to consummate sexually; yet they are seductive when they are not supposed to be, and they constantly provoke and imagine sexual advances on the part of others. Laymen call such behavior teasing.

Clinical experience would indicate that some couples, even though they have regular sexual consummation, never learn to court; they merely quasi-court and then have intercourse.

Since most Americans do not consciously differentiate between quasi-courting and courting, there is no way for such partners to become aware of their lack of preparation for sexuality. Dissatisfaction and pathology could result from this, for quasi-courting actually proscribes consummation.

On the other hand, some people do not seem able to deal with the leavening or ameliorative aspects of quasi-courting. They ignore the qualifiers and refuse any quasi-courting response by decourting, freezing, withdrawing, or criticizing. They alienate and are alienated in most groups and may, like the overcautious driver, have a provocative and disruptive effect, while they appear to be models of decorum and cooperativeness. I believe that frigidity, impotence, and other sexual disorders would be greatly clarified if looked at within this conceptual framework.

The effects of such miscommunication are, at the individual level, an ultimate loss of courtship readiness, attractiveness, attentiveness, and so on, on the part of one or more of the persons in a group. At the social level, the effect is alienation, temporary or permanent, between members, so that the processes of the group are interrupted or deterred.[27]

Quasi-courting as a technique in psychotherapy

I have argued that quasi-courting serves the purpose of clarifying aspects of a relationship that allow favorable states of attentiveness and involvement for specific tasks. If this is so, then quasi-courting is one device used covertly and automatically by patients and therapists to induce rapport and to maintain and regulate their relationship.

Since the psychotherapy relationship controls need gratification in order to further learning, some measure of impersonality is, of course, necessary; but this does not mean that a total impersonality is either necessary or desirable. The fact is that the patient and the therapist do have certain feelings for each other. These feelings are the cultural medium in which the data of psychotherapy are processed. They provide an environment for the learning experience which psychotherapy must be if it is to be successful. Thus, the psychotherapy relationship both *is* and *is not* personal. It *is* and *is not* sexual. Quasi-courting, with its affirmation and control of sexuality in one package, may be a mechanism by which this twofold aspect is announced, and by which the equilibrium between the affirmation and control is maintained. The quasi-courting metasignals are useful at points of excessive impersonalization or excessive personalization.

Certain modern psychotherapists appear to have purposely taken advantage of this point in communicative structure, using quasi-courting as a technique. They deliberately create ambiguities to force a patient to face and meet problems in these areas. Thus John Rosen may tell a patient to have sex with him and then interpret her various reactions.[28] Catherine L. Bacon and Warren Hampe have also experimented with such techniques.[29] In the Whitaker-Malone multiple therapy, one of the two therapists may quasi-court a patient elaborately, while one or both of them make interpretive comments to the patient about the process.[30]

NOTES

1. This research was supported by the Commonwealth of Pennsylvania. It was carried out in continuous cor-

roboration with Ray L. Birdwhistell, whose thinking helped shape many of the ideas and observations. Drawings for this paper were done by Sherl Winter and editorial work by Alice Schwar.

2. Ray L. Birdwhistell, J. D. Van Vlack, cinematographer, and the author constituted the film analysis team. The clinical team consisted of Catherine L. Bacon, O. Spurgeon English, Warren W. Hampe, and Max Katz, and at times Morris Brody, George Devereux, John Rosen, and others.

3. See, for example: Morris W. Brody, *Observations on "Direct Analysis";* New York, Vantage, 1959. O. Spurgeon English, Catherine L. Bacon, Warren W. Hampe, and Calvin F. Settlage, *Direct Analysis and Schizophrenia;* New York, Grune & Stratton, 1961. Albert E. Scheflen, *A Psychotherapy of Schizophrenia; A Study of Direct Analysis;* Springfield, Ill., Thomas, 1960. John N. Rosen, *Direct Analysis: Selected Papers;* New York, Grune & Stratton, 1953.

4. W. Ross Ashby, "General Systems Theory as a New Discipline," *General Systems* (1958) 3: 1–6. Ludwig von Bertalanffy, "An Outline of General Systems Theory," *British J. Philosophy of Science* (1950) 1:134. Bertalanffy, *Problems of Life;* New York, Harper, 1960.

5. Konrad Lorenz, *King Solomon's Ring;* New York, Crowell, 1952. Peter H. Klopfer, *Behavioral Aspects of Ecology;* Englewood Cliffs, N.J., Prentice-Hall, 1962.

6. Kurt Koffka, *Principles of Gestalt Psychology;* New York, Harcourt, 1935.

7. Henry A. Gleason, *An Introduction to Descriptive Linguistics;* New York, Holt, Rinehart, and Winston, 1955. Charles F. Hockett, *A Course in Modern Linguistics;* New York, Macmillan, 1958.

8. See, for example, Ruth Benedict, *Patterns of Culture;* New York, Mentor Books, 1946.

9. See, for example, E. E. Evans-Pritchard, *Social Anthropology;* London, Cohen and West, 1951.

10. Ray L. Birdwhistell, Chapter 3, in *The Natural History of an Interview,* edited by Norman McQuown; New York, Grune & Stratton, to be published in 1965. Birdwhistell, "Paralanguage: 25 Years After Sapir," in *Lectures on Experimental Psychiatry,* edited by Henry Brosin; Pittsburgh, Univ. of Pittsburgh Press, 1961. Birdwhistell, "The Frames in the Communication Process," paper read to the American Society of Clinical Hypnosis, October 10, 1959.

11. Albert E. Scheflen, "Communication and Regulation in Psychotherapy," *Psychiatry* (1963) 28: 126–136. Scheflen, "Natural History Method in Psychotherapy: Communicational Research," in *Methods of Research in Psychotherapy,* edited by Louis A. Gottschalk and Arthur H. Auerbach; New York, Appleton-Century-Crofts, 1965. Scheflen, *Stream and Structure of Communicational Behavior;* Philadelphia, Commonwealth Mental Health Research Foundation, 1965.

12. This relationship does not obtain at times when the partners share some mutual interest as a step in courtship—for example, when a man takes his girl to the movies. In these instances both partners are oriented outward, but they usually adopt the same bodily posture in mirror-imaged relationship.

13. Gregory Bateson, "The Message. 'This Is Play,'" in *Group Processes,* Vol. 2, edited by Bertram Schaffner; New York, Josiah Macy, Jr. Foundation, 1956.

14. See footnote 13.

15. See Scheflen, *Stream and Structure of Communicational Behavior,* in footnote 11.

16. There is an American middle-class

tendency to combine romantic love, which historically was a platonic concept, with active sexuality. It may be this combination that necessitates signals for differentiating courting and quasi-courting. Qualifers seem to be learned by middle-class children first in their relations with older relatives and later in the characteristic middle-class dating pattern with its ritualistic line-spieling flattery, dance programs, and nonprogressing courtshiplike routines. But the non-upwardly-mobile lower class, which separates romantic love and sexuality, has no developed dating pattern of this kind and apparently lacks the pattern of quasi-courting well known in the middle class. For discussions of middle-class dating patterns, see the following: D. D. Bromley and F. H. Britten, *Youth and Sex: A Study of 1300 College Students;* New York, Harper, 1938. Rayanne D. Cupps and Norman S. Hayner, "Dating at the University of Washington," *Marriage and Family Living* (1947) 9: 30–31. Winston Ehrmann, *Premarital Dating Behavior;* New York, Holt, 1959. C. Kirkpatrick and T. Caplow, "Courtship in a Group of Minnesota Students," *Amer. J. Sociology* (1945) 51: 114–125. Robert T. Ross, "Measures of the Sex Behavior of College Males Compared with Kinsey's Results," *J. Abnormal and Social Psychology* (1950) 45: 753–755. Geoffrey Gorer, *The American People: A Study in National Character,* New York, Norton, 1948.

17. Since quasi-courting contains courtship elements, it is tempting to say that quasi-courting is no more than aim-inhibited courtship. This idea is misleading, implying that interactants want to court or seduce and are merely dissuaded by circumstances or inhibition. On the contrary, quasi-courting is a distinct element in American middle-class culture, learned separately and earlier than courtship and having a very different function. Once this situation has evolved, whatever the origins of quasi-courting, a person "knows" at some level of consciousness that quasi-courting elicits different behavior from courting. He can therefore intend to quasi-court from the beginning of the relationship, and his behavior does not necessarily have to be attributed to any other intent.

18. This is why there is a serious risk of misinterpreting component behaviors of any pattern when they are observed out of context. If, for example, you hear only that two men exchanged kisses, without knowing that the context was a French military ceremony, you might wrongly interpret the kissing as homosexual. This is the shortcoming of the currently popular isolation-of-variables method of research in which this or that element of behavior is studied as an isolate.

19. The alarm bell rings when one party begins excluding others by seeking isolation or forming full and complete vis-à-vis postures with a partner, prolonging a quasi-courting involvement with one particular partner, or manifesting sexual responsivity, tactile contact, and so on.

20. The examples are taken from therapy sessions in which more than two persons were involved. We prefer to study sequences of quasi-courting in a larger group because behaviors of additional interactants form a context in which to test function.

21. Decourting is a term we use to indicate the withdrawal from a courtship or quasi-courtship. It includes, of course, cessation of courtship readiness and withholding of courting behaviors. But the effect can be more profound and

include actually becoming unattractive, withdrawing from relationship entirely, and so on. Decourting accounts for many of the well-known phenomena in which men and women who are ordinarily deemed attractive suddenly appear unattractive or even repellent. Often the other person attributes such changes, if he tries to explain them at all, as due to ill health, weight loss or weight gain, or something of the sort.

22. By American standards, this mother appeared to be courting, since qualifiers of the American type were absent. The monitoring by her family makes this conjecture probable.

23. See Scheflen, "Communication and Regulation In Psychotherapy," in footnote 11. Also, Ray L. Birdwhistell, personal communication.

24. This state can be put into terms that make it precisely definable and measurable. In our research we use a concept of modes of communication, as described by Ray L. Birdwhistell in Chapter 3 in *The Natural History of an Interview* (see footnote 10); and also in personal communications. The alertness and attentiveness associated with quasi-courting are usually seen as belonging to the *interpersonal* mode. Here an interactant projects his voice appropriately to the distance which lies between him and his partner, converges his eyes appropriately, and uses a moderate to high muscle tonus. On the other hand, an interactant who mumbles to himself, falls into hypotonus, seems to converge on his own body, and so on, is said to be in the *intrapersonal* mode. This mode is often seen in decourting persons.

25. Sigmund Freud, "New Introductory Lectures on Psychoanalysis," *Standard Edition of the Complete Psychological Works,* Vol. 22; London, Hogarth, 1964. Otto Fenichel, *The Psychoanalytic Theory of the Neuroses;* New York, Norton, 1945.

26. The theoretical assumption behind this way of conceptualizing these organismic states accords with current: thinking in psychoanalysis and other fields. It presumes there is an underlying state for sociability and relatedness that is basically libidinal or derived from sexualness. It is, of course, possible that sexualness is, rather, another derivative or activity that occurs in some basic organismic set of alertness.

27. It is incorrect to assume that all deviance in quasi-courting indicates pathology in the performer. Some deviances arise from participation in a group in which the rules are different from those to which one is accustomed. There is every reason to believe that each culture and subculture has its own ground rules and contexts for quasi-sexuality. For example, a middle-class male attending a party of the lower class may find that the attentions to women that are quite expected in his own class are frightening to these women and angering to their husbands. Similarly, the normal quasi-sexual exchanges at parties and meetings on the eastern seaboard are quite out of place in most of the Midwest, where relative segregation of the sexes in public is the rule. It is, therefore, important to separate two kinds of misperformance or misperception in quasi-courtship: (1) cross-cultural misunderstanding, and (2) pathological participation within the culture natural to the deviant.

28. See Scheflen, in footnote 3.

29. Catherine L. Bacon and Warren W. Hampe, personal communications, 1960–1965.

30. O. Spurgeon English, editor, *Strategy and Structure in Psychotherapy;* Philadelphia, Commonwealth Mental Health Research Foundation, 1965.

four

SPATIAL BEHAVIOR

Two major research traditions have been concerned with the social psychological use of space. *Proxemics,* introduced in Edward Hall's work, *The Hidden Dimension* (1966), is clearly linked to anthropology. The meaning and use of space in different cultures is a primary focus of study, and naturalistic methods of observation are generally used. Some thought is also given to the psychological significance of spacing, but that approach is more characteristic of the other school of thought, what we will call, *personal space,* discussed in a book by Robert Sommer (1969). This research tradition chiefly deals with the meaning of space to the individual in terms of the effects of crowding, territoriality, architectural design, and so on, and is only peripherally concerned with intercultural variations. Controlled laboratory and field studies are used, in contrast to proxemics, which mainly relies on observational studies. The difference between proxemic and personal space research is analogous to that between the structural and experimental approaches to body movement, discussed in Part 3.

However, there is considerable overlap between studies of proxemics and personal space, and the division between them is a very permeable one. Generally, when spatial behavior is studied within the purview of anthropology it is known as proxemics; when it comes under scrutiny by experimental social psychology and sociology, it is known as personal space. Both traditions are represented in this section: Hall and Watson on proxemics; and Sommer, and Sommer and Becker on personal space. We present a brief background for each area, while the articles give the reader more of a feeling for the difference between the two orientations.

Edward Hall, in the selection "Proxemics" (p. **205**) gives an excellent introduction. Readers desiring a fuller exposition of Hall's system are urged to read his book *The Hidden Dimension* (1966), a model of clarity and precision in social science writing. Hall defined proxemics as an area of study for anthropology and psychology and developed a helpful notational system (Hall, 1963) for describing proxemic behavior. He reviews the animal literature on the effects of crowding and the perception literature on the nature of spatial perception as a prelude to presenting his own view on proxemics. Hall's major contributions are the delineation of four social distances (intimate, personal, social, and public), which seem to be present in all cultures, and the discussion of the use of space in five cultures (Germany, England, France, Japan, Arab countries). The latter contribution is particularly noteworthy as he ties in national character to the use of space. For example, he notes that Germans are particularly orderly about marking off spatial boundaries and enforcing them. He says, "The door is taken very seriously by Germans . . . to close the door preserves the integrity of the room and provides a protective boundary between people" (Hall, 1966, p. 127). In Japan, he finds the concept of the center to be an organizing principle of Japanese society and sees this reflected in the use of space.

The beauty of Hall's book is the brilliance of his observations, which are in the tradition of the structural, ethological approach to behavior. O. Michael Watson has tested some of Hall's assertions in more controlled laboratory and field settings (Watson, 1970; Watson and Graves, 1966). In the 1966 study, Watson and Graves looked at the proxemic behavior of Arab and American students and found support for Hall's observations that Arabs interact more closely and more directly than Americans. Since Watson and Graves used Arab students studying in Colorado as their sample and typical Arab proxemic behavior was found, this indicates that proxemic behavior is a deeply embedded part of the person, not amenable to sudden change even after exposure to a foreign culture. On the other hand, Efron's (1941) study of gestures, discussed in the chapter on body movement, did show that after prolonged exposure to another culture, nonverbal behavior does change in the direction of the norms of the new culture. Watson's article (p. **230**) shows his present thinking on proxemics and discusses the issue of laboratory versus naturalistic research on proxemics.

Erving Goffman's *Behavior in Public Places* (1963) makes some good observations on the use of space in public places. Both physical and social barriers exist to control allocation of involvement, to prevent ones' getting too involved with the concerns of others in public places, and to protect oneself from the barrage of stimulation possible in a public place. Civil inattention is a mechanism Goffman postulates to ensure a manageable level of stimulation. For example, when we approach another person on a street, walking in opposite directions, we drop our gaze away from his when a certain critical distance is reached, about eight feet, where social and public distance cross (using Hall's terms). Being close to another person signals the possibility of an interaction. If this relationship is to be avoided, a negating signal, such as a cutoff in eye contact, must be given. Goffman dubs this particular maneuver of civil inattention, "a dimming of the lights."

The second research orientation on spatial behavior we shall term "personal space." Mainly experimental in design, these studies usually do not concern themselves with cross-cultural differences or with issues of national character, as do the anthropologically based proxemic studies. The effect of certain spatial arrangements on psychological states or social processes, and vice versa, is generally the focus of interest. (See Evans and Howard, 1973, for a review of personal space studies.) For example, Sommer's selection (p. **242**) presents evidence to support a spatial theory of leadership: persons placed in the center of group networks more often emerged as leaders than those in less advantageous positions. Aiello and Cooper (1972) report that persons liking each other stand closer to one another than those who do not; again, a relationship between spatial behavior and psychological state.

The study of crowd behavior has become part of the personal space tradition. The basic question is how does crowding affect psychological state and social behavior. Generally, the feeling has been that there must be a deleterious effect in both areas. Hall (1966) quotes animal evidence of pathological behavior in many species accompanying unchecked population expansion. Wynne-Edwards (1962) believes that animal social organizations have evolved as mechanisms for population control and dispersion. Indeed, much of the argument about the population crisis has to do with the lowering of the quality of life as a result of high density living (apart from the critical issue of competition for scarce resources). The picture of the crowd in social psychology is also a dim one. Writers as far back as Le Bon (1895) have been saying that man "descends several rungs on the ladder of civilization when he joins a crowd" (Le Bon, 1895). Presumably, some of the bad effects were caused by the physical closeness of people, which permitted such postulated crowd phenomena like mass suggestion and contagion to occur. The callous, pressured quality of urban life is commonly viewed as one consequence of high density living.

Psychologists studying crowding have found it to be a complex phenomenon. Zlutnick and Altman (1972) have noted that population density alone does not define the psychological feeling of being in a crowd. Such factors as the length of time spent in the area, the focus of attention, and expectation of interaction mediate the effects of population density. Desor (1972) found that the overall level of social stimulation was the determining factor for defining a crowd, not just the population density. Even when the number of people and size of the room are the same, individual reactions may differ. Ross, Layton, Erickson, and Schopler (1973) found that males rate others and themselves more favorably in a larger room, while females react more positively in a smaller room. Women tend to prefer the interpersonal closeness possible in smaller rooms, while men dislike the resulting higher population density. The psychological experience and effects of crowding, then, are only partially a function of physical conditions. The interpretation given these conditions is crucial, and for this we must know more about the individuals involved.

One aspect of spatial behavior which might tend to support the belief in the deleterious effects of crowding is the research on territoriality. Sommer and Becker's article (p. 252) presents some imaginative field and laboratory studies upholding this concept. They found that the use of personal markers to reserve space in public places was a very effective ploy to establish a territorial claim. Becker (1973) reports some new research on spatial markers, indicating that the concept of jurisdiction (temporary possession) may be more apt than that of territory (a more permanent claim). The concept of territoriality was popularized by Robert Ardrey's (1966) book, *The Territorial Imperative,* in which he sought to generalize from animal research to such human "territorial" behavior as nationalism. Much is known about animal territoriality, but the concept has not been applied to humans until recently. Lyman and Scott (1967) call territoriality "a neglected sociological dimension" and distinguish four types of territories in human societies: body territories, interactional territories, home territories, and public territories. Body territory covers the area that other researchers call personal space, the area immediately around the person. The others refer to various types of marked-off areas, where encroachment is possible and will be reacted to. Lyman and Scott enumerate three types of territorial encroachment: violation, invasion, and contamination, concepts that Hall (1966) also recognizes in a general way in his work.

Sommer's (1969) book *Personal Space: The Behavioral Basis of Design* discusses the way knowledge of human territoriality and spatial needs can be applied to architectural and urban design so as to maximize psychological comfort and social usage. For example, Sommer looked at classrooms from the point of view of proxemics. The usual spatial layout of straight rows of chairs oriented toward the teacher suggests on a nonverbal level the authority-oriented flow of communication from teacher to student. Audience participation is usually quite limited, and generally drops off radically as distance and eye contact decrease (farther away and at an angle from the teacher). Such interaction patterns are institutionalized in many schools by assigning seats to students and keeping them there throughout the year. Sommer quotes with favor Kohl's (1967) suggestion that students be given "spatial freedom" in the classroom, so they can change seats at will and keep the interaction pattern in a more fluid state, permitting individual differences to emerge in the free choice of seats and participation in class discussions.

Two other areas peripheral to proxemics deserve mention: posture and touch. An important aspect of body orientation in space is posture. Hewes (1955) has done an ambitious study of the world distribution of postural habits. He has found a wide variety of culturally patterned ways of sitting and standing and evidence that these habits are diffused to neighboring cultures much like other cultural traits. Mehrabian (1972) reports some work on postural orientation as a correlate of certain psychological states, such as liking and persuasiveness. There are also scattered reports in the psychiatric literature of certain postures associated with psychopathological states, such as depression.

The logical end of proxemics is touching. Once two people touch they have eliminated the space between them, and this act usually signifies that a special type of relationship exists between them. Studies of touching, or tactile behavior as it is more formally known, have appeared infrequently in the literature. Frank (1957) summarizes some of the psychiatric and anthropological literature on the subject, as does Montagu's (1971) more recent popular book. Research such as Harlows' (1971) tends to support the idea that monkeys seek tactile stimulation even at the expense of nourishment. In Harlows' classic study, monkeys clung to cloth "mothers" who did not provide food in preference to wire ones which did supply nourishment. The former provided tactile stimulation while the latter did not. Impressions of child behavior seem to give evidence of this need in the proclivity of children to seek tactile comfort and stimulation and to respond negatively to a deficit of such experience (Montagu, 1971).

As students of nonverbal communication, we should be most interested in the question of what *rules* regulate touching behavior. Jourard (1966) found that males and females had different kinds of tactile experiences with their mothers, fathers, same-sex and opposite-sex friends. For example, males were more likely than females to be touched by their mothers on the chest area, but females were more likely than males to be touched on the upper arm area by their mothers. Henley (1973) has recently studied what she calls "the politics of touch," indicating that status differences are reinforced by greater tactile accessibility to the lower status partner. Henley's contention is that in opposite-sex interaction, male dominance is partially established by touching the female. Certainly more work deserves to be done in the area of tactile communication, looking at it as an indicator of personality and the state of an interaction, as well as investigating cultural differences in the patterning of such behavior.

In conclusion, then, we have seen that study of the social use of space, in both the proxemic and personal space tradition, holds promise of deepening our understanding of interpersonal behavior and cultural differences, as well as of enabling us to improve the quality of life by tailoring our public places to the spatial needs of the human animal.

REFERENCES

Aiello, J. R., and Cooper, R. E., "Use of personal space as a function of social affect," *Proceedings,* 80th annual convention, American Psychological Association, 1972, 207–8.

Ardrey, R., *The Territorial Imperative,* Atheneum, New York, 1966.

Becker, F. D., "Study of spatial markers," *Journal of Personality and Social Psychology,* 1973, 26, 439–45.

Desor, J. A., "Toward a psychological

theory of crowding," *Journal of Personality and Social Psychology*, 1972, 21, 79–83.

Efron, D., *Gesture and Environment*, King's Crown Press, New York, 1941.

Evars, G. W., and Howard, R. B., "Personal Space," *Psychological Bulletin*, 1973, 80, 334–44.

Frank, L. K., "Tactile communication," *Genetic Psychology Monographs*, 1957, 56, 209–55.

Goffman, E., *Behavior in Public Places*, The Free Press, Glencoe, 1963.

Hall, E. T., "A system for the notation of proxemic behavior," *American Anthropologist*, 1963, 65, 1003–26.

Hall, E. T., *The Hidden Dimension*, Doubleday, New York, 1966.

Harlow, H. F., *Learning to Love*, Albion, San Francisco, 1971.

Henley, N. M., "The politics of touch," in *Radical Psychology*, P. Brown, ed., Harper & Row, New York, 1973, pp. 421–33.

Hewes, G. W., "World distribution of certain postural habits," *American Anthropologist*, 1955, 57, 231–44.

Jourard, S. M., "An exploratory study of body accessibility," *British Journal of Social and Clinical Psychology*, 1966, 5, 221–31.

Kohl, H., *36 Children*, New American Library, New York, 1967.

Le Bon, G., *The Crowd*, 1895 (reprinted 1960, Viking Press).

Lyman, S. M., and Scott, M. B., "Territoriality: a neglected sociological dimension," *Social Problems*, 1967, 15, 236–49.

Mehrabian, A., *Nonverbal Communication*, Aldine, Chicago, 1972.

Montagu, A., *Touching: The Human Significance of the Skin*, Columbia University Press, New York, 1971.

Ross, M., Layton, B., Erickson, B., and Schopler, J., "Affect, facial regard and reactions to crowding," *Journal of Personality and Social Psychology*, 1973, 28, 69–76.

Sommer, R., *Personal Space: The Behavioral Basis of Design*, Prentice Hall, Englewood Cliffs, 1969.

Watson, O. H., *Proxemic Behavior: A Cross Cultural Study*, Mouton, The Hague, 1970.

Watson, O. M., and Graves, T. D., "Quantitative research in proxemic behavior," *American Anthropologist*, 1966, 68, 971–85.

Wynne-Edwards, V. C., *Animal Dispersion in Relation to Social Behaviour*, Oliver and Boyd, Edinburgh and London, 1962.

Zlutnick, S., and Altman, I., "Crowding and human behavior," in *Environment and the Social Sciences: Perspectives and Applications*, J. Wohlwill and D. Carson, eds., American Psychological Association, Washington, D.C., 1972.

14

PROXEMICS [1]

EDWARD T. HALL

Western man has conceptualized space in many ways, ranging from Bogardus' (1933, 1959) social space and Sorokin's (1943) sociocultural space to Lewin's (1948) topologies. Chapple and Coon (1942) and Hallowell (1955) treated distance technically when they described how it is measured in different cultures.[2] Jammer (1960) has dealt with the concepts of space (including their historical underpinnings) in physics. Proxemics,[3] the study of man's perception and use of space, pertains to none of these directly. It is much closer, instead, to the behavioral complex of activities and their derivatives known to the ethologists as territoriality. It deals primarily with out-of-awareness distance-setting,[4] and owes much to the work of Sapir (1927) and Whorf (1956).

Because of my communications bias, the subjects of proxemic research have generally been members of my own culture. Like Bateson (1948), I have learned to depend more on what people do than what they say in response to a direct question, to pay close attention to that which cannot be consciously manipulated, and to look for patterns rather than content (Hall 1966). However, except in a few exceptional instances, I have never been able to be really certain of the correctness of my own interpretations of observed behavior in other cultures. In interpreting the actions of people in other cultures, the only thing about which I am reasonably certain is my own fleeting responses. Working in a detailed way on the micro-cultural level (Hall 1966: 96) and only where it was possible to detect responses on the affective, as well as the behavioral, level has motivated

From *Current Anthropology*, 1968, 9, 83–95, 106–8. Copyright © 1968 by the University of Chicago Press and reprinted by permission. The original of this article also included commentary by Ray L. Birdwhistell, Bernhard Bock, Paul Bohannan, A. Richard Diebold, Jr., Marshall Durbin, Munro S. Edmonson, J. L. Fischer, Dell Hymes, Solon T. Kimball, Weston La Barre, Frank Lynch, J. E. McClellan, Donald S. Marshall, G. B. Milner, Harvey B. Sarles, George L. Trager, and Andrew P. Vayda, as well as a reply from the author, Edward T. Hall. The reader is referred to the original source, cited above, for the commentary and reply (pp. 95–108).

me to concentrate on my own culture as it has been revealed against the contrasting backdrop of other cultures. In this sense, I am in agreement with Lévi-Strauss (1966b) when he speaks of the anthropology of the future as a science in which people study themselves. My approach has been to use myself and others as measuring devices (or "controls," if you like) at those times when we have been subjected to contrasting cultural environments. This last is important, for one can be no more than vaguely aware of one's own culture in the absence of face-to-face encounters with people of other cultures.[5]

I first became aware of my own interest in man's use of space when I was training Americans for service overseas and discovered that the way in which both time and space were handled constituted a form of communication which was responded to as if it were built into people and, therefore, universally valid. In 1963a, I wrote:

. . . Americans overseas were confronted with a variety of difficulties because of cultural differences in the handling of space. People stood "too close" during conversations, and when the Americans backed away to a comfortable conversational distance, this was taken to mean that Americans were cold, aloof, withdrawn, and disinterested in the people of the country.[6] U.S.A. housewives muttered about "waste-space" in houses in the Middle East. In England, Americans who were used to neighborliness were hurt when they discovered that their neighbors were no more accessible or friendly than other people, and in Latin America, exsuburbanites, accustomed to unfenced yards, found that the high walls there made them feel "shut out." Even in Germany, where so many of my countrymen felt at home, radically different patterns in the use of space led to unexpected tensions.

It was quite obvious that these apparently inconsequential differences in spatial behavior resulted in significant misunderstanding and intensified culture shock, often to the point of illness, for some members of the American overseas colonies. Examination of the very strong and deep responses to spatial cues on the part of overseas Americans highlighted many of the patterns implicit in the United States. These observations directed my thinking to Whorf. As I have stated elsewhere (1966):

. . . only to a handful of people have the implications of Whorf's thinking become apparent. Difficult to grasp, they become somewhat frightening when given careful thought. They strike at the root of the doctrine of "free will," because they indicate that all men are captives of the language they speak.[7]

It is my thesis that the principles laid down by Whorf and his followers in relation to language apply to all culturally patterned behavior, but particularly to those aspects of culture which are most often taken for granted and operate as Sapir (1927) so aptly put it ". . . in accordance with an elaborate and secret code that is written nowhere, known by none, and understood by all."[8] It is this elaborate and secret code that becomes confused with what is popularly conceived of as phenomenological experience. It has long been believed that experience is what men share and that it is possible to bypass language by referring back to experience in order to reach another human being. This implicit (and often explicit) belief concerning man's relation to experience is based on the assumption that when two human beings are subjected to the same "experience," virtually the same data is being fed to the two nervous systems and the two brains respond similarly. *Proxemic research casts serious doubts on the validity of this assumption, particularly when the cultures are different.* People from different cultures inhabit different sensory worlds (see Hall 1966: Chaps. 10, 11). They not only structure spaces differently, but experience it differently, because the sensorium is differently "programmed." [9] There is a selective screening or filtering that admits some types of data while rejecting others. Sometimes this is accomplished by individuals "tuning out" one or more of the senses or a portion of perception. Otherwise, it is accomplished by screening, which is one of the many important functions performed by architecture.

If the spatial experience is different by virtue of different patterning of the senses and selective attention and inattention to specific aspects of the environment, it would follow *what crowds one people does not necessarily crowd another.* Therefore, there can be no universal index of crowding, no known way of measuring crowding for all cultures. Instead, what one must ask is, "Are the people involved being stressed, and, if so, to what degree, and what senses are involved?" To answer questions such as these requires specialists from many disciplines, including pathology, biochemistry, experimental psychology, and kinesics.[10] The work of Gibson (1950) on perception and of Kilpatrick and others (1961) in transactional psychology have provided useful leads.

In 1953, Trager and I postulated a theory of culture based on a linguistic model.[11] We maintained that with the model we were using, it must be possible ultimately to link major cultural systems (of which there were several) to the physiology of the organism; i.e.,

that there should be not only a prelinguistic base (Trager 1949) but a precultural base as well. In 1959, I suggested the term "infra-culture" be used to designate those behavioral manifestations "that preceded culture but later became elaborated into culture." It followed from this that it might be helpful in the analysis of a primary cultural system, such as proxemics, to examine its infra-cultural base. A look at the various manifestations of territoriality (and these are many) should help provide both a foundation and a perspective to be used in considering more complex human elaborations of space.

Much can be learned in this regard from the ethologists.[12] It is difficult to consider man with other animals, yet, in the light of what is known of ethology, it may be appropriate to consider man as an organism that has elaborated and specialized his *extensions* [13] to the point where they are rapidly replacing nature. In other words, man has created a new dimension, the cultural dimension, in relation to which he maintains a state of dynamic equilibrium. This process is one in which both man and his environment participate in molding each other. Man is now in the position of creating his own biotope. He is, therefore, in the position of determining *what kind of organism* he will be. This is a frightening thought in view of how little we know about man and his needs. It also means that in a very deep sense, man is creating different types of people in his slums, his mental hospitals, his cities, and his suburbs. What is more, the problems man is facing in trying to create one world are much more complex than was formerly assumed. Within the United States we have discovered that one group's slum is another's sensorily enriched environment. (Fried and

Gleicher 1961, Gans 1960, Abrams 1965).

Hediger's unique work in zoology and animal behavior is particularly important to proxemics. He has devoted himself to the study of what occurs when men and animals interact in the wild, in zoos, and in circuses as well as in experimental situations. Hediger has demonstrated the very point that anthropologists would hope to make for man, namely that if one is to interact realistically with any organism, it is essential to gain a basic mastery of that organism's communications systems. Hediger is deeply committed to the position that the most common error in interpreting animal behavior is anthropomorphizing or interpreting the animals' communications as though they were human. His studies of the domestication process not only underline the necessity of thoroughly understanding the sensory symbolic world of a species (how it marks its territory, for example, or the components that go to make up its biotope), but also stress the importance of knowing the specific way in which the species handles distance beyond strictly territorial considerations (Hediger 1950, 1955, 1961). For example, the reduction or elimination of the flight reaction is essential for the survival of an organism in captivity. In addition, it provides us with an operational definition of domestication. Hediger distinguished between contact and non-contact species,[14] and he was the first to describe in operational terms personal and social distances (see Figures 1, 2, 3). He has also demonstrated that critical distance is so precise that it can be measured in centimeters.[15]

Schäfer (1956) has written about both, "critical space" and "critical situations." While he has stressed the danger of drawing analogies from non-human forms, his descriptions of social and group responses to crowding and his formulation of the concepts of the "critical densities" and "crises" are not only highly suggestive for man but appear to involve processes that embrace an extraordinarily broad spectrum of living substance.

Recent studies of spacing among animals reveal that one of the primary functions of proper spacing is to permit the completion of what Tinbergen (1952, 1958) terms "action chains." Tinbergen has demonstrated that the life of the stickleback and other species is made up of predictable behavioral sequences according to set paradigms. If a sequence is broken or interrupted, it is necessary to start over again from the beginning.[16] Both animals and man, according to Spitz (1964), require, at critical stages in life, specific amounts of space in order to act out the dialogues that lead to the consummation of most of the important acts in life.

The findings of ethologists and animal psychologists suggest that: (a) each organism inhabits its own subjective world,[17] which is a function of its perceptual apparatus, and the *arbitrary separation of the organism from that world alters context and in so doing distorts meaning;* [18] and (b) the dividing line between the organism's internal and external environment cannot be pinpointed precisely.[19] The organism-biotope relationship can only be understood if it is seen as a delicately balanced series of cybernetic mechanisms in which positive and negative feedback exert subtle but continuous control over life. *That is, the organism and its biotope constitute a single, cohesive system* (within a series of larger systems). To consider one without reference to the other is meaningless.

Two further ethological studies draw

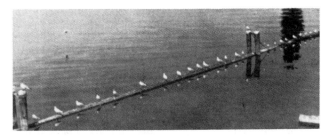

Fig. 1 Photo by H. Hediger, illustrating individual distance in the blackheaded gull. Hediger (1955, p. 66) was the first to systematically describe the various distances employed by animals and introduced the concept of individual distance 26 years ago.

Fig. 2 Personal distance in pelicans. [Photo by Edward T. Hall.]

Fig. 3 Pelicans on a rail. The maintenance of uniform distances between individuals of the species can be observed on the water (Fig. 2), on land, and while flying in the air. [Photo by Edward T. Hall.]

attention to the connection between territoriality and population control.[20] Christian's (1960) classic study of the James Island Sika deer advances the thesis that populations are controlled by physiological mechanisms that respond to density. In a summary made at a symposium on crowding, stress, and natural selection (Christian, Flyger, and Davis 1961), it was stated that:

Mortality evidently resulted from shock following severe metabolic disturbance, probably as a result of prolonged adrenocortical hyperactivity, judging from the histological material. There was no evidence of infection, starvation, or other obvious cause to explain the mass mortality.

Christian's study in only one of a number of similar studies of population collapse [21] due to stress from sensory overload (crowding).[22]

Calhoun's experiments and observations are also noteworthy for their behavioral data.[23] He allowed wild Norways rats, which were amply fed, to breed freely in a quarter-acre pen. Their number stabilized at 150 and never exceeded 200 (Calhoun 1950). With a population of 150, fighting became so disruptive to normal maternal care that only a few of the young survived. The rats did not distribute themselves evenly throughout the pen, but organized into a dozen colonies averaging 12 rats each (apparently the maximum number of rats that can live harmoniously in a natural group).

The disorders of Calhoun's overcrowded rats bear a striking resemblance to those of some contemporary Americans who live in densely packed urban conditions. Although comparative studies of humans are rare, Chombart de Lauwe (1959a, b) has gathered data on French workers' families and has demonstrated a statistical relationship between crowded living conditions and physical and social pathology. In the United States a health survey of Manhattan (Srole et al. 1962) showed that only 18% of a representative sample were free of emotional disorders while 23% were seriously disturbed or incapacitated.

Research methods and strategies

In the Foreword to Jammer's book *Concepts of Space*, Einstein has summarized many of the methodological problems in proxemics:

The eyes of the scientist are directed upon those phenomena which are accessible to observation, upon their appreciation and conceptual formulation. In the attempt to achieve a conceptual formulation of the confusingly immense body of observational data, the scientist makes use of a whole arsenal of concepts which he imbibed practically with his mother's milk; and seldom if ever is he aware of the eternally problematic character of his concepts. He uses this conceptual material, or, speaking more exactly, these conceptual tools of thought, as something obviously, immutably given; something having an objective value of truth which is hardly ever, and in any case not seriously, to be doubted.

In my study of proxemics, one of my objectives has been to examine a small slice of life in the United States—the experience of space—and to learn about some of the things Americans take for granted. My emphasis has not been on either the manifest or even the latent *content* but rather on the structural details, the implicit perceptual elements.

Most individuals, try as they will, can specify few if any of the elements that enter into perception.[24] They can only describe the end product. Thus, the student of proxemics is faced with the problem of developing techniques to isolate and identify the elements of space perception. What he aims to achieve is a sense-data equivalent of the morphophonemic structure of language or the chemist's periodic table of the elements. His data should be verifiable and the elements capable of being combined with predictable results. Where does one look for procedural models when exploring a new field? Descriptive linguistics, faced with similar problems, has provided methods applicable to proxemics.

Since the days of the Sanskrit grammarians, linguists have recognized that *language is a system* with structure and regularity. All writing systems are abstracted from the building blocks or sounds of the language represented. These are identifiable and finite in number. The way to isolate them is to obtain spoken texts as raw data and then to record the details of speech as precisely as possible, using a notation system that is based on identifiable physiological processes so that any trained observer can make the same transcriptions. In linguistics, the physiological structure points of the system have been worked out. These structure points were *not* known for proxemics when I began my research. It was clear, however, that in the perception of space, something more than the visual system was involved. The questions then became: What other systems? and, How do we know that they have been correctly indentified?

During the early stages of my research, I used a wide range of methods and techniques for identifying the elements of space perception—not just because proxemics appeared to involve many different types of variables, but on the theory that what I learned in one way could be used to check what I learned in other ways. Some of the research techniques, briefly described below, are: observation, experiment, interviews (structured and unstructured), analysis of the English lexicon, and the

study of space as it is recreated in literature and in art.

Observation

By observing people over a long period of time as they use and react to space, one can begin to discern definite patterns of proxemics behavior. While photography is only a supplement to other forms of observation—an extension of the visual memory, as it were —it is an absolutely indispensable aid in recording proxemic behavior (see Figures 4 and 5). It freezes actions and allows the investigator to examine sequences over and over again. The difficulty is to photograph people without intruding or altering their behavior. Practice in using a very small

Fig. 4 One of a series of photographs taken over a two year period to record personal distances in public settings. This particular setting was a streetcar loading platform of sufficient length that two cars would arrive and load simultaneously—a condition that reduced the bunching so characteristic of situations in which only one car at a time is loading. The loading platform was bounded on one side by streetcar tracks and the other by a street dense with traffic. This made it possible to observe spacing comparable to Hediger's gulls on a rail (see Fig. 1). [Photographs by Edward T. Hall.]

Fig. 5 Individual distances between Italians on a walkway overlooking the Rome Airport. Photograph was taken in early morning on a warm summer day. [Photo by Edward T. Hall.]

camera (Minox), which I carry with me at all times, has taught me how to photograph unobtrusively, and this has made it possible to use larger cameras as well.[25] Several thousand photographs have thus far been taken of people interacting under natural conditions in the United States, France, England, Italy, Greece, and Switzerland. These photographs have provided data against which visual observations can be checked.

The camera and the photographs it produces are extraordinarily subtle and complex tools (see Collier 1967, Byers 1966, Worth 1966). For proxemics, the camera has served as a record and reminder system and a training aid for students. It has also been very useful in investigating how subjects structure their particular perceptual worlds. One of my assistants, a German, illustrated this point when asked to take an "intimate" photograph followed by a "public" photograph of a female subject. I had expected distortion in the intimate shot and great detail in the public shot. Not at all. The intimate portrait was crisp and clear and the public shot deliberately out of focus ". . . because you aren't really supposed to look at people in public" (or photograph them, either).

In our recent investigations of proxemic behavior of various ethnic groups in the United States, my students and I have discovered that it is essential to use a member of the group we are studying as the photographer. Not only does the photographer constantly interact with his subjects (Byers 1966), but what he selects to photograph represents culture-bound choice. Photographer subjects have provided valuable insights on a number of points at which the groups involved were at odds. They also have noted serious omissions from

photographic texts taken by others (not of their own group). For example, in photographing lower class Negro, Puerto Rican, and Spanish-American subjects, our goal was to discover the specific ways in which these ethnic groups code and organize their senses in face-to-face encounters. (My experience in intercultural relations had taught me that differences in the proxemic behavior lead to what Goffman [1961] calls "alienation in encounters.") In the beginning, one of my assistants (a German photographer) photographed lower class American Negro subjects interacting with each other. Later these subjects were shown slides and 8×10 inch prints of themselves and were asked what was happening in the photographs. They were rarely able to tell us. However when one of the Negro subjects was given the control of a motorized drive camera and told to push the button whenever *he* saw something happening, he took frame after frame of what I, as a white, middle class American, considered identical pictures. Interviews with the Negro photographer and the subjects demonstrated that they were acting out and recording a highly structured dialogue in which the cues were more subtle than, and quite different from, those used by the white, middle class population. It would appear that in this particular lower class Negro group, a great deal of information is communicated by very small movements of the hands and fingers. These movements were almost imperceptible to my students and me.[26]

In addition to direct observation and photographs, another source of data is the unself-conscious comment people make as a result of some breach of spatial etiquette. Such comments often help identify the structure points in the proxemic system under study. Examples that occur frequently are statements like these:

I wish he would stop breathing down my neck. I can't stand *that!*
Have you noticed how she is always *touching* you. She can't seem *to* keep her hands to herself.
He was so close his face was all distorted.

Physical contact between people, breathing on people or directing one's breath away from people, direct eye contact or averting one's gaze, placing one's face so close to another that visual accommodation is not possible, are all examples of the kind of proxemic behavior that may be perfectly correct in one culture and absolutely taboo in another.

Experimental abstract situations

It is possible to learn a good deal about how members of a given culture structure space at various levels of abstraction by setting up simple situations in which they manipulate objects.[27] I used coins and pencils and asked my subjects to arrange them so that they were "close" and "far apart" and "side by side" and "next to each other" and then to tell me whether two objects were "together" or not. Arab subjects were unable or unwilling to make a judgment as to whether two objects were close together or not *if the surrounding area was not specified.* In other words, Arabs saw the objects *in a context;* Americans saw the objects only *in relation to each other.*

Structured interviews

My wife and I interviewed both American and foreign subjects in depth, following a detailed interview schedule. The shortest interviews took six hours; the longest lasted six months and was still producing data when that phase of the work was terminated. In the course of these studies, it became apparent that although the answers of different subjects to any particular question might vary, the interview schedule as a whole could teach us much about how the subjects structured and experienced space. Conclusions could be drawn from the way in which the questions were answered and from the difficulties encountered in understanding particular questions.

The protocol for the interviews began with a general question concerning the home and household, and the activities and named areas contained in the house. The home was chosen as a starting point not only because everyone has one, but also because it had been our experience that subjects can usually talk about the concrete features of the home even when they find it difficult or inappropriate to talk about other topics. Once the home picture had been recorded along with drawings and diagrams, the same material was covered in a different way by exploring such topics as privacy, boundaries, the rights of propinquity, and the place of the particular home in its social and geographic setting. Furniture arrangements in home and office provided added data on social relationships, and so did linguistic features such as words or concepts that were difficult to translate. Altogether, some 90 topics were covered.

One of the most valuable features of our protocol was that it was sufficiently culture-bound to cause foreign subjects to raise questions that revealed not only the structures of their own proxemic systems but the taken-for-granted aspects of our system as well. "Where do you go to be alone?"—a normal question for Americans—puzzled and sometimes angered Arabs. Some representative Arab replies are, "Who wants to be alone?" "Where do you go to be crazy?" "Paradise without people is Hell." Trespassing is thought of in the United States as a universally recognizable violation of the mores, yet our interviews failed to turn - up anything even approaching this concept among urban Arabs. The actual structure of the interview proved to be a valuable research instrument. The point is both subtle and important. By following a standard protocol, then, we were conducting research simultaneously on two different levels: level A was the manifest content, Answers to Questions; and level B (the more important and basic) was the contrast in structure of two cultural systems, one being used in context to elicit the other. The most valuable sessions turned out to be those in which foreign subjects took issue with our spatial categories.

One section of our questionnaire dealt with listening behavior [28] and was designed to elicit information on where subjects looked at the person being addressed for feedback. This proved to be one of the most productive sections of our questionnaire. What emerged from interviews with foreign subjects was not a direct answer to the questions but a series of complaints that Americans never listen or complaints about what Americans communicate by the *way* in which they listen. Arabs said we are ashamed all the time. What made them think so? The fact that we withhold our breath and direct it away from the other person. Latin American subjects complained that Americans never listened or were always breaking off, a conclusion they drew from the fact that our eyes wander. The information that we sought by this line of inquiry con-

cerned the type of perceptual involvement of the two subjects.

Analysis of the lexicon

I have long maintained (Hall and Trager 1953, Hall 1959) that *culture* is basically a communicative process. This process occurs simultaneously on many levels, some of them more explicit than others. Language is one of the explicit levels. Boas (1911) was the first anthropologist to emphasize the relationship between language and culture. He made his point in the simplest, most obvious way by analyzing lexicons of languages. Whorf (1956) went beyond Boas and suggested that language plays a prominent role in molding the perceptual world of a culture. He states,

We dissect nature along lines laid down by our natural languages. The categories and types that we isolate from the world of phenomena we do not find there. . . .

Whorf observed that in Hopi, time and space are inextricably bound up in each other; to alter one is to change the other. He says,

The Hopi thought world has no imaginary space. . . . In other words, the Hopi cannot as speakers of Indo-European languages do, "imagine" such a place as Heaven or Hell. Furthermore "hollow" spaces like room, chamber, hall are not really *named* objects but are rather located. . . .

Sapir's and Whorf's influence, extended far beyond the confines of descriptive linguistics, caused me to review the lexicon of the pocket Oxford Dictionary and to extract from it all the terms having spatial connotations such as: "over," "under," "away from," "together," "next to," "beside," "adjacent," "congruent," "level," "upright." Altogether, some 20% of this dictionary, or approximately 5,000 lexical items, were recorded.[29]

Interpretation of art

Paralleling Whorf's thinking about language, the transactional psychologists have demonstrated that perception is not passive but is learned and in fact highly patterned. It is a true transaction in which the world and the perceiver both participate. A painting or print must therefore conform to the Weltanschauung of the culture to which it is directed and to the perceptual patterns of the artist at the time he is creating. Artists know that perception is a transaction; in fact, they take it for granted.

The artist is both a sensitive observer and a communicator. How well he succeeds depends in part on the degree to which he has been able to analyze and organize perceptual data in ways that are meaningful to his audience. The manner in which sense impressions are employed by the artist reveals data about both the artist *and* his audience.

Gideon (1962), Dorner (1958), and Grosser (1951) have contributed to the specific understanding of the way European man has developed his perceptual organization through the ages.[30] For example, Grosser comments that the portrait is distinguished from any other kind of painting by a psychological nearness which ". . . depends directly on the actual interval—the distance in feet and inches between the model and painter. . . ." He sets this distance at four to eight feet and notes that it creates the characteristic "quality" of a portrait, "the peculiar sort of communication, almost a conversation, that the person who looks at the picture is able to hold with the person painted there." Grosser's discussion of the difficulties

of foreshortening and of the distortions that occur when the painter or perceiver gets too close to his subject closely parallels my subjects' descriptions of their perception of others when they are "too close."

The distinction made by Gibson (1950) between the *visual field* (the image cast on the retina) and the *visual world* (the stable image created in the mind) is essential to the comprehension of the differences in the work of two artists like Hobbema and Rembrandt. Hobbema depicted the visual world perceived in the same way a scene outside a window is perceived, as a summary of hundreds, if not thousands, of visual fields. Rembrandt, in contrast, painted visual fields.[31] In effect, he made static the scene which is generally perceived in an instant.

The principal difficulty in using art as cultural data is to distinguish between the artist's technique (which alone reveals the building blocks of his creation) and his subject matter, which may be designed to be persuasive and is often controversial [32] because tastes in art differ. Despite such complexities, the data are sufficiently rich to warrant any effort that is required.

Analysis of literature

An examination of the writer's sense impressions reveals much about his perceptual world. If a writer refers to vision to build his images it is possible to examine these images to determine what kind of vision he uses. Is it foveal, macular, or peripheral vision? Which of Gibson's numerous ways of seeing perspective does he employ? What is the role of olfaction and touch?

Writers express what readers already know and would have expressed if they had possessed the requisite analytic capability, training and skills. When the writer succeeds, there is a close register between his descriptions and his reader's own sensory pattern, since writers evoke spatial images in the reader. The question I asked myself was: "What clues does the writer provide the reader that enable him to construct a spatial image?" It seemed to me that an analysis of passages that are spatially evocative would be revealing. I asked subjects to mark such passages in a sample of over a hundred representative novels. The first texts used were those which contained spatial images that subjects vividly recalled from past reading. This group of passages, elicited from those who had spontaneously commented on them, ultimately proved to be of the most value.

As in painting, the representation of space in literature changes over time, and appears to reflect rather accurately growing awareness of the nature as well as the proxemic patterns of the culture. McLuhan (1963) notes, for example, that the first reference to three-dimensional visual perspective in literature occurs in *King Lear,* when Edgar seeks to persuade the blinded Duke of Gloucester that they indeed stand atop the cliffs of Dover. Thoreau's *Walden* is replete with spatial images. Referring to his small cabin and its influence on his conversation, he writes:

. . . our sentences wanted *room* to unfold and form their columns in the interval. *Individuals,* like nations, *must have* suitable broad and natural *boundaries, even a neutral ground* between them . . . If we are merely loquacious and loud talkers, then we can afford to stand very near together, *cheek to jowl, and feel each other's breath;* but if we speak reservedly and thoughtfully we want to be farther apart, *that all animal heat and moisture* may have a chance to evaporate (italics mine).

Mark Twain was fascinated with spatial imagery and its distortion. He set out to create impossible spatial paradoxes in which the reader "sees" intimate details at incredible distances, or experiences spaces so vast that the mind boggles at comprehending them. Most of Mark Twain's distances are visual and auditory. Kafka, in *The Trial,* emphasizes the body and the role of kinesthetic distance perception. The vitality of St. Exupery's images is in his use of kinesthetic, tactile, olfactory, and auditory perceptions.

Concepts and measures

Three categories of space

It has proved helpful in proxemic research to be able to refer to the degree to which cultures treat proxemic features as fixed, semi-fixed, or dynamic (Hall 1963a, 1966). In general, walls and territorial boundaries are treated as fixed features. However, territory may be a seasonal affair, as it is with the migrating Bedouin of Syria, and therefore, territory is sometimes classified as semi-fixed or dynamic. Furniture can be either fixed or semi-fixed. Interpersonal distance is usually treated informally [33] and is dynamic for most peoples of North European origin. These distinctions are important in intercultural encounters. If one person treats as moveable that which is considered fixed by someone else, it causes real anxiety. For example, a German subject (an immigrant to the United States), who treated furniture as fixed, had bolted to the floor the chair on which visitors sat in his office. This caused great consternation among American visitors. One of my Chinese subjects informed me that in China a visitor would not dream of adjusting the furniture to conform to his unwritten definition of an interaction distance unless specifically instructed to do so by his host. American students in my classes, who cover a wide spectrum of ethnic, class, and regional cultures within the United States, have been evenly divided between those who adjust the furniture to conform to an informal norm and those who do not.

Sociopetal and sociofugal space

Another type of observation to be made by proxemic fieldworkers is whether the space is organized so that it is conducive to communication between people (sociopetal) or whether it is organized to produce solitary (sociofugal) (Osmond 1957). What is sociofugal to one culture or subculture may be sociopetal to another. An Arab colleague has noted, for instance, that his small, paneled recreation room was "sehr gemütlich" or "cozy" to German friends but had just the opposite effect on Arabs, who found it oppressive.

The relationship of the spoken language to proxemics

The content of conversation is linked to distance and situation as well as to the relationship of the participants, their emotions, and their activity. Joos (1962) relates linguistic analysis to distance and situation in a manner applicable to a proxemic frame of reference. His five styles—intimate, casual, consultative, formal, and frozen—can be equated roughly with the intimate, personal, social-consultative, and public zones of United States proxemic patterns. The fact that Joos treats language as a transaction (introducing feedback) rather than as a one-way process makes his conceptual model especially applicable to proxemics. His work, is also relevant in that it intro-

duces the situational dialect (Hall 1960b).[34]

Hockett (1958) has defined communication as any event that triggers another organism. (This definition would include the environment, although it is not clear that Hockett intended this.) Originally, he listed seven design features for language:

1. duality (units or *cenemes* that build up)
2. interchangeability ("A" can play "B's" part, and vice-versa)
3. displacement (in time or space)
4. specialization (the attachment of specific meanings to specific things)
5. arbitrariness (there is no necessary connection between the event and the symbol)
6. productivity (novel forms can be created)
7. cultural transmission (as contrasted with genetic transmission)

Later, Hockett (1960) expanded the list to 13 in an effort to sharpen or clarify his definition of language. In the process he cleared up some problems while creating others. Hockett's concept of the design features represents a breakthrough in our understanding of communication. As a culturally elaborated form of communication, proxemics satisfies all of Hockett's seven original design features, even productivity (the architect or designer striving to create new forms). In general, the evolutionary studies of language as outlined by Hockett and the infra-cultural basis for proxemics seem to parallel each other. There are some points of departure. Displacement in time and space of an incipient but recognizable form occurs with territorial marking at the level of mammals. When ungulates are frightened by a panther they release an olfactory sign from the gland in their hoofs that warns others of their kind traveling the same trail later that there is danger in the bush. By presenting us with a well-laid-out scheme that compares communication systems across species and genera lines, Hockett not only has provided a series of specific points held up to the mirror of life but also has related them in a particular way. His points should be taken not as absolutes but as positions on a continuum. As an *absolute*, for instance, total feedback does not exist, because the speaker only hears and is aware of *part* of what he is saying. Duality of patterning, the "small arrangements of a relatively very small stock of distinguishable sounds which are in themselves wholly meaningless," would, by the substitution of a single word ("information" for "sounds"), prove to be a characteristic of all life beginning with RNA and DNA and ending with communicative forms that are present but have yet to be technically analysed. It is with language, then, that we complete the circle, beginning and ending with species other than man.

No known universal distance-setting mechanism

Observations, interviews, analysis of art and literature, all point to the fact that there is *no* fixed distance-sensing mechanism (or mechanisms) in man that is universal for all cultures. One of the complexities of proxemic research is the fact that not only are people unable to describe how they set distances, but each ethnic group sets distances in its own way. In fact, their measuring rods are different. Some of the perceived distances expand and shrink according to circumstances. *Interpersonal distance is a constellation of sensory inputs that is coded in a particular way.* For instance, middle class American subjects of North European extraction set many

of their interpersonal distances visually (Hall 1964a, b 1966).[35] This is accomplished to some extent by signals received from muscular feedback in the eyes, gauged by the point at which the subject begins to feel cross-eyed or has difficulty focusing, etc. Additional visual references used are the size of the retinal image, perceived detail, and peripheral movement. The visual interaction of Arabs is intense; they are directly and totally involved. The Arab stares; the American does not. The Arab's olfactory sense is actively involved in establishing and maintaining contact. Arabs tend to stay inside the olfactory bubble of their interlocutor, whereas Americans try to stay outside of it.

All the senses are ultimately involved in setting distance and bear the same relation to proxemics as the vocal apparatus (teeth, tongue, hard and soft palate, and vocal cords) does to phonetics. If man is thought of as being in a constant transaction with his environment, sometimes actively, sometimes passively, it can be seen that *selective screening* is as necessary as *patterned stimulation* of the senses. It is no wonder then that one of our subjects, a German professor, found even the solid architecture of early 20th century America unsatisfactory to him because it failed to screen out enough sound when he was working in his study. As a contrast in sensory needs, Fried and Gleicher (1961) and Fried (1963) found that West End Bostonians of Italian descent required great auditory involvement, and it is my interpretation that part of their shock at being relocated away from the Boston West Side to more modern buildings was due to an unfamiliar and uncongenial sensory mix. They felt shut off from people. American middle class subjects working in Latin America miss *visual* involvement with their neighbors and feel shut out by the adobe walls that make every Latin-American home a private affair. Frenchmen, accustomed to a wide assortment of pungent odors as they move along city streets, may suffer a form of sensory deprivation in the American urban setting with its uniform acrid smell.

Elsewhere (1963*b*), I have described a notation system based on eight different dimensions or scales for the senses (1) postural-sex; (2) sociofugal-sociopetal; (3) kinesthetic; (4) touch; (5) retinal; (6) thermal; (7) olfactory; (8) voice loudness. This system enables the fieldworker to focus his attention on specific behavioral segments that will ultimately enable him to distinguish between the behavior of one group and that of another.

. . . in spite of their *apparent* complexity, cultural systems are so organized that their context can be learned and controlled by all normal members of the group . . . The anthropologist knows that what he is looking for are patterned distinctions that transcend individual differences and are closely integrated into the social matrix in which they occur.

Table 1 shows the relationship of varying distances as experienced by Americans of North European heritage in relation to the different senses. Table 2 illustrates examples of various interaction distances.

Areas to be investigated

Research in proxemics underscores what anthropologists know, that what is taken for granted in one culture may not even exist in another. It is therefore impossible to make up a universal list of questions for revealing the structure of proxemic systems. Our experience with the extensive protocol referred to earlier was that it was at best only a culturally biased sounding board. Although great pains had been taken to make the protocol as culture-free as possible, this turned out to be impossible. The following list of problems for proxemic research will also reflect the biases of its originator's culture, not only in its organization but also in its content.

1. How many kinds of distance do people maintain? (It would be useful to know the total range of human behavior in this respect.)
2. How are these distances differentiated?
3. What relationships, activities, and emotions are associated with each distance?
4. In general, what can be classified as fixed feature, semi-fixed feature, and dynamic space?
5. What is sociofugal and what is sociopetal?
6. Boundaries:
   a. How are boundaries conceived?
   b. How permanent are they?
   c. What constitutes a violation of a boundary?
   d. How are boundaries marked?
   e. When and how do you know you are inside a boundary?
7. Is there a hierarchy of spaces from, for example, most intimate and most sacred to most public?
8. Related to both (1) and (7), is there a hierarchy of distances between people? Who is permitted in each, and under what circumstances?
9. Who is permitted to touch, and under what circumstances?
10. Are there taboos against touching, looking, listening, and smelling? To whom do they apply?
11. What screening needs are there?

TABLE I

Feet	0	1	2	3	4	5	6	7	8	10	12	14	16	18	20	22	30

INFORMAL DISTANCE CLASSIFICATION

INTIMATE { CLOSE / NOT CLOSE } — PERSONAL { CLOSE / NOT CLOSE } — SOCIAL-CONSULTIVE { CLOSE / NOT CLOSE } — PUBLIC

MANDATORY RECOGNITION DISTANCE BEGINS HERE — NOT CLOSE BEGINS AT 30'-40'

KINESTHESIA

HEAD, PELVIS, THIGHS, TRUNK CAN BE BROUGHT INTO CONTACT OR MEMBERS CAN ACCIDENTALLY TOUCH. HANDS CAN REACH AND MANIPULATE ANY PART OF TRUNK EASILY.

HANDS CAN REACH AND HOLD EXTREMITIES EASILY BUT WITH MUCH LESS FACILITY THAN ABOVE. SEATED CAN REACH AROUND AND TOUCH OTHER SIDE OF TRUNK. NOT SO CLOSE AS TO RESULT IN ACCIDENTAL TOUCHING.

ONE PERSON HAS ELBOW ROOM.

TWO PEOPLE BARELY HAVE ELBOW ROOM. ONE CAN REACH OUT AND GRASP AN EXTREMITY.

2 PEOPLE WHO'S HEADS ARE 8'-9' APART CAN PASS AN OBJECT BACK AND FORTH BY BOTH STRETCHING.

JUST OUTSIDE TOUCHING DISTANCE. — OUT OF INTERFERENCE DISTANCE. — BY REACHING ONE CAN JUST TOUCH THE OTHER.

THERMAL RECEPTORS

NORMALLY OUT OF AWARENESS. — CULTURAL ATTITUDE

ANIMAL HEAT AND MOISTURE DISSIPATE (THOREAU)

OLFACTION

WASHED SKIN & HAIR

SHAVING LOTION-PERFUME — OK

SEXUAL ODORS — OK — TABOO — Variable — TABOO

BREATH — ANTISEPTIC OK OTHERWISE TABOO — TABOO

BO — TABOO

SMELLY FEET — TABOO

VISION

DETAIL VISION (VIS ∠ AT MACULA FOVIA 1°): VISION — BLURRED DISTORTED | ENLARGED DETAILS OF IRIS, EYEBALL, PORES OF FACE, FINEST HAIRS | DETAILS OF FACE SEEN AT NORMAL SIZE. EYES, NOSE, SKIN, TEETH, CONDITION OF LASHES, HAIR ON BACK OF NECK | SMALLEST BLOOD VESSELS IN EYE LOST | FULL LINES OF FACE FADE, SLIGHT EYE WINK, LIP MOVEMENT | DEEP LINES STAND OUT, MENT SEEN CLEARLY | ENTIRE CENTRAL FACE INCLUDED | SHARP FEATURES DISSOLVE, EYE COLOR NOT DISCERNABLE, SMILE-SCOWL VISIBLE, HEAD BOBBING MORE PRONOUNCED | SNELLEN'S STANDARD FOR DISTANT VISION EMPLOYING ANGLE OF 1 MIN. GUILD OPTICIANS OF AMERICA EYE CHART. A PERSON WITH 20-40 VISION HAS TROUBLE SEEING EYES AND HEAD EXPRESSION AROUND EYES THOUGH EYE BLINK IS VISIBLE

CLEAR VISION (VIS ∠ 12° HOR., 3° VERT.): 20"-3" OR EYE NOSTRILS OR MOUTH | 3.75" x 84" UPPER OR LOWER FACE | 6.25" x 1.60" UPPER OR LOWER FACE | 10" x 2.5" UPPER OR LOWER FACE OR SHOULDERS | 20" x 5" 1 OR 2 FACES | 31" x 7.5 FACES OF TWO PEOPLE | 42" x 16" TORSOS OF TWO PEOPLE | 63" x 17" TORSOS OF 4 OR 5 PEOPLE

60° SCANNING: ½ OF FACE, EYE, EAR OR MOUTH AREA. FACE DISTORTED | NOSE PROJECTS, WHOLE FACE SEEN, FACE DISTORTED | UPPER BODY CAN'T COUNT FINGERS | UPPER BODY & GESTURES | WHOLE SEATED BODY VISIBLE. PEOPLE OFTEN KEEP FEET WITHIN OTHER PERSON'S 60° ANGLE OF VIEW | WHOLE BODY HAS SPACE AROUND IT. POSTURAL COMMUNICATION BEGINS TO ASSUME IMPORTANCE

PERIPHERAL VISION: HEAD AGAINST BACKGROUND | HEAD & SHOULDERS | WHOLE BODY MOVEMENT IN HANDS-FINGERS VISIBLE | WHOLE BODY | OTHER PEOPLE SEEN IF PRESENT | OTHER PEOPLE BECOME IMPORTANT IN PERIPHERAL VISION

HEAD SIZE: FILLS VISUAL FIELD FAR OVER LIFE SIZE | OVER NORMAL SIZE | NORMAL SIZE | NORMAL TO BEGINNING TO SHRINK | VERY SMALL

NOTE: PERCEIVED HEAD SIZE VARIES EVEN WITH SAME SUBJECTS & DISTANCE

ADDITIONAL NOTES: SENSATION OF BEING CROSSEYED | | | | | | | | PEOPLE AND OBJECTS SEEN AS ROUND UP TO 12—15 FEET | | | | ACCOMODATIVE CONVERGENCE ENDS AFTER 15' PEOPLE & OBJECTS BEGIN TO FLATTEN OUT

TASKS IN SUBMARINES: DIMMICH | | | FL & FARNSWORTH D | | VISUAL ACUITY TASKS IN A SUBMARINE | | NEW LONDON, 1951

TOO FAR CONVER- / TOO FAR CONVER-

FOR SATION BODY IS ⅓ SIZE

ARTISTS' OBSERVATIONS OF GROSSER: VERY PERSONAL DISTANCE | | A PICTURE PAINTED AT 4'6" OF A PERSON WHO IS NOT PAID TO "SIT" IS A PORTRAIT | | FULL LENGTH STATE PORTRAITS, HUMAN BODY SEEN AS WHOLE, COMPREHENDED AT A GLANCE WARMTH AND IDENTIFICATION CEASE

ORAL

GRUNTS / GROANS — WHISPER — SOFT VOICE INTIMATE STYLE — CONVENTIONAL MODIFIED VOICE CASUAL OR CONSULTIVE STYLE — LOUD VOICE WHEN TALKING TO A GROUP MUST RAISE VOICE TO GET ATTENTION CONVENTIONAL CONSULTIVE STYLE — FULL PUBLIC SPEAKING VOICE FORMAL STYLE

AURAL

67% OF TASKS IN THIS RANGE / 27% FALL IN THIS RANGE

NOTE: The boundaries associated with the transition from one voice level to the next have not been precisely determined.

The above chart makes it possible to see at a glance how middle class Americans of North European heritage are sensorially involved at different distances. It should be stressed that other cultures use different sensory mixes and often have a different set of sanctions.

TABLE 2

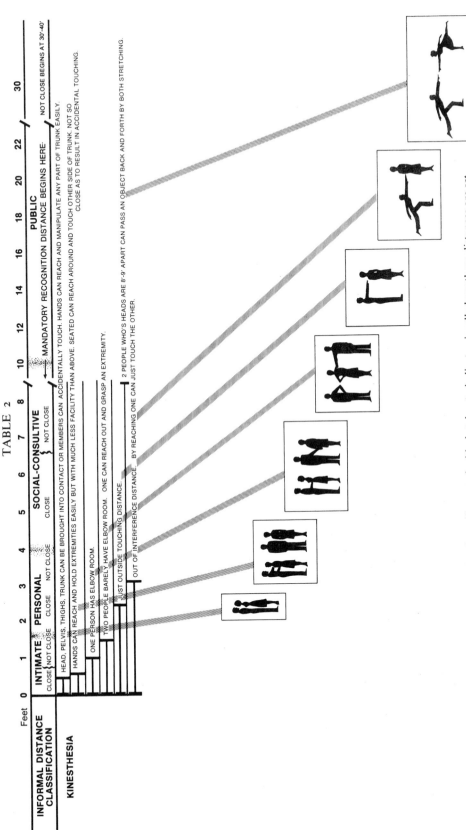

In this chart the kinesthetic portion has been illustrated with sketches to indicate visually how these distances are set.

For what senses and which relationships?

12. What is the nature of the sensory
involvement for the different relationships in the normal course of
everyday life?

13. What specific spatial needs are
there?

14. What are the spatial references in
the lexicon?

15. Is there a special handling of space
between superordinates and subor-
dinates?

NOTES

1. The research reported on in this
paper was supported by the National Institute of Mental Health
and the Wenner-Gren Foundation
for Anthropological Research.

2. Hallowell's introduction to his
Chapter 9 (Cultural Factors in Spatial Orientation) is particularly relevant to space perception.

3. In the course of the development
of proxemics, the work was spoken
of as "social space as bio-commu-
nication," and "micro-space in interpersonal encounters." These
were actually abbreviated technical
descriptions in which the proper
meanings of the terms of reference
were known only to a few specialists. Further, the widespread interest in activities connected with
outer space provided an incentive
to distinguish between my work
and that of the outer-space scientists. I decided to invent a new
term that would indicate, in general, what the field was about.
Among the terms I considered
were human topology, chaology,
the study of empty space, oriology,
the study of boundaries, chorology,
the study of organized space. I
finally chose "proxemics" as the
most suitable for that audience

most likely to encounter the topic
in the near future.

4. The following quote (Hall 1963)
speaks to the matter of levels of
awareness: "Any culture characteristically produces a simultaneous
array of patterned behavior on several different levels of awareness. It
is therefore important to specify
which levels of awareness one is
describing.

"Unlike much of the traditional
subject matter of anthropological
observation, proxemic patterns,
once learned, are maintained
largely out of conscious awareness
and thus have to be investigated
without resort to probing the conscious minds of one's subjects. Direct questioning will yield few if
any significant variables, as it will
with such topics as kinship and
house type. In proxemics one is
dealing with phenomena akin to
tone of voice, or even stress and
pitch in the English language. Since
these are built into the language,
they are hard for the speaker to
consciously manipulate."

Also see Hall (1959: Chap. 4)
for a more complete statement
concerning levels of awareness relating to change.

5. The problem of self-awareness has
been a stumbling-block for psychologists for years. We really do
not know by what means the brain
interprets the data fed to it by the
senses. Recently there has been
some progress in solving this problem. The solution appears to hinge
on *contrasts* built into the receptors rather than simple stimulation
leading to a specific response
(McCulloch 1964).

6. One can never be sure initially of
the true significance of this sort of
behavior. One learns with time to
pay attention to casual remarks engendered by the original response.
Instead of saying that a particular
American was cool, aloof, or dis-

tant, an Arab subject remarked: "What's the matter? Does he think I *smell* bad?" In this instance, the reference to olfaction provided an important clue to Arab distance-setting mechanisms.

7. By stressing the importance of Whorf's observations, I do not mean to imply that there is no external reality to be discovered, nor do I think that Whorf believed this. The reality can remain constant, but what different organisms perceive is determined largely by "what they intend to do about it," in the words of a colleague.

8. By "all" one assumes that Sapir meant the members of a given ethnic community.

9. The precise methods can only be surmised by which the young are taught to selectively attend some things while disregarding others and to favor one sense channel while suppressing another. It is reasonable to assume, however, that culture provides a pattern, among other things, for a rather elaborate and extraordinarily detailed, but less contrived, Skinnerian (1953) reinforcement schedule in which individual reinforcements are of such short duration that they are not ordinarily isolated out of the context in which they occur. The work of Condon (1967) and others has demonstrated the extraordinary degree to which people are capable of responding to each other and coordinating their behavior during conversations. Frame-by-frame examination of movies taken at 24 and 48 frames per second and study of simultaneous electroencephalograms reveals organized, coherent, synchronous behavior that is not normally observable without the aid of high-speed cameras. One can put forth the suggestion, in these terms, that positive and negative reinforcement can and does occur subliminally.

10. The relationship of proxemics to kinesics (Birdwhistell 1952, Hayes 1964, and Condon 1967) has been treated elsewhere (Hall 1963*b*). Basically, and in the simplest possible terms, proxemics is not primarily concerned with the observation and recording of the details of gestures and body movements. Proxemics deals with architecture, furniture, and the use of space, whereas kinesics, at present, is only indirectly concerned with the setting. Proxemic notation is simpler than that employed in kinesics. Proxemics seeks to determine the how of distance-setting (a question of epistemology). It is important for the proxemicist to know as much as possible about the physiology of the eye, and the many other ways in which man perceives distance.

11. A version of this original series of postulates was published in 1959.

12. Margaret Mead (1961) has also suggested that anthropologists have much to gain from the study of the works of ethologists.

13. The term "extension" summarizes a process in which evolution accelerates when it occurs outside the body (see Hall 1959, 1966).

14. McBride does not entirely agree with Hediger's basic distinction and, instead, holds that there are times when animals may be contact and other times when they may not. A three-way friendly polemic by mail between McBride, Hediger, and me has resolved many of McBride's objections. It now appears that, like dominance in genetics, contact/non-contact behavior is a matter of degree and situation.

15. For a description of these distances, see Hall (1966).

16. The territorial concept is complex, representing a wide variety of behavior patterns. Carpenter (1958), for example, lists 32 functions as-

sociated with territoriality. In the context in which I am using the term at present, what is important is that *the sensory paradigms are not broken or interfered with.*

17. Lissman (1963) has the following to say on this subject: "Study of the ingenious adaptations displayed in the anatomy, physiology, and behavior of animals leads to the familiar conclusion that each has evolved to suit life in its particular corner of the world. Each animal also inhabits a private subjective world that is not accessible to direct observation. This world is made up of information communicated to the creature from the outside in the form of messages picked up by its sense organs."

18. Social scientists trained in the North European tradition are familiar with the trap laid by a dichotomizing of language and culture. Some of the time we make our observations in context, but often we do not. Most, if not all, of Berelson and Steiner's (1964) "findings" separate the organism, including man, from the matrix of life both conceptually and operationally. Their interpretation of Lewin's (1935) adopted version of Zeigarnik's (1927) study is seen in terms of *drive* rather than of *social* acts. It remained for Spitz (1964) to place Zeignarnik's work in context again. Berelson and Steiner's chapter on culture is particularly fragmented. The work of the transactional psychologists is most conspicuous for its absence from their work. One is left with the impression that for many Americans one does not really "know" something *except when it is out of context.* At the risk of stating the obvious, I wish to underscore what appears to be a growing consensus among ethologists and ecologists that the organism and its environment are so inextricably intertwined that to

consider either as separate is an artifact of our own particular way of looking at things.

19. See "The Biochemistry of Crowding and Exocrinology", in Hall (1966).

20. Other studies that have contributed to the formation of my thinking are: Allee (1958); Bonner (1963); Calhoun (1962a; b); Christian (1963); Christian and Davis (1964); Christian, Flyger, and Davis (1961); Deevey (1960); Eibl-Eibesfeldt (1961); Errington (1956, 1957, 1961); Frake (1960); Gilliard (1960, 1963); Goffman (1959); Hediger (1950, 1955); Hinde and Tinbergen (1958); Howard (1920); Lévi-Strauss (1966a); Lissman (1963); Lorenz (1964); McBride (1964); McCulloch (1948); McCulloch and Pitts (1947); Parks and Bruce (1961); Portmann (1959); Rosenblith (1961); Schäfer (1956); Selye (1956); Snyder (1961); Sullivan (1947); Tinbergen (1952, 1958); and Wynne-Edwards (1962).

21. Notable among these is the work of Paul Errington (1956, 1957, 1961). His studies of muskrats and their behavioral response to the stress from crowding are most revealing. He states that *muskrats share with men* the propensity for growing savage under stress from crowding (italics mine).

22. See my 1966 summary of Christian's work.

23. It is impossible to do justice to Calhoun in any summary. The full implication of this thinking is comprehended only when virtually everything he has written has been mastered. To understand properly his experiments conducted under laboratory conditions, for example, one must be conversant with his earlier·studies conducted in the open in a natural setting.

24. Subjects included English, French, German, Swiss, Dutch, Spanish,

Arab, Armenian, Greek South Asian, Indian, Japanese, and West Africans.

25. For the past three years, a motorized drive, 250-exposure bulk film 35 mm Nikon has been used. The 35 mm negative enlarges well and provides excellent detail at low cost, and the camera is somewhat less bulky than a high-quality 16 mm movie camera. The half-frame 35 mm camera has also proved to be a very convenient, compact instrument. So far, the 8 mm and super-8 movie cameras have not provided either the quality or the slow speeds essential for this work.

26. The research referred to is currently under way and will appear in a handbook of procedures and methods in proxemic research.

27. Little (1965, 1967) has established that the correlation between the way a subject perceives two other people, two silhouettes, two dolls, or two cylinders of wood is such that for all practical purposes they are interchangeable. One must observe, however, that in all these contexts, the subject is judging spatial relations *as an outsider* and not *as a participant*.

28. It long has been taken for granted that the signal, sign, or message is what the social scientist concentrates on when doing communications research. I observed some years ago that much of the slippage in intercultural communication occurs because the speaker cannot tell whether the person he is addressing is listening or not (Hall 1964*b*).

29. It goes without saying that unless the anthropologist is thoroughly conversant with the language as it relates to the rest of the culture, the use of the lexicon as an analytic tool is not possible. In this regard, I have received invaluable aid from my colleague Moukhtar Ani, who has devoted years to the preparation of an Arab-English dictionary. Ani's immersion in the lexicons of the two languages has made it possible for him to deal explicitly with contrasts that would not otherwise be so obvious.

30. Western art is analyzable according to the perspective catagories identified by Gibson (1950). Linear perspective is only one of a great many different ways in which objects are seen in depth.

31. Like all great artists, Rembrandt painted in depth, communicating on many different levels. In some of his pictures, there are two or more visual fields, so that the eye jumps from one to the other. He undoubtedly was ahead of his time, and he certainly violated the art mores. His recording of the *instant* of perception appears to be extraordinarily accurate (for those of us who learned to see in the European tradition). It is only recently that popular culture has begun to catch up with him.

32. It is important to emphasize that the procedures used in this series of studies were not concerned with that level of analysis that deals with art styles or subject matter or content in the conventional sense. Both stylistic and content analyses represent valid points of entry into an analysis of art, but they are more suitable to intrasystemic analysis than to the comparison of *two or more different systems*.

33. The term informal, as used here, refers to one of three levels of culture. The other two levels are formal and technical. The formal level of culture is that which is integrated into the entire culture; everyone knows it and takes it for granted. The informal level is made up of those imprecise attitudes that are situational; the technical level is the fully explicated and analyzed activity (see Hall 1959).

34. The term "situational dialect" re-

fers to the different forms of language that are used in and are characteristic of specific *situations,* such as officialese, the language of the marketplace, and the specialized dialects of different occupational, professional, and subclass groups. Mastery of the situational dialect marks the individual as a member of the group. The term situational dialect was originally suggested to me by Edmund S. Glenn in a conversation in 1960. To my knowledge no adequate inventory of the situational dialects of any language exists. Such an inventory would provide an easy measure of relative social complexity of a given culture. Leach (1966) refers to the different "brands" of English embodying "social categories" in such a way as to indicate that he is referring to situational dialects. Lantis' (1960) article also pertains to the situational dialect.

35. They are not exclusively visual, but they do have a visual bias.

REFERENCES

Abrams, Charles. 1965. *The city is the frontier.* New York: Harper & Row.

Allee, Warder C. 1958. *The social life of animals.* Boston: Beacon Press.

Bain, A. D. 1949. Dominance in the Great Tit, Parus Major. *Scottish Naturalist* 61:369–472.

Bateson, Gregory. 1948. "Sex and culture," in *Personal character and cultural milieu,* pp. 94–107. Ann Arbor: Edwards Brothers.

Berelson, Bernard, and Gary A. Steiner. 1964. *Human behavior.* New York: Harcourt, Brace & World.

Birdwhistell, Raymond L. 1952. *Introduction to kinesics.* Louisville: University of Louisville Press.

Bloomfield, Leonard. 1933. *Language.* New York: H. Holt.

Boas, Franz. 1911. "Introduction," in *Handbook of American Indian Languages.* Bureau of American Ethology Bulletin 40.

Bonner, John T. 1963. How slime molds communicate. *Scientific American* 209(2):84–86.

Byers, Paul. 1966. Cameras don't take pictures. *Columbia University Forum* 9.

Calhoun, John B. 1950. The study of wild animals under controlled conditions. *Annals of the New York Academy of Sciences* 51:113–22.

———. 1962a. "A behavioral sink," in *Roots of behavior.* Edited by Eugene L. Bliss, pp. 295–316. New York: Harper & Brothers.

———. 1962b. Population density and social pathology. *Scientific American* 207:139–46.

Carpenter, C. R. 1958. "Territoriality: A review of concepts and problems," in *Behavior and evolution.* Edited by A. Roe and G. G. Simpson, pp. 224–50. New Haven: Yale University Press.

Carpenter, Edmund, Frederick Varley, and Robert Flaherty. 1959: *Eskimo.* Toronto: University of Toronto Press.

Chombart de Lauwe, Paul. 1959a. *Famille et habitation.* Paris: Editions du Centre National de al Recherche Scientifique.

———. 1959b. Le milieu et l'étude sociologique de cas individuels. *Informations Sociales* 2:41–54.

Chomsky, Noam. 1957. *Syntactic Stuctures.* The Hague: Mouton & Co.

Christian, John J. 1960. Factors in mass mortality of a herd of Sika deer (*Cervus nippon*). *Chesapeake Science* 1:79–95.

———. 1963. The pathology of overpopulation. *Military Medicine* 128:571–603.

Christian, John J., Vagh Flyger, and David E. Davis. 1961. Phenomena associated with population density. *Proceedings of the National Academy of Science* 47:428–49.

Christian, John J. and David E. Davis. 1964. Social and endocrine factors are integrated in the regulation of growth of mammalian populations. *Science* 146:1550–60.

Collier, John, Jr. 1967. Holt, Rinehart, & Winston. In press.

Condon, W. S. 1967. A segmentation of behavior. MS.

Condon, W. S., and W. D. Ogston. 1966. Sound film analysis of normal and pathological behavior patterns. *The Journal of Nervous and Mental Disease* 143(4):338–47.

Deevey, Edward S. 1960. The hare and the haruspex: A cautionary tale. *Yale Review*, Winter.

Dorner, Alexander. 1958. *The way beyond art*. New York: New York University Press.

Eibl-Eibesfeldt, I. 1961. The fighting behavior of animals. *Scientific American* 205(6):112–22.

Errington, Paul. 1956. Factors limiting higher vertebrate populations. *Science* 124:304–7.

———. 1957. *Of men and marshes.* New York: The Macmillan Company.

———. 1961. *Muskrats and marsh management.* Harrisburg: Stackpole Company.

Frake, Charles O. 1960. "Family and kinship in Eastern Subanun," in *Social structure in Southeast Asia.* Edited by G. P. Murdock, pp. 51–64. Viking Fund Publications in Anthropology no. 29.

Fried, Marc. 1963. "Grieving for a lost home," in *The urban condition.* Edited by Leonard J. Duhl. New York: Basic Books.

Fried, Marc, and Peggy Gleicher. 1961. Some sources of residential satisfaction in an urban slum. *Journal of the American Institute of Planners* 27:305–15.

Gans, Herbert, 1960. *The urban villagers.* Cambridge: The M.I.T. Press and Harvard University Press.

Gibson, James J. 1950. *The perception of the visual world.* Boston: Houghton Mifflin.

Giedion, Sigfried. 1962. *The eternal present: The beginnings of architecture.* Vol. II. New York: Bollingen Foundation, Pantheon Books.

Gilliard, E. Thomas. 1962. On the breeding behavior of the Cock-of-the-Rock (Aves. *Rupicola rupicola*). *Bulletin of the American Museum of Natural History* 124:31–68.

———. 1963. Evolution of bowerbirds. *Scientific American* 209(2):38–46.

Goffman, Erving. 1959. *The presentation of self in everyday life.* New York: Doubleday.

———. 1961. *Encounters.* Indianapolis: Bobbs-Merrill.

Grosser, Maurice. 1951. *The painter's eye.* New York: Rinehart.

Hall, Edward T. 1955. The anthropology of manners. *Scientific American* 192:85–89.

———. 1956. "A microcultural analysis of time." *Proceedings of the Fifth International Congress of Anthropological and Ethnological Sciences,* Philadelphia, Sept. 1–9, 1956, pp. 118–22.

———. 1959. *The silent language.* Garden City: Doubleday.

———. 1960a. The madding crowd. *Landscape,* Autumn, pp. 26–29.

———. 1960b. *ICA participant English language requirement guide, part I.* Washington, D.C.

———. 1963a. "Proxemics—The study of man's spatial relations and boundaries," in *Man's image in medicine and anthropology,* pp. 422–45. New York: International Universities Press.

———. 1963b. A system for the notation of proxemic behavior. *American Anthropologist* 65:1003–26.

———. 1964a. "Adumbration in intercultural communication," in *The ethnography of communication.* Edited by

American Anthropologist 66(6), part 2:154–63.

———. 1964b. "Silent assumptions in social communication," in *Disorders of communication* XLII. Edited by Rioch and Weinstein, pp. 41–55. Baltimore: Research Publications Association for Research in Nervous and Mental Disease.

———. 1966. *The hidden dimension.* New York: Doubleday.

Hall, Edward T., and George L. Trager. 1953. *The analysis of culture.* Washington, D.C.: American Council of Learned Societies.

Hall, Edward T., and William F. Whyte. 1960. Inter-cultural communication. *Human Organization* 19(1): 5–12.

Hallowell, A. Irving. 1955. "Cultural factors in spatial orientation," in *Culture and experience*, pp. 184–202. Philadelphia: University of Pennsylvania Press.

Hayes, Alfred S. 1964. "Paralinguistics and kinesics: Pedagogical perspectives," in *Approaches to semiotics.* Edited by T. H. Sebeok and A. S. Hayes. The Hague: Mouton.

Hediger, H. 1950. *Wild animals in captivity.* London: Butterworth.

———. 1955. *Studies of the psychology and behavior of captive animals in zoos and circuses.* London: Butterworth.

———. 1961. "The evolution of territorial behavior," in *Social life of Early Man.* Edited by S. L. Washburn, pp. 34–57. Viking Fund Publications in Anthropology no. 31.

Hellersberg, Elizabeth F. 1950. *Adaptation to reality of our culture.* Springfield: C. C. Thomas.

———. 1966. Spatial structures and images in Japan, a key to culture understanding. MS.

Hinde, R. A., and Niko Tinbergen. 1958. "The comparative study of species-specific behavior," in *Behavior and evolution.* Edited by A. Roe and G. G. Simpson, pp. 251–68. New Haven: Yale University Press.

Hockett, Charles F. 1958. *A course in modern linguistics.* New York: Macmillan.

———. 1960. The origin of speech. *Scientific American* 203:338–96.

Howard, H. E. 1920. *Territory in bird life.* London: Murray.

Jammer, Max. 1960. *Concepts of space.* New York: Harper.

Joos, Martin. 1962. The five clocks. *International Journal of American Linguistics* 28(2): Part V.

Kilpatrick, Franklin P. Editor. 1961. *Explorations in transactional psychology.* New York: New York University Press.

Lantis, Margaret. 1960. Vernacular culture. *American Anthropologist* 62: 202–16.

Leach, Edmund R. 1965. Culture and social cohesion: An anthropologist's view. *Daedalus*, Winter, pp. 24–38.

Lévi-Strauss, Claude. 1966a. The scope of anthropology. *Current Anthropology* 7:112–23.

———. 1966b. Anthropology: Its achievements and future. *Current Anthropology* 7:124–27.

Lissman, H. W. 1963. Electric location by fishes. *Scientific American* 208(3): 50–59.

Little, Kenneth B. 1965. Personal space. *Journal of Experimental Social Psychology* 1:237–47.

———. 1967. Value congruence and interaction distances. *Journal of Social Psychology.* In press.

Lorenz, Konrad. 1963. *On Agression.* New York: Harcourt, Brace & World.

———. 1964. *Das sogenannte Bose; zur naturgeschichte der Agression* (the biology of aggression). Vienna: Dr. G. Borotha-Schoeler.

Lynd, Robert S. 1948. *Knowledge for what?* Princeton: Princeton University Press.

McBride, Glen. 1964. *A general theory of social organization and behavior.* St. Lucia, Australia: University of Queensland Press.

McClellan, James E. 1966. Skinner's philosophy of human nature. *Studies in Philosophy and Education* 4:307–32.

McCulloch, Warren S. 1948. Teleological mechanisms. *Annals of the New York Academy of Sciences* 50:259–77.

———. 1964. "Reliable systems using unreliable units," in *Disorders of Communication* XLII. Edited by Rioch and Weinstein. Baltimore: Research Publications Association for Research in Nervous and Mental Disease.

McCulloch, Warren S., and Walter Pitts. 1947. How we know universals; the perception of auditory and visual forms. *Bulletin of Mathematical Biophysics* 9:127–47.

McHarg, Ian. 1963 "Man and his environment," in *The urban condition.* Edited by Leonard J. Duhl. New York: Basic Books.

McLuhan, Marshall. 1963. *The Gutenburg galaxy.* Toronto: University of Toronto Press.

———. 1964. *Understanding Media.* New York: McGraw-Hill.

Mead, Margaret, 1961. Anthropology among the sciences. *American Anthropologist* 63:475–82.

Osmond, Humphrey. 1957. Function as the basis of psychiatric ward design. *Mental Hospitals* (Architectural Supplement) April, pp. 23–29.

Parkes, A. A., and H. M. Bruce. 1961. Olfactory stimuli in mammalian reproduction. *Science* 134:1049–54.

Portmann, Adolf. 1959. *Animal camouflage.* Ann Arbor: University of Michigan Press.

Ruesch, Jurgen. 1961. *Therapeutic communication.* New York: Mouton.

Roe, Anne, and George G. Simpson. Editors. 1958. *Behavior and evolution.* New Haven: Yale University Press.

Rosenblith, Walter A. 1961. *Sensory communication.* New York: The M.I.T. Press and John Wiley & Sons.

Sapir, Edward. 1929. The status of linguistics as a science. Language 5:207–214.

———. 1949. *Selected writings of Edward Sapir* in *language, culture, and personality.* Edited by David Mandelbaum. Berkeley: University of California Press.

Schäfer, Wilhelm. 1956. *Der kritische raum und die kritische situation in der tierischen sozietät.* Frankfurt: Krämer.

Selye, Hans. 1956. *The stress of life.* New York: McGraw-Hill.

Snyder, Robert. 1961. Evolution and integration of mechanisms that regulate population growth. *National Academy of Sciences* 47:449–55.

Spitz, René A. 1964. The derailment of dialogue. Stimulus overload, action cycles, and the completion gradient. *Journal of the American Psychoanalytic Association* 12:752–75.

Srole, Leo, *et. al.* 1962. *Mental health in the metropolis: The Midtown Manhattan Study.* Thomas A. C. Rennie Series in Social Psychiatry. New York: McGraw-Hill.

Sullivan, Harry Stack. 1947. *Conceptions of modern psychiatry.* Washington: William Alanson White Psychiatric Foundation.

Thiel, Philip. 1961. A sequence-experience notation for architectural and urban space. *Town Planning Review,* April, pp. 33–52.

Tinbergen, Niko. 1958. *Curious naturalists.* New York: Basic Books.

Watson, Michael, and Theodore Graves. 1966. An analysis of proxemic behavior. *American Anthropologist* 68:971–85.

Whorf, Benjamin Lee. 1956. *Language, thought, and reality.* New York: The Technology Press and John Wiley & Sons.

Wynne-Edwards, V. C. 1962. *Animal dispersion in relation to social behavior.* New York: Hafner.

15

CONFLICTS AND DIRECTIONS IN PROXEMIC RESEARCH

O. MICHAEL WATSON

Descriptions and reviews of proxemics (under which rubic I include "environmental psychology") have recently been written or are forthcoming (Craik, 1970; Hall, 1968, 1973; Proshansky, Ittelson, and Rivlin, 1970; Watson, 1972; Watson and Graves, 1966). It is outside the intended scope of this paper to provide a detailed description of proxemic behavior or to review the literature of proxemic research. Instead, I have provided here a personal and therefore biased account of my own work in proxemics, which I will use as a foundation upon which to base some comments regarding the nature of conflicts, or potential conflicts, in proxemic research, and to give my views regarding the direction of future proxemic research.

Before I begin these tasks, let me make clear the way in which I will be using the term "proxemics" in this paper. Proxemics is concerned with the relationships of humans and space. Edward T. Hall, who coined the term "proxemics," defines it as ". . . the interrelated observations and theories of man's use of space as a specialized elaboration of culture" (Hall, 1966, p. 1), and, more explicitly, as ". . . the study of how man unconsciously structures microspace—the distance between men in conduct of daily transactions, the organization of space in his houses and buildings, and ultimately the layout of his towns." (Hall, 1963, p. 1003) From these definitions we can see the wide range of human behavior included within proxemics: spatial behavior from the manipulation of microspace in face-to-face interactions, through man's interaction with the architectural environment, to urban space. In keeping with the nature of the papers included in this volume, the discussion of proxemics is limited to the human perception, structuring, and use of space on the interpersonal level. ". . . how man structures microspace, how he relates physically to other persons with whom he is interacting, and what is communicated by these physical relationships." (Watson and Graves, 1966, p. 971)

In his book, *The Silent Language,*

From *Journal of Communication,* 1972, 22, 443–59. Copyright © 1972 by the International Communication Association and reprinted by permission.

Hall points out that people have a notion of what distances should be maintained between interactants in a given situation, and lists eight interaction distances for middle-class Anglo-Americans (Hall, 1959, pp. 162–4). In later writings Hall makes the point that it is less the concern of proxemics to measure distances between interactants than it is to understand the use of the senses to regulate these distances (Hall, 1964a, pp. 45–53; Hall, 1966, p. 22). The basis of proxemic behavior on the interpersonal level should be viewed as ". . . a constellation of sensory inputs that is coded in a particular way:" (Hall, 1968, p. 94) Thus, proxemic behavior is a *system* of interrelated variables which is operationally defined below [1] (Hall, 1963).

1. POSTURAL-SEX IDENTIFIERS This variable is scored to indicate the sex of the interactants and whether they are standing, sitting, squatting, or prone.
2. SOCIOFUGAL-SOCIOPETAL AXIS This variable concerns the relation of the axis of one person's shoulders to that of another person. Scoring is from face-to-face to back-to-back.
3. KINESTHETIC FACTORS This variable is scored to indicate the distance of one person from another in terms of the potential for touching the other person. The scoring range is from within body contact distance to just outside reaching distance.
4. TOUCH CODE This variable is scored to provide for the amount and kind of touching which takes place during an interaction.
5. VISUAL CODE The coding of this variable provides an index of the amount of visual contact during an interaction, from eye-to-eye to gazing off into space.
6. VOICE LOUDNESS The measurement of the intensity of a person's voice during an interaction.

7. THERMAL CODE The measurement of this variable provides information concerning the detection of thermal radiation or conduction from an interactant's body.
8. OLFACTION CODE The measurement of this variable is concerned with the detection of undifferentiated body and breath odors.

Controlled observation of proxemic behavior

Using the system of variables which operationally define proxemic behavior and the notation system devised by Hall, briefly outlined above, the researcher of proxemic behavior has several procedural options available. The option I have taken in my own research, initially by necessity and more recently by choice, has been one of controlled observation of proxemic behavior in a laboratory setting (Watson, 1970; Watson and Graves, 1966).

As subjects I have used both Anglo-American college students and foreign students, from many different parts of the world, who were studying in the United States. All subjects were males. I have had each subject get together with a friend from his country (or region, in the case of the U.S.), and come to the laboratory at the appointed time. The pair was shown into the laboratory and asked to seat themselves at a table, on chairs which were arranged side-by-side in a standard position. Each pair of subjects was told only that I was interested in the ways people from different countries behave when they talk to each other; to talk about anything that they wanted to in their native language; and that I would be observing them from behind a one-way glass. Following these instructions I would leave the room, take up my position behind the one-way glass and, allow the subjects a couple of minutes of "warm up" time, and then observe and record their proxemic behavior [2] over a five minute period. In an initial study, involving Arab and Anglo-American students, one line of notation of proxemic behavior for each subject was recorded every minute (Watson and Graves, 1966). In a later study, with foreign students from several different countries, the same procedures were used, except that a line of notation was recorded for each subject every ten seconds (Watson, 1970). In both studies the pencil and paper method of recording was used.

Having summarized the research procedure, let me elaborate on some points that I consider important in the context of the theme of this paper.

Laboratories

There are, in the social sciences, at least two ways in which to deal with human behavioral phenomena. One of these methods requires a keen observational eye, an insightful mind with the ability to sort out and synthesize the bits and pieces of human behavior and make a presentation in a meaningful (and preferably fresh) way. This approach is creative, intellectually stimulating, exciting, and almost always precludes replicability. The other method involves experimentation, control, a high tolerance for boredom (for me, anyway), and a standardized format in presenting the products of ones labors. This latter method almost always has replicability built into it. It is less often as creative, less often as intellectually stimulating, and almost always less exciting than the first method, but always of equal importance. I don't see these two approaches as competitive but, at least in the case of proxemics (and

there's no way I can say this without sounding like a martyr), I see the second approach as more necessary. [3]

At the time the two studies mentioned above were undertaken (1966–1967) there did not exist, to my knowledge, any empirical data concerning the observation and measurement of proxemic behavior using Hall's system of notation (Hall, 1963). I therefore felt, and continue to feel, that a necessary step in studying proxemic behavior was to establish a baseline derived from laboratory research. Human interaction is, of course, a global phenomenon, and the fields of study that slice the material of communication in face-to-face encounters into its component parts (linguistics, paralinguistics, kinesics, proxemics, etc.) are intellectual constructs, analytic products of academic minds. In order to isolate one's chosen component and to keep it free from various factors which may have a contaminating effect on it, it is necessary to have a large degree of observational control over it. So, in order to study proxemic behavior under conditions which were as constant as possible for all subjects, a laboratory setting was the only practicable situation which allowed the degree of control which I felt was necessary to isolate proxemic behavior from factors which may have had an influence on it.

At this point a problem arises: what kinds of factors must be neutralized, rendered constant, in order to isolate proxemic behavior from their differential influence? A model that I have found helpful in approaching this problem is one proposed by Altman and Lett. The model is concerned with the ecology of interpersonal relationships, defined as "the nature of the *mutual* interaction between man and his environment." (Altman and Lett, 1969). Central to the model is the notion of the definition of the situation in which interactants find themselves. The model hypothesizes that when people engage in face-to-face interaction, they derive from certain factors antecedent to the interaction the definition of the situation. These antecedent factors on which interactants base their definitions of the situation are reducible to two categories: environmental characteristics and interactant characteristics. Included in the category of environmental characteristics are those features of the physical environment which are external to the interaction but which may play a role in influencing the interaction (e.g., light, temperature, noise, available space, etc.). Interactant characteristics are, of course, attributes of the interactants themselves, and include physical factors (height, weight, disfigurement, etc.), physiological factors (states of fatigue, anger, excitement, etc.), personal factors ("personality properties"), social factors (status, role, etc.), and interpersonal factors (past relationships between the interactants, degree of acquaintance, etc.). The two general categories of antecedent factors, environmental and interactant, provide a basis for defining the situation and aid interactants in forming expectations of the interaction and in making judgments about appropriate (in the case of the interests represented in this paper) proxemic behavior.

Given varying environmental characteristics and/or varying interactant characteristics, one would expect to find varying definitions of the situation and, thus, varying proxemic behavior. One could obviously control one set of antecedent factors and manipulate another set in order to observe the effect on interaction, but in an attempt to establish a cross-cultural "baseline" of proxemic behavior, I chose to keep both sets of antecedent factors as constant as possible.

In the laboratory setting environmental characteristics were relatively easy to control. All subjects were observed interacting in the same room, sitting at the same table on chairs that were placed in a standard position before each interaction (it was up to the subjects to move the chairs any way they wished). Therefore, the architectural environment was controlled. Other environmental factors which were external to the interaction but potentially influential were also controlled: light, temperature, and noise level were kept constant. It was, unfortunately, impossible to control for the time of day during which the interactions took place, but all observations were made during daylight hours.

Control of interactant characteristics was a more difficult matter. It seemed to me that the best way to approach consistency in terms of interactant characteristics was not only to have each member of an observed pair be from the same country, speak the same native language, and be of the same sex (all males), but that each be friends with the other member of the dyad. I assumed that by being friends, each member of the dyad had already found the other member acceptable as a conversational partner and each would be comfortable in the presence of the other. As a further aid to neutrality, prior to each interaction I told the subjects to talk about anything they wished during the interaction. This was an attempt to avoid contamination by assigning a topic to be discussed (one can assume that Arabs would have discussed the then-recent "June War" with relatively more vigor, than, say Norwegians).

Even granted that environmental and interactant characteristics were as rigorously controlled as they needed to be in order to establish the proxemic baseline I mentioned above, it could be argued that a laboratory setting makes it obvious to a subject that his behavior is under scrutiny. More important in this regard than the laboratory setting itself, I think, is whether or not the subject is conscious of *what* behavior is being observed and therefore potentially manipulable by the subject (and lots of chicanery goes on in psychology to keep the subject unaware of the focus of an experiment), and whether or not the subject is even aware that he is under observation. Concerning the point of conscious manipulation, it appears that "proxemic patterns, once learned, are maintained largely outside awareness. . ." (Hall, 1963, p. 1003). Thus, it would be difficult for a person to manipulate behavior which was outside of awareness. As to a person's awareness that he is being observed, modern technology makes possible all sorts of ways in which to observe without being observed (disregarding the ethical problems raised by doing so).

There does remain, however, one nagging, seemingly insoluble, difficulty involved in cross-cultural proxemic research in a laboratory setting, and this problem concerns the subjects' definitions of the laboratory setting itself. Perhaps, to an Anglo-American college sophomore, participating in a laboratory experiment is a part of everyday life, but a foreign student might define such a setting as highly unusual and artificial.

This problem leads to the argument between observing behavior in a laboratory *vs.* a "natural" setting. Ethologists, as well as most of my colleagues in cultural anthropology, would argue that behavior observed in a laboratory environment is abnormal behavior and therefore is useless in understanding how people behave in "real life." I would argue that people do what they do, no matter where they are, according to a set of rules and, as an anthropologist, I'm interested in the patterning of these rules, in whatever setting they are manifested. Still, the proponents of the observation of behavior in a natural setting do have a point. Although the findings in the two studies under discussion reveal that there was an extremely high degree of proxemic homogeneity within a national group, this could (in a rigidly empirical system of knowledge) only reveal the ways members of a particular culture behave in a laboratory.

I am not arguing for laboratory experimentation in the study of proxemic behavior (although I still feel that more laboratory research is necessary), but for *controlled* observation. I would urge proxemic research in natural settings, but in a controlled manner. The researcher *must* know the meaning of the context in which the interaction takes place, as well as the various interactant and environmental characteristics involved. There is, as most ethologists ignore, much more than biology involved in studying human behavior— an understanding of the cultural components of human interaction are absolutely essential.

Dyads

The units of observation in my two studies were dyads. This in itself seems a perfectly acceptable procedure and therefore unworthy of comment, but recent statements by Birdwhistell lead me to comment very briefly on the use of dyads as units of observation (Bird-whistell, 1972). Essentially, Bird-whistell's argument is that dyadic interaction occurs so seldom in the everyday world, and when it does occur it is as part of a larger context, that one wastes ones time in studying such units. Again, my argument in defense of dyads is that people who interact in dyads do what they do, and that what they do is highly patterned (at least proxemically) and varies across cultures, and that the study of these patterns is worthy of attention.

Another, more pragmatic, argument for the observation of the proxemic behavior of dyads is that adding more persons, even one more, to a dyadic interaction makes things incredibly more complicated. At the level of understanding on which proxemic research currently finds itself, I feel we should attempt to make the simpler forms comprehensible before we move on to the more complicated.

Pencil and paper method
of recording

In the two studies being discussed, proxemic behavior was observed and recorded, using Hall's system of notation, by the simple method of writing down on a piece of paper a subject's score for each variable in the system of proxemic behavior. In the first study, using Arab and American subjects, a line of notation was taken every minute. In the second study, involving foreign students from several different countries, a line of notation was taken every ten seconds. The method was, looking through the one-way glass, to start with the subject on my left and record a line of notation, recording each variable in turn, and then repeating the procedure for the subject on my right.

Although inter-observer reliability checks yielded almost 100% agreement, the pencil and paper method is highly insufficient. The source of the insufficiency relates to the fact that there is no visual record, either still or moving, of the interactions. The behavior has vanished, and all that remains are some scores punched on IBM cards.

Using the pencil and paper method, one observer is unable to get a synchronous slice of behavior, i.e., he cannot record *all* variables for *both* subjects at the same time. Initiating recording for the first subject on the first variable, I would judge that there was an elapsed time of five to eight seconds by the time I recorded the last variable for the second subject. Still photographs could remedy this problem, but even with still pictures taken a few seconds apart the record of the behavior is frozen, with gaps in between, with no information concerning what went on between the photographs. If one had a record of an interaction on motion picture film or videotape, then one would have the opportunity to plot a continuous account of what went on during an interaction. I have more to say about the use of continuous accounts below.

The point I'm trying to make here is simple and obvious: the use of visual recording devices, preferably motion pictures or video tape, is absolutely indispensable in the observation of proxemic behavior. While we're on the point of visual records, let me say a few words about the *misuse* of these methods. In a study published in this journal, Forston and Larson reported on the proxemic behavior of Anglo-American and Latin American students (Forston and Larson, 1968). The subjects interacted in dyads for a period of five minutes, and although an observer noted the proxemic behavior of the interactants, it appears that the mean distance between the members of an interacting dyad was derived from two polaroid photographs taken during the interaction. I would advise a more copious visual record.

Foreign students as subjects

All the subjects in the two studies, with the exception of 16 Anglo-Americans, were foreign students studying in the United States. There are both problems and advantages in using this type of sample.

Among the problems is the fact, mentioned above that there was no reliable way to determine if the definition of the laboratory setting was comparable for all subjects. In addition, it would be quite correct to argue that foreign students studying in this country are not representative of the populations of their respective countries: my subjects were mostly urban, highly educated, well-traveled, and members of the higher socio-economic stratum. It would have been better, of course, to observe and record proxemic behavior as it occurs in indigenous settings but such research was beyond the limits of my budget.

Among the advantages of using foreign students as subjects is the fact that while in this country many of their proxemic norms are constantly violated, and I feel that a good way to discover the rules of any system of behavior is to have them broken. Thus, most foreign students found it easy to answer the question: "When you [talk] to Americans, in what ways [do] they act that [are] different from the ways people act in your country?" (Watson, 1970).

All subjects were males

This fact was mentioned above in regard to avoiding any confusion which might result from cross-sex interaction. Further, no female dyads were observed due to the scarcity of female foreign students at the time of the research.

The lack of a female sample portends, obviously, a serious deficiency in the understanding of proxemic behavior, and a study is now underway in an attempt to correct this deficiency.[4] The research project is concerned with the observation and measurement, from videotape recordings, of the proxemic behavior of American college students, both black and white, and both male and female. The observations and measures were made of pairs of students from the same racial and sexual subgroups interacting in a laboratory setting. Data analysis is incomplete and interpretation of the data is tentative at this point, but some interesting suggestions are emerging. Comparisons between the various subgroups in the sample suggested the following:

ALL BLACKS VS ALL WHITES No striking differences on any variables were suggested.

ALL FEMALES VS ALL MALES Eye contact was the only variable on which a difference emerged. It appears that females tend to look each other in the eye more than males.

BLACK MALES VS WHITE MALES Males, when compared by race, appear to differ on three variables. White males tend to face each other more directly, black males tend to interact at closer distances, and white males tend to display more eye contact.

BLACK FEMALES VS WHITE FEMALES Voice loudness was the only variable which suggested a difference when females were compared by race. Black females appear to interact with a higher voice level than do white females.

BLACK FEMALES VS BLACK MALES When blacks were compared across sex, it appeared that females interacted at closer distances and display more eye contact than males.

WHITE FEMALES VS WHITE MALES Across sex comparisons of whites yielded a slight association between females and less voice loudness.

WHITE FEMALES VS BLACK MALES Black males are strongly associated with sitting closer and employing less eye contact than white females. There is a less strong association with white females facing more directly, and employing a lower voice level.

BLACK FEMALES VS WHITE MALES Eye contact showed a rather weak association with black females displaying more eye contact.

A full demonstration of the accuracy of these preliminary findings will have to await the completion of the data analysis.

Directions in proxemic research

For me to explicate what I feel should be some directions in proxemic research, it is necessary to point out gaps that exist in our knowledge of proxemic behavior as a system of nonverbal communication. I will attempt to achieve this goal by discussing proxemic behavior within two contexts: levels of analysis in proxemic research, and proxemic behavior as a process of semiosis.

Using as an analogy the analytical distinctions made by linguists between phonetic and phonemic approaches to sound systems, the terms "etic" and "emic" have been coined by Kenneth Pike and applied to two different approaches, or levels of analysis, to the study of systems of human behavior (Pike, 1966). The *etic* approach involves viewing a system of behavior from outside the system, using criteria which are external to the system: ". . . phenomenal distinctions judged appropriate by the community of scientific observers." (Harris, 1968, p. 575). The *etic* approach provides an initial base from which the observer can begin his analysis of the system.

The *emic* approach, on the other hand, is concerned with studying behavior from inside a single, culturally specific system of behavior. Criteria used in an emic description are drawn from the contrasts made within the system itself and are relevant to the internal functioning of the system. Emic distinctions are those that are recognized as meaningful to the "users" of the system themselves.

Thus, within this framework, an investigator has two approaches available to him in his study of human behavioral systems: using an etic point of view he would use "objective" units and categories in describing behavior as it occurs around the world or, if he were interested in describing a form of behavior in a single, culturally specific system, the etic categories would provide an entrance into the system, but his goal would be to discover the internal structure of the behavioral system.

So far, proxemic research has been cast almost entirely in an etic framework, and thus the subject matter of this paper is in fact *proxetics*, and not proxemics. This fact accounts for a serious gap in our understanding of proxemic behavior. Using Hall's system of notation, which consists of criteria which are external to any particular system of proxemic behavior, a researcher has the etic methodological equipment to observe, measure, and quantify the proxemic behavior of all the peoples of the world. Indeed, it could be argued that the task of recording, using etic categories, the proxemic behavior of as many cultures, particularly those of the rapidly diminishing "primitive" world, is a top priority task. While the results of such etic research would be of enormous value, I would argue that a grasp of proxemic behavior as a system of communication is dependent upon a better understanding of the emic aspects, i.e., what relationships exist between variables in various culturally specific systems of proxemic behavior. Using an etic approach we can describe the differences *between* different culturally specific systems of proxemic behavior, but only emic research can tell us much about the contrasts made *within* each system.

I feel that the most important, and largely neglected, area of proxemic research lies in the need to isolate *proxemes*—contrastive units of proxemic behavior—within culturally specific systems. For example, the variable "eye contact" has four analytic subdivisions, which amount to: looking another person directly in the eye; directing the gaze at the other person's face; looking in his general direction; and directing the gaze away from the other person. These are etic subdivisions, four phenomenally distinct, observable units of behavior. But, in emic terms, the boundaries between these units might not be significant in a particular proxemic system. It is conceivable, for instance, that in a given culturally specific system of proxemic behavior looking another person directly in the eye and looking at his face might not be contrastive units and,

thus, would be alloproxes of the same proxeme. The same would apply, of course, to the observational subdivisions of the other proxemic variables. Emic analysis would also be necessary in the investigation of problems discussed below in connection with the consideration of proxemic behavior as a process of semiosis.

Charles Morris has defined semiosis as "the process in which something functions as a sign. . ." (Morris, 1938, p. 3). In Morris' view, semiosis has three principal components: the sign vehicle ("that which acts as a sign"), the designatum ("that which the sign refers to"), and the interpretant ("that effect on some interpreter in virtue of which the thing in question is a sign to that interpreter") (Morris, 1938, p. 3). Morris, further, has abstracted the relationships between these three principal components of semiosis into three different dimensions (the semantic, the pragmatic, and the syntactic), each of which will be discussed below as it relates to proxemics.

The semantic dimension of semiosis deals with the relationship of signs to the things signified, or, in terms of proxemics, the relationship between a proxemic sign and the meaning attached thereto. We are immediately confronted with a problem: what is a proxemic sign and what meanings, in what contexts, are attached to it? An attempt to answer these questions demonstrates a serious gap in our knowledge of the communicative dimension of proxemic behavior. For a definition of "proxemic sign" we are dependent on etic categories: a proxemic sign is that element of behavior which is subsumed within each of the analytically distinct subdivisions of the variables which operationally define the system of proxemic behavior. Using, once again, "eye contact" as an example, there are subsumed under this variable four proxemic signs at the etic level (direct eye contact, etc.). But our information regarding the semantic dimension in any particular system of proxemic behavior is extremely limited, consisting almost entirely of statements to the effect that Arabs employ more direct eye contact during an interaction than do Anglo-Americans (Watson, 1970). Statements of this kind, concerning proxemic norms, are of only limited use in establishing the meanings attached to these norms. Proxemic norms, once internalized, appear to be maintained largely outside awareness, i.e., people are not aware of the importance of the norms (Hall, 1964a, p. 41; Hall, 1966, p. 109). Thus, when questioned about the meaning of these norms, people are very probably unable to state a set of rules that govern the use of proxemic signs. The meaning of proxemic signs becomes clearer when the norms are violated. A discovery procedure in the investigation of the semantic aspect of proxemic behavior that I have found useful in my own research is to question foreign students about the violation of their proxemic norms. Since students from other countries are likely to be exposed, to a greater or lesser degree, to violations of their proxemic norms while resident in this country, they are often able to answer questions concerning the norms. Arabs can be asked, for instance, what it means to an Arab to employ the lesser amount of eye contact typical of Anglo-American interaction.

Turning to the pragmatic dimension of proxemic behavior, which concerns the relationship of a proxemic sign to the response that it elicits from an interpreter, it is again more illuminating to talk about violations of proxemic norms than their maintenance, and to employ the distinction that Hall makes between adumbrations and cues (Hall, 1964b). Adumbrations are precedents and accompaniments to the "formal" topic of an interaction and serve as feedback mechanisms in adjusting or maintaining behavior. An adumbration "is a perceivable manifestation of A's feelings of which he may not even be aware," while a "cue is a short message of minimal redundancy in full awareness from A to B that indicates what A wants B to do." (Hall, 1964b, p. 157) The principal difference between adumbrations and cues is the level of awareness at which each is transmitted. Proxemic signs can be used both as adumbrations or cues within a culturally specific system of proxemic behavior, but in a cross-cultural situation proxemic signs frequently occur as cues (or, more properly, miscues).

In a culturally specific context proxemic signs are useful in gauging the smoothness of an interaction or as indicators of hostility, but the signs are usually interpreted correctly and elicit the expected response. But in communication across cultures, correct interpretation of proxemic signs is often not the case. My Arab, Latin American, and Southern European subjects gave a composite picture of Anglo-American males which characterized them as shy, uninterested, and generally "cold." (Watson, 1970) In large part these impressions are due to a misinterpretation of proxemic signs. An Arab and an Anglo-American engaged in a conversation would perhaps define the situation in the same way, but the proxemic signs appropriate to that situation could differ between the two cultures. Again, we know very little about the pragmatic aspect of proxemic behavior.

Finally, let's turn to the syntactic dimension of proxemic behavior, which concerns the relationship of proxemic signs to other proxemic signs. The task in investigating the syntactic aspect of proxemic behavior is to attempt to construct networks and concatenations of proxemic signs. Given the lack of information concerning proxemic signs in culturally specific systems, we have no choice but to use the operationally defined, phenomenally distinct, etic units in approaching proxemic behavior within a syntactic context. I have recently begun to look at my own proxemic data in regard to the syntactic aspect of semiosis, and some interesting relationships between proxemic signs are emerging. It appears that the relationship between proxemic signs in different culturally specific systems bear different relationships to each other, i.e., different proxemic systems seem to be structured differently. But confirmation of these differing relationships is dependent upon further analysis. Again, viewing proxemic behavior in the syntactic dimension serves to emphasize how little we know about the subject.

The point of this section of the paper is to demonstrate our incomplete knowledge of any culturally specific system of proxemic behavior and my belief that the investigation of such systems is an important direction in proxemic research. The way the term "proxemic sign" has been used in this paper is a convenient analytical device which may or may not have relevance within a culturally specific system of proxemic behavior. The isolation of proxemes—contrastive units of proxemic behavior which are relevant within culturally specific systems—is, in my view, a task which must be undertaken if meaningful statements about the communicative aspects of proxemic behavior are to be under-stood. We must find out what the culturally meaningful signs are before we can determine the ways in which they are used. To determine the boundaries between proxemes will be a difficult task, but one that will be necessary to advance our understanding of proxemic behavior.

NOTES

1. For the complete system of notation and scoring, the reader is referred to Hall, 1963.
2. The olfactory and thermal factors in Hall's system were not used in my studies because I was interested in direct observation and, obviously, these variables cannot be directly observed.
3. Psychologists and other behavioral scientists who participate in the traditions of rigid control and experimentation will perhaps be amused at my comments on laboratory settings, but they should keep in mind that I am a cultural anthropologist, a practitioner of a discipline that has generally eschewed controlled observations of human behavior.
4. These data were collected by J. S. Griswald, a Ph.D. student under my direction. It is hoped that seeing his name in print will inspire Mr. Griswald to finish his dissertation.

REFERENCES

Altman, I., and E. E. Lett. "The Ecology of Interpersonal Relationships: A Classification System and Conceptual Model." In *Social and Psychological Factors in Stress* (edited by J. E. McGrath). New York: Holt, Rinehart and Winston, 1969.

Birdwhistell, R. Personal Communication, 1972.

Craik, K. H. "Environmental Psychology." In *New Directions in Psychology* 4 (edited by T. M. Newcomb). New York: Holt, Rinehart, and Winston, 1970.

Forston, R. F., and C. U. Larson. "The Dynamics of Space: An Experimental Study in Proxemic Behavior Among Latin Americans and North Americans." *Journal of Communication*, 18:109–16, 1968.

Hall, E. T. *The Silent Language.* Greenwich, Conn.: Fawcett, 1959.

Hall, E. T. "A System for the Notation of Proxemic Behavior." *American Anthropologist*, 65:1003–26, 1963.

Hall, E. T. "Adumbrations as a Feature in Intercultural Communication." *American Anthropologist*, 66:154–63, 1964a.

Hall, E. T. "Silent Assumptions in Social Communication." *Disorders of Communication*, 42:41–55, 1964b.

Hall, E. T. *The Hidden Dimension.* New York: Random House, 1966.

Hall, E. T. "Proxemics," *Current Anthropology*, 9:83–108, 1968.

Hall, E. T. *Handbook of Proxemic Research.* In preparation.

Harris, M. *The Rise of Anthropological Theory.* New York: Crowell, 1968.

Morris, C. W. *Foundations of the Theory of Signs.* Chicago: Univ. of Chicago Press, 1938.

Pike, K. L. "Etic and Emic Standpoints for the Description of Behavior." In *Communication and Culture* (edited by A. G. Smith). New York: Holt, Rinehart and Winston, 1966.

Proshansky, H. M., W. H. Ittelson, and L. G. Rivlin, editors. *Environmental Psychology: Man and his Physical Setting.* New York: Holt, Rinehart and Winston, 1970.

Watson, O. M. *Proxemic Behavior: A Cross-Cultural Study.* The Hague: Mouton, 1970.

Watson, O. M. "Symbolic and Expressive Uses of Space: An Introduction to Proxemic Behavior." *Module #20.* Reading, Mass.: Addison-Wesley, 1972.

Watson, O. M. "Proxemics." In *Current Trends in Linguistics* (edited by T. A. Sebeok). The Hague: Mouton, (in press).

Watson, O. M., and T. D. Graves. "Quantitative Research in Proxemic Behavior." *American Anthropologist*, 68:971–85, 1966.

16

SMALL GROUP ECOLOGY

ROBERT SOMMER

Systematic study of spatial arrangements in face-to-face groups, or small group ecology as the field has been termed, is a comparatively recent development. Typically, the arrangement of people has been an incidental or background variable in psychological experimentation. The use of spatial arrangements as an independent variable in small group research can be traced to Steinzor (1950), who noted some unusual spatial effects while he was doing a study on other aspects of interaction. This pattern persists to the present, since at least half the published studies of small group arrangements involve the reanalysis of data collected for other purposes. Despite consistent and clear data, psychologists seem reluctant to make the arrangement of people a major independent variable. As Hall (1959) put it, "We treat space somewhat as we treat sex, it is there but we don't talk about it." Yet, enough studies, experimental as well as ex post facto, have accumulated to warrant some attempt to integrate the findings

and indicate what directions further studies may profitably take.

This review focuses upon the arrangement of individuals in face-to-face groups. Studies of residential living units such as dormitories, housing developments, and communities are omitted. These phenomena require a different level of analysis (community or societal) than the relationship between individuals in face-to-face groups. The study of larger stable human aggregations has fallen to the fields of demography, human ecology, and geography. Because of space limitations, studies of crowding and density are excluded from consideration since these important topics deserve treatment in their own right. This study concentrates instead on two aspects of small group ecology—the way groups arrange themselves under various conditions, and the ways in which the resulting arrangements affect communication, productivity, and social relationships.

From *Psychological Bulletin*, 1967, 67, 145–52. Copyright © 1967 by the American Psychological Association and reprinted by permission.

Leadership and spatial arrangements

Many of the concepts used in discussion of leadership, such as central figure, dominant position, upper echelon, and high status are based on spatial analogies. Studies of group dynamics and leadership have shown that concepts such as social distance, inner circle, and isolate have some geographic reference but there is no simple isomorphism between psychological and geographic concepts. While investigating discussion groups, Steinzor noticed a participant changing his seat in order to sit opposite another person with whom he had recently had a verbal altercation. In an ex post facto design using data already collected, Steinzor found that when one person stopped speaking, someone opposite rather than alongside was next to speak, an effect he attributed to the greater physical and expressive value a person has for those opposite him in a circle. Following this, Bass and Klubeck (1952) reanalyzed their discussion group data to determine if leadership ratings varied as a function of location in an inverted V or a parallel row arrangement. Although they found that persons occupying end positions attained higher status than people in middle seats, there were so many confounding factors, including a nonrandom selection of seats by people of different status levels, that their results were equivocal. Hearn (1957) reanalyzed small group data collected for other purposes and found that leadership style had a significant influence on what was termed the "Steinzor effect." With minimal leadership, members of a discussion group would direct more comments to people sitting opposite than people adjacent; when a strong leader was present, people directed more comments to adjacent seats than to people opposite; and when direction of the group was shared equally among the members, no spatial effect appeared. These results may be explained in terms of eye contact. Since it is impermissible to look directly at a dominant individual at close quarters, the individual restricts his gaze to his immediate neighbors when a strong leader is close by. Steinzor's expressive contact hypothesis has been further refined by Argyle and Dean (1965), who studied the connection between eye contact, distance, and affiliation. A one-way mirror was used to chart interaction between a naïve subject and a confederate who gazed continually at the subject. There was less eye contact and glances were shorter when the people were close together, and this effect was most pronounced for mixed-sex pairs. The authors believed that eye contact is a component of intimacy, which is governed by both approach and avoidance forces kept in a state of equilibrium during any given encounter. When this equilibrium is disturbed by increasing physical proximity or decreasing eye contact, there are compensatory changes along the other dimensions.

Communication flow as a function of spatial relationship was emphasized by Leavitt (1951), who continued the work of Bavelas (1950). Leavitt used groups of five subjects each, who were seated at a table but separated from one another by vertical partitions. Channels of communication could be changed by manipulating slots in the partitions. Group leadership was closely correlated with a member's position in the communication net. Centrally located individuals enjoyed the task most and those in the peripheral positions enjoyed it least. Howells and

Becker (1962) hypothesized that people who received greater numbers of messages would be more likely to be designated leaders than people who received fewer messages. They arranged groups of five subjects around small rectangular tables with three people on one side, two on the other. The results confirmed their predictions that more leaders than would be expected by chance would emerge from the two-man side of the table.

The studies described thus far have involved *relational* space, or the way people orient themselves towards one another. A second line of research has emphasized the cultural import of various fixed locations. In studies of leadership, the head chair at the table has a special significance. Sommer (1959) found that leaders in small discussion groups gravitated to the head position at rectangular tables. Strodtbeck and Hook (1961) reanalyzed data from experimental jury deliberations and found that people at end positions participated more and were rated as having greater influence on the decision process than people at the sides. It was also found that jurors from the managerial and professional classes selected the head chair more than did individuals of lower status. Hare and Bales (1963) did not work with leadership per se, but rather with dominance as measured by a paper-and-pencil personality test. Reanalyzing the data collected by Bales and his associates from five-man discussion groups, they found that subjects high on dominance tended to choose the central seats and do the most talking. Felipe (1966) used the semantic differential to assess dyadic seating arrangements along these dimensions: intimate-unacquainted, hostile-friendly, talkative-untalkative, and unequal-equal. The cultural influence

of the head position was evident on the equality dimension—if one member of a pair was at the head of the table, this pair was rated significantly less equal than if members were both at ends of the table or only at the sides.

A weakness of all these studies is the limited range of cultures and populations sampled, almost all taking place in the United States. This would not be a serious limitation except that Hall indicated that leaders in other parts of the world use space differently. An equally serious problem concerns the confounding of location, status, and personality. All studies agreed that choice of seats is nonrandom with respect to status and personality. High status, dominant individuals in American culture gravitate to the head position, and people who occupy the head position participate more than people at the side positions (Strodtbeck & Hook, 1961), but there is no way to disentangle status from location in these studies. It is possible that occupancy of certain locations automatically raises an individual's status and/or dominance. On the other hand, it may be that dominant individuals choose these locations for reasons of tradition and would participate more wherever they sat, and thus their location has no essential connection with their participation. It may be that high status people tend to participate more *and* certain locations also increase participation, but the combination of the two results in greater participation than either by itself. The only way to disentangle these variables is to conduct experiments in which people are assigned randomly to various locations and their relative contributions noted. It must be recognized that these conditions are highly artificial in a society that typically allocates space according to status considerations. From the standpoint of designing experiments in natural settings, the policies of random assignments of location are not always adhered to in practice. In the prison camp studied by Grusky (1959), inmate leaders received the most desirable job assignments as well as the bottom bunks (which were status symbols in the dormitories) despite the official policy of random bed assignment. It is likely that the same pressures responsible for the connection between status and location operate against any assignment scheme in conflict with accepted spatial norms.

Task and location

The quest for effective spatial arrangements in working units such as relay assembly teams, seminars, and buzz groups has been a subject of considerable concern to applied psychologists. Textbooks of group dynamics recommend horseshoe or semicircular rather than straight-row arrangements for discussion groups and classrooms, rectangular tables have been criticized for fostering authoritarian leadership, and the improper location of individuals has been blamed for the failure of the working teams. Intuitively it would seem that the proper arrangement of people would increase production, smooth the flow of communication, and reduce the "friction of space," but the data are largely of the anecdotal variety. Perhaps more convincing data lie buried somewhere in applied psychology or human engineering journals and, if so, a valuable service could be rendered by bringing them to light.

Several recent studies have explored the connection between spatial arrangement and group task. Sommer (1965) and Norum (1966) studied the arrangement of conversing, competing, co-acting, and cooperating individuals. At a rectangular table, cooperating pairs sat side-by-side, conversing pairs sat corner-to-corner, and competing pairs sat across from one another, while coacting individuals sat in distant arrangements. In a separate study of cooperative and competive working conditions using a like-sex decoy, the subjects sat opposite the decoy in the competitive condition and on the same side of the table in the cooperative condition.

The extent to which similar attitudes produce greater physical proximity remains in some dispute. Little, Ulehla, and Henderson (1965), using silhouette figures, found that pairs reputed to be Goldwater supporters were placed closer together than Goldwater-Johnson pairs, but the effect did not occur with Johnson-Johnson pairs. However, Elkin (1964), using actual discussion groups involving pro-pro, pro-anti, and anti-anti Medicare pairs of college students, found no differences in seating between concordant and discordant pairs. It is possible that the intensity of the discussion and the interest shown by each of the participants influences proximity more than attitude concordance or discordance.

Several psychiatrists and clinical psychologists have written speculative articles on the significance of various spatial arrangements in psychotherapy. Goodman (1959) made an intriguing comparison between the Freudian use of the couch, Sullivan's cross-the-table therapy, and the spatial freedom of the Gestalt therapists. Wilmer (1958), Winick and Holt (1961), and Horowitz (1965) all discussed seating position from the standpoint of nonverbal communication in group psychotherapy.

Individual distance

The term individual distance was first used by Burkhardt (1944) to refer to the spacing that animals maintain between themselves and others of the same species. Several studies have been directed toward the question of how close people come to one another and to physical objects. Hall (1959) developed a detailed schema for conversational distance under various conditions of social and psychological closeness which ranged from 3–6 inches for soft intimate whispers to 8–20 feet for talking across the room in a loud voice. It is also likely that noise, bustle, or threat brings people together. To measure conversational distance, Sommer (1961) sent pairs into a large lounge where they could sit either side-by-side or across from one another to discuss designated topics. On the basis of previous work, it was assumed that people would sit across from one another rather than side-by-side unless the distance across was too great. It was found that the upper limit for comfortable conversation *under these specified conditions* was approximately 5.5 feet between individuals. A subsequent study used four chairs instead of couches so that the distance side-by-side as well as the distance across could be varied. Again the 5.5-foot conversational distance prevailed. However, a cursory examination of conversational distance in private homes revealed a much greater conversational range than this, something like 8–10 feet between chairs.

Other investigators have used paper-and-pencil or projective tests to study individual distance. Kuethe (1962, 1964) instructed students to pin yellow felt figures (a woman, man, child, dog, rectangles of various sizes) on a blue felt background in various combinations. Kuethe found that the woman and the child were placed closer together than the man and the child, while the dog was typically placed closer to the man than the woman. In all conditions, the people were placed closer together than the rectangles. Little (1965) used line drawings of males and females to examine concepts of individual distance. It was found that the degree of prior acquaintance attributed to cardboard figures influenced the distance they were placed apart. A replication using silhouettes and another using live actresses who were posed by the subject in scenes involving different activities also showed that the distance apart which the figures were placed was a function of the closeness of the relationship between them.

Horowitz, Duff, and Stratton (1964) investigated individual distance among schizophrenic and nonschizophrenic mental patients. Each subject was instructed to walk over to either another person or a hatrack, and the distance between his goal and his stopping place was measured. It was found that both groups approached the hatrack closer than they approached a person. Each subject tended to have a characteristic individual distance which was shorter for inanimate objects than for people. McBride, King, and James (1965) did a similar study testing GSR to varying amounts of closeness between subject and male or female experimenters. It was considered that GSR effects would provide an indication of the level of arousal associated with the proximity of neighbors. The authors found that GSR was greatest (skin resistance was least) when the subject was approached frontally, while a side approach yielded a greater response than a rear approach. The response to experimenters of the same sex was less than to experimenters of the opposite sex. Being touched by an object produced less of a GSR than being touched by a person. Argyle and Dean (1965) invited the subjects to participate in a perceptual experiment in which they were to "stand as close as comfortable to see well" to a book, a plaster head, and a cutout life-sized photograph of the senior author with his eyes closed and another with his eyes open. Among other results, the subjects placed themselves closer to the eyes-closed photograph than the eyes-open photograph.

Systematic violation of individual distance was undertaken by Garfinkel (1964) and Felipe and Sommer (1966). Garfinkel reported that the violation of individual distance produced avoidance, bewilderment, and embarrassment, and that these effects were most pronounced among males. Felipe and Sommer systematically staged invasion sequences under natural conditions (people seated on benches and at library tables) and demonstrated observable flight reactions. Two recent studies have dealt with the relationship between individual distance and personality variables. Williams (1963) showed that introverts placed themselves further from other people than did extroverts. The same conclusion was reached by Leipold (1963), who noted the chair a person occupied vis-à-vis a seated decoy under anxiety and praise conditions. There was greater closeness under the praise than the anxiety conditions, and extroverts placed themselves closer to the decoy than introverts.

Sex differences in spacing have been found on a number of occasions, but the number of cultures sampled is limited. Several investigators (Elkin, 1964;

Norum, 1966; Sommer, 1959) have found that females make more use of the side-by-side arrangement than do males. Side-by-side seating, which is generally considered to be the most intimate of all seating arrangements for people already acquainted, is comparatively rare among males if they are given the opportunity to sit across from one another. The idea that females can tolerate closer physical presence than males is underscored by the observations of women holding hands or kissing one another, practices which are uncommon between males in this culture.

Campbell, Kruskal, and Wallace (1966) used seating arrangements of Negroes and whites as an index of attitude in three Chicago colleges. Clustering of Negroes and whites was found to be associated with differences in ethnic attitudes in the three schools. These authors and Strodtbeck and Hook (1951) attempted to develop appropriate statistical techniques for analyzing aggregation data. Tabulating the results of a single observation involving a large number of individuals whose behavior at times relates to one another and at times to aspects of the physical environment is no small achievement, but when one assembles the records of repeated observations of individuals, some observed many times and some just one, the difficulties multiply. It is fortunate that animal ecologists and zoologists have encountered these problems over the years and have developed useful methods for measuring aggregation, dispersion, home range, and social distance. McBride (1964) has developed computer programs to assess the degree of nonrandomness within an aggregation. Esser (1965), working on a closed research ward of a mental hospital with the available area divided into squares so that the location of each patient can be charted during the entire working day, has obtained detailed records of individual spatial behavior similar to those of the better tracking studies by animal biologists, but he has not yet reached the same level of precision in relating the individual patients' locations one to another. The problems in analyzing the interdependency between a large number of individuals with $n(n-1)$ dyadic relationships has led some investigators to use physical aspects of the environment such as walls, partitions, and chairs as coordinates for locating individuals. A new approach (Bechtel & Srivastava, 1966) is the development of the Hodometer, an electronic recording device placed on the floor of a building to measure use of given areas as well as pathways. A much cruder index of area usage was suggested by Webb, Campbell, Schwartz, and Sechrest (1966), who examined the wear on floortiles in front of different museum exhibits.

Discussion

Knowledge of how groups arrange themselves can assist in fostering or discouraging group relationships. A library which is intended to be *sociofugal space* (Osmond, 1957), aimed at discouraging interaction, requires knowledge of how to arrange people to minimize unwanted contact. It may be possible to use the rank order of preferred arrangements by interacting groups as arrangements *to be avoided* in sociofugal space. On this basis, corner-to-corner seating would be less satisfactory than opposite or distant seating in a sociofugal setting. An Emily Post or Amy Vanderbilt may know these principles intuitively, and diplomatic protocol may codify them, but there is value in making them explicit

and subjecting them to empirical test. To an increasingly greater extent we find ourselves being arranged by impersonal environments in lecture halls, airports, waiting rooms, and lobbies. Many aspects of the proximate environment, including furniture and room dividers, have been placed for ease of maintenance and efficient cleaning with little cognizance to their social functions. These principles will be of most help in institutional settings such as schools, hospitals, public buildings, and old folks' homes where the occupants have little control over their surroundings. The straight-row arrangement of most classrooms has been taken for granted for too long. The typical long narrow shape of a classroom resulted from a desire to get light across the room. The front of each room was determined by window location, since pupils had to be seated so that window light came over the left shoulder. However, new developments in lighting, acoustics, ventilation, and fireproofing have rendered invalid many of the arguments for the boxlike room with straight rows. In mental hospitals, the isolation of schizophrenic individuals can be furthered by sociofugal settings which minimize social contact, or reduced through sociopetal buildings aimed at reinforcing social behavior. The former approach is valid if one wants to provide an optimal environment in terms of the individual's present needs, the latter if society desires to shape the patient's social behavior to facilitate his return to society. It is mindless to design mental hospitals without taking cognizance of the connection between physical environment and social behavior. The study of small group ecology is important not only from the standpoint of developing an adequate theory of relationships that takes into account the context of social relationships, but also from the practical standpoint of designing and maintaining functional contexts in which human relationships can develop.

Several problems of method must be resolved before a relevant theory of group ecology can be developed. Having reviewed the studies themselves, problems in recording and some special characteristics of the settings in which the studies have taken place should be mentioned. The studies described have generally tabulated gross categories of behavior without any real specificity or precision. A person's location has been plotted as if this described his orientation, head angle, arm position, etc. Stated another way, the investigators whose work has been described here have relied almost exclusively on the eyeball technique of recording. Some, such as Esser and McBride, are moving into the electronic processing of observational data, but the improved precision is in data analysis rather than the integration of various facets of spatial behavior. Very little use has been made of photographic recordings. One would hardly undertake the study of comparative linguistics without a tape recorder, but only a handful of investigators whose work we have discussed have used still photographs, much less moving pictures. Twenty-five years ago, Efron (1941) hired a professional artist to sketch conversing groups. A few anthropologists, such as Birdwhistell and Hall, are currently accumulating film libraries of interaction data. McBride found it necessary to photograph aggregations of fowl from small towers above the coops. It is difficult to get good photographs of the spatial arrangements of people from the horizontal plane, particularly if there are more than two individuals involved. Yet, it seems likely that the real breakthroughs in this field will occur when methods for monitoring angle of orientation, eye contact, and various other nonverbal cues are developed for use in standard interaction situations. The arguments for and against laboratory studies of group behavior which involve one-way mirrors, microphones, and hidden photographic equipment compared to field studies in playgrounds, schools, and city streets will not be reviewed here. However, a promising solution is the field-laboratory method used by Sherif (1954) in his camp studies where he employed a standard controlled situation, in the sense that relevant variables were specified in advance and introduced in specified ways by the experimenter but always under conditions that appeared natural and appropriate to the subjects. Another limiting element in the work to date is that almost all the studies have involved discussion groups around tables and chairs. We know little about the ecology of working groups (apart from sociometric data) or coacting individuals, particularly if they are standing or moving. Again, the technical problems of recording interaction patterns of moving individuals are much greater than if the individuals are seated in a classroom or around a conference table.

Along with this is a disproportionate number of environmental studies that have taken place under conditions of confinement, particulary in mental hospitals. At this time there are at least seven studies underway on the use of space by mental patients. As far as the writer knows, this exceeds the number of current studies of spatial behavior of nonhospitalized individuals. Mental hospital studies allow greater control and environmental manipulation than can be achieved outside a total institution, but they also confound the effects of schizophrenia and institutionalization as a social process over time with the effects of captivity and locked doors as spatial variables.

REFERENCES

Argyle, M., & Dean, J. Eye contact, distance, and affiliation. *Sociometry,* 1965, 28, 289–304.

Bass, B. M., & Klubeck, S. Effects of seating arrangements on leaderless group discussions. *Journal of Abnormal and Social Psychology,* 1952, 47, 724–727.

Bavelas, A. Communication processes in task-oriented groups. *Journal of the Acoustical Society of America,* 1950, 22, 725–730.

Bechtel, R. B., & Srivastava, R. Human movement and architectural environment. *Milieu,* 1966, 2, 7–8.

Burckhardt, D. Mowenbeobachtungen in Basel. *Ornithologische Beobachter,* 1944, 5, 49–76.

Campbell, D. T., Kruskal, W. H., & Wallace, W. P. Seating aggregation as an index of attitude. *Sociometry,* 1966, 29, 1–15.

Efron, D. *Gesture and environment.* New York: Kings Crown Press, 1941.

Elkin, L. The behavioral use of space, Unpublished master's thesis, University of Saskatchewan, 1964.

Esser, A., et al. Territoriality of patients on a research ward. In, *Recent advances in biological psychiatry.* Vol. 7. New York: Plenum Press, 1965.

Felipe, N. Interpersonal distance and small group interaction. *Cornell Journal of Social Relations,* 1966, 1, 59–64.

Felipe, N., & Sommer, R. Invasions of personal space. *Social Problems,* in press.

Garfinkel, H. Studies of the routine grounds of everyday activities. *Social Problems,* 1964, 11, 225–250.

Goodman, P. Meaning of functionalism. *Journal of Architectural Education,* 1959, 14, 32–38.

Grusky, O. Organization goals and the behavior of informal leaders. *American Journal of Sociology,* 1959, 65, 59–67.

Hall, E. T. *The silent language.* Garden City, N. Y.: Doubleday, 1959.

Hare, A. P., & Bales, R. F. Seating position and small group interaction. *Sociometry,* 1963, 26, 480–486.

Hearn, G. Leadership and the spatial factor in small groups. *Journal of Abnormal and Social Psychology,* 1957, 54, 269–272.

Horowitz, M. J. Human spatial behavior. *American Journal of Psychotherapy,* 1965, 19, 20–28.

Horowitz, M. J., Duff, D. F., & Stratton, L. O. Body-buffer zone. *Archives of General Psychiatry,* 1964, 11, 651–656.

Howells, L. T., & Becker, S. W. Seating arrangement and leadership emergence. *Journal of Abnormal and Social Psychology,* 1962, 64, 148–150.

Kuethe, J. L. Social schemas. *Journal of Abnormal and Social Psychology,* 1962, 64, 31–38.

Kuethe, J. L. Pervasive influence of social schemata. *Journal of Abnormal and Social Psychology,* 1964, 68 248–254.

Leavitt, H. J. Some effects of certain communication patterns in group performance. *Journal of Abnormal and Social Psychology,* 1951, 46, 38–50.

Leipold, W. D. Psychological distance in a dyadic interview. Unpublished doctoral dissertation, University of North Dakota, 1963.

Little, K. B. Personal space. *Journal of Experimental Social Psychology,* 1965, 1, 237–247.

Little, K. B. Ulehla, J., & Henderson, C. Value homophily and interaction distance. Unpublished manuscript, University of Denver, 1965.

McBride, G. *A general theory of social*

organization and behaviour. St. Lucia: University of Queensland Press, 1964.

McBride, G., King, M. G., & James, J. W. Social proximity effects on GSR in adult humans. *Journal of Psychology*, 1965, 61, 153–157.

Norum, G. A. Perceived interpersonal relationships and spatial arrangements. Unpublished master's thesis, University of California, Davis, 1966.

Osmond, H. Function as a basis of psychiatric ward design. *Mental Hospitals*, 1957, 8, 23–29.

Sherif, M. Integrating field work and laboratory in small group research. *American Sociological Review*, 1954, 19, 759–771.

Sommer, R. Studies in personal space. *Sociometry*, 1959, 22, 247–260.

Sommer, R. Leadership and group geography. *Sociometry*, 1961, 24, 99–110.

Sommer, R. Further studies in small group ecology. *Sociometry*, 1965, 28, 337–348.

Steinzor, B. The spatial factor in face to face discussion groups. *Journal of Abnormal and Social Psychology*, 1950, 45, 552–555.

Stodtbeck, F. L., & Hook, L. H. The social dimensions of a twelve man jury table. *Sociometry*, 1961, 24, 397–415.

Webb, E. J., Campbell, D. T., Schwartz, R. D., & Sechrest, L. *Unobtrusive measures: Nonreactive research in the social sciences*. Chicago: Rand McNally, 1966.

Williams, J. L. Personal space and its relation to extroversion-introversion. Unpublished master's thesis, University of Alberta, 1963.

Wilmer, H. A. Graphic ways of representing some aspects of a therapeutic community. In, *Symposium of preventive and social psychiatry*. Washington, D. C.: United States Government Printing Office, 1958.

Winick, C., & Holt, H. Seating position as nonverbal communication in group analysis. *Psychiatry*, 1961, 24, 171–182.

17

TERRITORIAL DEFENSE AND THE GOOD NEIGHBOR [1]

ROBERT SOMMER AND FRANKLIN D. BECKER

The concept of human territoriality is receiving increased attention. In addition to the popular books by Ardrey (1961, 1966), a number of social scientists have become impressed with the utility of the concept (Altman & Haythorn, 1967; Esser et al., 1965; Hall, 1966; Lipman, 1967; Lyman & Scott, 1967). Hediger (1950) defined a territory as "an area which is first rendered distinctive by its owner in a particular way and, secondly, is defended by the owner." When the term is used by social scientists to refer to human behavior, there is no implication that the underlying mechanisms are identical to those described in animal research. The major components of Hediger's definition are *personalization* and *defense*. Roos (1968) uses the term *range* as the total area an individual traverses, *territory* as the area he defends, *core area* as the area he preponderantly occupies, and *home* as the area in which he sleeps. Goffman (1963) makes the further distinction between a territory and a *jurisdiction,* such as that exercised by a janitor sweeping the floor of an office and keeping other people away. Territories are defended on two grounds, "you keep off" and "this space is mine." Jurisdictions are controlled only on the former ground; no claim of ownership, no matter how transitory, is made.

In a previous study, the reactions to staged spatial invasions were investigated (Felipe & Sommer, 1966). There was no single reaction to a person coming too close; some people averted their heads and placed an elbow between themselves and the intruder, others treated him as a nonperson, while still others left the area when he came too close. The range of defensive gestures, postures, and acts suggested that a systematic study of defensive procedures would contribute materially to our knowledge of human spatial behavior. Following the tradition of ecological research, the studies would be undertaken in naturally occurring environments.

From *Journal of Personality and Social Psychology,* 1969, 11, 85–92. Copyright © 1969 by the American Psychological Association and reprinted by permission.

Questionnaire studies

During previous observations of library study halls Sommer (1967) was impressed by the heavy concentration of readers at the side-end chairs. Interviewing made it clear that students believed that it was polite to sit at an end chair. Someone who sat, for example, at a center chair of an empty six-chair table (three chairs on each side) was considered to be "hogging the table." There appeared to be two styles by which students gained privacy in the library areas. One method was avoidance, to sit as far away from other people as one could. The other method was offensive ownership of the entire area. To study the two methods of gaining privacy, a brief questionnaire was constructed which presented the student with table diagrams containing 6, 8, and 10 chairs, respectively (Sommer, 1967). Two forms of the questionnaire were distributed randomly within a class of 45 students. Twenty-four students received avoidance instructions: "If you wanted to be as far as possible from the distraction of other people, where would you sit at the table?" Twenty-one other students in the same class were shown the same diagrams and given the offensive display instructions: "If you wanted to have the table to yourself, where would you sit to discourage anyone else from occupying it?" Even though both sets of instructions were aimed at insuring privacy, the two tactics produced a striking difference in seats chosen. Those students who wanted to sit by themselves as far as possible from other people overwhelmingly chose the *end* chairs at the table, while those students who wanted to keep other people away from the table almost unanimously chose the *middle* chair.

When the findings were discussed with architect James Marston Fitch, his first question concerned the location of the door in regards to the table. This seemed a good question, since the preferred location for retreat or active defense should be guided by the path the invaders would take or by the most accessible escape route. The previous diagrams had depicted only a table and chairs, so it seemed necessary to undertake another study in which the entrance to the room was indicated. This conception of the study suggested that additional information could be obtained on the ecology of retreat and active defense by varying the location of walls and aisles and the table size.

Method

The present study involved four diagrams, each one drawn on a separate 8½ × 11-inch sheet.

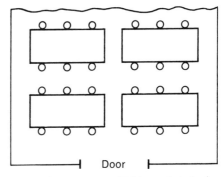

Fig. 1 Arrangement of tables and chairs in Form G.

FORM G showed eight rectangular six-chair tables, with a large aisle down the center and two smaller aisles along the walls. (See Figure 1.)

FORM H was the same as Form G, only the tables were set against the wall and the center aisle was wider.

FORM J was a hybrid of G and H, with the right row of tables against the wall and the left row of tables away from the wall.

FORM I contained one row of four-chair tables and one row of eight-chair tables, with aisles in the center and along both walls.

Four different sets of instructions were used with the forms (two defense styles and two densities), but any single subject received only one set. One form asked the subject where he would sit if he wanted to be by himself and away from other people—the retreat instructions. The other form asked where he would sit if he wanted to keep other people away from the table—the active defense instructions. In each case, the prospective room density was also indicated. On half the questionnaires, it was stated that room density was likely to be low throughout the day and very few people would be using the room, while remaining subjects were told that room density was likely to be high and many people would be using the room. All the instructions described the room as a study hall such as that already existing in the campus library, and the respondent was informed that he was the first occupant in the room, so he could take any seat he wanted. Booklets containing some combination of instructional set (Defense Style × Room Density) and two diagrams in random order were passed out randomly among 280 students in introductory psychology classes.

Results

HYPOTHESIS I stated that during the retreat condition people gravitate to the end chair closest to the wall. During the active defense condition they make greater use of the center and aisle chairs. Hypothesis I was confirmed beyond the .01 level. During the retreat conditions 76% of the subjects occupied a wall chair compared to 48% during the active defense condition.

HYPOTHESIS 2 stated that with the retreat instructions the subjects face away from the door, while they face towards the door with the active defense instructions. The data disclose a preference in all conditions for a subject to sit with his back to the door—60% of the subjects faced away from the door compared to 40% who faced towards it. However, the results were still in the predicted direction since 44% of the subjects in the active defense condition faced the door compared to 36% in the retreat condition ($p < .05$).

Although the authors had imagined that the use of different-sized tables and the variation in wall placement would influence seating patterns, specific hypotheses had not been formulated. In all conditions there was a marked preference for chairs towards the rear of the room. Overall, 79% selected chairs in the rear half of the room. However, occupancy of the rear was significantly higher with the retreat instructions under high room density than in any of the other conditions ($p < .05$). There was also a highly significant preference for the four-chair tables when they were paired with the eight-chair tables, with 73% selecting a small table compared with 27% selecting a large table. There was a slight trend in the active defense condition to make greater use of the small tables, but this was not statistically significant.

When tables against the wall were paired with tables with aisles on both sides, 62% of the subjects selected a table against the wall compared to 38% who chose a table with aisles on both sides ($p < .001$). As an independent variable, description of the projected room density as high or low made very little difference in where people sat. However, density interacted with the defense instructions on several of the tabulations. With high density *and* retreat instructions, there was significantly greater use of (*a*) the rear half of the room, (*b*) a wall compared to an aisle table, and (*c*) the chair closest to the wall. In essence, the attribution of high room density increased the degree of physical retreat. It had no observable effects on the active defense conditions.

The results make it clear that room dimension and the location of barriers must be considered if we are to understand the ecology of spatial defense. In a library reading room, the best chair for retreat is at the rear, facing away from the door, next to a wall, and at a small table if one is available. Distance from the door protects the person against people simply walking by as well as lazy intruders who are more likely to sit in the first available chair; facing away from the door tends to minimize distraction and also displays an antipathy toward social intercourse; a wall table protects a person's entire left (or right) side; and a small table reduces the number of invaders in close proximity. At this point the authors felt they had derived many useful hypotheses from the questionnaire data which they wanted to extend using an experimental approach under natural conditions. The first experimental studies took place in two soda fountains, and the remainder took place in library areas.

Experimental Studies

Most territories are marked and bounded in some clear way. In the animal kingdom, markers may be auditory (bird song), olfactory (glandular secretions by deer), or visual (bear-claw marks on a tree). Since humans rely almost exclusively on visual markers, the authors decided to test the strength of various markers ranging from the physical presence of a person to impersonal artifacts.

Study 1

The first study took place in a popular soda fountain on campus. The soda fountain was located in a converted office building which still contained a number of small rooms. Patrons would obtain their refreshments at a central counter and then repair to one of the smaller rooms to eat and chat informally. Prior to the study, the authors had been struck by the sight of students walking up and down the corridor looking for an empty room. One of the small rooms which contained three square tables, each surrounded by four chairs, was used for the study. A 20-year-old-girl who appeared to be studying stationed herself at a table facing the door. On other occasions during the same hours she stationed herself down the hall so she could observe who entered the experimental room. A session took place only when the room was unoccupied at the outset.

If an all-or-none criterion of room occupancy is applied, the experimenter's defense was not very successful. During only 1 of the 10 experimental sessions was she able to keep the entire room to herself. The average length of time before the room was occupied during the experimental sessions was 5.8 minutes compared to 2.6 minutes during the control sessions, but the difference was not statistically reliable. Although the experimenter was unable to keep the room to herself, she was able to protect the table at which she studied. The remaining three seats were occupied only once during the experimental sessions compared to 13 occupancies during the control sessions ($p < .01$). It seems clear that territorial defense in a public area is not an all-or-none affair. The defender's presence may be seen in a delay in occupancy rather than an absence of invaders and in the avoidance of a subarea within the larger area.

Study 2

The next study took place in a more traditional open-plan soda fountain and, instead of the physical presence of the experimenter, three sorts of objects were used as territorial markers—a sandwich wrapped in cellophane, a sweater draped over a chair, and two paperback books stacked on the table. In each case the experimenter located two adjacent empty tables and arbitrarily placed a marker on one with the other as a control. Seating himself some distance away, he was able to record the duration of time before each table was occupied. The sessions all took place at moderate room density. There were 8 sessions with a sandwich marker, 13 with a sweater, and 20 with the books.

The authors were interested in whether a marker would reserve an entire table as well as the marked chair. The answer for all of the markers was affirmed. The unmarked control tables were occupied significantly sooner than were the marked tables, and the difference was significant for each of the three markers. In fact, in all 41 sessions the control table was occupied sooner or at the same time as the marked table. In only three of the sessions did anyone sit at the marked *chair*. All three were occupied by males, a finding whose significance will be discussed

later. It is also interesting to examine the occupancy patterns at the two sorts of tables. The marked tables were eventually occupied by 34 lone individuals and 4 groups of 2 persons, while the unmarked tables were occupied by 18 lone individuals and 20 groups. It can be noted that a group of 2 or 3 could easily be accommodated at a marked table even assuming that the marker represented one person, yet virtually all the groups sat at unmarked tables. It is clear that the markers were able to (a) protect the particular chair almost totally, (b) delay occupancy of the entire table, and (c) divert groups away from the table.

Study 3

A similar study using books and newspapers as markers was undertaken in a dormitory study hall at a time of very light room density. Virtually all the markers proved effective in reserving the marked chair. The only exceptions were two sessions when the school paper which had been used as a marker was treated as litter and pushed aside. After more than 30 individual sessions where virtually all the markers were respected, the authors decided to move the experiments to the main university library where room density was much heavier. It seemed clear that at low densities almost any marker is effective. One qualification is that the object must be perceived as a marker and not as something discarded and unwanted by its former owner. Certain forms of litter such as old newspapers or magazines may, indeed, attract people to a given location.

The locus of study was switched to the periodical room in the university library where room density was high and pressure for seats was great. This room contained rectangular six-chair tables, three chairs to a side. The experimenter arrived at one of the six seats at a designated table at 6:50 P.M., deposited a marker, and then departed to another table at 7:00 P.M. to view any occupancy at the marked position by a student seeking space. During each session, a similarly situated empty chair which was unmarked was used as the control. There were 25 experimental sessions, each lasting 2 hours. The markers included two notebooks and a textbook, four library journals piled in a neat stack, four library journals randomly scattered on the table, a sports jacket draped over the chair, and a sports jacket draped over the chair in addition to the notebooks on the table.

If one compares the average time before occupancy of the marked and the control chairs, it is apparent that all markers were effective. Seventeen of the 25 marked chairs remained vacant the entire 2-hour period, while *all* control chairs were occupied. The average interval before the control chairs were occupied was 20 minutes. Some of the markers were more potent than others. Only one student occupied a chair that was marked either by a sports jacket or a notebook-and-text. Chairs marked by the neatly-piled journals were occupied three of the five sessions, while chairs marked by the randomly placed journals were occupied all five sessions, even though the interval in each case exceeded that of the control chairs. It is clear that the personal markers, such as the sports jacket and notebooks, were able to keep away intruders entirely, while the impersonal library-owned markers (journals) could only delay occupancy of the marked chairs.

An interesting sidelight is that eight of the nine students who sat down de-spite the markers were males. Since there were more females than males in the control chairs at the same time, the high incidence of males is quite significant. It may be recalled in the previous study that the only three individuals who pushed aside the marker and sat at a marked chair were also males. It is likely that some sort of dominance or risk-taking factor is at work in the decision to disregard a territorial marker. The relationship between personality characteristics and the likelihood of invading someone else's space seems an exciting topic for further investigation.

Another serendipitous finding concerns the role of the neighbor, the person sitting alongside the marked chair, in defending the marked space. In all five trials with the scattered journals, the potential invader questioned the person sitting alongside the marked chair (the neighbor) as to whether the space was vacant. Early in the 2-hour session, the neighbor unknowingly served as the protector of the space. He informed all inquisitive intruders that the space was taken, since he believed the experimenter would return in view of the marker left on the table. As time passed, the neighbor's belief that the experimenter would return to the chair began to wane. At this point he would impart his new conception of the situation to potential invaders, "Yes, somebody was sitting there, but that was over an hour ago. Maybe he's not coming back."

Study 4

Since the role of the neighbor seemed an important aspect of a property-ownership system, the authors decided to investigate it experimentally. The first of such studies involved two experimenters and a person sitting alongside an empty chair. One experimenter seated himself next to a stranger (the neighbor) for 15 minutes and then departed, leaving behind an open book and an open notebook upon the table as territorial markers. After a fixed interval, the second experimenter, in the role of a student looking for a chair, came and inquired about the marked space nonverbally. The nonverbal questionning was a pantomime which included catching the neighbor's eye, pulling out the chair slightly, hesitating, looking at the place markers and at the neighbor, and then back at the markers. The authors had very little experience with such nonverbal cues, but expected that the neighbor's reactions might include verbal defenses ("That seat is taken") and nonverbal defenses (moving the books to reinforce the marker). The independent variable was the length of time between the departure of the first experimenter and the arrival of the second—which was either a 5- or a 20-minute interval. Some sessions had to be terminated when the neighbor departed before the second experimenter arrived on the scene.

Overall the results were discouraging. In only 6 of the 55 trials did the neighbor respond to the nonverbal gestures of the second experimenter in what could be described as a space-defending manner, such as a statement that the seat was taken. Five of the six defensive acts occurred when the experimenter had been away 5 minutes, compared to only one defensive act when he had been away 20 minutes, but considering that there were 55 trials the difference was unimpressive.

Study 5

The authors decided to make another attempt to see if the neighbor could be involved in property defense on a spontaneous basis—that is, if he would defend marked space without being questioned directly. Unlike in the preceding study, the "owner" attempted to establish a relationship with the neighbor prior to the "owner's" departure. There were two phases of the study; when it seemed that the first approach was not leading anywhere, another approach was used. The markers were a neat stack of three paperback books left on the table in front of a chair. The sessions took place at six-chair tables where there was at least 1 empty seat between the marker and the neighbor. The first experimenter entered the room and found the location meeting the experimental requirements (a person sitting at the end chair of a six-person table with two empty chairs alongside him—O-O-S). The experimenter (a girl) sat down on the same side of the table but one seat away (E-O-S). There were 13 trials in each of the following conditions: (*a*) The experimenter sat 5 minutes and then departed from the table, leaving her books neatly stacked on the table. During this time she did not interact with her neighbor. (*b*) Similar to Condition *a*, the experimenter sat for 5 minutes except that during the 5-minute wait, the experimenter asked the neighbor "Excuse me, could you tell me what time it is?" (*c*) Similar to Condition *a,* the experimenter sat for 5 minutes except that during the 5-minute wait the experimenter engaged the neighbor in conversation four times and, while leaving and placing the stack of three paperback books on the table, declared, "See you later." Fifteen minutes later, the second experimenter (a male) entered the room, walked directly to the marked chair, pushed the books directly ahead of him, and sat down at the table.

The results were again discouraging. In none of the 39 trials involving Conditions a, b, and c did the neighbor inform the intruder that the seat was taken. The authors therefore decided to strengthen the conditions by having the "owner" return and directly confront the intruder. Seven of such trials were added to Condition a, six to Condition b, and 6 to Condition c, making 19 trials in all when the "owner" came back and told the intruder "You are sitting in my chair." Each time she hesitated about 30 seconds to see if the neighbor would intervene, and then she picked up her books and departed. There was no verbal response from the neighbor in any of the 19 sessions. The most that occurred would be a frown or a look of surprise on the part of the neighbor, or some nonverbal communication with someone else at the table. Stated simply, despite a flagrant usurpation of a marked space, all neighbors chose to remain uninvolved. It became clear that if one wanted to study the neighbor's role in such an informal regulatory system one would have to question him directly as to whether the seat was occupied.

Study 6

The next study employed two experimenters, a male and a female, and the same three paperback books as markers. Two different girls were used as experimenters, and the sessions occurred in two different, nearby college libraries. The experimental situation involved six-chair tables where the first experimenter (female) sat down at the same side of a table with a subject, leaving an empty chair between them (E-O-S). The goal of the study was to learn whether a greater amount of interaction between the former occupant and the neighbor would increase the neighbor's likelihood of defending the chair. Unlike in the previous study, the neighbor was questioned directly as to whether the seat was taken. There were three different instructional sets, and these took place according to a prearranged random order. In 14 trials, the first experimenter sat at the chair for 5 minutes without saying anything, deposited the marker (three paperback books), and left. Fourteen other sessions were similar except that at some time during her 5-minute stay, the first experimenter asked the neighbor for the time. Ten other sessions were similar except that the experimenter engaged the neighbor in conversation as to where to get a coke, what was happening on campus, and other minor matters. Fifteen minutes after the first experimenter departed, the second experimenter (a male) entered the room, walked over to the marked chair, and asked the neighbor "Excuse me, is there anyone sitting here?"

The results differ markedly from those in the previous study. A total of 22 out of the 38 neighbors defended the seat when questioned directly on the matter. The typical defense response was "Yes, there is" or "There is a girl who left those books." [2] However, the amount of contact between the first experimenter and the neighbor made little difference in defensive behavior. When there had been no contact, or minimal contact, between the first experimenter and neighbor the seat was protected 58% of the time, while the use of several items of conversation between the experimenter and her neighbor raised the percentage of defensive responses only to 66%. The difference between conditions is small and statistically unreliable; what is impressive is the great increase in defensive behavior when the neighbor was questioned directly. Two other parameters of the situation are (a) the time that the first experimenter remained in the seat before depositing her marker, and (b) the length of time that the first experimenter was out of room before the second experimenter approached the marked chair.

Study 7

The final study employed two experimenters, both males, and the same three paperback books. The sessions took place at six-chair tables in the library, where the first experimenter again sat down on the same side of the table with a subject, leaving an empty chair between them (E-O-S). He remained either 5 minutes or 20 minutes, depending upon the experimental condition, and then departed, leaving on the table a neat stack of three paperback books. After a designated interval of either 15 or 60 minutes, the second experimenter entered the room and asked the neighbor whether the (marked) chair was taken. The second experimenter recorded the neighbor's reply verbatim just as soon as he was able to sit down somewhere. Since both experimenters were males, it was decided to use only male neighbors in the experiment.

The independent variables were (a) the length of time the first experimenter had been seated before he left his marker and departed and (b) the length of time the first experimenter was absent before the neighbor was questioned by the second experimenter. Some sessions were unusable since the neighbor departed before the designated time and could not be interviewed. Most of the unusable sessions occurred when the experimenter had

been absent for 60 minutes. The sessions took place at times of light-to-moderate room density.

Although the design had not called for comparison of marked and unmarked chairs, it is noteworthy that the markers were effective in keeping people away. Not one of the 64 marked chairs was ever occupied. Regarding the inclination of the neighbor to defend the marked space when questioned by the second experimenter, a content analysis of the neighbor's responses to the query "Is this seat taken?" into defense and nondefense categories revealed that 44 neighbors defended the marked space by indicating that it was taken, while 20 failed to do so either by pleading ignorance or by stating that the chair was empty. The response to a direct question stands in contrast to the lack of involvement when neighbors were approached nonverbally. The length of time that the first experimenter had originally occupied the chair (his tenure period) had no effect on the willingness of the neighbor to defend the chair. However, the length of time that the previous owner was away—either 15 or 60 minutes—had a significant effect. When the former owner had been absent 15 minutes, 80% of the neighbors defended the space compared to 54% defending it when the former owner had been away a full hour ($p < .05$).

Several aspects of the results require elaboration. It is possible that initial tenure periods of 5 and 20 minutes were not sufficiently different. Yet it seems noteworthy that even with a rather impersonal marker, more than two-thirds of the neighbors defended the marked chair upon direct questioning. Most of those who didn't defend it simply pleaded ignorance ("I don't know if it's taken") rather than indicating that the seat was vacant.

After the experiments had been completed, 15 additional students in the library were interviewed on the question of how personal belongings could reserve space. Each student was asked how he would react if he saw someone intrude into a marked space, particularly if the original owner came back and claimed the space (i.e., the actual experimental situation was described to him). The replies were at variance with what the authors had actually found in such a situation. Most of the respondents maintained that they would indeed protect a marked space, although some of them added qualifications that they would defend the space only if the person were away a short time. Typical responses were: "I would protect the person's books and state (to the intruder) that the place was obviously taken by the presence of the books," and "Yes, I would mention that someone was sitting there." Although the majority mentioned specifically that they would protect a marked chair, in the actual situation no one had done so unless approached directly. The ethic regarding space ownership in the library exists, but is paid lip service, probably because institutional means of enforcement do not exist.

Discussion

The present article represents a small beginning toward understanding how markers reserve space and receive their legitimacy from people in the area (neighbors) and potential intruders. Psychologists have paid little attention to boundary markers in social interaction, perhaps because such markers were regarded as physical objects relegated to the cultural system (the province of the anthropologist) rather than an interpersonal system which is the true province of the social psychologist. Generally it is the geographers and lawyers who are most concerned with boundaries and markers. Since the present studies took place in public spaces, we are dealing more with norms and customs than with legal statutes. Stated another way, the situations involve an interpersonal system where sanctions are enforced by the individuals immediately present. Goffman (1963) labels the situations the authors used in the experiments *temporary territories*. It is clear that a person placing his coat over the back of a chair desires to reserve the space, and most people in the immediate vicinity will support his claim if questioned (although they will remain uninvolved if they can); such behavior meets Hediger's (1950) definition of territory presented previously as well as the more simple one provided by Noble (1939) that a territory represents "any defended area." The phenomena the present authors have studied do not belong under other available rubrics of spatial behavior, such as home range, biotope, niche, or life space. The major differences between the experimental situations and more enduring territories is that the latter are meshed with a legal-cultural framework and supported in the end by laws, police, and armies. The marked spaces in the present authors' experiments have no legal status and are supported only by the immediate social system. Occasionally it became necessary to articulate the structure of the system by "requiring" neighbors to enter the situation.

People are now spending an increasing portion of their time in public or institutional spaces, including theaters, airport lobbies, buses, schools, and hospitals, where the use of personal belongings to mark out temporary territories is a common phenomenon. The study of territories, temporary as well as enduring ones, deserves study by psychologists. There is some danger that such work will lose much of its force if some semantic clarity is not obtained. While the ethologist's definition of a territory as "any defended area" has considerable heuristic value, there is no need to assume that the mechanisms underlying human and animal behavior are identical. The paucity of data about human territorial behavior makes it most reasonsable to assume that the mechanisms are analogous rather than homologous.

In conclusion, the present series of studies suggests that further investigation of spatial markers is feasible and warranted. The physical environment has for too long been considered the background variable in psychological research. The time is past when we can have theories of man that do not take into account his surroundings. Boundary markers not only define what belongs to a person and what belongs to his neighbor, but also who he is and what it means to be a neighbor in a complex society.

NOTES

1. The authors are grateful to Harriet Becker, Martha Connell, Ann Gibbs, Lee Mohr, Tighe O'Hanrahan, Pamela Pearce, Ralph Requa, Sally Robison, and Nancy Russo for their assistance.
2. The neighbors' replies to the intruder's question were scored separately by two coders as indicating defense of the space ("Yes, that seat is taken") or nondefense ("No, it isn't taken" or "I don't know"). There was 100% agreement between the two raters in scoring the replies into defense or nondefense categories.

REFERENCES

Altman, I., & Haythorn, W. W. The ecology of isolated groups. *Behavioral Science,* 1967, 12, 169–182.

Ardrey, R. *African genesis.* London: Collins, 1961.

Ardrey, S. *The territorial imperative.* New York: Atheneum, 1966.

Esser, A. H. et al. Territoriality of patients on a research ward. In J. Wortis (Ed.), *Recent advances in biological psychiatry.* Vol. 8. New York: Plenum Press, 1965.

Felipe, N., & Sommer, R. Invasions of personal space. *Social Problems,* 1966, 14, 206–214.

Goffman, E. *Behavior in public places.* New York: Free Press of Glencoe, 1963.

Hall, E. T. *The hidden dimension.* Garden City: Doubleday, 1966.

Hediger, H. *Wild animals in captivity.* London: Butterworths, 1950.

Lipman, A. Old peoples homes: Siting and neighborhood integration. *The Sociological Review,* 1967, 15, 323–338.

Lyman, S. M., & Scott, M. B. Territoriality: A neglected sociological dimension. *Social Problems,* 1967, 15, 236–249.

Noble, G. K. The role of dominance in the social life of birds, *Auk,* 1939, 263–273.

Roos, P. D. Jurisdiction: An ecological concept. *Human Relations,* 1968, 21, 75–84.

Sommer, R. Sociofugal space. *American Journal of Sociology,* 1967, 72, 654–660.

five

MULTICHANNEL COMMUNICATION

We have been discussing nonverbal communication as if messages arrived in discrete packages: facial expression, voice, spatial distance, eye contact, and so on. Of course, this is not the case at all. What we are confronted with is an alive, reacting person giving off all sorts of messages simultaneously in competing channels. The structural approach, exemplified by Birdwhistell, Kendon, and Scheflen, discussed earlier (Part 3) in this book is totally concerned with multichannel communication. Dittmann (1972) addresses this problem directly in his communications theory approach. Other researchers have recognized the problem but have studied one area at a time as a matter of research strategy and conceptual economy. Nevertheless, the problem still remains: after we have decided what each piece looks like, we must put the interacting organism back together again. Several researchers have begun to address this issue, and it is to their efforts that we turn in this section. Ekman and Friesen (p. **269**) deal with deception as a case study in multichannel communication, while Mehrabian and Ferris (p. **291**) develop a model for combining information from two channels. Duncan (p. **298**) has provided a valuable case study of the set of multichannel cues needed to facilitate the taking of speaking turns in ordinary conversation. Next, Mehrabian and Ksionzky (p. **312**) put forward a factor analytic model of social interaction based on Mehrabian's (1972) extensive research program in verbal and nonverbal communication. Finally, Smith (p. **331**) takes a broad view of human communication by setting it in the context of animal displays and messages.

Combining information from several channels is an ever-present part of decoding nonverbal displays. Both the Ekman and Friesen, and the Mehrabian and Ferris studies address this problem. When there is a conscious or unconscious attempt to deceive oneself and/or others about one's emotional state, inconsistent messages are often sent. Since the head and the face can be more easily controlled, nonverbal leakage is likely to occur from body cues. Ekman and Friesen report that observers who attended to body cues more often caught the "true" emotion than those who directed their attention to the more deceptive face and head areas. The difference between the information given by head and by body cues is an interesting one. In an early study, Ekman (1965) reported that head cues reveal the type of emotion experienced, while body cues indicate the intensity of the affect (in a situation without deception). Ekman and Friesen (1967) later reformulated their position to say that nonverbal *acts* (observable body movements) can convey the nature of an emotion, while *positions* (lack of such movement) can reveal the gross affect state (negative or positive; pleasant or unpleasant), but not the specific emotion. Head and body cues can appear as either acts or positions, although more information is usually obtained from facial cues in general. When head and body cues conflict, as in deception situations, body movements will "leak" more than facial expressions and lead to a more accurate assessment of the individual's emotional state, as described in the Ekman and Friesen article. Mehrabian (1971) looked directly at the differences between truthful and deceitful communicators and found that deceitful communicators (who were lying in their verbal statements) moved less, were less immediate in their body positions, spoke less and more slowly and with more speech errors, and smiled more than their truthful counterparts. More negative evaluations of affect were made in the deceitful condition than in the truthful state.

A special type of conflict situation occurs when nonverbal and verbal information differ. Mehrabian and Ferris's study (p. **291**) indicates that facial expressions are given slightly more weight than vocal cues in formulating a judgment of emotional state. Bugental, Kaswan, and Love (1970) also found that facial and vocal cues are combined in a linear model of impression formation. They also report that negative information is more heavily weighted than positive information, so that if both are combined in the same message, it tends to be read as negative. This effect is especially true for children, who may be puzzled and upset by joking messages, tending to interpret them as negative ridicule. Adults display less of this effect, being more sophisticated in emotional decoding. Another age difference was reported in the interpretation of conflicting communications. The "perfidious" female smile (as Bugental, Love, and Gianetto, 1971, term it) cannot convince children of the positive tone of otherwise negative vocal messages. Children interpret such messages negatively (although adults do not). This study (Bugental, Love, and Gianetto, 1971) actually found that female smiling was unrelated to the evaluative content of their verbal messages (they smiled a lot, through both negative and positive messages), unlike male smiling which mainly accompanied friendly messages. This effect was true only for middle class Ss, since lower class women smiled very rarely, regardless of message content. Bugental, Kaswan, Love, and Fox (1970) also found that negative facial expressions in males were weighted less heavily in rating the total message than similar female input, presumably because the basal male facial expression was closer to the neutral pole and such "negativity" could be interpreted as determination or concentration rather than negative affect. Since the basal female facial expression was more decidedly positive, negative deviation from it would be closely attended to, while remaining in the positive female "neutral" position would not be. Bugental et al. (1970) also report that their model of combining information from several channels is a modified additive one, in which reduced weight is given to successive inputs which reinforce the direction of the initial cue.

An active line of research in mental illness contends that the genesis of emotional disorder is often a disturbed parent-child communications network, in which conflicting messages are sent from parent (usually mother) to child. The double-bind hypothesis (Bateson, Jackson, Haley, and Weakland, 1956) of schizophrenia is based on the proposed existence of this disordered communications network, although empirical research has not supported this position very strongly (Shuham, 1967). One may directly look at verbal-nonverbal conflict as an index of such disturbance in parental messages, so that mothers may be sending positive messages in the more regulated verbal channel, coupled with negative cues coming from the less controllable nonverbal channels. Bugental, Love, Kaswan, and April (1971) found that mothers of emotionally disturbed children did send more conflicting verbal-nonverbal messages than mothers of normal children, and that the sons of mothers sending conflicting messages manifested a higher level of aggressive behavior than the other disturbed children. A typical conflicting message would be negative in verbal content and positive paralinguistically and nonverbally. Earlier research (Bugental, Kaswan, and Love, 1970) discussed above, indicated that children weight negative inputs more heavily, especially when attending to female communicators. The effect of such conflicting cues might be that of "arousing the negative feelings of the child (due to the negative evaluative component) while simultaneously inhibiting a direct negative response to her (because of the positive component)" (Bugental, Love, Kaswan, and April, 1971, p. 9). Of course, one must always consider the possibility that the disordered communication is an effect rather than a cause of the child's behavioral problems.

An excellent example of applying multichannel analysis to a small, but important segment of social encounter is Starkey Duncan's study (p. 298) of "signals and rules for taking speaking turns in conversations." Various paralinguistic, linguistic, and kinesic cues are combined to indicate that a speaker has ended his statement and that another may speak. An interactant may also send "attempt-suppressing" signals (chiefly hand movements) if he has been mistakingly "read" as being ready to give up his turn when he really wishes to continue. Duncan's research is based on the careful transcription of nineteen minutes of two video-taped dyadic interviews. As in linguistic analysis, a very small sample of behavior from a few informants is considered adequate to reconstruct the nature of the structures underlying the interaction. In this way, Duncan's research is similar to the tradition established by Birdwhistell (discussed in this book on p. **128**).

In the final two articles, we take a broader view of multichannel communication by looking at two different overall views of the structure of interaction. Mehrabian and Ksionzky (p. **312**) report on a factor analytic approach to analyzing social interaction and come up with three factors: affiliation, status, and responsiveness, that are well-supported in the literature. Smith (p. **331**) takes an ethological view of multichannel communication in animals and man.

First, we will consider Mehrabian's study. The summary table on p. **314** enumerates the multichannel components of each factor, in terms of both verbal and nonverbal cues. Thus, affiliative behavior is indicated by such cues as talkativeness, positive verbal content, head nods, hand and arm gestures, and pleasantness of facial expression. Mehrabian cites many theoretical models of interaction and emotion which turn up a similar three factor structure. The present study is an extension of some earlier work (Mehrabian, 1970) in which a "semantic space" for nonverbal behavior was proposed. The same three factors were put forth as dimensions of nonverbal communication, and the same methodology (factor analysis) was used. A fuller discussion of Mehrabian's ten-year program of experimental research in nonverbal communication can be found in his recent book (Mehrabian, 1972). We earlier (p. **93**) discussed his work on immediacy in verbal interaction (Wiener and Mehrabian, 1968). Note the type of experimental analytic approach Mehrabian takes to nonverbal communication (exemplified by his two articles in this section) and how it differs from the structuralist approach of Birdwhistell and others.

Finally, Smith's article (p. **331**) takes the broadest view yet of nonverbal communication by placing it in an evolutionary perspective. Smith sees a gradual overtaking of kinesic and paralinguistic communication by language in man but asserts that the more primitive forms of communication still persist and are important sources of intraspecific messages. The new science of semiotics (Sebeok, Hayes, and Bateson, 1964; Sebeok and Ramsey, 1969) takes as its subject matter, "patterned communications in all modalities," and its concern ranges from animal communication to linguistic analysis. According to Sebeok, human semiotic systems consist of two varieties: (1) anthroposemiotic systems, chiefly language communication, unique to man, and (2) zoosemiotic systems, paralinguistic and nonverbal behavior, characteristic of other animals as well as man. Linguistics is the science concerned with the first area, nonverbal communication with the second. Semiotics urges an ultimate joining of the two concerns, an aim shared by such researchers as Birdwhistell, whose work was discussed earlier in the section on body movement. The founders of the semiotic movement publish their own journal, *Semiotica,* from which the Smith article, as well as the earlier Ekman, Friesen, and Tomkins piece (p. **34**) are taken.

Smith (1974) has also reported some work on tracing a distinctive facial display, sticking out the tongue, through several species, including man, to determine how it is used and how this usage evolved. Generally, Smith finds, this display is used to signal an aversion to social encounter. The well-known "Bronx cheer" is one stylized example of this display, but it is used frequently on a more casual basis as well. Smith speculates that the tongue display may have originated as a rejection of food, with feeding being a prototype for other forms of social interaction. Smith is one of the most active researchers in evolutionary biology studying nonverbal communication, but the general ethological perspective is very concerned with evolutionary questions (see Eibl-Eibesfeldt article, p. **20,** as well as discussion on p. **11,** also Hinde, 1972, Eibl-Eibesfeldt, 1970, 1971).

The understanding of multichannel communication, then, is the ultimate goal of all research on the human communications system, both verbal and nonverbal. Although a unified approach seems to lie in the future, present work in the field offers the hope that that day may not be too far off.

REFERENCES

Bateson, G., Jackson, D. D., Haley, J., and Weakland, J., "Toward a theory of schizophrenia," *Behavioral Science,* 1956, 1, 251–64.

Bugental, D. E., Kaswan, J. W., and Love, L. R., "Perception of contradictory meanings conveyed by verbal and nonverbal channels," *Journal of Personality and Social Psychology,* 1970, 16, 647–55.

Bugental, D. E., Kaswan, J. W., Love, L. R., and Fox, M. N., "Child versus adult perception of evaluative messages in verbal, vocal and visual channels," *Developmental Psychology,* 1970, 2, 367–75.

Bugental, D. E., Love, L. R., and Gianetto, R. M., "Perfidious feminine faces," *Journal of Personality and Social Psychology,* 1971, 17, 314–18.

Bugental, D. E., Love, L. R., Kaswan, J. W., and April, C., "Verbal-nonverbal conflict in parental messages to normal and disturbed children," *Journal of Abnormal Psychology,* 1971, 77, 6–10.

Dittmann, A. T., *Interpersonal Messages of Emotion,* Springer, New York, 1972.

Eibl-Eibesfeldt, I., *Ethology: The Biology of Behavior,* Holt, Rinehart, and Winston, New York, 1970.

Eibl-Eibesfeldt, I., *Love and Hate: The Natural History of Behavioral Patterns,* G. Strachen transl., Holt, Rinehart and Winston, New York, 1971.

Ekman, P., "Differential communication of affect by head and body cues," *Journal of Personality and Social Psychology,* 1965, 2, 726–35.

Ekman, P., and Friesen, W. V., "Head and body cues in the judgment of emotion," *Perceptual and Motor Skills,* 1967, 24, 711–24.

Hinde, R. A., ed., *Nonverbal Communication,* Cambridge University Press, Cambridge, 1972.

Mehrabian, A., "A semantic space for nonverbal behavior," *Journal of Consulting and Clinical Psychology,* 1970, 35, 248–57.

Mehrabian, A., "Nonverbal betrayal of

feeling," *Journal of Experimental Research in Personality,* 1971, 5, 64–73.

Mehrabian, A., *Nonverbal Communication,* Aldine, Chicago, 1972.

Sebeok, T. A., Hayes, A. S., and Bateson, M. C., eds., *Approaches to Semiotics: Transactions of the Indiana University Conference on Paralinguistics and Kinesics,* Mouton Publishers, The Hague, 1964.

Sebeok, T. A., and Ramsay, A., *Approaches to Animal Communication,* Mouton, The Hague, 1969.

Shuham, A. I., "The double-bind hypothesis a decade later," *Psychological Bulletin,* 1967, 68, 409–16.

Smith, W. J., Chase, J., and Leiblich, A., "Tongue showing: a facial display of humans and other primate species," in *Interaction Analysis,* A. Kendon, J. Sherzer, W. J. Smith, J. Chase, and A. Leiblich, eds., Mouton, 1974, in press.

Wiener, M., and Mehrabian, A., *Language within Language: Immediacy, A Channel in Verbal Communication,* Appleton-Century-Crofts, New York, 1968.

18

NONVERBAL LEAKAGE AND CLUES TO DECEPTION [1]

PAUL EKMAN AND WALLACE V. FRIESEN

In the last few years there has been a resurgence of interest in facial expression and body movement, both in research relevant to psychotherapy,[2] and in the development of psychotherapeutic techniques which emphasize this mode of behavior.[3] Most of the research has shown that the kind of information which can be gleaned from the patient's words—information about affects, attitudes, interpersonal styles, psychodynamics—can also be derived from his concomitant nonverbal behavior. Yet, if body movements and facial expressions were only redundant with verbal behavior, there would be little need for the therapist to carefully attend to it, or the psychotherapy researcher to bear the burden of recording and analyzing visual records. Two years ago we argued (1968a) that the central problem for those investigators interested in the application of their work to psychotherapy research or practice was to provide evidence of how nonverbal behavior can provide information which differs from that provided by words. We suggested that demographic variables, changes in ego states, situational variables, and message content would all be relevant in determining when actions speak louder than words. In this article we will explore only one of these variables, the interaction situation, and will consider how within deception interactions differences in neuroanatomy and cultural influences combine to produce specific types of body movements and facial expressions which escape efforts to deceive and emerge as *leakage* or *deception clues*.

The proposal that nonverbal behavior may escape efforts to deceive, may evade self-censoring, or may betray dissimulation is by no means new. Darwin wrote:

Some actions ordinarily associated through habit with certain states of mind may be partially repressed through the will, and in such cases the muscles which are least under the separate control of the will are the most liable still to act, causing movements

From *Psychiatry*, 1969, 32, 88–106. Copyright © 1969 by The William Alanson White Psychiatric Foundation, Inc., and reprinted by special permission.

which we recognize as expressive. In certain other cases the checking of one habitual movement requires other slight movements; and these are likewise expressive. [pp. 48–49]

Darwin did not, however, clearly specify which movements are susceptible to control of the "will," and which escape such control or are themselves a product of the control.

Freud was persuaded of the importance of nonverbal behavior when he wrote:

He that has eyes to see and ears to hear may convince himself that no mortal can keep a secret. If his lips are silent, he chatters with his finger-tips; betrayal oozes out of him at every pore. [p. 94]

But Freud was less concerned with nonverbal behavior than with the intricacies of verbal behavior, and such forms of verbal leakage as slips of the tongue and dreams.

Goffman is the contemporary writer whose general framework is most relevant to deception and nonverbal behavior. Social interactions are all in a sense deceptive; the participants are engaged in a dramatic performance to manage impressions that are given off.

The legitimate performances of everyday life are not "acted" or "put on" in the sense that the performer knows in advance just what he is going to do, and does this solely because of the effect it is likely to have. The expressions it is felt that he is giving off will be especially "inaccessible" to him. But as in the case of less legitimate performers, the incapacity of the ordinary individual to formulate in advance the movements of his eyes and body does not mean that he will not express himself through these devices in a way that is dramatized and pre-formed in his repertoire of acts. In short, we all act better than we know how. [pp. 73–74]

Our view of deception situations differs from Goffman's in emphasis; we will isolate specific types of interactions which differ from other performances in terms of the focus upon withholding information and dissimulating. Goffman has also described how nonverbal actions may inadvertently distract from the performance. He considers unmeant gestures as problems in that the audience may treat them seriously, questioning the honesty of a performance because of accidental expressive cues. We will emphasize the other side of the coin, how certain nonverbal acts should be treated as important evidence that the performance is deceptive and the information being provided is false.

We will distinguish two types of deception, and then consider three dimensions which distinguish deceptive situations from other forms of social interaction. We will then postulate differences in the sending capacity of the face, hands, and feet based largely upon neuroanatomical considerations, and discuss how these sending differences combine with sociocultural variables to bring about differences among face, hands and feet in internal and external feedback. These differences in feedback form the basis for our predictions about the types of nonverbal activities which provide leakage and deception clues. Finally, we will present evidence from our study of psychiatric interviews which illustrates our general hypotheses.

Definitions

We will consider two forms of deception: alter-deception, where ego,[4] the deceiver, conceals information from the other interactant, alter; and self-deception, where ego is the object of his own deception, concealing information from himself. Alter is not deceived if he perceives either deception clues or leakage. Deception clues tip him off that deception is in progress but do not reveal the concealed information; the betrayal of that withheld information we call leakage. Alter may become aware of deception clues or leakage regardless of whether ego is aware of their occurrence or of alter's cognizance of them. During alter-deception, if ego realizes alter is on to him, he may give up his deception; or he may continue it, since explicit acknowledgment of engaging in deception may be more embarrassing than maintaining a deception tacitly discovered. During self-deception, it is likely that alter may be aware of deception clues and leakage of which ego is oblivious; if ego becomes aware of his own deception clues he may have an uncanny feeling that something is amiss, or that he has some conflicting feelings; presumably ego does not become aware of his own leakage during self-deception because to learn the information he has concealed from himself would produce severe anxiety.

Ego plans his behavior during alter-deception and is usually quite aware of what he wishes to conceal from alter. The information withheld might refer to ego's feelings and attitudes toward alter, or toward some other person or object; or it might be about some past activity or future plan of his own, or of alter's, or of some third party of interest to alter. Ego has two choices, if he is to succeed in his deception: inhibit or simulate. Most often he will do both. Simply inhibiting, cutting off communication entirely, is the safest way to prevent leakage, but it usually is a giveaway to alter that something is amiss. Instead ego will attempt to maintain the communicative flow, pretending that nothing is being concealed while he carefully and selectively omits certain messages.

Simulation comes about for three reasons. The first reason, just described, is that the gaps left by omitting specific messages must be filled if the gaps are not to become conspicuous deception clues. A second motive for simulation is to maintain a barrier against the breakthrough of inhibited behavior. When there is considerable pressure behind the matters being concealed the only way to prevent their leakage is by simulating antithetical feelings. A neutral face probably will not succeed in masking uproarious laughter, particularly if there is continuing mirthful provocation; the trace of the smile, the quiver in the corners of the lips, can best be withheld over time by setting the jaw, biting the lip, or compressing the lips.

A third reason for simulation is more intrinsic to the structure of the social setting and the goal of the deception. Most deceptive situations not only dictate the need to conceal one item of information but also require the substitution of a false message. It is not sufficient, for example, for the job applicant to inhibit signs of nervousness or inexperience, or for the hospitalized depressive patient to inhibit signs of melancholia; the goal of the deception requires that to gain employment the applicant simulate cool confidence, that to gain release from the hospital the patient simulate feelings of optimism, well-being and insight. The extent of simulating is thus related to how extensive the lie may be, how many gaps are created by omission, how much motivational force is associated with the information concealed, and how extensive the requirements are for substituted false messages in order to achieve the goal of the deception. Later we will describe how simulations may be improperly performed because of defects in internal feedback about certain types of nonverbal behavior, and how such imperfect nonverbal simulations are major forms of deception clues.

While alter-deception involves a dyad in which one member deceives the other, self-deception is a more individual phenomenon, where the presence of the other person is not necessarily relevant to the deception. Alter is not the primary target; instead the purpose of the deception is to conceal information from the self-aware part of the self. There is a division within the individual such that one part of the self can inhibit and conceal information from the more conscious or self-aware part of the individual. Such a formulation of individual behavior is, of course, completely consistent with the psychoanalytic theory of defense mechanisms. The term "blocking" would be applied to those self-deceptive situations in which ego realizes that he has concealed something from himself, or that he can't remember something, or that he can't describe or be sure of how he feels. The terms "repression" or "dissociation" would refer to a more complete manifestation of self-deception, where ego is totally unaware that part of his self has engaged in concealing information from the self-aware part. And the situation of ambivalence has similarities, which we will discuss later, in both alter- and self-deception.

Simulation typically accompanies the inhibition of information in self-deception. In order for ego to maintain the required image of himself and the desired social face to others, it is usually not sufficient that he conceal certain information; he must adopt as his own, feelings and attitudes which help disconfirm the matters being withheld. The person who dissociates anger not only may need to omit all such feelings, but also may need to appear to himself and others as altruistic and generous. The simulated behavior during self-deception differs from the simulation during alter-deception; it is less explicitly managed and the false message is actually felt, but it is not all that is felt. The simulation and its degree of genuineness is much like the feelings involved in the psychoanalytic defense mechanism of reaction-formation, and this is far more actually experienced than the simulations of alter-deception.

Dimensions of deceptive situations

At least three aspects of deceptive interactions need to be considered in order to distinguish deceptions from other forms of social interaction, and also to distinguish among types of deceptive encounters. For both ego and alter we must specify the *saliency* of deception, the adoption of deceptive and detective *roles,* and whether there is *collaboration* or *antagonism* between ego and alter about the discovery or maintenance of deception.

"Saliency" refers to the degree to which deception is an explicit focus of conscious concern by ego and/or alter; it is in large part determined by the social definition of the situation, although variations in past experience or deviations in personality [5] also influence saliency. The encounter of a jury (alter) with a murderer (ego), on trial for his life and testifying to his innocence, is an example of symmetrical saliency. Both ego and alter are quite aware of the likelihood that ego may be engaged in deception; both are highly aware that ego's honesty is in question and that they must respectively conceal or discover deception. Bargaining, between labor and management or between unfriendly world powers, is another example of symmetrical saliency. Both parties distrust their counterpart, both recognize that the opponent may attempt to deceive about his state of satisfaction with any set of proposed outcomes or about threatened actions if bargains are not made or kept. In these situations both ego and alter are vigilant about the possibility of deception.

There are, of course, asymmetical saliency situations. If ego is an applicant for a job, and is trying to conceal his past criminal or mental hospital record, the employment interview may be a situation where deception is not expected and has low saliency for the interviewer (alter) but high saliency for the applicant (ego).

In all of these examples, saliency means not only that ego has focused upon attempting to deceive (or alter upon detecting deception), but that in addition the stakes are high, ego wishes to succeed in his deception, and alter wishes to succeed in his detection (if the situation is also salient for him). But there are situations where deception is salient in terms of the focus on concealment or dissimulation, by either ego or alter, but little is at stake, and success is not important. Deception within games, at least for those who don't take their games too seriously, would be one such example; the telling of "white lies" is another. In our terms, deception is not salient in situations in which the stakes are low. We shall consider only interactions where there is a focus upon deception for at least one participant, and where there are important issues at stake which motivate at least one of the participants to care about success. Later we will briefly discuss how leakage may occur because the deceiver, even though motivated to deceive, feels guilty and wishes to be caught in his lie.

The second dimension of the deceptive situation is the number of *roles* adopted by each participant. Both parties may adopt the roles of deceiver and detector. Or, one party may be cast as deceiver, the other as detector. In the example of murderer and jury, the murderer is primarily a deceiver and the jury a detector. To the extent that the jury conceals its evaluation of the prisoner, it is also a deceiver, and inasmuch as the prisoner wishes to determine the jury's belief in his story, he must become detector as well as deceiver. Still, the situation dictates that one be the primary deceiver and the other the primary detector.

Bargaining is a situation where the roles adopted by ego and alter are symmetrical; both parties equally tend to emphasize deceiver and detector roles and are cognizant that both roles are salient for each. The job interview situation described earlier shows asymmetry; only the applicant has a salient concern with deception, although, like the prisoner, he may wish to learn alter's view of him. While the interviewer is primarily focused on evaluating, and detection has low saliency for him, his evaluating may be unwitting detection, and he is seen by the applicant as a detector. Similarly, low or nil saliency can result in a situation in which both parties are deceivers and neither is a detector. When saliency is high for one party and low for the other, there may be a deceiver and no detector, or a detector and no deceiver.

Collaboration or *antagonism* refers to the implicit or explicit pact between alter and ego about the discovery or maintenance of deception. In the jury situation there is antagonism; ego, the prisoner, wishes to maintain deception, but realizes that alter, the jury, wishes to uncover or discover deception. The same is true for the bargaining example. An example of collaboration about maintenance of deception would be a situation in which two students, after finishing a difficult examination, quiz each other about their reactions and fears, with tacit agreement not to discuss their anxieties; they thus collaborate in maintaining the deceptive behavior each displays in acting "cool." The philandering husband and the wife who doesn't wish to confront his infidelities collaborate to maintain the deception.

There can also be collaboration to *discover* deception rather than to maintain it. Psychotherapy is probably such a situation, in that the patient agrees at least in part to work with the therapist in uncovering his own alter- or self-deceptive maneuvers. In terms of the other dimensions of deceptive situations, psychotherapy is characterized by role asymmetry, with patient probably in both deceiver and detector roles, and the therapist more in the role of detector. And, in psychotherapy, the saliency of deception will fluctuate, perhaps being maximal for both participants at periods of therapeutic crisis or intense resistance. We do not claim that psychotherapy is best conceived of as a deceptive situation, but rather that there are points in psychotherapy when deception occurs and our formulation would be applicable.

Convincing deceptive performances should be most difficult under the following conditions: saliency for both ego and alter; role asymmetry, with ego in the role of both deceiver and detector, and alter only in the role of detector and thus able to concentrate upon ego's behavior without concern about monitoring or dissimulating his own performance; and, antagonism, with

ego wishing to maintain and alter wishing to uncover deception.

The easiest deceptive situation for ego would be the following: asymmetry in saliency, with ego focused upon deceiving but the probability of being deceived having low saliency for alter; role asymmetry, with ego focused primarily upon deceiving and not concerned with detecting, and alter attempting both to detect and deceive; and some collaboration to maintain the deception, such that alter would be embarrassed to admit discovery of ego's deception. The encounter of prisoner and jury is an example of the most difficult deceptive situation. An easy deceptive situation may be illustrated by the following. A teacher is telling his student that he was unable to read the student's paper the previous night because of a visit of out-of-town relatives, while in actual fact the teacher was wildly drunk at a jazz spot, and observed by the student; while the teacher is himself engaged in deception, the student is amused or has contempt for the teacher, but does not want to reveal these feelings or his knowledge of the teacher's lie; the student, as ego, has an easy time in his deception. Another situation where deception is easy is when ego engages in alter-deception, withholding information which alter is also withholding from himself in a self-deceptive maneuver; for example, ego tells a very unattractive alter, "You're a beautiful gal," and the gal in question has deceived herself about her own appearance and therefore will collaborate with her deceiver to maintain the deception.

In terms of these dimensions of deceptive situations, Goffman has been most interested in interactions where there is moderate to low saliency about deception and collaboration to maintain the deception. We will emphasize in our discussion situations where the deception is highly salient, at least for ego; where there is antagonism, such that ego wishes to maintain and alter wishes to uncover the deception; and where there tends to be role asymmetry, such that ego is primarily deceiver, and alter is primarily detector.

In such deceptive interactions ego must be skilled in both inhibition and simulation maneuvers. In order either to prevent his own action or to act falsely in terms of his real feelings or experience, ego needs to know what he can do with his body; he needs to be aware of his own actions through both internal and external feedback; and he needs knowledge of how to program his actions. We will suggest that the internal feedback available varies for the face, hands, and feet.[6] These differences in internal feedback arise from differences in sending capacities and differences in external feedback usually given these body areas.

Sending capacity, external feedback, and internal feedback

The *sending capacity* of a part of the body can be measured by three indexes: average transmission time, number of discriminable stimulus patterns which can be emitted, and visibility. In these terms the face is the best sender, the feet/legs the worst. The face has the shortest potential transmission; most "macro" facial expressions, those that can be easily seen and readily labeled in terms of emotion, last less than a second, often about half a second. "Micro" facial expressions are even shorter; by definition their duration is

so short that they are at the threshold of recognition unless slow motion projection is utilized.[7] The facial musculature allows for a great number of discriminable stimuli patterns,[8] far more than are provided by legs/feet. The face has the greatest visibility; it is covered only by sunglasses, make-up or hair, except in cultures that frequently use masks or veils. It is difficult to hide the face without being obvious about concealment; there are no inhibition maneuvers for the face equivalent to putting the hands in the pocket or sitting upon them. A frozen, immobile poker face is more noticeable than are interlocked fingers or tensely held feet.

The feet and legs are in almost all respects the worst nonverbal senders. Their transmission time is slow, far slower than that for the face or hands. The number of discriminable stimulus patterns which can be emitted is also limited. When a person is standing, his foot movements are restricted by the requirements of staying erect; even when seated, he is limited to what foot and leg movements can occur without his falling or sliding out of the chair. Feet/legs are not very visible; the toes are usually covered by socks and shoes, much of the leg by pants or a skirt (the popularity of mini-skirts makes for some change in visibility, although inhibitions about looking may still apply). In Western society at least, furniture is usually arranged so that the feet or legs cannot be easily viewed, and people become uncomfortable during conversations if they are totally exposed without the screen of a desk, table, or speaker's podium. Even when furniture does not directly interfere with the gaze, seating distance usually does. While talking, people usually sit or stand too close for inspection of the feet/legs area to take place without a noticeable look downwards.

Anatomically, hands are intermediate between face and feet/legs, and this is also true of their sending capacity. Although small hand movements may be as brief as most macro facial expressions, most hand activity, whether it be in space or touching the body, requires a longer duration for performance. The independent movements of the ten fingers, the different spatial patterns which may be described, the accelerations, the choice of areas of the body to contact, and the actions which may occur at the apex of the movement provide the hands with many more discriminable stimulus patterns than the legs/feet, perhaps as many as the face. Hands are much more visible than the legs/feet, rarely covered by clothing or obscured by furniture, but, unlike the face, they can be easily hidden.

External feedback from alter closely parallels these differences in sending capacity. External feedback can be defined as behavior by alter which ego is likely to perceive as reactive to his own nonverbal behavior. The most obvious external feedback would be alter's verbal comment on ego's nonverbal behavior; alter's gaze direction may also provide external feedback to ego, at least in terms of alter's interest in a nonverbal act. There can be other forms of external feedback, such as imitative behavior or other changes in verbal or nonverbal behavior which are responsive to ego's nonverbal behavior, but ego usually will not associate them with his own nonverbal behavior. The term "external feedback" does not refer to what alter perceives, but more narrowly to those aspects of alter's behavior which explicitly inform ego what alter has perceived and evaluated.

The most external feedback is provided for the face; people are most willing to comment verbally on and hold the person responsible for what is shown facially. There is less external feedback directed at the hands, and very little to the feet/legs, which not only are rarely the subject of verbal comment but also are rarely the conspicuous target of eye gaze. The differences in sending capacity among body areas may partially explain these differences in external feedback: People look most at the best sender, the face. But there are other reasons for looking at and commenting on facial behavior. As the input site for seeing, hearing, smelling, tasting, breathing, and ingesting, and the output site for words, most other sounds, and lipreading cues, it commands attention. In Western culture there is almost a fetish about facial attractiveness; at least part of the self is identified with the face; there is belief in the ability to read character and intelligence from facial cues; and the most idiosyncratic personal sector of the individual is thought to reside in or be reflected in the face. The face is the primary site for the display of affects, and in particular for eye-contacts, which are important in regulating the relationship between ego and alter.

There are, however, limits to the attention that can be directed toward the face. The face cannot be watched as continually as the voice can supposedly be listened to. If alter looks too long he suggests intimacy or a power struggle; if he looks too little he suggests disinterest, dishonesty, or suspicion. In Western society a dyadic conversation usually occurs in a seating position where the rest positions of the faces are not directly vis-à-vis. People sit at slight angles to each other rather than directly face to face, particularly if no table is interposed. Looking at the other person requires an act, moving the eyes or the head from center, and the act ends by returning to the resting position where it is easy not to look or not to be looked at. Seating a dyad in direct face-to-face confrontation can produce the same discomfort as removing all screens blocking the view of the body below the waist. Such seating positions connote interrogation and severe role inequality.

Alter may give external feedback regarding ego's hands if those hands are moving in space, particularly if they are enacting what we have called "illustrator" movements, motions which in some fashion illustrate what is being verbalized. But there is a taboo about being caught looking at hand acts when they involve contact with the body, particularly if hands contact a body orifice or genital area. It is not that people are polite and constrained and don't do these things their parents would scold about; but people are polite observers. When the rules of Emily Post are broken and people rub, pick, or massage their noses, ears, anus, or crotch, they believe that others won't look, and this is generally true. Rudeness seems to reside as much in watching such behavior as in emitting it. An interesting sidelight on this phenomenon is found in interactions between drivers of automobiles. Many people act in their cars as if they had the privacy of their bathrooms, and a convention has developed of not looking through the open window or clear glass at such bathroom behavior, so that the "embarrassed" party is not the groomer but the one caught watching the grooming.

Even less external feedback is given to the feet/legs than to the hands. Alter might directly comment on a facial expression, describing or mimicking it and asking ego what it means, and might similarly comment on a hand movement in space. But just as it would be extraordinary for alter to ask about ego's nose picking, ear scratching, or genital rubbing, so it would be unusual for him to comment on leg squeezing or foot arching. These differences in what alter will comment upon are paralleled in any looking behavior which occurs in a fashion easily noted by ego.

Let us repeat that in this discussion of external feedback we have not meant to claim that alter will not see hand movements or leg/foot movements; he may, just as he may actually see facial behaviors on which he does not provide feedback. Instead, our use of the term "external feedback" rather than "visual focus" was to limit our concern to those behaviors of alter which conspicuously provide information to ego that ego's nonverbal behavior is the subject of alter's scrutiny and evaluation. In such terms, the face receives more commentary than the hands or the legs/feet.

Internal feedback, our conscious awareness of what we are doing and our ability to recall, repeat, or specifically enact a planned sequence of motor behavior, parallels both sending capacity and external feedback in terms of the differences among face, hands, and feet. People have the greatest internal feedback about their face, next most about their hands and least about their legs and feet. Why might this be so? As we have explained, the face, as the best sender, receives the most external feedback; such feedback may teach ego to pay more attention to his face, amplifying and focusing upon whatever internal feedback cues are available. Conversely, ego may learn that people pay little attention to his legs/feet, and therefore conclude that he can afford to be less vigilant about what he does in this body area.

Further, our verbal vocabulary is most extensive for facial behaviors, next most for hands, and least for legs/feet. While it is reasonable to presume that the verbal labels develop because of the greater sending capacity of the face and the need for a simple means of communicating about facial messages, the existence of labels amplifies any already existing differences, in that cognitive processes of retrieval, sorting, and recognition of logical or temporal relationships are aided by the availability of a simple means of referring to or tagging nonverbal events.

Another consideration is that just as people are held responsible for what they show facially, so they take more responsibility for what is shown in their face. Most people identify at least some part of their self with their face, but do so to a much lesser degree with other areas of the body.

A last consideration relates to the neuroanatomical properties of the face, hands and legs/feet. Internal feedback may be more developed and accentuated for the face than for hands and legs/feet because of the relative rapidity of facial muscular movements, and because of the possible neural linkage of the facial muscles as affect programs, as suggested by Silvan Tomkins. Ego may have to monitor facial behaviors very closely because they are such a fast system, capable of being ennervated by involuntary as well as voluntary events.

Our hypotheses about the nonverbal sources for leakage and deception clues can be derived from what has been outlined about sending capacity, internal feedback, and external feedback. Ego will not expend much effort inhibiting

or dissimulating with areas of the body largely ignored by alter. Equally important, ego cannot inhibit or dissimulate actions in areas of the body about which he has learned to disregard internal feedback or in which he receives little internal feedback. If an action is to be withheld, that area of the body must be closely monitored; if a false message is to be sent, then ego must be able to retrieve easily information about actions he has customarily employed to express the particular feeling he wishes to convey misleadingly at this moment. Before specifying hypotheses, we must digress to consider two types of nonverbal behavior which are of central importance as leakage and deception clues: affect displays and adaptors.[9]

The face is the major site of the *affect displays*. We and others [10] have accumulated evidence which indicates distinctive movements of the facial muscles for each of some seven primary affect states: happiness, anger, fear, surprise, sadness, disgust, interest. Most affect displays, at least those shown in public places, and perhaps all those shown during even the most intimate interaction, are managed or controlled by display rules. Display rules determine whether an affect display is intensified, de-intensified, neutralized, or masked with a covering affect. The particular display rule which operates upon a particular affect is determined by culture, well mapped in terms of social situations, role, age, sex, and status of the person emitting the display. Display rules may also be idiosyncratic within a culture, shaped by peculiarities of the family interaction.

Micro affect displays result from the operation of any of the display rules; they are expressions which are so brief that they are barely perceptible to the untrained observer. Micro displays may be fragments of a squelched, neutralized, or masked display. Micro displays may also show the full muscular movements associated with a macro affect display, but may be greatly reduced in time. We have found [11] that such micro displays when shown in slow motion do convey emotional information to observers, and that expert clinical observers can see micro displays and read the emotional information without the benefit of slow motion projection.

If the micro display results from squelching and that squelching is fast enough, the affect may be completely obscured, and the display may provide deception clues rather than leakage. If there is a brief but relatively complete display of affect, then the micro display may provide leakage. Such micro displays are often followed by or covered by simulated, antithetical, macro affect displays, and the untrained observer will usually miss or minimize micro displays.

Eye-contacts (which we consider part of the affect display of interest) which deviate in duration or frequency from the norm for a given social interaction can provide important deception clues, stemming from ego's guilt regarding deception or fear of being uncovered, or, conversely, his attempt to simulate confidence and candor.

Adaptors develop from movements which are first learned by a person in early life as part of his adaptive efforts to satisfy self or bodily needs, to perform bodily actions, to manage emotions, to develop or maintain prototypic interpersonal contacts, and to learn instrumental activities. The confusing aspect of adaptors is that while they were first learned as part of a total adaptive pattern in which the goal of the activity was obvious, they are emit-

ted by the adult, particularly during social conversations, in a form in which only a fragment of the original adaptive behavior can be seen. These fragments or reductions of previously learned adaptive acts are maintained by habit. When originally learned, the adaptive behavior was associated with certain drives, with certain felt emotions, with expectancies, with types of interpersonal interaction, or with a given setting. When the adaptor appears in the adult, it is a response to something in the current environment that triggers the old habit; something occurs which is relevant to the drive, emotion, relationship, or setting originally associated with the learning of the adaptive pattern. But the original total adaptive activity is rarely carried through to completion; and, when seen without knowledge of the origin of the activity, it may appear as random, or noisy behavior. By this definition, adaptors emitted by the adult are habitual, are not intended to communicate, and occur usually without awareness. We can distinguish among self-adaptors, alter-adaptors, and object-adaptors.

Self-adaptors are based on behavior learned to master or manage a variety of problems and needs: to facilitate or block sensory input; to perform ingestive and excretive functions; to engage in autoerotic activity; to groom, cleanse or modify the attractiveness of the face and body; and to facilitate or block sound-making and speech. Alter-directed adaptors originate in movements learned in early, perhaps prototypic, interpersonal contacts. They include movements necessary to giving and taking, attacking or defending, establishing closeness and intimacy or withdrawal and flight, and establishing sexual contact. Object-adaptors include movements originally learned in the performance of some instrumental task: driving a car, smoking, wielding a tool or weapon, and so forth.

Since the adaptors are habitually based, and primarily involve the body rather than the face, they are less likely than facial acts to be inhibited, and they are rarely employed as part of a simulation. Ego receives less external feedback and maintains less internal feedback about the adaptors. Often, ego will be uncomfortable about engaging in deception, and adaptors will emerge as deception clues which betray this discomfort and stand out as discordant with the primary dissimulated message. For example, ego may scratch or pick at himself to punish himself for deceiving, or he may tend to hide his face with his hands, an adaptor for concealing embarrassment, or he may engage in abortive flight movements with his legs / feet. The relevance of the adaptors and micro affect displays will emerge in the general discussion of the differences among the face, hands, and feet / legs.

Leakage and deception clues

Earlier we traced how sending capacity and external and internal feedback are greater for the face than for the hands and feet. From this we hypothesized that ego will attempt much less inhibition or dissimulation in the areas of the hands and feet. Thus, the face is likely to be the major nonverbal liar, maximally redundant with the verbal behavior during deception, subject to lies of both omission and commission. The chief exceptions are micro facial displays, which can serve as leakage or deception clues. Because the face is such a fast sending system, even during alter-deception, there may be affect displays which begin to emerge before ego

is fully aware of them and can squelch them. Other forms of deception clues in the face are imperfectly performed simulations of affect. These might include performances of too long duration, with too extensive a scope to the expression, or without the usual blend of affects. Examples are the smile that lasts too long, the frown that is too severe, the look of fear that is not sufficiently blended with surprise.

The full affect reduced time micro displays may well be those which ego is not aware of, while the squelched micro displays may be those which ego senses and interrupts in midperformance. If that is so, we would expect the time reduced full affect displays to be more prevalent in self-deception than in alter-deception, and the reverse to be true of the micro, squelched affect displays.

In a sense the face is equipped to lie the most and leak the most, and thus can be a very confusing source of information during deception. Generally, ego can get away with and best perpetuate deception through his face. Although he must monitor quickly and work continually to inhibit this fast responsive system, he has most awareness of his facial displays and is usually well practiced in the display rules for modulating facial affects. In contrast to either the hands or legs / feet, the face is the major site for lies of commission, for simulated messages; ego has the internal feedback to retrieve information about what facial muscles to move to create the appearance of an affect which he does not feel at present. The success of facial deception depends upon alter's ignoring or disregarding the leakage through micro displays and the rough edges on the simulated displays. The evidence cited earlier suggests that most persons do disregard such important forms of leakage and deception clues, and one would expect the usual observer of the face typically to be misled. One would expect the keen observer, on the other hand, to receive contradictory information from facial cues: simulated messages, micro leakage of information which contradicts the simulations, and deception clues of squelched displays and improperly performed simulations.

The hands are easier to inhibit than the face; as mentioned earlier, they can be hidden from view without the hiding itself becoming salient as a deception clue. But the hands, unlike the face, are not fakers; most people will not use their hands to dissimulate. The hands commit lies of omission but not of commission. Major forms of leakage in the hands are the adaptors, particularly the self-adaptors. While facially smiling and pleasant, ego may be tearing at a fingernail, digging into his cheek, protectively holding his knees, and so forth. Self-adaptors can also serve as deception clues, betraying discomfort about the deception. Alter-adaptors in the hands and legs/feet can provide leakage or deception clues—for example, a fist can leak interest in attack, a beseeching hand movement can leak fear which is otherwise disavowed. Object-adaptors can provide deception clues, such as the restless tapping of a cigarette; or leakage, such as the displacement of withheld anger into the snapping of a pencil.

The legs/feet, which have a limited repertoire of information, are a primary source of both leakage and deception clues.[12] Like the hands, they are relatively easy to inhibit, although not as totally as the hands, and the legs/feet are employed even less than the hands in dissimulations. Leakage in the legs/feet could include aggressive foot kicks, flirtatious leg displays, auto-erotic or soothing leg squeezing, abortive restless flight movements. Deception clues can be seen in tense leg positions, frequent shift of leg posture, and in restless or repetitive leg and foot acts.

Another form of deception clues in both the hands and legs/feet results from ego's neglecting to perform simulations which should accompany the verbal and facial simulations. The lack of the usually associated self- and alter-adaptors, the lack of the usual illustrative hand movements, can create the impression in alter that ego does not really mean what he says; ego just doesn't look natural. But, generally, these areas of the body are not watched too closely by alter, and deficiencies can pass.

To summarize, the availability of leakage and deception clues reverses the pattern described for differences in sending capacity, internal feedback, and external feedback. The worst sender, the legs/feet, is also the least responded to and the least within ego's awareness, and thus a good source for leakage and deception clues. The best sender, the face, is most closely watched by alter, most carefully monitored by ego, most subject to inhibition and dissimulation, and thus the most confusing source of information during deception; apart from micro expressions, it is not a major source of leakage and deception clues. The hands are intermediate on both counts, as a source of leakage and deception clues, and in regard to sending capacity and internal and external feedback.

Illustrative experiments

We have conducted some preliminary experiments employing records of natural occurrences of deception. Sound motion-picture films had already been collected of 120 brief interviews with 40 female psychiatric inpatients at different points in their hospitalization. The films of each patient, the interviewer's notes about her, the ward records, and information obtained after her discharge were examined in order to isolate interviews in which the patient had probably been engaging in either self- or alter-deception. We could be certain that deception occurred and could specify the concealed information on only three interviews.

The basic design of the experiments was to show a film of one of the interviews silently to one of two different groups of naive observers, one group viewing only the face and head, the other viewing the body from the neck down. The observers were not told they were seeing a psychiatric patient; the film was identified as a record of a conversation. After viewing the film, both groups of observers described their impressions by checking words from Gough's Adjective Check List, 300 words descriptive of attitudes, traits, affects, manners. To test hypotheses about the source of leakage of withheld information, the information conveyed by head/face cues was contrasted with information conveyed by body cues.

An example of alter-deception

Patient A was admitted to the hospital with depressed affect, angry outbursts, screaming, threats of suicide; there was disagreement about whether the diagnosis was agitated depression or schizophrenia. She was given amitriptyline hydrochloride and psychotherapy. Within two and a half weeks she had begun to attempt to manage her affect expression, and to inhibit the display of her anxiety, anger, and dysphoria. Films were taken on the first day of hospitalization, in the middle of hospitalization and shortly before discharge. At the middle of hospitalization it appeared that Miss A was engaged in alter-deception, attempting to conceal information about how upset she still actually was, and simulating optimism, control of affect, and feelings of well-being. Our evidence that such deception occurred during this interview included the interviewer's impression and the ward psychiatrist's impression; the patient's behavior at the conclusion of the interview when she broke down, cried and admitted she did not feel as well as she had earlier claimed; and posthospitalization discussions of this film with the patient.

HYPOTHESIS The observers who view the face/head cues, more than those who view the body cues, will miss concealed information about depression and agitation, and instead will pick up the simulated message about well-being. While we anticipated that there would be both micro leakage and deception clues in the face, we expected that naive observers viewing the head/face at normal projection speed would fail to pick up these occurrences and would instead be more misled by the patient's deception than those who viewed the body.

The head/face version of the film was viewed by 18 observers; 28 observers viewed the body version of the film. In data analysis a word from the Adjective Check List was considered a "head" message if it was checked by $\geq 50\%$ of the observers who saw the head, $\leq 49\%$ of the observers who saw the body, and if there was $\geq 20\%$ difference in the head and body percent-

TABLE I

Alter-deception: patient A, withholding information about depression and agitation, simulating health and well-being

Head messages	% Head	% Body	Body messages	% Head	% Body	Head & body messages	% Head	% Body
Sensitive	83	36	Tense	44	82	Anxious	89	100
Friendly	50	14	Excitable	22	79	Emotional	89	82
Coopera-tive	50	14	High strung	39	75	Confused	72	82
			Fearful	33	68	Defensive	72	71
Self-pun-ishing	50	02	Hurried	0	61	Worrying	50	68
			Changeable	39	61	Dissatisfied	56	57
			Awkward	33	61	Despondent	56	50
			Complaining	11	54			
			Touchy	28	54			
			Affected	33	54			
			Restless	06	50			
			Impulsive	17	50			
			Impatient	0	50			
			Rigid	17	50			

ages. The same criterion was used for determining a "body" message. A word was considered to be a message for both head and body if it was checked by $\geq 50\%$ of both head and body observers and if there was $\leq 19\%$ difference in the head and body percentages.

Table I shows the head messages, body messages, and messages common to both cue areas. Our hypothesis is supported only in part. While the head messages contained the expected dissimulated information and the body messages conveyed the expected concealed information, the messages conveyed by *both* head and body contained some of what we expected to be concealed (anxious, confused, worrying, etc.). We believe that this was due to the fact that near the end of the film the patient ceased her efforts to deceive and cried openly, thus providing previously concealed information in her face.

Self-deception: Example I

The same patient, Miss A, was in a hypomanic state shortly before discharge. At this time she engaged in a great deal of girlish, seductive, flirtatious behavior, showing coquettish interest in the males she encountered. On the basis of her verbal behavior in the interview, the impressions of the interviewer, and posthospitalization discussions with the patient, who within a few months had a recurrence of her depression, the flirtatious, immature seductiveness seemed quite outside of her awareness.

HYPOTHESIS The observers who view only the head/face will tend to see only the appearance of a healthy, cooperative patient, while those who view the body will perceive the coquettish, excited, seductive picture.

The head/face version was seen by

TABLE 2

Self-deception: patient A, withholding information about seductive, immature, impulsive behavior, and simulating cooperativeness

Head messages	% Head	% Body	Body messages	% Head	% Body	Head & body messages	% Head	% Body
Talkative	68	30	Confused	48	83	Emotional	65	83
Alert	65	39	Awkward	47	78	Active	74	74
Cheerful	61	30	Excitable	42	78	Changeable	68	74
Cooperative	59	35	Restless	32	74	Nervous	65	74
Serious	52	22	Impulsive	39	65	Defensive	52	61
			High strung	29	65			
			Feminine	32	65			

31 observers; 23 observers saw the body version of the film. Table 2 shows the results of the comparative analysis of head and body messages. These results provide some support for the hypothesis; the expected differences in head and body messages appear to have been conveyed, and the messages conveyed by both head and body do not contain the information which we expected to be concealed.

In other research on this film we found many legs/feet movements which we considered to be flirtatious, autoerotic, and appropriate to a woman much younger than the patient. We showed just the legs/feet movements of this film to another group of observers, and when we compared their impressions with those of persons who had seen just the head/face, the legs/feet messages generally supported our impression. We also found that the observers of the legs/feet guessed that the patient was in her teens, while those who saw the face/head guessed her to be in her thirties. This difference in age perception was not found when comparing observers of head and observers of feet for the same patient's admission-to-the-hospital film.

Self-deception: Example 2

Patient B was admitted to the hospital with hallucinations, delusions, and ideas of reference, with a diagnosis of acute schizophrenia. She was treated with fluphenazine hydrochloride and nine days after admission the acute signs of the psychosis began to fade and the patient began to rationalize and deny her acute disorder. A film was taken at this time. Her interviewer, the attending psychiatrist, and the patient herself in later discussion substantiated the impression that despite her claims that she was no longer disturbed, she was actually still experiencing considerable anxiety, confusion, and delusions during the filming session.

HYPOTHESIS Observers who view the face/head cues more than those who view the body cues will miss concealed information about anxiety, confusion and delusions, and instead will pick up the simulated message of well-being and health.

The head/face version of the film was viewed by 27 observers; 28 observers viewed the body version of the film. Table 3 shows the results of the com-

TABLE 3

Self-deception: patient B, withholding information about confusion, anxiety, and delusions, simulating well-being and health

Head messages	% Head	% Body	Body messages	% Head	% Body	Head & body messages	% Head	% Body
Cooperative	85	36	Tense	18	68	Active	59	53
Friendly	81	25	Nervous	44	64	Changeable	55	53
Cheerful	70	11	Defensive	26	57	Alert	63	50
Sensitive	63	39	Confused	33	53			
Affectionate	59	28	Cautious	30	53			
Appreciative	59	18	Worrying	30	50			
Pleasant	59	11						
Warm	59	18						
Kind	55	32						
Talkative	55	21						
Considerate	52	25						
Good-natured	52	25						
Honest	52	28						

parative analysis of head and body messages.

These results provide the best illustration of our formulation of the source of leakage and deception clues.

These studies show a difference in the information conveyed by the head as compared to the hands/legs/feet, which is in the direction predicted by our formulation of leakage and deception clues. They do not, however, directly test our theory; there is no comparison of the information conveyed by nonverbal and verbal behavior, no comparison of the micro and macro facial displays, and no determination of whether the specific hand and legs/feet acts which we described as sources of leakage and deception clues were actually responsible for conveying the messages listed in the tables. Further, they suffer from an uncertainty, which probably can never be fully resolved in studying naturalistic occurrences of deception, about whether we were correct in our assessment of what information was withheld and what was dissimulated. To remedy some of these deficiencies, our work in progress is employing an experimental, laboratory, dyadic interaction in which ego is immersed in a positive or negative affect-inducing experience and instructed to engage in alter-deception by simulating positive affect when experiencing negative affect, and vice versa.

Before closing, some mention should be made of the major exceptions to what we have presented. There are some people who do not leak very much, if at all; they are professional, convincing nonverbal liars—for example, the professional dancer or actor, the skilled courtroom lawyer, the shrewd diplomat or negotiator, and the successful (sometimes psychopathically so) used-car salesman. An explanation of why there is less nonverbal leakage with the dancer and actor can be inferred from the earlier discussion of internal and external feedback. The dancer and actor have focused their attention on the use of their body as a communicative instrument; they have heightened their internal awareness of their nonverbal behavior and engaged in continual training which involves focused external feedback from coach, director, audience, about the effectiveness of their simulations. Thus, they are exceptions to our formulation because they have what most people lack, the feedback necessary to monitor, tune, and thus disguise through the nonverbal channel. But, why would the diplomat or car salesman or con man be a convincing nonverbal liar, providing little leakage and few deception clues? Do they simply become more skilled through practice, or are there personality variables which influence the selection of such persons and which also are related to skill in nonverbal dissimulating? Or might it be that in some social settings there is little guilt or ambivalence about deceiving? If so, to the extent that leakage is motivated by an attempt to be caught, this would explain why such people do not leak.[13] Certainly some of the behavior which leads to the discovery of deception may be attributed to a deliberate wish to be caught, but this should be distinguished from the leakage and deception clues which result when the subject is motivated to deceive but secondarily becomes ashamed, guilty, or anxious, and unwittingly gives away his deception.

If one considers why a person does not succeed in deception, one finds at least three explanations and they are not mutually exclusive. The simplest one is that the person has a conscious wish to be caught or not to succeed in deception. In such cases, one would not expect the concealed information to be manifest in the micro displays, or adaptors, but instead to be conveyed by macro facial displays, postural cues, and other more easily and usually attended to forms of nonverbal behavior.

This situation, where the person consciously wants to deceive but wants to be caught, is quite similar to that of the ambivalent person who is aware of both sides of his ambivalence. Here, the part of the message the person wishes to take least responsibility for will probably be channeled into nonverbal behavior. The consciously ambivalent person can have his cake and eat it too, by communicating the less acceptable feelings through his nonverbal behavior; he conveys his message but in a form where alter is less likely to explicitly respond, and in a manner which will allow him to deny responsibility for it, or even to deny its occurrence. But, like the person who wants to be caught, the consciously ambivalent person should not be considered as wanting to conceal information, but as wanting to convey one of his messages in such a way that he will be less accountable for it. While such messages may tend to be manifest in nonverbal behavior, they will not be shown in the types of activities we have described as leakage (i.e., micro displays), for these would not be likely to get the messages across. Instead, macro facial displays, postural cues, hand in space movements, and other forms of nonverbal activity which customarily receive attention from alter will de employed. These are the forms of nonverbal behavior which we have not previously discussed as sources of leakage and deception clues, because ego customarily has good internal and external feedback about them and can successfully utilize such nonverbal behaviors to dissimulate. In conscious ambivalence the person does not have the same problem of concealing information which he has in alter-deception; instead he conveys contradictory information, with the verbal and nonverbal channels dividing in some part the more and less socially acceptable parts of the ambivalence.

The second explanation of why a person does not succeed in deception is that he may feel secondary guilt, shame, and/or anxiety about engaging in the deception or about the possibility of being discovered, and these feelings add to his problem of concealing information. Here we assume that the person does not wish to be caught; he may not even be aware of his guilt, shame, and/or anxiety, but he must withhold both the original concealed information and also those affective reactions about deception which, if manifest, would serve at least as deception clues. The manifestations of leakage should be as we have predicted, although their content may pertain either to the secondary affective reaction about deception or to the original concealed information.

The last explanation of why a person fails in deception is the one provided in the main argument of the paper. Ego cannot monitor and disguise those forms of nonverbal behavior to which he has customarily not attended and about which he does not maintain feedback; and, if he has learned that most people do not usually watch certain types of activities, then he does not bother trying to inhibit or dissimulate in regard to those activities.

While we have just distinguished conscious ambivalence from deception, ambivalence in which one feeling or message is not conscious fits our description of self-deception. The manifestations of the unconscious feeling or thought in the ambivalence presumably appear in the forms we have described as leakage and deception clues.

There are a number of applications of this description of leakage and deception clues. People could be trained to become better nonverbal liars, utilizing videotape feedback to enhance their internal feedback, and focusing external feedback to help them plug up leaks and better eliminate deception clues; the most benevolent use of such procedures would be in the dramatic arts. Our description of deceptive situations should help begin to specify those types of interactions or points during an interaction when ego and alter might best attend to nonverbal behavior or as a source of information which will be least repetitive with the verbal behavior. Moreover, we have suggested specific types of behaviors for which the diagnostician or clinician should look; these may be useful either in evaluation or as a focus in bringing problems to the attention of the patient. Training could be developed which would improve recognition of micro expressions as well as alert the observer to particular nonverbal acts. Knowledge of nonverbal leakage and deception clues could also perhaps be utilized in an attempt to develop lie detection procedures which rely upon nonverbal behavior.

It is interesting to note that our formulation of the origin of leakage and deception clues contains a suggestion that the phenomenon may considerably change—and may even partially disappear—as attention is brought to bear upon it. If the reader believes what has been said, then when he is engaged as ego in deceptive situations he may monitor his own behavior more closely, and be more alert about what to inhibit and which body areas to scrutinize; paradoxically, the leakage through hands and legs/feet should be relatively easy to eliminate once a person is aware of it. In the role of alter he should also be more attentive to the areas of leakage in others. If we are correct, such an increase in both internal and external feedback may start to diminish the information revealed through nonverbal leakage and clues to deception.

NOTES

1. Part of this paper was read at the Western Psychological Association Convention, 1967. The research was supported by a grant from the National Institute of Mental Health (MH 11976-03) and by a Research Scientist Development Award (3 KO3 MH 06092-02S1). The authors are indebted to Patricia W. Garlan for her helpful contributions on the content and editorial criticisms of style.

2. See, for example: Argyle; Birdwhistell; Dittmann, Parloff, and Boomer; Freedman and Hoffman; Mahl; Ruesch and Kees.

3. See Paredes and Cornelison; Gruenberg, Liston, and Wayne; and Wilmer.

4. The term ego is used to refer to the party of principal interest in a dyad, not in the psychoanalytic sense.

5. Paranoid persons might be considered to typically enter interactions with salient expectations that they will be deceived.

6. We have excluded posture from our discussion, as we do not think it is a major source of either leakage or deception clues. Posture, while standing or sitting, and gait are paradoxical forms of nonverbal behavior. They are, we believe, highly determined by basic characterological aspects of the individual and, in particular, by identification models and yet are easily modified by training or exercise, such as is given in certain vocations. Conversational postures are in our terms *regulators*, or, as Scheflen has described them, *markers*; they serve to set the stage for the interaction, defining the degree of formality, task orientation, etc. Shifts in posture note changes in topic, affect, or role during conversations. Conversational postural positions are quite standardized in terms of the social setting and the roles of the participants, and easily assumed. We thus believe that simulation of posture is quite easy, and that postural cues rarely provide leakage or deception clues, if ego cares at all about deceiving.

7. This distinction between macro and micro expressions will be discussed later. While Haggard and Isaacs first described micro facial expressions as being actually not detectable at normal viewing, our own research and the evidence from the neurophysiology of visual perception strongly suggest that micro expressions that are as short as one motion-picture frame (1/50 of a second) can be perceived. That these micro expressions are not usually seen must depend upon their being embedded in other expressions which distract attention, their infrequency, or some learned perceptual habit of ignoring fast facial expressions.

8. In developing a coding scheme for describing the relevant cue properties of 7 primary affect states, we have had to deal with over 20 separate facial items.

9. We have distinguished among five types of nonverbal behaviors—emblems, illustrators, regulators, affect displays, and adaptors—in

terms of their origins, coding and usage (Ekman and Friesen, 1968b). Emblems are those actions which are consciously intended to be communicative signals, where there is high agreement among members of a subculture or culture about the meaning of the signal—e.g., the thumb-to-index-finger circle, with other fingers extended is an emblem for O.K. Illustrators are those actions which are intimately related to the verbal discourse, illustrating what is being said by emphasis, pointing, pictorial enactment, rhythmic movements, or kinetic actions. Regulators are those nonverbal actions which have as their sole function the management of the conversational flow or exchange. While leakage and deception clues can be manifest in emblems, illustrators, or regulators, we believe that they are less important for this discussion than the affect displays and adaptors.

10. See Ekman, Sorenson, and Friesen; and Izard.

11. Paul Ekman, Grant Progress Report, Oct., 1968.

12. Overall posture, like the legs/feet, is limited in the repertoire of information which can be conveyed. But it differs from legs/feet in terms of being highly visible, and, importantly for our discussion, there are well-established standards of posture for given social situations, while such standards are not nearly as well formulated for legs/feet movements independent of total posture. Thus, it would be unlikely that ego would show inappropriate posture as a form of leakage or deception clues; he knows too well how he should sit or stand in a given situation; for the same reason, he can simulate the postural position he may need to convey a false message.

13. This explanation was suggested by Erving Goffman.

REFERENCES

Argyle, Michael. *The Psychology of Interpersonal Behavior;* Baltimore, Pelican, 1967.

Birdwhistell, Ray L. "Contribution of Linguistic-Kinesic Studies to the Understanding of Schizophrenia," in Alfred Auerback (Ed.), *Schizophrenia: An Integrated Approach;* Ronald Press, 1959.

Darwin, Charles. *The Expression of the Emotions in Man and Animals;* Philosophical Library, 1955.

Dittmann, Allen T., Parloff, Morris B., and Boomer, Donald S. "Facial and Bodily Expression: A Study of Receptivity of Emotional Cues," PSYCHIATRY (1965) 28:239–244.

Ekman, Paul, and Friesen, Wallace V. "Nonverbal Behavior in Psychotherapy Research," in John Shlien (Ed.), *Research in Psychotherapy,* Vol. 3; Washington, D. C., Amer. Psychol. Assn., 1968. (a)

Ekman, Paul, and Friesen, Wallace V. "The Repertoire of Nonverbal Behavior: Origins, Usage, Coding and Categories," Studies in Semiotics, in *Social Science Information,* in press, 1968. (b)

Ekman, Paul, Sorenson, E. Richard, and Friesen, Wallace V. "Pan-cultural Elements in Facial Displays of Emotion," submitted for publication, 1968.

Freedman, Norbert, and Hoffman, Stanley P. "Kinetic Behavior in Altered Clinical States: Approach to Objective Analysis of Motor Behavior During Clinical Interviews," *Perceptual and Motor Skills* (1967) 24:527–539.

Freud, Sigmund. "Fragment of an Analysis of a Case of Hysteria (1905)," *Collected Papers,* Vol. 3; Basic Books, 1959.

Goffman, Erving. *The Presentation of Self in Everyday Life;* Doubleday, 1959.

Gruenberg, Peter B., Liston, Edward H., and Wayne, George J. "Intensive Supervision of Psychotherapy with Videotape Recording," paper presented at the meetings of the Amer. Psychiatric Assn., 1967.

Haggard, Ernest A., and Isaacs, Kenneth S. "Micro-Momentary Facial Expressions as Indicators of Ego Mechanisms in Psychotherapy," in Louis A. Gottschalk and Arthur H. Auerbach (Eds.), *Methods of Research in Psychotherapy;* Appleton-Century-Crofts, 1966.

Izard, Carroll E. "The Emotions and Emotion Constructs in Personality and Culture Research," in R. B. Cattell (Ed.), *Handbook of Modern Personality Theory;* Aldine, 1968, in press.

Mahl, George F. "Gestures and Body Movements in Interviews," in John Shlien (Ed.), *Research in Psychotherapy,* Vol. 3; Washington, D. C., Amer. Psychol. Assn., 1968.

Paredes, Alfonso F., and Cornelison, Floyd S. "An Audiovisual Method for Eliciting Attitude Changes in Alcoholics," panel on videotape feedback, presented at the meetings of the Amer. Psychiatric Assn., 1967.

Ruesch, Jurgen, and Kees, Weldon. *Nonverbal Communication;* Berkeley, Univ. of Calif. Press, 1956.

Scheflen, Albert E. "The Significance of Posture in Communication Systems," PSYCHIATRY (1964) 27:316–331.

Tomkins, Silvan S. *Affect, Imagery, Consciousness,* Vol. 1, *The Postive Affects;* Springer, 1962. Vol. 2, *The Negative Affects;* 1963.

Wilmer, Harry A. "Television as Participant Observer," paper presented at the meetings of the Amer. Psychiatric Assn., 1967.

INFERENCE OF ATTITUDES FROM NONVERBAL COMMUNICATION IN TWO CHANNELS [1]

ALBERT MEHRABIAN AND SUSAN R. FERRIS

While there are many studies of non-verbal attitude or feeling communication in single channels (e.g., reviews by Davitz, 1964 or Mahl & Schulze, 1964), investigators are only beginning to explore simultaneously transmitted feelings or attitudes in two or more channels. Gates' (1927) investigation of single-channel decoding of facial and vocal stimuli is relevant to the present study. She found that children are more accurate in their judgments of facial compared to vocal expressions of feeling. Unfortunately, her method only allows a tentative conclusion that discrimination of feeling on the basis of facial cues is easier than discrimination of feeling on the basis of vocal cues. There is, however, some corroboration of Gates' findings in a study by Levitt (1964). Communicators were filmed as they attempted to communicate six emotions facially and vocally, using neutral verbal materials. The decoding of facial and vocal stimuli in combination was only as accurate as the decoding of facial stimuli alone,

and both conditions were more accurate than the decoding of vocal stimuli alone. This finding can be interpreted to indicate that in a two-channel facial-vocal communication of emotion, the facial channel contributes more to the decoding of the total message than the vocal channel.

There is one other study in which the characteristics of two-channel communications of emotion have been explored. Williams and Sundene (1965) used the semantic differential method (Osgood, Suci, & Tannenbaum, 1957) to obtain judgments of the same emotions communicated facially, vocally, and in facial-vocal combinations. All three modes of communication of emotion were found to be recognized in terms of the three factors of general evaluation, social control, and activity.

It should be noted that none of the foregoing studies investigated two-channel communications in which the emotion communicated in the facial expression was inconsistent with that communicated vocally. Despite the

From *Journal of Consulting Psychology*, 1967, 31, 248–52. Copyright © 1967 by the American Psychological Association and reprinted by permission.

paucity of experimental studies of decoding of multichannel communications of feeling or attitude by any particular population (e.g., children or adults), there is some theoretical consideration of the effects of such communications. Bateson, Jackson, Haley, and Weakland (1956) proposed a "double bind" theory of schizophrenia. They consider the maladaptive responses of schizophrenics to be a consequence of their being the frequent recipients of inconsistent attitude communications. The double bind communication can be defined as typically consisting of two or more inconsistent attitude messages which are assumed to elicit incompatible responses from the addressee. For example, a mother asks her son to come over and kiss her while she nonverbally communicates disinterest in what he is requested to do. The child is assumed to be left with the difficult task of responding to either the verbal or the nonverbal component, with the knowledge that response to the former will elicit a rebuff and response to the latter will elicit indignation. The recipients of frequent double-bind messages are assumed to learn to respond with their own double-bind messages. In the example considered, the child may respond with, "I can't come because my leg hurts," or "I can't come because Trap is holding me," the hurt leg and Trap being figments of his imagination.

While double-bind communications are assumed to lead to the development of maladaptive patterns of interpersonal functioning, Haley (1963) also conceptualized most psychotherapeutic processes as being interpretable within a beneficial double-bind paradigm. Haley's thesis is that applications of the beneficial double bind serve the function of successfully eliminating the secondary gain which is associated with a symptomic behavior and therefore eliminating the behavior.

The above assumptions about the change-inducing properties of inconsistent communications require clarification through investigation of the ways in which multichannel attitude communications are decoded. Since the quantification of degree of consistency or inconsistency between communications in two channels is only possible if the two communications can be scaled along a common dimension, the general evaluation dimension obtained in the Williams and Sundene (1965) study seems appropriate. Mehrabian and Wiener (1967) pursued these considerations by investigating the decoding of two-channel vocal-verbal communications in which three degrees of attitude (i.e., positive, neutral, and negative) in the vocal component were each combined with three degrees of attitude in the verbal component (i.e., meanings of words). They found that when vocal communication of attitude is inconsistent with verbal communication of attitude, normal addressees respond to the two-channel communication by subordinating the verbal component to the vocal component. If, for example, the word "scram" is said in a tone of voice which is independently judged as communicating positive attitude towards the addressee, the consensual interpretation of the total communication is positive.

The present study was designed to investigate the decoding of inconsistent and consistent communications of attitude in facial and vocal channels. Three degrees of attitude (i.e., positive, neutral, and negative) communicated in facial expressions were each combined with three degrees of attitude communicated vocally. In accordance with Gates' and Levitt's findings, it was expected that the decoding of a consistent facial-vocal communication would yield a judgment equivalent to that obtained from the decoding of the facial component only—that is, the facial component would be dominant. Furthermore, since Mehrabian and Wiener's (1967) study indicated that the dominant component in a two-channel communication determines the meaning of inconsistent communications, it was expected that the decoding of an inconsistent facial-vocal communication would yield a judgment equivalent to that obtained from the decoding of the facial component only. It was therefore hypothesized that judgments of attitude, on the basis of consistent and inconsistent pairings of facial and vocal attitude communications, would yield a main effect due to variations in the facial component and no effect due to variations in the vocal component or its interaction with the facial component.

Method

Subjects

A group of 25 subjects (Ss) was used in the preliminary selection of a neutral word. A second group of 17 Ss was used to assess the independent effects of facial and vocal communications. A third group of 20 Ss was used to obtain the combined effects of facial-vocal communications. All 62 Ss were female University of California undergraduates who participated in the study in partial fulfillment of introductory psychology course requirements.

Materials

For the selection of a neutral attitude-communicating word, 25 Ss were asked to judge the attitude of a speaker towards her addressee when saying each of 15 words. The 15 words were each presented in written form and Ss recorded their judgments of attitude on a 9-point scale designated "like very much," $+4$ and "dislike very much," -4 at its poles. The word "maybe" was selected as an appropriate neutral verbal carrier of vocal communications, since it was rated .28 on the attitude scale with a standard deviation of .72.

For the selection of vocal communications of three degrees of attitude, three female speakers were instructed to vary their tone of voice while saying the word "maybe," so as to communicate like, neutrality, and dislike towards an imagined addressee. Each speaker was instructed to say the word "maybe" twice in the same way while her communications were being recorded on magnetic tape. The 18 items, consisting of two instances each of positive, neutral, and negative vocal attitude communications obtained from the three speakers, were presented to 17 female Ss with the following written instructions:

The purpose of this study is to find out how well people can judge the feelings of others. In this part, you will hear a recording on which the word "maybe" is spoken in different tones of voice. You are to imagine that the speaker is saying this word to another person, the addressee. For each tone, indicate on the scale what you think the speaker's attitude is towards the addressee.

A modified form of the semantic differential instructions (Osgood, Suci, & Tannenbaum, 1957, pp. 80–85) was used to direct Ss' use of an attitude scale designated "like," $+3$ and "dislike," -3 at its poles. The 18 items were presented in a different random order to each S. The positioning of positive and negative poles of the scale was counter-balanced and was random in the 18-item sequence.

The facial communications of three degrees of attitude were selected in a similar manner. Photographs of three female models were taken as they attempted to use facial expressions to communicate like, neutrality, and dislike towards another person. The photographs were 3½ × 4½ inch black and white prints of head only against a neutral background. Eighteen items, consisting of two photographs for each degree of attitude communicated by each of the three models, were presented to the same 17 Ss who judged the vocal communications. The instructions for recording judgments of the facial communications of attitude were analogous to those used with the vocal communications. The Ss were randomly assigned so that eight of them judged facial communications prior to judging vocal communications and nine made their judgments in reverse order.

On the basis of Ss' judgments of the vocal and facial communications, three vocal communications (i.e., positive, neutral, and negative), obtained from each of two speakers, and three facial communications, obtained from each of two models, were selected. As the data in Table 1 indicate, the facial attitude communications of a given value (e.g., positive) were selected to match the vocal attitude communications of the same value. Standard deviations of judgments as well as their means were approximately matched. A 3 Attitude × 4 Communicator × 17 Subject analysis of variance of the data summarized in Table 1 indicated a significant effect due to the Attitude factor ($F = 333.47$, $df = 2/32$; $MS_e = 1.12$, $p < .001$), no significant effect due to the Communicator factor ($F < 1$, $df = 3/48$; $MS_e = .37$, $p > .25$), and no significant Attitude × Communicator effect ($F = 1.05$, $df = 6/96$; $MS_e = .70$, $p > .25$). Thus, the independent effects of all vocal communications of attitude are comparable to the independent effects of all facial communications of attitude within each of the three levels of attitude investigated.

Design

The three vocal attitude communications of each speaker were each paired with the three facial attitude communications of each model. Therefore, there were 36 experimental conditions, con-

---

TABLE 1

Independent effects of vocal and facial communications: degree of positive attitude inferred from three kinds of vocal attitude communication by two speakers and three kinds of facial attitude communication by two models

	INFERRED ATTITUDE SCORES CORRESPONDING TO COMMUNICATIONS CONSIDERED					
Communi-cator	POSITIVE		NEUTRAL		NEGATIVE	
	M	*SD*	*M*	*SD*	*M*	*SD*
Speaker 1	2.41	0.79	0.06	0.82	−2.29	0.77
Speaker 2	2.35	0.70	−1.12	1.11	−2.18	0.73
Model 1	2.12	0.70	0.35	0.61	−2.65	1.00
Model 2	2.35	0.61	−0.24	1.15	−2.53	0.62

sisting of 3 Vocal Attitude × 3 Facial Attitude × 2 Speaker × 2 Model interactions. All 36 conditions were administered to each of 20 Ss, thus yielding a $3 \times 3 \times 2 \times 2$ factorial design with repeated measures on all factors.

Procedure

The experiment was individually administered to each S. The written instructions presented to the Ss were:

The purpose of this study is to find out how well people can judge the feelings of others. You will be shown photographs of different facial expressions and at the same time you will hear a recording of the word "maybe" spoken in different tones of voice. You are to imagine that the person you see and hear (A) is looking at and talking to another person (B). For each presentation, indicate on the scale what you think A's attitude is towards B.

A second form of instructions was identical to those presented above with the exception that references to facial expressions and seeing, and tones of voice and hearing, were made in reverse order. The Ss were randomly assigned so that half received the first form and half received the second form of instructions. A modified form of the semantic differential instructions was again used to direct Ss' use of an attitude scale designated "like," $+3$ and "dislike," -3 at its poles.

The 36 two-channel communications were presented in a different random order to each of 20 Ss. In each experimental condition, the vocal and facial components of the communication were presented simultaneously, so that Ss heard the vocal component only while seeing the facial component and vice versa.

Results

Each S recorded 36 responses, corresponding to all possible combinations of three facial communications of each of two models with three vocal communications of each of two speakers. The responses, which had a possible range of $+3$ to -3, were analyzed in a $3 \times 3 \times 2 \times 2$ factorial design with repeated measures on all factors. The analysis indicated a significant effect due to Facial Attitude ($F = 233.14$, $df = 2/38$; $MS_e = 2.37$, $p < .001$) and a significant effect due to Vocal Attitude ($F = 77.49$, $df = 2/38$; $MS_e = 3.33$, $p < .001$). None of the other main or interaction effects attained the .05 level of significance. The Facial Attitude × Vocal Attitude interactions with $MS_e = 2.21$ are summarized in Table 2. The Newman-Keuls method (Winer, 1962) yielded significant differences at the .01 level for all comparisons within each level of both factors.

The Facial Attitude factor accounted for 41.4% of the total sum of squares, whereas the Vocal Attitude factor accounted for 19.3% of the total sum of squares. Furthermore, the effects of the facial and vocal components were strongly linear. The linear trend accounted for 97% of the effect due to the facial component and 99% of the effect due to the vocal component. Moreover, the combined effect of

TABLE 2

Effects of two channel facial-vocal communications: degree of inferred positive attitude corresponding to the facial attitude × vocal attitude interactions

Vocal component	FACIAL COMPONENT		
	Positive	*Neutral*	*Negative*
Positive	2.45	1.31	−0.91
Neutral	1.33	0.50	−1.62
Negative	0.20	−1.07	−2.47

the facial and vocal components was a weighted sum of their independent effects, since there was no significant interaction between them. The following regression equation summarizes the relative contributions of facial and vocal components to interpretations of combined facial-vocal attitude communications:

$$A_T = 1.50 A_F + 1.03 A_V$$

A_T represents attitude inferred on a -3 to $+3$ scale from the two-channel communications. A_F represents attitude communicated in the facial component alone and is assigned values of $+1$, 0, and -1 for positive, neutral, and negative attitude, respectively. Similarly, A_V represents attitude communicated in the vocal component alone. The .95 confidence interval for the coefficient of A_F is 1.32 to 1.68, while that of the coefficient of A_V is .79 to 1.28. The absence of overlap between the two intervals indicated that the effect due to the facial component was significantly greater than that due to the vocal component.

Discussion

The hypothesis of the present study was only partially supported. A main effect due to variations in the facial component and no effect due to variations in the vocal component or its interaction with the facial component had been expected. The results of the study indicate that the facial and vocal components do not interact and that the facial component has a stronger effect than the vocal component. However, in contrast to the hypothesis, the effect due to the vocal component is also significant. Thus, the results of the study can be summarized as follows: Attitudes inferred from two-channel facial-vocal attitude communications are a linear function of the attitude communicated in each component, with the facial component receiving approximately 3/2 the weight received by the vocal component.

The above results were obtained from a sample of normal adult female *S*s who were communicators and addressees. However, it is likely that the linear model for two-channel communications of attitude obtained for female communicator-addressee combinations has broader applicability. For instance, the model (with, perhaps, slightly different relative weights for the facial and vocal components) may be applicable to same- and different-sex communicator-addressee pairs of various ages.

One interesting implication of the linear model with positive coefficients relates to redundant multichannel communications of attitude. The model indicates that the effect of redundancy (i.e., consistent attitude communication in two or more channels) is to intensify the attitude communicated in any one of the component channels. Thus, pushing a child away while turning away from him is assumed to communicate a more negative attitude toward the child than only pushing him away or only turning away from him. Similarly, holding and kissing a child is assumed to communicate a more positive attitude toward the child than only holding or only kissing the child.

A final comment is required to integrate the implications of the findings of the present study with the findings of the Mehrabian and Wiener study (1967). It is suggested that the combined effect of simultaneous verbal, vocal, and facial attitude communications is a weighted sum of their independent effects—with the coefficients of .07, .38, and .55, respectively. Analytic procedures outlined by Anderson (1962, 1964) can presently be employed to test this proposed weighted-sum model for any single decoder. In view of these extrapolations of experimental findings from the decoding of multichannel inconsistent communications, the assumptions underlying the effects of double-bind communications can be questioned. Further experimentation with schizophrenics or children as addressees is needed to clarify the pathology-inducing or behavior-modifying effects of inconsistent communications of attitude.

NOTE

1. This study was supported in part by United States Public Health Service Grant 1 R03-MH-12629-01 and in part by University of California Grant No. 2189. The authors wish to thank Dee Nieto, Nina Spitzer, and Barbara Ullman, who acted as models, and Elaine Blackman and Katherine Nelson, who, along with one of the authors, acted as speakers in preparing the experimental materials.

REFERENCES

Anderson, N. H. Application of an additive model to impression formation. *Science,* 1962, 138, 817–818.

Anderson, N. H. Note on weighted sum and linear operator models. *Psychonomic Science,* 1964, 1, 189–190.

Bateson, G., Jackson, D., Haley, J., & Weakland, J. Toward a theory of schizophrenia. *Behavioral Science,* 1956, 1, 251–264.

Davitz, J. R. (Ed.) *The communication of emotional meaning.* New York: McGraw-Hill, 1964.

Gates, G. S. The role of the auditory element in the interpretation of emotion. *Psychological Bulletin,* 1927, 24, 175. (Abstract)

Haley, J. *Strategies of psychotherapy.* New York: Grune & Stratton, 1963.

Levitt, E. A. The relationship between abilities to express emotional meanings vocally and facially. In J. R. Davitz (Ed.), *The communication of emotional meaning.* New York: McGraw-Hill, 1964. Pp. 87–100.

Mahl, G. R., & Schulze, C. Psychological research in the extra-linguistic area. In T. A. Sebeok, A. S. Hayes, & M. C. Bateson (Eds.), *Approaches to semiotics.* The Hague: Mouton, 1964. Pp. 51–124.

Mehrabian, A., & Wiener, M. Decoding of inconsistent communications. *Journal of Personality and Social Psychology,* 1967, 6, 108–114.

Osgood, C. E., Suci, G. J., & Tannenbaum, P. H. *The measurement of meaning.* Urbana: University of Illinois, 1957.

Williams, F., & Sundene, B. Dimensions of recognition: Visual vs. vocal expression of emotion. *Audio Visual Communications Review,* 1965, 13, 44–52.

Winer, B. J. *Statistical principles in experimental design.* New York: McGraw-Hill, 1962.

20

SOME SIGNALS AND RULES FOR TAKING SPEAKING TURNS IN CONVERSATIONS [1]

STARKEY DUNCAN, JR.

E. Goffman (personal communication, August 7, 1969) has asked rhetorically how people manage to walk down the street without continually bumping into each other. Part of the answer is that in our culture there are rules for walking down the street and for managing situations in which individuals find themselves on collision courses. Goffman (1963) has suggested some rules for these situations.

Just as it is desirable to avoid bumping into people on the street, it is desirable to avoid in conversations an inordinate amount of simultaneous talking. Beyond considerations of etiquette, it is difficult to maintain adequate mutual comprehensibility when participants in a conversation are talking at the same time.

The fact that participants in a conversation tend to take turns in speaking and listening has been frequently observed and discussed by other investigators. Yngve (1970) has commented that this phenomenon "is nearly the most obvious aspect of conversation [p. 568]." Jaffe and Feldstein (1970) also refer to the saliency of turn taking and the importance of avoiding interruptions. They cite Sullivan (1947), who observed careful turn taking in conversations between chronic mental hospital patients, and Miller (1963), who suggests that turn taking is a language universal. Kendon (1967) deals in detail with the role of gaze direction in turn taking. Schegloff (1968) proposed the "basic rule for conversations: *one party at a time* [p. 1076, italics in original]," and discussed some implications of this rule. Leighton, Stollak, and Ferguson (1971) found more interrupting and simultaneous talking in the interaction of families waiting for psychotherapy than in the interaction of "normal" families.

The question may be asked, again rhetorically, how participants in a conversation can avoid continually bumping into each other in a verbal sense. The thesis of this paper is that there is a regular communication mechanism in our culture for managing the taking of speaking turns in face-to-face interac-

From *Journal of Personality and Social Psychology*, 1972, 23, 283–92. Copyright © 1972 by the American Psychological Association and reprinted by permission.

tion (Goffman, 1963). Through this mechanism, participants in an interaction can effect the smooth and appropriate exchange of speaking turns. (The term "turn taking" has been independently suggested by Yngve, 1970, and by Goffman, personal communication, June 5, 1970).

The proposed turn-taking mechanism is mediated through signals composed of clear-cut behavioral cues, considered to be perceived as discrete. The turn-taking signals are used and responded to according to rules. Signals, cues, and rules are described in detail below.

Turn taking is considered to be one of a number of communication mechanisms, such as those discussed by Scheflen (1968), operating in face-to-face interaction. These mechanisms serve the function of integrating the performances of the participants in a variety of ways, for example, regulating the pace at which the communication proceeds, and monitoring deviations from appropriate conduct.

Goffman (1955) commented on these integrating mechanisms in general and on turn taking in particular:

In any society, whenever the physical possibility of spoken interaction arises, it seems that a system of practices, conventions, and procedural rules comes into play which functions as a means of guiding and organizing the flow of messages [p. 226].

The notion that a set of rules operates to integrate the turn-taking behavior of participants in a conversation is supported by Jaffe and Feldstein (1970), who also studied temporal patterns of speech and silence in dyadic conversations. Although they limited their data to the information provided by a "pair of voice-actuated relays

which treat any sound above threshold as equivalent [p. 113]," their findings suggested to them

further interactional rules that govern the matching of speech rates of the participants, the prohibition of interruption, and the requirement for properly timed signals that acknowledge understanding and confirm the continued attention of the listener [p. 6].

Source of Data

INTERVIEWS The results to be reported were based on meticulous transcriptions of speech and body motion behaviors during the first 19 minutes of two dyadic interviews, as recorded on videotape.

The first interview was a preliminary interview held at the Counseling and Psychotherapy Research Center at the University of Chicago. This preliminary interview is part of the routine intake procedure at the Counseling and Psychotherapy Research Center, and the client was a regular applicant for therapy. A preliminary interview was chosen for intensive transcription of communication behaviors because within a rather compressed period of time a wide variety of types of interaction may be encountered, from simple information giving, such as address, etc., to more emotionally laden discussion of the client's reasons for applying for therapy. At the same time, there is a strong intrinsic motivation for the interview, namely, an application for therapy, thereby avoiding the more artificial experimental situation in which unacquainted subjects are brought together and asked to discuss anything which might be of mutual interest.

The client was in her early twenties, working as a secretary, and had not completed college. The therapist-interviewer was a 40-year-old-male, an experienced therapist, who had been doing preliminary interviews for many years.

The second interview was between the therapist who participated in the first interview, and a second male therapist, also 40 years old. The two therapists were good friends and had known each other for about 10 years. Their interaction was relaxed and lively. The topic in this case was another client whom the first therapist had seen in a preliminary interview, and whom the second therapist had at that time seen in therapy for two interviews.

The preliminary interview is designated as Interview 1, and the second, peer interaction, is designated as Interview 2. The client is designated as Participant A; the preliminary interviewer, B; and the second therapist, C. Thus, the participants in Interview 1 were A and B, and the participants in Interview 2 were B and C.

VIDEOTAPING To videotape the interactions, the camera was placed so that both participants in each interaction were fully visible from head to foot on the tape at all times. No zoom techniques or other special focusing effects were used. A single camera was set up in full view of the participants. The camera and tape were left running prior to the participants' entry into the room and were not touched again until after the interview.

Despite the fact that a wide-angle lens was used, the camera was necessarily at such distance from the participants that more subtle details of facial expressions were not discriminable on the videotape. Less subtle expressions, such as broad smiles and grimaces, were readily discernible. In contrast, very small movements of the hands and fingers, for example, were clearly evident on the tapes, so that fine discriminations of these movements could be made and were on the transcription. A high-quality monophonic, audiotrack was obtained on the videotape.

TRANSCRIPTION For this study, the principal requirements for the transcription were those of maximum behavioral breadth and of continuity (no breaks or interruptions). Maximum breadth is desirable in analysis because it is not yet known which behavioral cues are the primary mediators of any given communication function. Continuity of transcription permits the complete analysis of sequences of events: the basic concern of this study.

In terms of size, two 19-minute transcriptions of interaction are simultaneously very small and very large, depending upon one's perspective. From the point of view of the wealth of communication engaged in each day by an individual, the transcriptions are quite brief. On the other hand, these transcriptions are believed to be unique in their breadth and duration. As described below, there was a detailed transcription of English segmental and suprasegmental phonemes, paralanguage, and body motion of both participants in the two interviews. The time involved in making the two transcriptions was great, involving the better part of 2 academic years.

Phonemes

SEGMENTAL PHONEMES Transcription of segmental phonemes, which describe the way syllables are pronounced within the framework of the English sound system, followed the scheme developed by Trager and Smith (1957). The segmental phonemes were the least important components of the study.

SUPRASEGMENTAL PHONEMES The suprasegmental phonemes are commonly referred to as intonation. They include the phenomena of stress, pitch, and juncture.

The Trager-Smith scheme for transcribing suprasegmental phonemes was used, with minor modifications identical to those described in previous studies by the present author (Duncan, Rosenberg, & Finkelstein, 1969; Duncan & Rosenthal, 1968).

Three terminal junctures—rising, falling, and sustained—were transcribed in accordance with the Trager-Smith system. These junctures are composed of contours of pitch, intensity, and duration occurring on the final syllable of phonemic clauses.

The point of departure for all subsequent analysis in this study was the phonemic clause (Trager & Smith, 1957). A phonemic clause is a phonological unit, defined by Trager and Smith as containing one and only one primary stress and one terminal juncture. Transcribing primary stresses and terminal junctures automatically identifies the phonemic clauses in a corpus.

Paralanguage

Paralanguage refers to the wide variety of vocal behaviors that occur in speech but that are not part of the sound system of language, as traditionally conceived. Comprehensive catalogs of paralinguistic behaviors have been compiled by Trager (1958), Crystal and Quirk (1964), and Crystal (1969). Any one speaker will probably use only a small fraction of the total behaviors available. The following list, which uses Trager's (1958) terminology, includes only those behaviors that play a part in the turn-taking signals: (*a*) intensity (overloud-oversoft); (*b*) pitch height (overhigh-overlow); and (*c*) extent (drawl-clipping of individual syllables). The terms in parentheses define the anchor point for each behavioral continuum. A wide variety of paralinguistic behaviors was actually encountered in the two dyads and included in the transcriptions.

Body motion

In contrast to paralanguage, there was no available transcription system for body motion which could be readily applied to our video-tapes. This situation led to a transcribing method based on the behaviors actually found in each interview. The transcription system for the first interview was created by first making an inventory of the movements used by the two participants and then assigning either arbitrary or descriptive labels to these movements. This system was then applied to the second interview, after expanding it to include new movements observed in the second interview.

While there is no pretense that the resulting transcription system is able to encompass all movements occurring in this culture, every attempt was made to include all movements observed in the dyads under study. The transcription was in this sense comprehensive. Included were (*a*) head gestures and movements (nodding, turning, pointing, shaking, etc.) and direction of head orientation; (*b*) shoulder movements (e.g., shrugs); (*c*) facial expressions, such as could be clearly seen; (*d*) hand gestures and movements of all sorts (each hand transcribed independently); (*e*) foot movements (each foot independently); (*f*) leg movements; (*g*) postures and posture shifts; and (*h*) use of artifacts, such as pipe, kleenex, papers, and clip-board.

Coordination of body motion and speech transcriptions

Speech syllables were used to locate all transcribed events. Thus, the movements of both participants in an interview were located with respect to the syllables emitted by the participant who happened to be speaking at the time, or to the pause between two syllables.

The turn-taking mechanism

The variables for the turn-taking mechanism were formulated as signals by which each participant indicated his state with regard to the speaking turn. Given the display or absence of a given turn-taking signal by one participant, rules delimit the appropriate responses by the other participant.

The rules and signals, considered together, establish empirical expectations with respect to turn-taking activities at any given moment in a conversation, assuming that the participants in the conversations under analysis are rule abiding for the most part. Data relevant to evaluating the turn-taking mechanisms are presented in the Results section.

DEFINITIONS Definitions of "speaker," "auditor," and "simultaneous turns" are required to begin. A *speaker* is a participant in a conversation who claims the speaking turn at any given moment. An *auditor* (Kendon, 1967) is a participant who does not claim the speaking turn at any given moment.

In general, with the help of the turn-taking mechanism, the turn need not be disputed in the course of the conversation. However, when both par-ticipants claim the speaking turn at the same time, then the state of *simultaneous turns* obtains in the conversation and the turn-taking mechanism may be said to have broken down, or perhaps to have been discarded, for the duration of that state.

The term "simultaneous turns" is used here instead of the more usual term "simultaneous talking" because there will be certain circumstances, described below, in which talking by the auditor, even simultaneously with the speaker, does not imply a claim for the speaking turn. Therefore, the two terms should be differentiated.

When simultaneous turns occurs, the auditor attempts to take his turn, and the original speaker continues with his turn. The turn-taking mechanism is not designated to explain how the state of simultaneous turns is resolved, that is, which one of the two speakers will continue and which one will fall silent. Meltzer, Morris, and Hayes (1971) reported some interesting findings, based on techniques of "social psychophysics [p. 401]," on one mode of resolution.

Just as both participants may become speakers, claiming simultaneous turns, both participants may also become auditors, not claiming a turn. In this case, the obvious result is silence for the duration of that mutual state. The phenomenon—apparent avoidance of the turn by both participants—was not observed in the two interviews analyzed for this study and thus will not be discussed in this paper.

Turn yielding

RULE The auditor may take his speaking turn when the speaker gives a turn-yielding signal. Under proper operation of the turn-taking mechanism, if the auditor acts to take his turn in response to a yielding signal by the speaker, the speaker will immediately yield his turn.

A state of simultaneous turns can be created in two ways: (*a*) if the auditor attempts to take his speaking turn in the absence of a turn-yielding signal by the speaker or (*b*) if the speaker displays a yielding signal, and the auditor acts to take his turn, and the original speaker then continues to claim his speaking turn. Neither of these sequences of events will occur in interaction when the participants are adhering to the turn-taking mechanism.

The auditor is not obliged to take his speaking turn in response to a regular turn-yielding signal by the speaker. The auditor may alternatively communicate in the back channel (Yngve, 1970) or remain silent. (Portions of the back channel are briefly described below.)

SIGNAL A turn-yielding signal for a speaker is described as the display of at least one of a set of six discrete behavioral cues. These cues may be displayed either singly or together. When displayed together, they may occur either simultaneously or in tight sequences.

The six turn-yielding cues are listed below.

1. Intonation: the use of any pitch level—terminal junction combination other than 2 2| at the end of a phonemic clause. Following the Trager-Smith (1957) notation, the 2 refers to an intermediate pitch level, neither high (3) nor low (1). The single bar juncture "|" at the end of the clause refers to a sustention of the pitch at the level previously indicated. Thus, 2 2| refers to a phonemic clause ending on an intermediate pitch level, which is sustained, neither rising nor falling, at the juncture between clauses.

A frequent pattern of phonemic clauses in American English is a series of 2 2| clauses, which terminates in a final clause with a rising or falling pitch level–juncture combination. Any of these rising or falling combinations qualifies as a regular turn-yielding cue. A phonemic clause containing one of these rising or falling combinations is referred to as a "terminal clause."

2. Paralanguage: Drawl: drawl on the final syllable or on the stressed syllable of a terminal clause.

3. Body motion: the termination of any hand gesticulation (Kendon, 1967) used during a speaking turn or the relaxation of a tensed hand position (e.g., a fist) during a turn.

To account for the gesticulations observed in the two interviews, it is sufficient to define gesticulations as those hand movements generally away from the body, which commonly accompany, and which appear to bear a direct relationship to, speech.

Specifically excluded from the definition of gesticulation are self-adaptors and object adaptors (Ekman & Friesen, 1969). Self-adaptors involving the hands are movements in which the hand comes in contact with one's own body, often with the appearance of grooming. Examples would be rubbing the chin, scratching the cheek, smoothing the hair, brushing off the pants leg, picking lint (real or imaginary) from the socks, etc. Such self-adaptors are very frequent for many individuals both while they are speakers and while they are auditors. For present purposes, the definition of object adaptors is construed more narrowly than in Ekman and Friesen's definition. Movements considered to be object adaptors in the first interview were those movements having to do with Participant B's maintaining his pipe, and some movements in which the paper on his clipboard was wrinkled. Highly similar behaviors, termed "self-manipulatory gestures," were also studied by Rosenfeld (1966).

4. Sociocentric sequences: the appearance of one of several stereotyped expressions, typically following a substantive statement. Examples are "but uh," "or something," or "you know." The three participants varied in the particular expressions used and in the frequency of their use. They were most common for the client. They were generally preceded by other yielding cues, and were often accompanied by a marked paralinguistic "trailing off" effect. The term sociocentric sequences was coined by Bernstein (1962), who commented on these expressions in another context. These expressions do not add substantive information to the speech content that they follow. Instances in which the auditor proceeded to take his speaking turn during the completion of a sociocentric sequence are not considered as a state of simultaneous turns in the conversation. Rather, such an act is considered to be an instance of permissible simultaneous talking.

5. Paralanguage: Pitch/loudness: a drop in paralinguistic pitch and/or loudness in conjunction with one of the sociocentric sequences described above. When used, these expressions typically followed a terminal clause but did not often share the same paralanguage.

6. Syntax: the completion of a grammatical clause, involving a subject–predicate combination.

Attempt-suppressing signal

RULE An attempt-suppressing signal displayed by the speaker maintains the turn for him, regardless of the number of yielding cues concurrently being displayed. Auditors almost never attempted to take their turn when this signal was being displayed.

SIGNAL The attempt-suppressing signal consists of one or both of the speaker's hands being engaged in gesticulation. Self- and object adaptors do not operate as attempt-suppressing signals. Dropping of the gesticulating hand or hands into a rest position, as on the arm of a chair, constitutes a turn-yielding cue (see 3 described above). It should be noted that much speech is not accompanied by gesticulation, and therefore neither the attempt-suppressing signal nor its coordinate yielding cue would be applicable for that speech.

Back-channel communication

RULE The term "back channel" was introduced in the context of turn taking by Yngve (1970) to cover such messages as "mm-hmm" and head nods from the auditor. In this sense, the term is roughly equivalent to Kendon's (1967) "accompaniment behavior" and Dittmann and Llewellyn's (1968) "listener response."

For the purposes of this study, it is sufficient to point out that a back-channel communication does not constitute a turn or a claim for a turn. To the contrary, it appears that, when a speaker is displaying a turn-yielding signal, the back channel is often used by the auditor to avoid taking his speaking turn. In this sense, taking a turn and communicating in the back channel may be considered to be contrasting tacks an auditor, faced with a yielding signal, may take.

It is important to note that, because back-channel signals do not constitute a turn or a claim for a turn, their display by the auditor simultaneously with the speaker's speech is not considered to be a state of simultaneous turns in the dyad.

SIGNAL It is suspected that back-channel communication comprises a large and complex set of signals, which at present may not be well understood. These signals may participate in a variety of communication functions, including the regulation of speaking turns. It is proposed that "back channel" be expanded to refer to this broader class of signals, as it is progressively documented.

In addition to the back-channel signals such as "mm-hmm," "yeah," and head nods mentioned above, the following back-channel signals were observed in our interviews: (a) sentence completions, in which the auditor completed a sentence that the speaker had begun (independently reported by Yngve, 1970); (b) brief requests for clarification; and (c) restatement in a few words of an immediately preceding thought expressed by the speaker.

Unit of analysis

In order to subdivide the interviews, a unit of analysis was chosen which in size lay between the phonemic clause and the speaking turn. Every cue display and every instance of smooth exchange of turns or simultaneous turns occurring in the interviews was located with respect to these units. As with the yielding signal, the unit was defined in terms of the display of at least one of a number of behaviors in syntax, intonation, paralanguage, and body motion.

Specifically, boundaries of the units were defined as being (a) at the ends of phonemic clauses (b) which additionally were marked by the display of one or more of the floor-yielding cues described above, and/or by the display of one or more of the following cues.

1. Unfilled pause: an appreciable unfilled pause following the phonemic clause.

2. Head direction: turning of the speaker's head toward the auditor. This cue is identical to the speaker's part of the gaze-direction pattern discovered by Kendon (1967).

3. Paralanguage: a drop in paralinguistic pitch and/or loudness in conjunction with a phonemic clause, either across the entire clause or across its final syllable or syllables.

4. Body motion (for Participant A only): a relaxation of the foot from a marked dorsal flexion. (Throughout the interview the client's legs were stretched out in front of her and were crossed at the ankle.) Fom time to time one or both feet would be flexed dorsally, such that they assumed a nearly perpendicular angle to the floor. Their falling, as a result of relaxing the flexion, was the cue.

Each of these behaviors appeared to play a part in the speaker's segmenting of his communication and in the timing and placement of the auditor's turn-taking and back-channel responses.

Results

The rules for turn yielding and attempt suppressing lead to the expectations that (a) the occurrence of simultaneous turns will be associated primarily with the auditor's turn-taking attempts when zero yielding cues (i.e., the absence of a yielding signal) are being displayed by the speaker, and (b) display of the attempt-suppressing signal by the speaker will sharply reduce the auditor's turn-taking attempts in response to yielding cues. In addition, auditor attempts to take the floor appeared to vary as a function of the number of yielding cues conjointly displayed. Data analyses are presented relevant to these three empirical issues.

Table I, on which the analyses were based, presents the data, summed over the two interviews, for auditor turn-taking attempts and resulting simultaneous turns, in terms of (a) the number of turn-yielding cues conjointly displayed and (b) the display or absence of the attempt-suppressing signal. Percentages of auditor attempts in response to a given number of cues were calculated as the number of attempts divided by the number of displays of those cues. Percentages of simultaneous turns were calculated by dividing the number of simultaneous turns by the number of attempts.

The relationship between the display of zero yielding cues by the speaker and the occurrence of simultaneous turns resulting from a turn-taking attempt by the auditor may be tested by applying chi-square to Table 2, a 2 × 2 contingency table derived from Table

TABLE I

Auditor turn-taking attempts and resulting simultaneous turns as a function of number of turn-yielding cues displayed and the display of the attempt-suppressing signal

SPEAKER YIELDING CUE DISPLAY		AUDITOR TURN-TAKING ATTEMPT			SIMULTANEOUS TURNS RESULTING FROM AUDITOR ATTEMPT		
	A	*B*	*C*		*D*	*E*	
N conjointly displayed	*Frequency of display*	*N*	*P*[a]	*SD*[b]	*N*	*P*[c]	*SD*[b]
No attempt-suppressing signal displayed							
0	52	5	.10	.04	5	1.00	.00
1	123	12	.10	.03	2	.17	.11
2	146	25	.17	.03	2	.08	.05
3	89	29	.33	.05	2	.07	.05
4	47	15	.32	.07	0	.00	.00
5	9	4	.44	.17	0	.00	.00
6	2	1	.50	.35	0	.00	.00
Σ	468	91			11		
Attempt-suppressing signal displayed							
0	56	7	.13	.04	7	1.00	.00
1	109	0	.00	.00			
2	138	0	.00	.00			
3	105	2	.02	.01	1	.50	.35
4	6	0	.00	.00			
5	3	0	.00	.00			
Σ	417	9			8		

[a] column B/column A.
[b] Standard error of the proportion $= \sqrt{\dfrac{PQ}{N}}$.
[c] column D/column B.

TABLE 2

Smooth exchanges of turns and simultaneous turns resulting from auditor's turn-taking attempts in response to the speaker's display of zero yielding cues and of ≥1 yielding cues

No. yielding cues displayed	Smooth exchange of turns	Simultaneous turns
0	0	12
≥1	81	7

NOTE $N = 100$.

1 ($x^2 = 52.31$, corrected for continuity, $df = 1$, a chi-square of 10.8 has an associated probability of .001).

When no attempt-suppressing signal was displayed, the correlation between number of yielding cues displayed and percentage of auditor turn-taking attempts was .96 ($df = 4$). This correlation accounts for 92% of the variance. The analysis of variance for the regression is presented in Table 3. The F value for the analysis was 50.53. (When $df = 1/4$, and F value of 21.2 is significant at the .01 level of significance.) The data points and the regression line are plotted in the left half of Figure 1.

TABLE 3

Percentage of auditor turn-taking attempts in response to number of yielding cues displayed: analysis of variance for the regression

Source of variation	df	SS	MS	F
Attributable to regression	1	.09367	.09367	50.53
Deviation from regression	4	.00741	.00185	
Total	5	.10109		

It should be noted that the data point for the display of six cues was not included in the regression because there were only two such cases, thereby giving a relatively unreliable estimate for that point. It happens, however, that the data point falls precisely on the regression line, as may be seen in Figure 1.

The results on auditor attempts were sharply different when the speaker was displaying an attempt-suppressing signal along with his yielding cues. Data on auditor attempts in the presence of a suppressing signal are presented in the lower half of Table 1 and in the right half of Figure 1. With the exception of the display of zero yielding cues, the auditor attempt curve was virtually flat

at 0%, with no increase of turn-taking attempts as the number of yielding cues increases.

Discussion

The results reflect strong regularities in interview behaviors with respect to turn taking. It should be borne in mind that the data presented here were generated through the coordinated action of two individuals. As an integrating mechanism, turn taking appears capable of being remarkably successful in dyadic conversations.

The chance of simultaneous turns was sharply decreased when the auditor attempted to take his turn after the display of a yielding signal by the speaker.

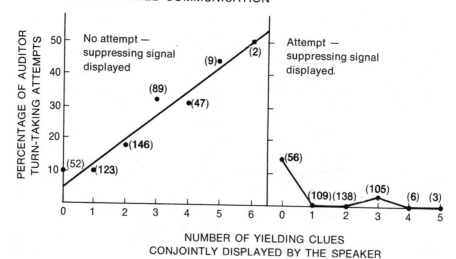

Fig. 1 Auditor's turn-taking attempts in response to the display of yielding cues and attempt-suppressing signals (*n*s are shown in parentheses).

As more yielding cues were conjointly displayed, the probability of a turn-taking attempt by the auditor increased in a strictly linear fashion.

On the other hand, the display of an attempt-suppressing signal essentially eliminated the auditor's tendency to take his turn regardless of the number of yielding cues concomitantly displayed. Because the auditor's attempts were so thoroughly suppressed by the signal, it was not possible to infer from the data the likelihood of simultaneous turns resulting from turn-taking responses to the suppressing signal.

It should be noted that the display of any number of yielding cues by the speaker, in the absence of a suppressing signal, did not automatically result in an attempt by the auditor. At best, the probability of an auditor attempt appears to be about .50. Thus, the auditor retains considerable discretion over his responses.

Either the speaker or the auditor may disregard the turn-taking mechanism, so that a state of simultaneous turns is produced. In the present data

the occurrence of auditor turn-taking attempts when zero yielding cues were being displayed may be straightforwardly interpreted as an interruption of the speaker. On those six occasions on which simultaneous turns were associated with the display of yielding cues by the speaker, the blame may be laid to him for not properly yielding when he had so signaled.

This study was based on two behaviorally inclusive transcriptions of dyadic face-to-face interaction. The emphasis on inclusiveness required joint consideration of the linguistic, paralinguistic, and body motion components of face-to-face interaction, as opposed to focusing exclusively on any one or two of these modalities. As mentioned above, this behavioral inclusiveness is desirable at this stage of our understanding of face-to-face interaction because it is not known a priori which behaviors in the stream of communication are the important cues for any given communication function.

A primary obstacle to research of this type is the laboriousness of making fine-grained transcriptions of multiple interaction behaviors. Despite the difficulty of the task, these detailed comprehensive transcriptions are valuable for their potential contribution to the discovery and documentation of various communication functions. It is important at this stage of research to be able to specify, quite accurately, what happens where in interactions. Considering the wealth of transcribed data on languages throughout the world, the raw transcribed data available on face-to-face interaction in its broader aspect are deplorably scant.

Once important signals are identified for any given communication function, further research on that function can proceed at a much more rapid pace. In Scheflen's (1966) words, the signals become *"recognizable at a glance and recordable with a stroke* [p. 277, original italics]." Accordingly, work is presently underway to transcribe the turn-taking signals (and a few other potentially significant behaviors) for brief sections of additional interviews. In this manner it is possible to capitalize on existing knowledge of turn taking, both to extend our understanding of it and to validate further our original findings.

The findings on the turn-yielding signal provide an example of the usefulness of behaviorally comprehensive research. The cues comprising this signal were found in every communication modality examined: content, syntax, intonation, paralanguage, and body motion.

The behavioral breadth in the yielding signal provides it with the desirable property of flexibility. No single communication modality is required in order to display a signal. The yielding signal may also be said to possess the property of generality, in that the cues for the signal are formulated in terms

of general properties of behaviors, rather than specific acts. For example, it is not a specific intonation pattern that served as a cue, but simply any deviation from the 2 2| pattern; not a specific gesticulation, but cessation of the gesture, or relaxation of a tensed hand position; not a specific paralinguistic pattern, but a drop from the preceding pattern in pitch and/or loudness, and so on.

Further research is underway on various aspects of the turn-taking mechanism using our transcriptions. The distribution and functions of the impressively large and complex class of back-channel signals are being investigated. The notion of floor-requesting signals by the auditor, suggested by Yngve (1970), is being explored, including the possibility that there may in some sense be an ongoing negotiation for the floor by speaker and auditor.

By positing three types of signals and as many rules, a turn-taking mechanism can be described which accounts for extensive portions of the turn-taking behavior in the two interviews under examination. The overall strength of the results underscores the potential of further research on the rule-governed aspects of behavior.

The rules for turn taking were designed to be applicable across a wide range of individual styles and communication contexts. There is room for appreciable variation in their use. For example, variation may be found in the use of (*a*) the attempt-suppressing signal, (*b*) back-channel communications in lieu of turn-taking attempts, (*c*) the number of simultaneous turns created either by the speaker or by the auditor, and (*d*) the number of turn-yielding signals composed of large numbers of cues. If such variations actually exist, they may be related to other variables of interest. These variations in the use of basic structural elements of conversations may be the source of many of the subtle effects which, while difficult to specify explicitly, often have telling consequences on impression formation and on the developmental course of interactions.

NOTES

1. This study was supported in part by Grants MH-16,210 and MH-17,756 from the National Institute of Mental Health, and by Grant GS-3033 from the Division of Social Sciences on the National Science Foundation. The author is grateful to Erving Goffman, Adam Kendon, and Allen Dittmann, who made valuable constructive criticisms of an earlier draft of this paper. The author wishes to express his appreciation to Susan Beekman, Mark Cary, Diane Martin, Ray O'Cain, Tom Shanks, and Andrew Szasz, who contributed to the transcriptions and data analysis. I am indebted to Dick Jenney, Wayne Anderson, and the client, who generously consented to serve as participants in this study.

REFERENCES

Bernstein, B. Social class, linguistic codes, and grammatical elements. *Language and Speech*, 1962, 5, 221–240.

Crystal, D. *Prosodic systems and intonation in English*. Cambridge: Cambridge University Press, 1969.

Crystal, D., & Quirk, R. *Systems of prosodic and paralinguistic features in English*. The Hague: Mouton, 1964.

Dittmann, A. T., & Llewellyn, L. G. Relationship between vocalizations and head nods as listener responses. *Journal of Personality and Social Psychology*, 1968, 9, 79–84.

Duncan, S. D., Jr., Rosenberg, M. J., & Finkelstein, J. The paralanguage of experimenter bias. *Sociometry*, 1969, 32, 207–219.

Duncan, S. D., Jr., & Rosenthal, R. Vocal emphasis in experimenters' instruction reading as unintended determinant of subjects' responses. *Language and Speech*, 1968, 11, 20–26.

Ekman, P., & Friesen, W. V. The repertoire of nonverbal behavior: Categories, origins, usage, and coding. *Semiotica*, 1969, 1, 49–98.

Goffman, E. On face work: An analysis of ritual elements in social interaction. *Psychiatry*, 1955, 18, 213–231.

Goffman, E. *Behavior in public places: Notes on the social organization of gatherings*. New York: Free Press of Glencoe, 1963.

Jaffe, J., & Feldstein, S. *Rhythms of dialogue*. New York: Academic Press, 1970.

Kendon, A. Some functions of gaze-direction in social interaction. *Acta Psychologica*, 1967, 26, 22–63.

Leighton, L. A., Stollak, G. E., & Ferguson, L. R. Patterns of communication in normal and clinic families. *Journal of Consulting and Clinical Psychology*, 1971, 36, 252–256.

Meltzer, L., Morris, W. N., & Hayes, D. P. Interruption outcomes and vocal amplitude: Explorations in social psychophysics. *Journal of Personality and Social Psychology*, 1971, 18, 392–402.

Miller, G. A. Review of J. H. Greenberg (Ed.), *Universals of language*. *Contemporary Psychology*, 1963, 8, 417–418.

Rosenfeld, H. M. Instrumental affiliative functions of facial and gestural expressions. *Journal of Personality and Social Psychology*, 1966, 4, 65–72.

Scheflen, A. E. Natural history method in psychotherapy: Communicational research. In L. A. Gottschalk & A. H. Auerbach (Eds.), *Methods of research in psychotherapy*. New York: Appleton-Century-Crofts, 1966.

Scheflen, A. E. Human communication: Behavioral programs and their integration in interaction. *Behavioral Science,* 1968, 13, 44–55.

Schegloff, E. A. Sequencing in conversational openings. *American Anthropologist,* 1968, 70, 1075–1095.

Sullivan, H. S. *Conceptions of modern psychiatry.* New York: Norton, 1947.

Trager, G. L. Paralanguage: A first approximation. *Studies in Linguistics,* 1958, 13, 1–12.

Trager, G. L., & Smith, H. L., Jr. *An outline of English structure.* Washington, D.C.: American Council of Learned Societies, 1957.

Yngve, V. H. On getting a word in edgewise. *Papers from the sixth regional meeting of the Chicago Linguistic Society.* Chicago: Chicago Linguistic Society, 1970.

21

SOME DETERMINERS OF SOCIAL INTERACTION [1]

ALBERT MEHRABIAN AND SHELDON KSIONZKY

The study of social interaction can be viewed as having at least two phases: first, the description and measurement of the various behavioral aspects of social interaction; and second, the study of the main and interactive effects of the situational determiners and individual difference correlates of these behaviors.

The description of social interaction has been the subject of considerable study. Findings have repeatedly demonstrated the importance of certain basic factors that may be used to describe and measure it. Several studies which used Bales' (1950) Interaction Process Analysis consistly yielded three dimensions of social evaluation: power, affection (positive-negative evaluation), and contribution to group tasks (e.g., Carter, 1954; Couch, 1960; Bales, 1950, 1968). Borgatta (1962, 1963) attempted to revise and improve the original scoring categories of Bales (1950) and in one experiment obtained the factors of sociability (which relates to affection) and assertiveness (which relates to power). Other results relating to Bales' (1950) category system and descriptions and criticisms of that approach showed a need for studies to use (a) non-task oriented methodologies and (b) more specific and reliable scoring criteria for the nonverbal behavior as well as for the verbal report or verbal behavior measures (Weick, 1968).

In one such study by Mehrabian and Ksionzky (1972a), the behaviors of participants in a social situation were measured using reliably scored cues (e.g., sideways lean of the body, facial pleasantness, number of questions per minute). The 26 selected measures used had demonstrated unambiguous significance in studies described by Mehrabian (1972a). Factor analyses of the 26 cues provided the six factors of Table 1. The first, affiliative behavior, included the amount of verbal interaction as well as positiveness of both verbal and nonverbal cues, thus relating to the "affection" factor identified in earlier studies. The second factor,

From *Sociometry*, 1972, 35, 588–609. Copyright © 1972 by the American Sociological Association and reprinted by permission.

responsiveness, was primarily an index of one's awareness of another's presence and one's reaction to him, and was scored in terms of the activity measures identified in studies of nonverbal communication (e.g., Osgood, 1966; Mehrabian, 1970a, 1971b). Relaxation, the third factor, has been repeatedly shown to imply dominance (e.g., Mehrabian, 1972a, b) and related to the "power" factor identified in earlier studies. The fourth factor, ingratiation, exhibited a small positive correlation with affilative behavior, and has been found to be part of a somewhat forced attempt to elicit a harmonious relationship with another (e.g., during the awkward initial moments of interaction with a stranger). It included positive nonverbal cues in combination with questions designed to ensure a friendly exchange. The fifth factor, distress, included active avoidance of another by walking about and preoccupation with various objects in the interaction setting. Finally, the sixth factor, intimate position, was indexed by a close position.

Of this group of factors, the first three are of major importance and serve to characterize not only actual social behavior, but also the perceptions and judgments of social events, persons, and objects. For example, factor analyses of ratings of verbal cues yielded the three semantic differential factors of activity (responsiveness), dominance (power), and evaluation (Osgood, Suci and Tannenbaum, 1957; Snider and Osgood, 1969). Mehrabian (1972b) used these three dimensions to characterize nonverbal behavior, and demonstrated the relevance of these three dimensions across a wide range of social situations.

Some of the factors in Table 1 were also repeatedly identified in earlier

theoretical accounts and empirical findings. Leary (1957) proposed a two-dimensional structure—dominance-submission (power) and love-hostility (affection)—to account for interpersonal behavior. Focusing on interpersonal needs rather than interpersonal behavior, Schutz (1958) proposed three interpersonal drives: control (power), affection, and inclusion.

Empirical support for these factors has primarily come from factor analytic studies. In a review of these studies, Foa (1961) found that the two factors of dominance-submission and love-hostility were common to all of them. Lorr and Suziedelis (1969) factor analyzed ratings of the social behavior of three groups of subjects (two patient groups and one normal group). The factor structure contained two of the major factors—a control factor (power), and a sociability (affiliation) factor. These two factors were also relevant to ratings of maternal behavior. Schaefer (1969) factor analyzed three sets of ratings of mothers' social and emotional behavior toward their children. The two factors of control-autonomy (power) and love-hostility emerged.

Cross-cultural generality of some of the factors has also been demonstrated. Longabaugh (1966) factor analyzed the group behavior of children in six different cultures and obtained a three factor structure which showed cross-cultural generality. This three factor structure was likened to Carter's (1954) factors of individual prominence (power), sociability, and aiding attainment of the group. Triandis, Vassiliou and Nassiakou (1968) factor analyzed judgments of (1) role perceptions, (2) behavioral intentions, and (3) perceptions of social behavior from two different cultures and yielded four culture-com-

mon factors: affect, intimacy, dominance, and hostility.

Thus, the factors of Table 1 have
been shown to be of significance in a
wide range of social situations. The
present study uses these factors as a
starting point, and deals with the second concern, namely, the study of the
situational determiners and individual
difference correlates of factors (ob-

TABLE 1[a]

Factors of social behavior

	Loading direction on factor
Factor I: Affiliative Behavior	
Total number of statements per minute	(+)
Number of declarative statements per minute	(+)
Percent duration of eye contact with confederate	(+)
Percent duration of subject's speech	(+)
Percent duration of confederate's speech	(+)
Positive verbal content	(+)
Head nods per minute	(+)
Hand and arm gestures per minute	(+)
Pleasantness of facial expressions	(+)
Factor II: Responsiveness	
Vocal activity	(+)
Speech rate	(+)
Speech volume	(+)
Factor III: Relaxation	
Rocking movements per minute	(−)
Leg and foot movements per minute	(−)
Body lean	(+)
Factor IV: Ingratiation	
Pleasantness of vocal expressions	(+)
Negative verbal content	(−)
Verbal reinforcers given per minute	(+)
Number of questions per minute	(+)
Self-manipulations per minute	(+)
Factor V: Distress	
Percent duration of walking	(+)
Object manipulations per minute	(+)
Arm position asymmetry	(+)
Factor VI: Intimacy	
Shoulder orientation away from confederate	(+)
Distance from confederate	(−)
Head turns per minute (looking around)	(+)

[a] This is a modified version of Table 8.3 of Mehrabian's *Nonverbal Communication*, published
by Aldine-Atherton, Inc., in 1972. Reproduced by permission.

tained by Mehrabian and Ksionzky, 1972a) which described social interaction. Several experimental manipulations were used to elicit a variety of behaviors and to relate these to the individual differences of the participants.

Since a previous experiment employing similar procedures had shown that affiliative behavior was the primary aspect of social interaction (Mehrabian, 1971a), most of the experimental manipulations were introduced to induce variability in such behavior. These manipulations were based directly upon a model of affiliative behavior proposed by Mehrabian and Ksionzky (1970). According to that model, a person's affiliative behavior increased with the target's positive, and decreased with his negative, reinforcing quality. Therefore, two experimental factors were (1) the degree of positive evaluation and (2) the degree of negative evaluation received from the target prior to interacting with him.

The preceding analysis of affiliative behavior provided a framework for discussing other familiar aspects of social interaction such as independence versus conformity (Mehrabian and Kzionzky, 1970); ingratiation (Jones, 1964); or competition versus cooperation. Cooperation-competition was included as a factor in this experiment because it related most directly to the model for affiliative behavior. Cooperative situations, compared to competitive ones, involve a greater exchange of positive, and a lesser exchange of negative, reinforcers. In addition, the competition condition was expected to elicit social behaviors different from those obtained in the task-oriented social interactions of the studies already reviewed. An individual difference measure of achieving tendency (Mehrabian, 1968, 1969b)

was also included, since it was expected to interact with the cooperation-competition factor in determining nonaffiliative behaviors.

Four other individual difference measures employed in the experiment related to affiliative behavior: sex, birth order, affiliative tendency, and sensitivity to rejection. For the sex variable, Anastasi (1958) and Mehrabian (1970c, 1971a) have shown that females are generally more affilative and convey more positiveness to others. The relevance of birth order in studies of affiliation was demonstrated by Schachter's (1959) studies. The first-born relative to the later born among his female subjects showed a greater desire to wait with others while anticipating a painful experience. The model proposed by Mehrabian and Ksionzky (1970) indicated that, averaging over a representative sample of unfamiliar targets, affiliative behavior increased with affiliative tendency and decreased with sensitivity to rejection—the former making a greater contribution. In this experiment, affiliative tendency and sensitivity to rejection were assessed using Mehrabian's (1970b) questionnaire measures. Evidence of validity and reliability of these measures are provided by Mehrabian (1970b).

In sum, the independent effects of the experiment were the degree of positive evaluation from the target, the degree of negative evaluation from him, and anticipated cooperation versus competition with the target. Based on their relevance to these experimental manipulations and the dependent measures of the study, five individual difference variables (affiliative tendency, sensitivity to rejection, achieving tendency, sex, and birth order) were also included. The dependent measures were to be based on the factor analytic results reported in Table 1, and constituted the basic categories of social interaction. Some of the hypotheses have already been noted in describing the rationale for the introduction of the various independent effects and individual difference factors. Additional hypotheses could be stated at this point. However, it is important to note that the study was primarily exploratory in quality and the object was to identify some replicable relationships among this large set of independent and dependent variables.

Method

Subjects

University of California undergraduates were paid to participate in the study, both as subjects and confederates. There were 256 subjects and 22 experimental confederates, all of whom were recruited by an advertisement in the student newspaper. Each confederate was trained for one hour before his participation in the study and served as a confederate with approximately 12 subjects.

Procedure

Subjects first responded to questionnaire measures of affiliative tendency and sensitivity to rejection (Mehrabian, 1970b), achieving tendency (Mehrabian, 1968, 1969a), and an attitude questionnaire. They also provided information about their birth order. The attitude questionnaire elicited the subject's attitudes toward a variety of social, economic, esthetic, political, and school-related issues. When a subject had completed all the questionnaires, he received the following instructions.

This is the first half of a two-part experiment. You and another subject have just filled out some personality and attitude questionnaires, and now we are going to exchange your answers with those of the other subject. After you receive his questionnaires, look them over carefully, then write a brief character sketch of him below, and complete the Interpersonal Judgment scale. Although you may work with any and all of the questionnaire answers in writing your character sketch of him (her), you will probably find his (her) Attitude scale answers the most helpful in forming your impression. You will have fifteen minutes, after which the second part of the experiment will be described.

The subject then received the questionnaire responses of his "partner," who was actually a confederate in the experiment and was waiting in another room. He then proceeded to write a personality sketch of the partner-confederate and to rate him on the Interpersonal Judgment scale (Byrne, 1966). The questionnaire responses of the partner-confederate were noncommittal, so that in all conditions subjects produced a sketch and completed the Interpersonal Judgment scale for their partners on the basis of neutral cues. The Interpersonal Judgment scale asked for estimates of the partner's level of intelligence, knowledge of current events, morality, psychological adjustment, liking of the partner, and the subject's willingness to work with the partner. When the subject had completed his personality sketch of the confederate, he was told that their two sketches would be exchanged so that each could read the other's opinions of himself. The sketch given to the subject was actually one of four standard descriptions, pre-written to be primarily positively reinforcing, primarily negatively reinforcing, mixed positively and negatively reinforcing, or neutral. The sketches for males and females were identical except for the appropriate pronoun changes. The four personality sketches for male subjects read as follows:

POSITIVE This person seems to be very likable. I think he has thought very deeply about the serious problems facing the United States today, because his answers seem very conscientious. Even though his opinions are not well liked by everyone, he is not afraid to state them. He impresses me as an honest, sincere person who tells you exactly what he thinks instead of talking behind your back. He is the kind of person who will go out of his way to help a friend, sticking with that friend through difficult times. In addition, he seems to have a wide range of interests, which probably makes him very interesting to talk to.

NEGATIVE Although it is difficult to evaluate someone merely on the basis of his answers to questionnaires, I have received a rather unfavorable impression of this person. He seems to show an irresponsible attitude on many issues, leading me to believe that he has not thought very deeply about the serious problems facing the United States today. Possibly he has been more interested in having a good time than in developing an interest in intellectual matters. I also think he is too concerned with impressing his friends favorably, and his answers on one of the personality questionnaires led me to suspect that he is a phony—never saying what he really thinks of you except behind your back. I don't think I would want this person for a friend, because I don't think I could trust him to help me out when I needed it—especially if helping me might embarrass him in any way.

AMBIVALENT I have mixed feelings about this person. On the one hand, his attitudes reflect humanistic feelings and concerns. I believe that he has thought deeply about the serious problems facing the United States today. Yet at the same time, most of his attitudes conform to what the majority of college students believe. I believe he holds these opinions merely to please others. He therefore seems to have a narrow range of interests. He also impresses me as being a phony—never telling what he thinks of you except behind your back. However, he is also the kind of person who will go out of his way to help a friend, sticking with that friend through difficult times. I believe that this person might be more likable if he were more straightforward.

NEUTRAL This person is a male college student with beliefs which are generally representative of the college student population. He is probably at the freshman or sophomore level. He has probably not yet decided what field he is going to enter after completing college. If I had to guess I would say he will choose a field connected with the humanities. His answers to the music, art and literature questions do not allow me to draw any specific conclusion about his personality. But I would say that he enjoys going to the movies. This is about all I can say about this person with the limited amount of information I was given about him.

These four sketches were handwritten, complete with writing errors and scratched-out portions, to make them look authentic. Also, the sketches received by males and females were written in the appropriate masculine or feminine handwriting.

The subject and confederate also exchanged their responses to the Interpersonal Judgment scale. On that scale, the confederate's judgments of the subject for the positive reinforcement condition were primarily positive; in the negative reinforcement condition his judgments were negative; in the mixed condition half of the judgments were negative and half positive; in the neutral condition the confederate had written at the top of the scale that, "based on the information given, I could not answer the questions below." The subject was allowed five minutes to read the personality sketch and the Interpersonal Judgment scale completed by the confederate. He then received instructions which led him to anticipate either a cooperative or a competitive task with the confederate. Instructions for the cooperative condition are given below. The italicized portions were replaced by the changes noted in brackets for the competition condition.

This experiment is designed to explore the relationship between how people see and describe each other, and how they are able to function *cooperatively* [competitively]. In the next part of this experiment, we are going to ask you and your partner to perform a very difficult task which will require a considerable amount of *close cooperative* [competitive] effort *between the two* [from each] of you. In order to maximize your involvement in the task, we will pay you *each a bonus if the two of you are able to successfully complete the task* [a bonus if you are able to successfully complete the task first]. We will explain the rest of this task to you after you have entered the room in which it will be performed.

After the subject had studied these instructions for about two minutes, he was asked to accompany the experimenter. On their way to the waiting room the experimenter also asked the confederate, who was sitting at a desk and who was always of the same sex as the subject, to come along. As the confederate got up he picked up his books and was told to leave them on the desk. The subject usually did the same; if not, he was told to do so, and both were led into the waiting room. The prearranged movements of the experimenter and the confederate insured that the latter would enter the empty, $9' \times 20'$ room first and assume a preassigned position. The experimenter then said, "Wait here for a while, I'll be back," and closed the door. They were left standing for two minutes, during which time the confederate, who had been coached beforehand, behaved in ways which conveyed a moderately positive attitude to the subject. He stood near one corner of the room, facing the opposite corner, with a moderately relaxed and natural posture—arms and legs slightly asymmentrical. As they entered the room, the confederate smiled once at the subject, and during the waiting period he looked in the subject's direction 30% of the time, which included eye contact when the subject spoke to him. When the subject made a statement or asked a question, the confederate responded with a statement of about five words. For every three such initiations by the subject, the confederate initiated one topic himself.

Following the waiting period, the subject was carefully debriefed. There was no actual competition or cooperation task, as the subject had expected. So, as a substitute for the bonus payment he had been promised, he received pay for one full hour instead of the half hour he actually spent in participation.

Confederates knew that the subjects

would receive bogus descriptions, supposedly written by them; however, they did not know which description each subject received, nor did they know whether a subject was anticipating cooperation or competition. Nonetheless, in a few cases a subject's comments during the waiting period revealed the condition to the confederate. Those who were observing and recording through a one-way mirror likewise did not know the experimental conditions; they had only the subject's name. Since facial expressions and distances are somewhat difficult to measure from video recordings, one of the observers scored the subject's distances from the confederate as he moved around in the room, and also recorded the exact total amount of time that the subject spent in the room. Another observer scored the subject's facial expressions.

The audio and video recordings were scored using categories given in Table I. The measures of Table I are mostly self-explanatory. All measures except "percent duration of confederate's speech" pertain to a subject. "Total number of statements" was an overall measure of the amount of conversation of a subject and also was scored as consisting of "declarative statements" and "questions." "Verbal reinforcers" were short utterances of agreement and recognition (e.g., *uh huh, yeah, same here*). "Positive (or negative) verbal content" was assessed from the meaning of the statements (e.g., whether the contents showed concern, desire for friendship, or whether they were inconsiderate, sarcastic, or openly insulting). "Vocal activity" was scored from paralinguistic features (e.g., fundamental frequency range). "Speech rate" was number of words per minute. "Rocking movements" referred to the standing subjects' body move-

ments back and forth or sideways. "Body lean" referred to the average lean over time of the torso away from the vertical. "Self-manipulation" was scratching or rubbing of part of the body, whereas "object manipulation" was the handling of a piece of chalk or some other object taken out of the pocket. "Shoulder orientation" was the degree to which the subject's shoulders were turned away from the confederate, that is, the degree to which he was bodily facing away from the confederate.

Average rater reliability for these measures is 0.85 and detailed scoring criteria for each measure have been provided by Mehrabian (1972b, Appendix A). The latter list is essentially a scoring manual for nonverbal behaviors and can be referred to for a more detailed consideration of the findings. In the present experiment, two raters independently scored each category and their scores were averaged. No information about subjects' individual difference test scores was available to the raters, since those questionnaires were scored last.

Results and discussion

To analyze the data, the information of Table I was first used to obtain a composite index for each subject on each factor. These composite indexes were algebraic sums of the normalized values of all the variables subsumed under a given factor. Except in the case of the affiliative behavior factor, all the measures within each factor were used to compute a composite score for that factor. For affiliative behavior, a number of the variables were quite similar to "total statement rate" and would have disproportionately emphasized that variable within the total set of contributing measures. In this case the composite index was as follows:

Affiliative Behavior = total statements per minute + percent duration of eye contact with the confederate + positive verbal content + head nods per minute + hand and arm gestures per minute + pleasantness of facial expressions

The six composite indexes were the dependent measures in the regression analyses reported below. As already noted, the experiment included five individual difference variables: affiliative tendency (R_1), sensitivity to rejection (R_2), achieving tendency (A), sex, and birth order; and there were three experimental factors: positive reinforcement-evaluation received from the confederate prior to the waiting period (r_1), negative reinforcement-evaluation received from the confederate (r_2), and anticipated cooperation versus competition with the confederate (C). For each composite index, two regression analyses were performed. The first analysis explored the main and interactive effects of affiliative tendency and sensitivity to rejection, along with the effects of the experimental conditions. A second analysis explored the contribution of achieving tendency and its interactions with the experimental conditions. Sex and birth order were correlated only with the six dependent measures, and the significant correlations are reported.

For each composite index, the effects of affiliative tendency (R_1) and sensitivity to rejection (R_2) were tested in the same regression analysis because these two individual difference measures had been shown to contribute jointly to social behavior (Mehrabian and Ksionzky, 1970). However, a separate regression analysis was employed to test the effects of achieving tendency (A) because $A \times R_1$, $A \times R_2$, and $A \times R_1 \times R_2$ interactions (or higher order interactions including these) had not been hypothesized and were of little interest in the present study.

Regression analyses were selected in preference to the traditional analysis of variance technique since they do not necessitate the elimination of some cases to achieve cell proportionality. Cohen (1968) described the specific techniques that can be used not only to assess main but also interaction effects with regression analysis, and he pointed out several advantages of this more general method.

Table 2 summarizes the results of all the regression analyses and provides a list of all the effects found to be significant at the .05 level. The A and B equations in that table correspond respectively to the two separate regression analyses described in the preceding paragraph. The main effects of Table 2 are readily interpreted by considering the coefficients of these terms. However, cell means are of further help in discussing the various interactions, and these are reported in Tables 3 through 6. For all these tables, t-tests were used to assess the significance of simple effects, and arrows connect those means which differed significantly at the .01 level.

Before proceeding to the detailed discussion of findings, it is helpful to consider the effectiveness of the positive reinforcement-evaluation (r_1) and the negative reinforcement-evaluation (r_2) factors. First, these manipulations were intended to convince subjects of having the particular qualities enumerated in the evaluations. That is, the intent was not to change the self-perceptions of subjects, but rather to have them know they were being evaluated

TABLE 2
Summary of all regression analyses [a]

1A. Affiliative behavior $= .16\ R_1 + .13\ C - .20\ R_1 r_2$
$+ .12\ r_1 r_2 C - .13\ R_1 R_2 r_1 r_2$ (.37)

2A. Responsiveness $= .15\ R_1 R_2 r_1$ (.15)

2B. Responsiveness $= .14\ AC - .14\ ACr_1 r_2$ (.19)

3A. Relaxation $= -.17\ r_1 r_2 C$ (.17)

4A. Ingratiating Behavior $= .17\ R_1 r_2$ (.17)

4B. Ingratiating Behavior $= -.20\ Ar_2$ (.20)

5A. Distress $= .23\ r_2$ (.23)

6A. Intimate Position $= -.26\ r_2$ (.26)

NOTATION

A   = achieving tendency
R_1 = affiliative tendency
R_2 = sensitivity to rejection
r_1 = received positive evaluation (reinforcement)
r_2 = received negative evaluation (reinforcement)
C   = (cooperation $= +1.0$) $-$ (competition $= -1.0$)

[a] All the variables in these equations are normalized to facilitate comparisons of the magnitudes of the various effects. When no equation is listed for the B regressions, this is because no corresponding significant effects involving achieving tendency were obtained.

in a certain way by another person. Second, those cases where the received evaluations were incongruous with self-perceptions probably produced error variance. Thus, the results reported below tend to be conservative estimates of real effects.

Affiliative behavior

The first, third, and fifth effects in equation 1A are interrelated and provide increasingly precise predictions for affiliative behavior as a function of affiliative tendency, sensitivity to rejection, and the positive and negative confederate evaluations. Therefore, only the fifth effect is interpreted in detail. The first effect shows that, as expected, subjects who scored higher on a measure of affiliative tendency were more affiliative. The cell means for the $R_1 \times r_2$ effect in Table 3 show that more affiliative persons (a designation

which is used henceforth to refer to persons scoring higher on the measure of affiliative tendency) behaved in a more affiliative way only when they did not receive negative evaluations from the target prior to the interaction period.

The $R_1 \times R_2 \times r_1 \times r_2$ effect of equation 1A provides even more specific information about the differential sensitivity of subjects differing in affiliative tendency and sensitivity to rejection to the four evaluation conditions.

To consider the cell means in Table 3 for this fourth order interaction, it is helpful to note that dichotomizing the R_1 and R_2 scales leads to four types of affiliative personality: *positive* affiliators, who are high on affiliative tendency and low on sensitivity to rejection; *negative* affiliators, who are low on affiliative tendency and high on sensitivity to rejection; *ambivalent af-*

TABLE 3
Cell means for the interactions affecting affiliative behavior[a]

CELL MEANS FOR THE $R_1 \times r_2$ EFFECT

	High r_2	Low r_2
Affiliator (High R_1)	$-.23 \longleftrightarrow$	$.53$
Nonaffiliator (Low R_1)	$-.15$	$-.18$

CELL MEANS FOR THE $r_1 \times r_2 \times C$ EFFECT

	High r_2	Low r_2
High r_1	$.26$	$.33$
Anticipated Cooperation		
Low r_1	$-.19$	$.24$
High r_1	$-.61 \longleftrightarrow$	$.14$
Anticipated Competition		
Low r_1	$-.22$	$.03$

CELL MEANS FOR THE $R_1 \times R_2 \times r_1 \times r_2$ EFFECT

	High r_2	Low r_2
High r_1	$-.41 \longleftrightarrow$	$.51$
Ambivalent Affiliator		
(High R_1, High R_2)		
Low r_1	$-.20$	$-.14$
High r_1	$-.18 \longleftrightarrow$	$.57$
Positive Affiliator		
(High R_1, Low R_2)		
Low r_1	$-.14 \longleftrightarrow$	$.82$
High r_1	$-.10$	$-.30$
Negative Affiliator		
(Low R_1, High R_2)		
Low r_1	$-.34$	$-.27$
High r_1	$.01$	$.03$
Neutral Affiliator		
(Low R_1, Low R_2)		
Low r_1	$-.15$	$-.21$

[a] Arrows connect cell means which differed significantly at the .01 level. See Table 1 for the definition of symbols used here.

filiators, who are high on both dimensions; and *neutral* affiliators, who are low on both dimensions. This terminology will be used in our discussions to follow.

Positive and ambivalent types exhibited a significantly higher degree of affiliative behavior relative to negative and neutral types when they received positive (i.e., high r_1 and low r_2) evaluations from the target. However, there was an important difference between the behavior of ambivalent and positive types. Whereas positive affiliators continued to exhibit a very high level of affiliative behavior when they received a neutral evaluation (i.e., low r_1 and low r_2) this was not so for the ambivalent affiliators. They affiliated significantly less than positive types in that condition. The positive affiliators' increased affiliative effort in the neutral condition was possibly an attempt to elicit positive attitude and evaluation, thereby providing confirmation for their generalized expectation that interpersonal experiences are rewarding.

The second main effect in equation 1A shows that subjects were more affiliative with the target when they anticipated cooperation, as opposed to competition. The $r_1 \times r_2 \times C$ effect and the corresponding cell means in Table 3 show that this was significant for only one of the four evaluation conditions: subjects who received mixed (i.e., high r_1 and high r_2) evaluations affiliated significantly less while anticipating competition than while anticipating cooperation. Our interpretation of this effect is based on the assumption that anticipated competition, compared to cooperation, highlighted subjects' sensitivities to dominance-submissiveness issues. Since the amount of evaluation is a correlate of the implied status of the evaluator, the target's implied dominance was highest in the mixed evaluation condition where he made both positive and negative evaluations. In contrast, the other three conditions involved either only one (positive or negative) or no (neutral) evaluations and thus implied a less dominant attitude. Therefore, relative to those anticipating cooperation, subjects who anticipated competition may have resented the implied dominance of targets who had provided them with mixed evaluations. This resentment in turn was reflected in a lower level of affiliative behavior.

Equation 1B does not show any effects for achieving tendency or its interactions with the experimental conditions in determining affiliative behavior. This finding is encouraging since the measure of achievement used (Mehrabian, 1969a) was designed to be independent of characteristic affiliative behavior.

Responsiveness

For the results in equations 2A and 2B, it is important to note that although reponsiveness is slightly correlated with affiliative behavior, it is primarily a measure of another's salience in a situation. The cell means for the only significant effect of equation 2A show that there were no differences among the four affiliator types when they received positive evaluations. Compared to the other three affiliator types, however, positive affiliators were more responsive to the target when they received no positive evaluations from him. Because of their generalized expectations of positive interpersonal relationships, positive affiliators were especially attuned to those partners who evaluated them in a neutral way: their increased responsiveness to these noncommittal targets was in anticipation of additional reactions or evaluations.

The two interaction effects of equation 2B are related and the first one shows that high achievers were most responsive to their confederates when they anticipated cooperation (see the $A \times C$ cell means in Table 4. Since high achievers generally function independently or competitively, having to work with and depend on someone else was more ususual for them than for the low achievers. Their increased responsiveness was due to the salience of the confederate for them, and was not associated with more affiliation—note the absence of an $A \times C$ effect in equation 1B.

There were several significant simple effects among the cell means for the $A \times C \times r_1 \times r_2$ effect of equation 2B. Examination of the corresponding cell means in Table 4 shows that, while anticipating cooperation, high achievers were most responsive to those targets

TABLE 4
Cell means for the interactions affecting responsiveness[a]

CELL MEANS FOR THE R_1 x R_2 x r_1 EFFECT

	High r_1	Low r_1
Ambivalent Affiliator	−.07	−.07
		↕
Positive Affiliator	−.14	.24
Negative Affiliator	.03	.10
Neutral Affiliator	−.07	−.05

CELL MEANS FOR THE A x C EFFECT

	Anticipated Cooperation	Anticipated Competition
High Achiever	.26 ←———————→	−.08
	↕	
Low Achiever	−.14	.00

CELL MEANS FOR THE A x C x r_1 x r_2 EFFECT

		High Achiever	Low Achiever
High r_1, High r_2	Anticipated Cooperation	.36	−.04
	Anticipated Competition	.04	−.11
High r_1, Low r_2	Anticipated Cooperation	.25	−.53
	Anticipated Competition	−.46	.15
		↕	
Low r_1, High r_2	Anticipated Cooperation	.35	−.09
	Anticipated Competition	−.04	−.16
Low r_1, Low r_2	Anticipated Cooperation	.12	.01
	Anticipated Competition	.17	.19

[a] Arrows connect cell means which differed significantly at the .01 level. See Table 1 for the definition of symbols used above.

who had expressed some negative attitudes toward them (i.e., in the high r_1 and high r_2, or the low r_1, and high r_2 conditions). In the cooperation condition, subjects' attainment of their goals were to be contingent on assistance from the target, and the targets who had expressed dislike of the high achievers were implicitly threatening the latter's characteristic efforts to succeed. Thus, even though the high achievers were not significantly more or less affiliative in this condition (note the absence of a corresponding fourth order effect in equation 1B), they were highly attuned to these particular targets—spending more time "sizing them up."

While anticipating competition, high achievers exhibited their lowest level of responsiveness to partners who had evaluated them positively (i.e., high r_1 and low r_2). Persons who were very complimentary and flattering were not as challenging to high achievers, posing much less of a threat in competitive situations.

Low achievers, on the other hand, exhibited their lowest level of responsiveness while anticipating cooperation with someone who had evaluated them positively. For them, the absence of the threat of individual failure (that would have been present in the competitive condition) was further emphasized by the presence of a friendly target, thus making it unnecessary to be especially attentive to him.

tween relaxation and affiliative behavior, thus showing that for the interactions among these strangers, tension signified respect and positive attitudes.

The results for relaxation, summarized in equation 3A, show only one significant effect. The cell means in Table 5 for the r_1 x r_2 x C effect of equation 3A show that subjects who anticipated cooperation were least relaxed with targets who had evaluated them neutrally. They were significantly more relaxed while anticipating competition with such a partner. This finding

---

TABLE 5
Cell means for the interactions affecting relaxation *

CELL MEANS FOR THE r_1 X r_2 X C EFFECT	Anticipated Cooperation	Anticipated Competition
High r_1, High r_2	.03	.25
High r_1, Low r_2	.12	− .08
Low r_1, High r_2	.18	− .13
Low r_1, Low r_2	− .55	.19

* Arrows connect cell means which differed significantly at the .01 level. See Table 1 for the definition of symbols used above.

Relaxation

Previous research indicated that two kinds of significance can be attached to relaxation, or its converse, tension. Moderate tension can imply either (1) respect for the listener, or (2) vigilance associated with "sizing up" the listener and/or an ambiguous situation (Mehrabian, 1969b). The criterion for assigning one or the other interpretation to tension is the presence or absence of positive affect communication cues. When tension and positive affect are combined, respect is inferred; however, when tension occurs without positive affect, it indicates vigilance. A −.26 correlation ($p < .01$) was obtained be-

can be interpreted in a way similar to that of the r_1 x r_2 x C effect of equation 1A. It was assumed that the amount of evaluation from the target implicitly conveyed his dominance versus submissiveness. Thus, the implied dominance of the target was greatest in the mixed, and was least in the neutral, evaluation condition. The present effect shows, then, that subjects who anticipated cooperation assumed a tense posture (which conveyed submissiveness) to reciprocate the cautious attitude from the target, whereas such a reciprocation was not necessary or even desirable in the anticipated competition condition.

Ingratiating behavior

Such behaviors can be instrumental in eliciting a harmonious and beneficial relationship, particularly with one of higher status (e.g., Jones, 1964). They have also been shown to be most frequent during the initial and awkward moments of encounter between peers who are strangers (Mehrabian and Ksionzky, 1972b). The interaction effect in equation 4A and the cell means in Table 6 show that more affiliative subjects were more ingratiating with their targets, but only when the latter had not been negative. There was no corresponding significant difference in the behavior of less affiliative subjects. Also, a .39 correlation ($p < .01$) between affiliative and ingratiating behaviors was obtained. Thus, it is not surprising that these two behaviors of more affiliative subjects were similarly determined by the evaluations received from targets (note that the R_1 x r_2 effect occurs in both equations 1A and 4A). The higher level of ingratiation from affiliative subjects is consistent with their greater concern to have positive exchanges with others, but these results show that there is a limit to how far they will extend such efforts.

The effect in equation 4B shows that high achievers who received negative evaluations were least ingratiating toward their partners (Table 6). These subjects, who are generally independent of others, were less prone to make special efforts to have a friendly exchange with a person who had evaluated them negatively.

Distress

The result in equation 5A provided support for referring to this particular group of variables as a measure of "distress." Subjects who received more negative evaluations were more distressed. Also, the correlations showed that males were more distressed than females. The latter finding is consistent with others which have shown that, relative to females, males have greater difficulty coping with the initial awkward moments of an encounter with a stranger (e.g., Mehrabian and Ksionzky, 1972b).

Intimate position

Only one significant effect was obtained for this measure. Since intimate position is one way of conveying a positive

---

TABLE 6

Cell means for the interactions affecting ingratiating behavior *

CELL MEANS FOR THE R_1 x r_2 EFFECT

	High r_2	Low r_2
Affiliator (High R_1)	$-.16 \longleftrightarrow$	$.24$
Nonaffiliator (Low R_1)	.00	$-.09$

CELL MEANS FOR THE A x r_2 EFFECT

	High r_2	Low r_2
High Achiever	$-.29 \longleftrightarrow$	$.08$
Low Achiever	.08	.08

* Arrows connect cell means which differed significantly at the .01 level. See Table 1 for the definition of symbols used above.

feeling to another, it is not assumed with persons who are disliked (e.g., Mehrabian, 1969b), or in this experiment, with persons who evaluated the subjects negatively.

Summary

This study investigated some determiners of social interaction between pairs of strangers in a waiting situation. The dyads were always of the same sex and were standing. The behaviors of the subjects yielded the following set of composite scores which describe social interaction: affiliative behavior, responsiveness, relaxation, ingratiation, distress, and intimacy. The effects of the experimental conditions are summarized in the regression equations of Table 2. Affiliative behavior, as expected, was a function of affiliative tendency and was greater in the more interpersonally positive cooperative condition. Affiliative behavior was also a function of the social reinforcers received. Both positive and ambivalent affiliators, compared to neutral and negative types, were more affiliative when they received positive evaluations from the confederate.

The behaviors of the high achievers provided corroboration for the meaning assigned to the responsiveness factor. These subjects were more responsive to the target in the cooperative condition, particularly when the confederate provided negative evaluations. Confederates who were implicitly threatening the high achievers' efforts to succeed in the cooperative condition were understandably more salient in that situation.

Tension-relaxation can signify two quite different attitudes: in conjunction with liking it conveys respect, whereas with a neutral or negative attitude it signifies vigilance. The inverse correlation between relaxation and affiliative behavior indicated that, in the present study, tension signified respect for the confederate.

Although in some experiments the ingratiation cues have been included within a factor of affiliative behavior, the present results showed that the distinction between affiliative and ingratiating behaviors can be useful. Ingratiation has been found to be greatest during the initial awkward moments of interaction with a stranger. Positive affiliators, who are more concerned about having friendly exchanges, were more ingratiating with the targets, except when the targets evaluated them negatively.

Distress generally occurred in interpersonally difficult situations. Subjects who received negative evaluations were more distressed. In addition, males, who have greater difficulty in encounters with strangers, were more distressed than females.

Incidentally, two sets of interaction cell means were readily interpreted in terms of the following assumption: the amount of evaluation a person gives to another is a subtle communication of his dominance-submissiveness, with more evaluation of any kind being suggestive of a higher status. Thus, experimental manipulations, such as those for the r_1 and r_2 factors of the present study, can be used to test the effects of subtle communications of a higher or lower status on social interaction. It should be noted, however, that such manipulations are more likely to have the intended effects when the actual status levels of subjects are equal (e.g., as in this study where the subjects were peer students).

In this study, the objective measures of affiliative tendency, sensitivity to rejection, and achievement did not significantly relate to birth order. In Rosenfeld's (1966) and Mehrabian's (1971a) studies where birth order was correlated with personality questionnaire scores, or actual affiliative behavior, no relationships were found. Mehrabian (1971a) suggested that given the presently available questionnaire measures of affiliation, it is preferable to use the latter than to rely on birth order as a convenient, but less valid, index of affiliative tendency.

Most of the results obtained in this and related studies can be integrated, and additional future ones anticipated, in terms of the concepts of (1) expectation of positive reinforcement and (2) expectation of negative reinforcement from social interaction with another. The expectation of positive reinforcement is higher when the subject is female rather than male, when he is a high scorer on a questionnaire measure of affiliative tendency (R_1), when he has already received more positive reinforcement-evaluation (r_1) from the other, or when he expects to cooperate rather than to compete. On the other hand, there is a higher expectation of negative reinforcement when the subject is a high scorer on a questionnaire measure of sensitivity to rejection (R_2), when he has already received negative reinforcement-evaluation from the other, or when he expects to compete rather than to cooperate. Positive expectations encourage affiliative behavior and positive interpersonal exchanges, thus reinforcing the initial positive expectations and creating a beneficial cycle for social interaction. Conversely, negative expectations discourage affiliative behavior and are likely to inhibit positive enchanges while making negative exchanges more likely, thus reinforcing the negative expectations and creating a vicious cycle

for social interaction. The present findings also showed that the interactions of positive expectations with negative ones (i.e., when due to individual differences, R_1 x R_2; when due to received evaluations, r_1 x r_2) are additional important determiners of social interaction.

The above integration is consistent with reinforcement theory (Byrne and Clore, 1970; Staats and Staats, 1967) and exchange theory (Thibaut and Kelley, 1959), which view interpersonal interaction to be a function of the positive and negative reinforcements exchanged. Further, our conclusions, based on *in vivo* behavior, complement those (e.g., Byrne and Clore, 1970) which were based primarily on questionnaire data.

NOTE

1. This study was supported by United States Public Health Service grant MH 13509.

REFERENCES

Anastasi, A. 1958 Differential Psychology. New York: Macmillan.

Bales, R. F. 1950 Interaction Process Analysis. Reading, Massachusetts: Addison Wesley: 1968 "Interaction process analysis." In D. L. Sills (Ed.), International encyclopedia of the sicial sciences. New York: Crowell-Collier and Macmillan. Pp. 465–471.

Borgatta, E. F. 1962 "A systematic study of interaction process scores, peer and self-assessments, personality and other variables. Genetic Psychology Monographs 65:219–291. 1963 "A new systematic interaction observation system: Behavior scores system (BSs system)." Journal of Psychological Studies 14:24–44.

Byrne, D. 1966 An Introduction to Personality: A Research Approach. Englewood Cliffs, New Jersey: Prentice-Hall.

Byrne, D. and G. L. Clore 1970 "A reinforcement model of evaluative responses." Personality: An International Journal 1:103–128.

Carter, L. F. 1954 "Evaluating the performance of individuals as members of small groups." Personnel Psychology 7:477–484.

Cohen, J. 1968 "Multiple regression as a general data-analytic system." Psychological Bulletin 70:426–443.

Couch, A. S. 1960 "Psychological determinants of interpersonal behavior." Unpublished doctoral dissertation, Harvard University.

Foa, U. G. 1961 "Convergences in the analysis of the structure of interpersonal behavior." Psychological Review 68:341–353.

Jones, E. E. 1964 Ingratiation. New York: Appleton-Century-Crofts.

Leary, T. 1957 Interpersonal Diagnosis of Personality. New York: Ronald Press.

Longabaugh, R. 1966 "The structure of interpersonal behavior." Sociometry 29:441–460.

Lorr, M. and A. Suziedelis 1969 "Modes of interpersonal behaviour." British Journal of Social and Clinical Psychology 8:124–132.

Lott, B. E. and A. J. Lott 1960 "The formation of positive attitudes toward group members." Journal of Abnormal and Social Psychology 61:297–300.

Mehrabian, A. 1968 "Male and female scales of the tendency to achieve." Educational and Psychological Measurement 28:493–502.

———. 1969a. "Measures of achieving tendency." Educational and Psychological Measurement 29:445–451.

———. 1969b. "Significance of posture and position in the communication of attitude and status relationships." Psychological Bulletin 71:359–372.

———. 1970a. "A semantic space for nonverbal behavior." Journal of Consulting and Clinical Psychology 35:248–257.

———. 1970b. "The development and validation of measures of affiliative tendency and sensitivity to rejection." Educational and Psychological Measurement 30:417–428.

———. 1970c. "Some determinants of affiliation and conformity." Psychological Reports 27:19–29.

———. 1971a. "Verbal and nonverbal interaction of strangers in a waiting situation." Journal of Experimental Research in Personality 5:127–138.

———. 1971b. Silent Messages. Belmont, California: Wadsworth.

———. 1972a. "Nonverbal communication." In J. K. Cole (Ed.), Nebraska symposium on motivation, 1971. Lincoln, Nebraska: University of Nebraska Press. Pp. 107–161.

———. 1972b. Nonverbal Communication. Chicago: Aldine-Atherton.

Mehrabian, A. and S. Ksionzky 1970 "Models for affiliative and conformity behavior." Psychological Bulletin 74:110–126.

———. 1972a. "Categories of social behavior." Comparative Group Studies.

———. 1972b. "Social behavior under interpersonal stress." Unpublished manuscript, UCLA.

Osgood, C. E. 1966 "Dimensionality of the semantic space for communication via facial expressions." Scandinavian Journal of Psychology 7:1–30.

Osgood, C. E., G. J. Suci and P. H. Tannenbaum 1957 The Measurement of Meaning. Urbana: University of Illinois Press.

Rosenfeld, H. M. 1966 "Relationships of ordinal position to affiliation and achievement motives: Direction and generality." Journal of Personality 34:467–480.

Schachter, S. 1959 The Psychology of Affiliation. Stanford, California: Stanford University Press.

Schaefer, E. S. 1959 "A circumplex model for maternal behavior." Journal of Abnormal and Social Psychology 59:226–235.

Schutz, W. C. 1958 FIRO: A Three-Dimensional Theory of Interpersonal Behavior. New York: Holt, Rinehart and Winston.

Snider, J. C. and C. E. Osgood (Eds.) 1969 Semantic Differential Technique. Chicago: Aldine.

Staats, A. W. and C. K. Staats 1967 "An outline of an integrated learning theory of attitude formation and function." In M. Fishbein (Ed.), Readings in Attitude Theory and Measurement. New York: Wiley, Pp. 373–381.

Thibaut, J. W. and H. H. Kelley 1959 The Social Psychology of Groups. New York: Wiley.

Triandis, H. C., V. Vassiliou and M. Nassiakou 1968 "Three cross-cultural studies of subjective culture." Journal of Personality and Social Psychology 8: Monograph Supplement.

Weick, K. E. 1968 "Systematic observational methods." In G. Lindzey and E. Aronson (Eds.), The handbook of social psychology. Vol. II. Reading, Massachusetts: Addison Wesley, Pp. 357–451.

22

DISPLAYS AND MESSAGES IN INTRASPECIFIC COMMUNICATION

W. JOHN SMITH

Evolution of intraspecific communication

It is characteristic of most animals that they respond actively to their environments, and have a variety of responses among which they select as environmental features change. To respond selectively they must obtain information about the environment upon which they can base changes in their behavior.

Obtaining information from a changing environment has been an important problem throughout the evolution of animals. Over evolutionary time there have always existed opportunities for animals to tap more and more different kinds of sources, larger sources, and sources of more detailed information. Animals which could use these opportunities, however slightly at first, have inevitably received the evolutionary advantage of greater fitness.[1]

Any environmental feature can become a source of information. An obvious source for any individual animal is another animal. For instance, if the other individual is strange it may be dangerous. If it is a customary associate, some of its activities (e.g., fleeing) may also indicate a source of danger in the environment.

Indirect advantages can accrue to an animal that provides its associates with information—that is, that becomes a better information source. This is adaptive when the information it provides is likely to modify the behavior of a recipient individual in a way appropriate to the needs of the communicator. For example, if the information leads the recipient to escape danger this is adaptive if the continued existence of that individual is in any sense valuable to the provider of the information. Or the recipient may become more ready to accept a mating approach of the communicator—which is very important, considering that the measure of evolutionary fitness is contribution of genetic material to future generations. What constitutes an appropriate response varies enormously, of course,

From *Semiotica*, 1969, 1, 357–69. Copyright © 1969 by Mouton & Co., Edicom N. V. and reprinted by permission.

depending on the situation. But it varies within one important limitation: the response must be appropriate from the standpoints of BOTH recipient and communicator if evolution is to occur.

Intraspecific communication is not just the result of evolving better means of providing information, since the provision of information does not require specialized signalling. With respect to the evolution of communication there are three classes of behavior patterns:

1. All activities are potentially informative. For instance, Altmann (1965, p. 492) treats as "communicative" any behavior pattern whose occurrence changes the probability of behavior patterns of other individuals in the social group. Most acts, however, are not SPECIALIZED to be more informative.

2. Some acts occur MORE OFTEN, or are more prolonged, than is necessary to accomplish their direct function. The additional usage apparently makes some aspect(s) of their information available more frequently or for longer periods.

3. Some acts appear to be specialized to function ONLY to carry information, and are distinct in FORM from more directly functional events.

Both the second and third classes involve evolutionary specialization for communicative functions. Both are customarily called DISPLAYS, following the definition of Moynihan (1960) who set as the criterion special adaptation in "physical form or frequency to subserve social signal functions." In nonhuman species, this adaptation is usually the result of the evolutionary process of RITUALIZATION which has been considered by Tinbergen (1959, p. 44) and Blest (1961).

Like any evolutionary novelty, displays cannot arise *de novo* but must be ritualized from precursors. Most thought on these precursors has been devoted to visible displays, which likely arise from such acts as intention movements, redirected activities, displacement activities, and comfort movements (see Tinbergen, 1952) or from activities having a close temporal correlation with motor patterns directly related to the referents of the signalling (see Moynihan, 1955). Chemical displaying *via* release of pheromones (see Wilson, 1965) probably began with such sources as metabolic waste products. It is harder to account for vocal displays. Much of the extant diversity is probably the result of vocalizations evolving from preexisting vocalizations, but vocalizations may have originated as ritualizations of what Spurway and Haldane (1953) called displacement breathing, or by amplification and modification of the loud, sustained breathing of terrified or sexually aroused animals (apparently what Darwin, 1872, was suggesting).

Kinds of displays

Whatever their origin, the two classes of especially informative events subsumed under the definition of 'displays' have different evolutionary histories. Since the first class involves an evolutionary increase in the frequency of usage of the precursor, it may be said to comprise ritualized iteration displays. Similarly, the second class comprises ritualized transformation displays. Their evolutionary characteristics include the following:

1. The first must evolve by the increasingly iterative employment of non-display precursor acts which carry useful information, and which do not become disadvantageous when done to excess. Ritualized transformations, on

the other hand, need not increase in frequency, and can arise from acts the excessive repetition of which would be harmful.

2. Ritualized iterations appear to involve primarily social acts, or acts that were social in the phylogenetic lineage concerned. That is, their evolutionary sources appear to be behavior patterns performed by at least two interacting individuals. The relationship between the individuals may have to be bonded—*i.e.,* one in which the individuals remain socially inter-related with conventionally defined statuses, and recognize each other individually. But the precursors of ritualized transformations need not be social acts. For example, most intention movements are locomotory acts of a general sort, such as taking flight or turning around. Redirected acts may usually be social: the grass-pulling display of Herring Gulls appears to derive from redirected attack movements (Moynihan, 1955). Comfort acts often are not social: a courting drake pointing at the bright speculum feathers on his wing is probably using a display ritualized from a preening movement (Lorenz, 1941, and Moynihan, 1955).

3. Ritualized iterations are no more conspicuous than their precursors, except by virtue of being used more. Ritualized transformations often are more conspicuous and need to be, as they are more likely to be evanescent, and to be performed outside of close social encounters. They are always distinctive from other acts, whether those are displays or not.

4. The only social function of ritualized transformations is communication. A ritualized iteration, however, is not distinguishable from its evolutionary precursor, an act which retains its initial, non-communicative function.

Thus birds allopreen and mammals allogroom—they cleanse each other's plumage or pelage of dirt and ectoparasites. Allopreening or allogrooming is also considered to be a display in most species because it occurs much more often than seems necessary for hygiene, and its usage follows definite social patterns.

Yet in some cases it can be very difficult to decide whether or not a particular sort of social activity is always directly functional, or whether it is used in part as a display. For instance, mated birds often associate with one another. One, usually the male, follows its mate about, not approaching for contact but maintaining a distance. Some direct advantages must accrue: a male is able to see and forestall any approaches to his mate by another male, each member of the pair gains the protection offered by the presence of another bird which can warn of the approach of a predator, and so forth. But the behavior also informs each individual of the other's acceptance of its special status, and it is difficult to know whether this has been an evolutionary pressure to maintain or extend the use of associating behavior.

5. Ritualized transformations may, in some circumstances, evolve from or replace ritualized iterations, particularly if the initial direct function of the iterated act changes. For example, in many species of New World flycatchers (*Aves: Tyrannidae*) males make apparently standard nest-forming movements in appropriate nest sites during the period when they are 'courting' mates (*e.g.,* Smith, 1966, 1969a, and in prep.). Used by females, the same movements apparently function in testing the suitability of potential nest sites, and later in shaping the nest. But under normal circumstances, males of

most tyrannid species neither select nest sites nor help to build nests, although they remain close to the nest site or female as she builds. Their use of these movements thus represents an increase from an expected frequency of occurrence of near zero. Males of many other passerine bird species do help build the nest, and in yet many other species do not. Males of many of the latter species also do not make the nest-forming movements in most cases (*e.g.,* Pokrovskaya, 1968).

The movements in the Tyrannidae constitute a ritualized iteration display. In at least one tyrannid genus (*Sayornis*) males appear to lack nest-forming movements, although they do visit and squat in potential nest sites. These males usually flutter their wings at such sites. That is, they have replaced nest-forming movements with a new component, a ritualized transformation display, perhaps evolutionarily derived from balancing movements used in landing on the narrow ledges that serve as nest sites, or from a flight display with which their Nest-Site-Showing usually shares vocalizations (Smith, 1969a, and in prep.).

The messages of displays

Every display encodes messages which are descriptive of the state of the communicator, and which provide recipients with information about the communicator (Smith, 1965, 1968). In order to study the messages of a particular display in a particular species, it is necessary to know all of the ways in which a communicator can perform when using that display—and most displays are employed in a variety of circumstances. The criteria for recognizing messages are found in features of the communicator's behavior which are consistent for all occurrences of the display. A simplified synopsis of behavioral criteria for the known messages of a selection of vertebrate animals (see Smith, 1969b) is provided in Table 1.

In practice, there are two exceptions to this procedure for determining messages. First, the probability that a given sort of behavior will occur if a display is used is recognized as a modifying message. Second, another message identifies the classes to which the communicator belongs, classes that have characteristic behavioral repertoire. This is usually determined not by studying the entire behavioral repertoire of the classes, but merely by assuring that the display differs consistently in physical form from otherwise comparable displays used by members of different classes. A class may be as small as one individual, or much larger than a species (as, for instance, when vocalizations converge in evolution due to selective advantage dependent upon interspecific interaction).

At least most vertebrate animals have only from about 15 to 45 displays per species. Each display encodes identifying information, and some probability information about one or more other messages.

An even smaller number of messages, usually fewer than 12 per species, is encoded by each species' display repertoire. But unlike displays, which differ among species, most animals probably share more or less the same small message set (discussed more fully by Smith, 1969b). A tentative list of the basic set of messages is provided in Fig. 1, organized to show that most messages indicate some selection within the behavioral repertoire of the communicator, although few narrowly specify only one particular act.

The differences among messages in

TABLE I

A tentative message list, and a simplified synopsis of the sorts of criteria used in research to determine the messages of a display

Message	Criteria
general set	Virtually any act within the behavioral repertoire of the communicator's class may occur (further research may indicate that this message is somewhat narrower than it appears on the basis of current evidence)
locomotion	Communicator is locomoting, beginning or terminating locomotion, or using locomotory 'intention movements'; the functional significance of the locomotion is not indicated
attack	Communicator attacks, soon attacks, or appears ambivalent between attacking and conflicting behavior and does not always attack
escape	Communicator flees, soon flees, or tends to orient away, partially withdraw, or sometimes flee
non-agonistic subset	Communicator does or may do any non-agonistic act
association	Communicator joins and stays near a social partner, avoiding contact, or accepts association but not contact from a partner
bond-limited subset	Communicator interacts non-aggressively with individuals with which a social bond has been established
play	Communicator plays or attempts to initiate play
copulation	Communicator copulates or attempts to initiate copulation
frustration	Communicator displays when the opportunity for a particular more directly functional behavior pattern (such as attack, escape, associating) is unavailable
probability	Each act specified by each message encoded in a particular display has a specifiable probability of occurring
identification	The form of each display is specific to a class of communicators (the form is evolutionarily selected for an identifying function only in ritualized transformations)

selectivity effect a categorization of the behavioral repertoire of a species. For instance, the 'general set' message, while probably not as inclusive as it appears on the basis of present evidence, is very much more inclusive than any other message. Acts are divided into those that are agonistic (*i.e.*, attack, escape, and ambivalent mixtures) and those which are not, although the former categories are much more selective than the latter. One message deals only with the probability of locomoting, an act that is often necessary if, in different contexts, the communicator is to initiate, extend, or terminate a social encounter. The bond-limited subset message occurs in displays used by an animal behaving, or about to behave, in ways characteristic of a member of an organized group of two or more individuals in which the organization is based upon mutual recognition and special status (that is, a group such as a

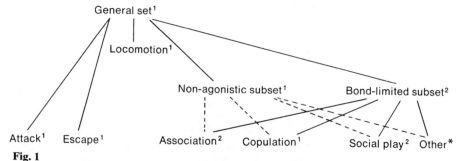

Fig. 1

Legend:

a. the list is least selective at the top, most selective at the bottom; the bond-limited subset should perhaps appear below the non-agonistic subset.

b. messages subsumed below the bond-limited subset may not, when more is known, always be bond-limited; hence the solid lines connecting them to the non-agonistic subset.

c. * "other" refers to as yet undiscovered or unsubstantiated messages. For instance, as yet incomplete analyses of infant displays will yield one or more messages peculiar to relationships of dependency (usually offspring-parent).

d. superscripts:

    1 = message encoded primarily or solely by transformation displays.

    2 = message apparently encoded by both iteration and transformation displays.

e. three additional basic messages act essentially as modifiers to the above: identification, probability, and frustration.

troop of monkeys, but not a fish school). Probably the more narrow messages now listed under it (*e.g.,* copulation) will be found not to be restricted to species that employ them only in bond-limited situations. The narrowest messages (specifying only one type of act) appear to be used only when information from sources contextual to the display cannot efficiently assist a recipient in selecting an appropriate response. This varies from species to species: for instance, even among birds with basically similar social behavior some species have displays with copulation messages and others do not. Specifying particular kinds of non-aggressive contact usually does not seem to have been sufficiently important in the evolution of a species' display repertoire to merit the 'assignment' of displays to such narrow messages. (Evolu-

tionary 'assigning' is viewed as a result of natural selection; the phrasing is teleonomic, not teleological).

Not only are social behavior patterns categorized, so also are basic acts which may be employed much more often in non-social than in social behavior. Thus one of the most-used messages in many species simply indicates (as mentioned above) that the communicator is locomoting, or will begin or cease locomotion, but does not specify the function of the locomotion in any case.

Contextual information and the process of communication

The basic behavior patterns of which social behavior is comprised are adjustable, and are modified in many ways as continuously variable circumstances shift. But it appears as if animals do not employ displays to communicate about the multitude of variables. Parameters such as established social relationships of individuals, the sequence of events before a display, the spatial location of an interaction within a non-uniform area such as a territory, and others, supply information that is contextual to displays. From the nature of the messages known, it appears that a communicator uses stylized communication patterns that enable a recipient to know he is present and whether or not he will undertake the categories of behavior discussed above.

Since communicators do not provide highly selective information in most events involving displays, it is important to study the various other sources of information available to a recipient. Most of these are contextual. It does not help an understanding of the process of animal communication to contend, as many ethologists do, that because (i) a communicator may be in different motivational states at different times when using the same display, and (ii) a recipient may do different things on perceiving the same display at different times, therefore the display IT-SELF contains different information at different times. How is a recipient to know which information, when? In most vertebrate animals a display alone does not simply 'release' a response, it primes recipients to select from a particular set of responses. The information deciding selection is contextual. The information in most displays provides only a sufficient basis to make contextual information functional. This is accomplished because the information encoded in the display (its message) does not vary, but always enables prediction of the same range of communicator activities. In most known ritualized iterations and in many ritual-

ized transformations the range of activities is often wide, but it is nonetheless useful—for example in priming recipients for long-duration responses such as acceptance of the communicator as a social partner.

One of the best examples of the difference between releasing and priming functions was provided by David Lack in 1940. He experimentally tested the releaser concept, *i.e.,* the notion that evolutionary processes produce features that, on being perceived by a recipient, automatically evoke an appropriate response independently of other clues. Instead of a display, he used what amounts to an evolved 'badge'— the red breast of the European robin *Erithacus rubecula.* During the breeding season, when strange robins appear within the territory of a pair the resident male attacks them. Lack was able to show that stuffed models without red breasts are not attacked, but that all other parts could be removed, one at a time or even all together, and the red breast alone would elicit threat posturing and even attack by a resident male. That is, this patch of feathers which apparently evolved in part to identify its wearer as an adult of the species, appeared to release aggressive behavior. But, as Lack pointed out, the male's mate wears an identical patch of red feathers, and he rarely attacks her—so the same patch does not always release attack. Lack did not carry the experiments further, but it is clear that some contextual features of the experiment (such as novelty—Lack's models were not familiar individuals to the males tested) decided that aggressive responses would occur, or that contextual information which might have inhibited aggression had been removed. It is not possible to present a patch of red feathers alone without contextual information, even though the experiments did eliminate all of the most expected context (*i.e.,* the remainder of the robin).

Implications for the evolution of human communication

Sebeok (1965) pointed out that "any viable hypothesis about the origin and nature of language will have to incorporate the findings of zoosemiotics." But Lenneberg (1967, p. 234) has indicated that the antecedents of what he calls "the human propensity for language" are not obvious, and that "logical commonalities among communication systems are not necessarily indicators of a common biological origin" (p. 237). In arguing (Lenneberg, 1967, 1968) that language is a product of discontinuous evolution (*i.e.,* that it is a new departure, not developed by continuous modification of previously existing modes of animal communication) he tends to overlook one important feature. Our prehuman hominoid ancestors must have evolved this new approach AT THE SAME TIME they were communicating by other means. Whatever novel features linguistic communication has, they initially supplemented and were at least partially in competition with an already existing mode of communication. This prelinguistic mode must, therefore, have had some influence in shaping at least the directions of the origins of linguistic communication.

What implication this may have for an understanding of language is very uncertain, but as a first step it will be necessary to attempt to delimit the nature of the stylized communication of which these hominoids were capable. As we have seen, it can confidently be said to have comprised two sorts of displays with different evolutionary histories. Less confidently, at this stage of research into messages, it can be said that it probably was based on a small set of messages, shared with many other vertebrate species. A list not unlike that presented in Table 1. The contextual mode of operation of animal communication, plus the fact that the display repertoires of most or all species are small, leads to the prediction of a small, widespread, message set (Smith, 1969b). But confirmation of the prediction and identification of the component messages can only be done empirically. If a general message set can be established, however, we shall know the 'communication environment' which formed the background for the origin of language.

Yet, even if the study of animal communication should lack implications for the study of the evolutionary origins of language, it cannot lack implications for other aspects of human communication. As Sebeok (1968, p. 8–9) has made clear: "Man's total communicative repertoire consists of two sorts of sign systems: the anthroposemiotic . . . and the zoosemiotic." The zoosemiotic are so unlike the anthroposemiotic (language, and language-based communication) that they cannot profitably be studied by linguistic techniques, although profitable comparisons can be made (*e.g.,* Hockett and Altmann, 1968). Yet the zoosemiotic forms are wide-ranging and found, with modifications, in all cultures. They are not unlike the stylized communication patterns of other animals, and can be studied with the same techniques applicable there.

The zoosemiotic forms of human communication may be important in a number of ways. First, they are the only stylized communicative tools available to prelinguistic infants, and some children (*e.g.,* the deaf) who remain prelinguistic for relatively long periods. They may be the only tools left to certain aphasic adults, they may be the only reliable tools left to, say, schizophrenics. And they may be useful, to some degree, in understanding the behavior of (culturally or genetically) retarded children, a possibility I am now exploring in cooperation with C. Ristau and M. Bernstein. Second, even normal adults provide considerable information *via* paralinguistic and kinesic signalling. Whatever we can learn about displays and messages in other animal species is certain to be of value in learning to interpret the zoosemiotic forms of human communication, even if primarily by teaching us what methods can appropriately be applied.

NOTE

1. For a discussion of modern evolutionary theory, and of the concept of evolutionary fitness, see Mayr, 1963.

REFERENCES

Altmann, Stuart A., 1965 "Sociobiology of Rhesus Monkeys: II, Stochastics of Social Communication", *Journal of Theoretical Biology* 8 (1965), 490–522.

Blest, A. D. 1961 "The Concept of Ritualization", *Current Problems in Animal Behaviour*, ed. by W. H. Thorpe and O. L. Zangwill (Cambridge, Cambridge University Press), 102–124.

Darwin, Charles, 1872 *The Expression of the Emotions in Man and Animals* (London, Appleton). (Reprinted 1965, University of Chicago Press.)

Hockett, Charles F., and Stuart A. Altmann, 1968 "A Note on Design Features", *Animal Communication*, ed. by Thomas A. Sebeok (Bloomington, Indiana University Press), 61–72.

Lack, David, 1940 "The Releaser Concept of Bird Behaviour", *Nature* 145, 107–108.

Lenneberg, Eric H., 1967 *Biological Foundations of Language* (New York, Wiley).

————, 1968 "Language in the Light of Evolution", *Animal Communication*, ed. by Thomas A. Sebeok (Bloomington, Indiana University Press), 592–613.

Lorenz, Konrad, 1941 "Vergleichende Bewegungsstudien an Anatinen", *Journal für Ornithologie* 89 Ergänzungsband, 19–29 and 194–293.

Mayr, Ernst, 1963 *Animal Species and Evolution* (Cambridge, Harvard University Press).

Moynihan, Martin H., 1955 "Remarks on the Original Sources of Display", *Auk* 72, 240–246.

————, 1960 "Some Adaptations which Help to Promote Gregariousness", *Proceedings of the 12th International Ornithological Congress*, 523–541.

Pokrovskaya, I. V., 1968 "Observations on Nest Site Selection in Some Passerines", *Ibis* 110, 571–573.

Sebeok, Thomas A., 1965 "Animal Communication", *Science* 147, 1006–1014.

————, 1968 "Goals and Limitations of the Study of Animal Communication", *Animal Communication*, ed by Thomas A. Sebeok (Bloomington, Indiana University Press), 3–14.

Smith, W. John, 1965 "Message, Meaning, and Context in Ethology", *American Naturalist* 99, 405–409.

————, 1966 "Communication and Relationships in the Genus *Tyrannus*", *Publications of the Nuttall Ornithological Club* 6, 1–250.

————, 1968 "Message-Meaning Analyses", *Animal Communication*, ed. by Thomas A. Sebeok (Bloomington, Indiana University Press), 44–60.

————, 1969a "Displays of *Sayornis phoebe* (Aves: Tyrannidae)", *Behaviour* 33, 283–322.

————, 1969b "Messages of Vertebrate Communication", *Science* 165, 145–150.

Spurway, H., and J. B. S. Haldane, 1953 "The Comparative Ethology of Vertebrate Breathing: I. Breathing in Newts, with a General Survey", *Behaviour* 6, 8–34.

Tinbergen, Niko, 1952 " 'Derived' Activities: their Causation, Biological Significance, Origin and Emancipation during Evolution", *Quarterly Review of Biology* 27, 1–32.

————, 1959 "Comparative Studies of the Behaviour of Gulls (Laridae): a Progress Report", *Behaviour* 15, 1–70.

Wilson, Edward O., 1965 "Chemical Communication in the Social Insects", *Science* 149, 1064–1071.

NAME INDEX

SUBJECT INDEX